KISS HIM, NOT ME!

8

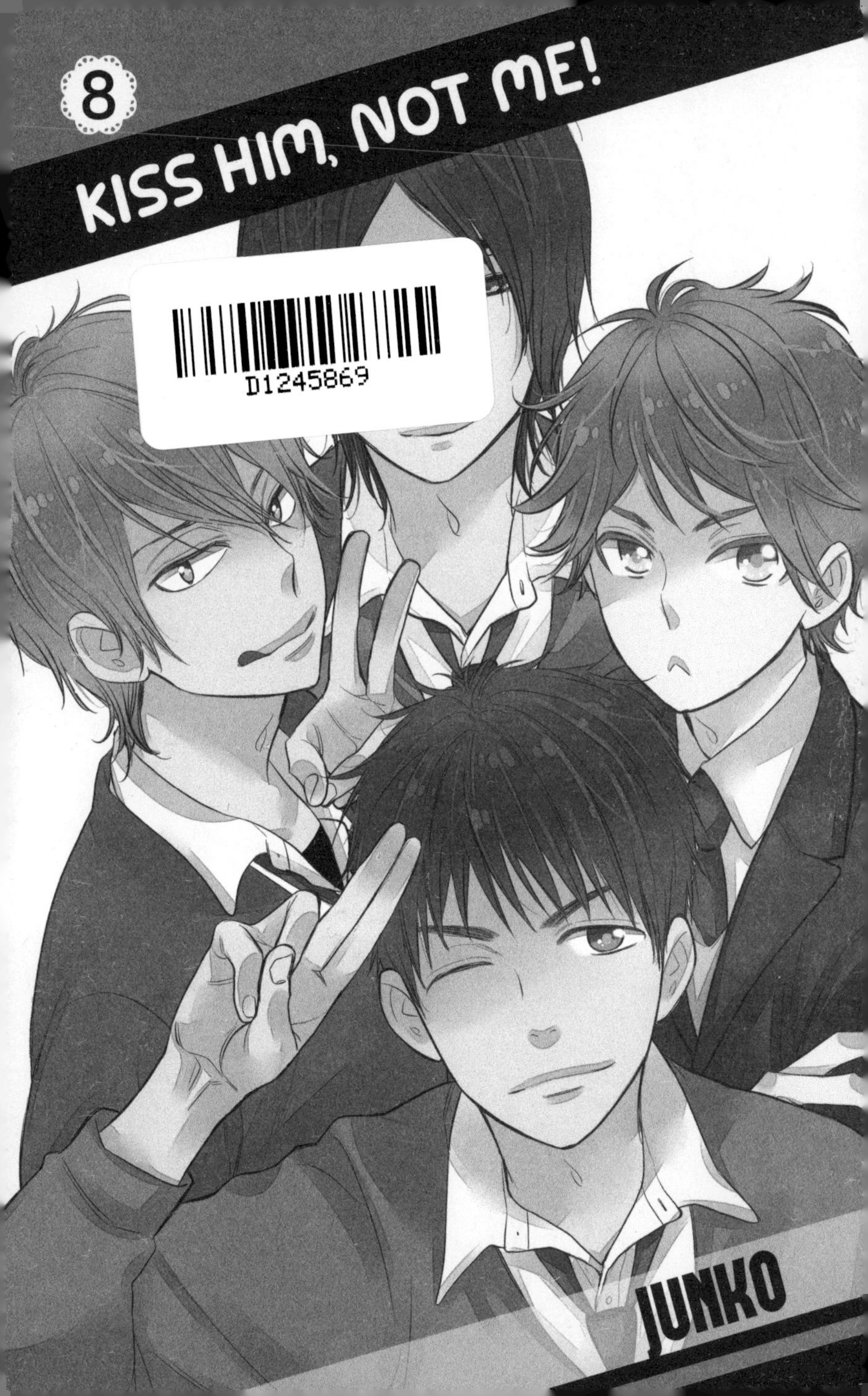

JUNKO

CONTENTS

STORY

WITH THE ALL TOO EVENTFUL TRIP TO THE HOLY LANDS NOW OVER, IT'S BACK TO THE ROUTINE OF EVERYDAY LIFE.

THAT'S WHEN IT DAWNS ON **NANASHIMA**... THE OTHER GUYS HAVE MADE MORE PROGRESS WITH KAE THAN HE HAS!

NANASHIMA DECIDES TO STEP UP HIS GAME, AND **HE STARTS A PART-TIME JOB** AT USAMI LAND WITH **KAE** IN ORDER TO GET CLOSER TO HER!

HOWEVER, **NANASHIMA** OVEREXERTS HIMSELF DURING PRACTICE AND COLLAPSES! NOT JUST THAT, WHILE IN A FEVERISH HAZE AND HALF-ASLEEP, HE ENDS UP **KISSING KAE**!!

I ♥ BL

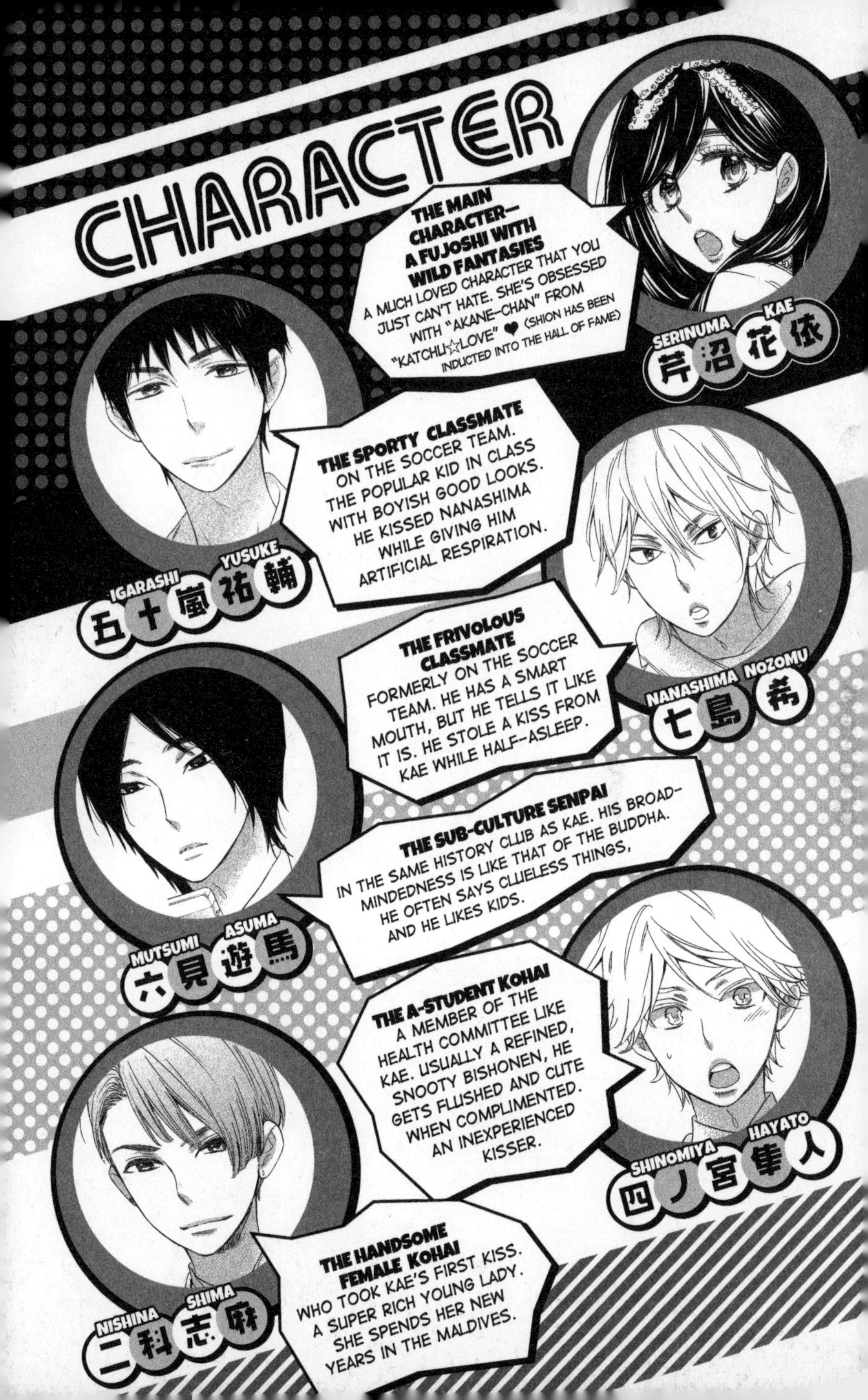
CHARACTER
THE MAIN CHARACTER—A FUJOSHI WITH WILD FANTASIES
A MUCH LOVED CHARACTER THAT YOU JUST CAN'T HATE. SHE'S OBSESSED WITH "AKANE-CHAN" FROM "KATCHU☆LOVE" ♥ (SHION HAS BEEN INDUCTED INTO THE HALL OF FAME)
SERINUMA KAE
芹沼花依
THE SPORTY CLASSMATE
ON THE SOCCER TEAM. THE POPULAR KID IN CLASS WITH BOYISH GOOD LOOKS. HE KISSED NANASHIMA WHILE GIVING HIM ARTIFICIAL RESPIRATION.
IGARASHI YUSUKE
五十嵐祐輔
THE FRIVOLOUS CLASSMATE
FORMERLY ON THE SOCCER TEAM. HE HAS A SMART MOUTH, BUT HE TELLS IT LIKE IT IS. HE STOLE A KISS FROM KAE WHILE HALF-ASLEEP.
NANASHIMA NOZOMU
七島希
THE SUB-CULTURE SENPAI
IN THE SAME HISTORY CLUB AS KAE. HIS BROAD-MINDEDNESS IS LIKE THAT OF THE BUDDHA. HE OFTEN SAYS CLUELESS THINGS, AND HE LIKES KIDS.
MUTSUMI ASUMA
六見遊馬
THE A-STUDENT KOHAI
A MEMBER OF THE HEALTH COMMITTEE LIKE KAE. USUALLY A REFINED, SNOOTY BISHONEN, HE GETS FLUSHED AND CUTE WHEN COMPLIMENTED. AN INEXPERIENCED KISSER.
SHINOMIYA HAYATO
四ノ宮隼人
THE HANDSOME FEMALE KOHAI
WHO TOOK KAE'S FIRST KISS. A SUPER RICH YOUNG LADY. SHE SPENDS HER NEW YEARS IN THE MALDIVES.
NISHINA SHIMA
二科志麻

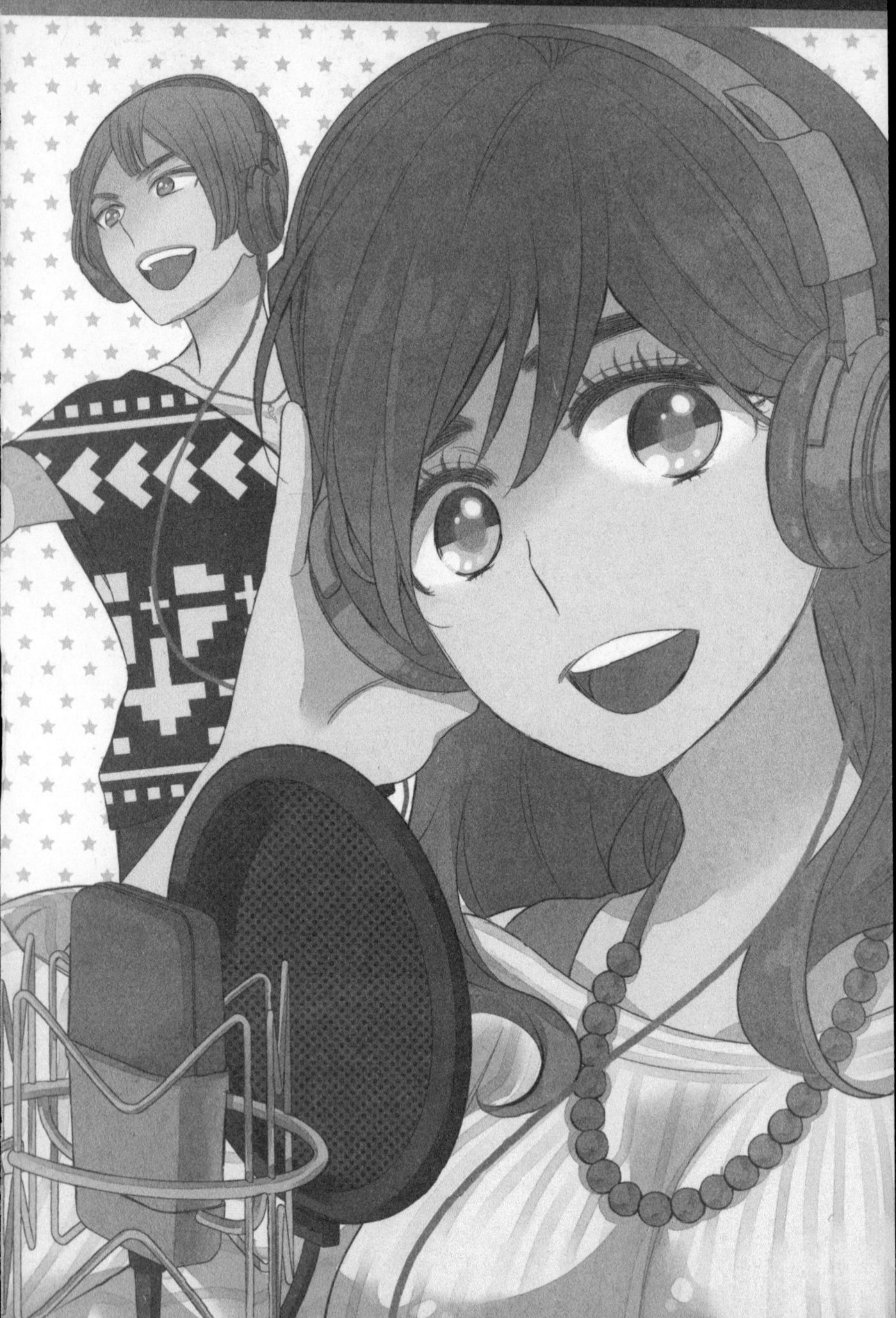

#29 NEVER HURT YOU AGAIN

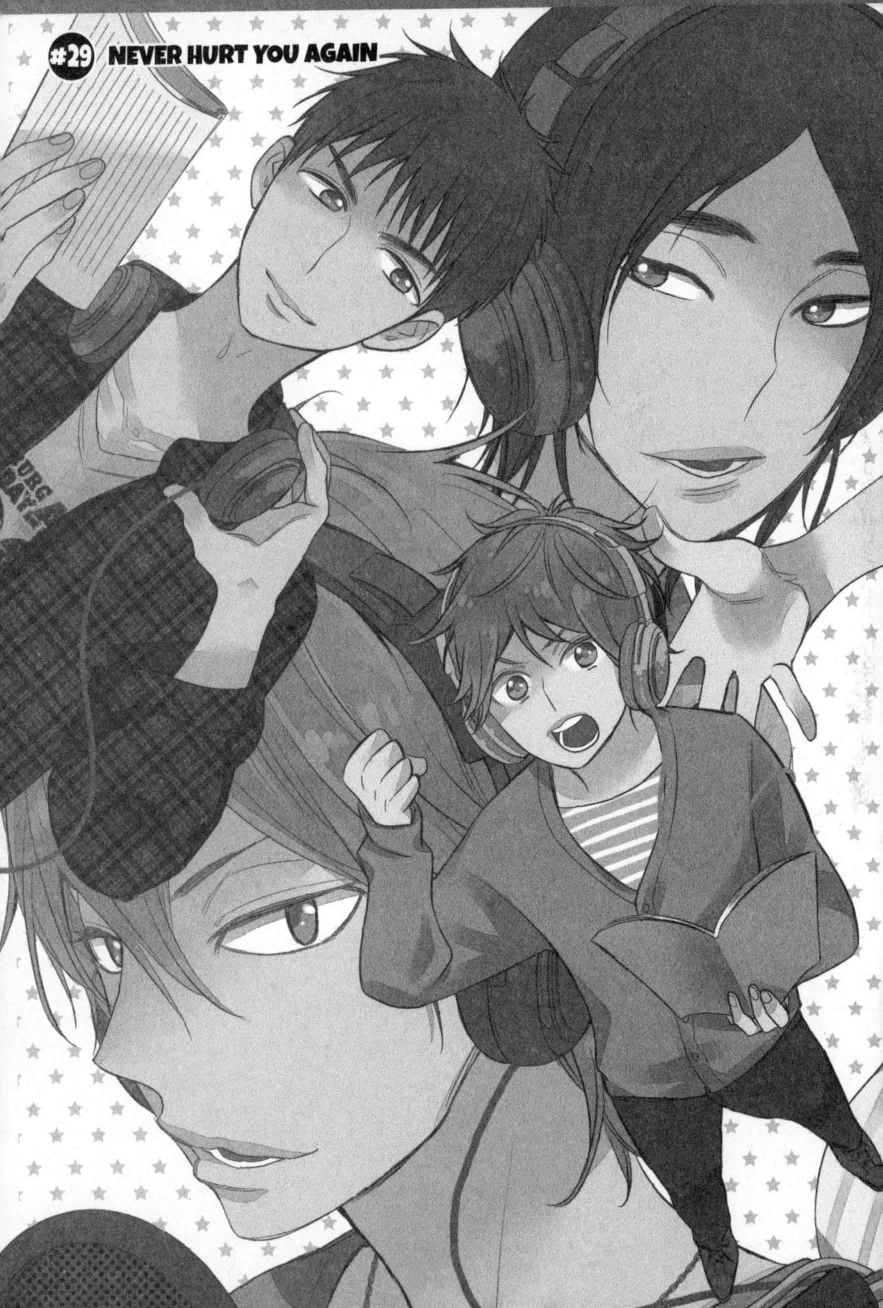

KiSS HiM, NOT ME!

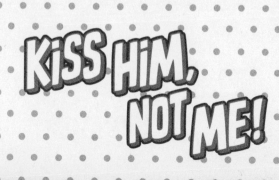

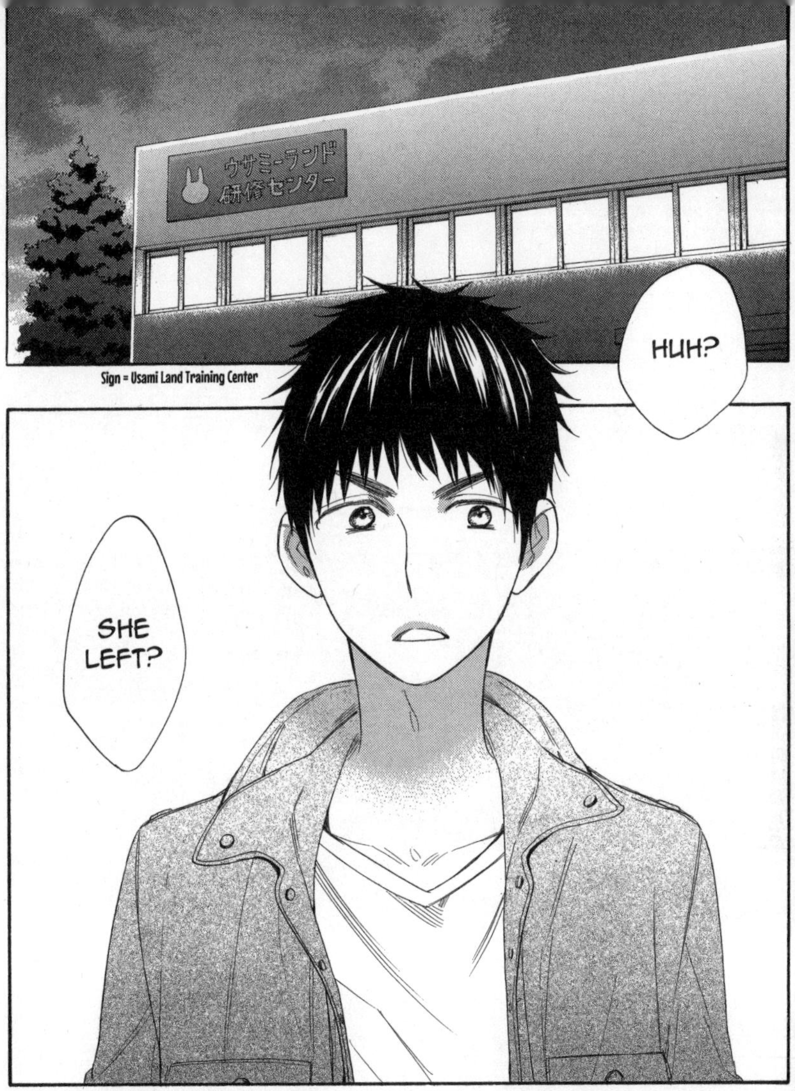
ウサミーランド
研修センター
HUH?
SHE LEFT?
Sign = Usami Land Training Center

KiSS HiM, NOT ME!

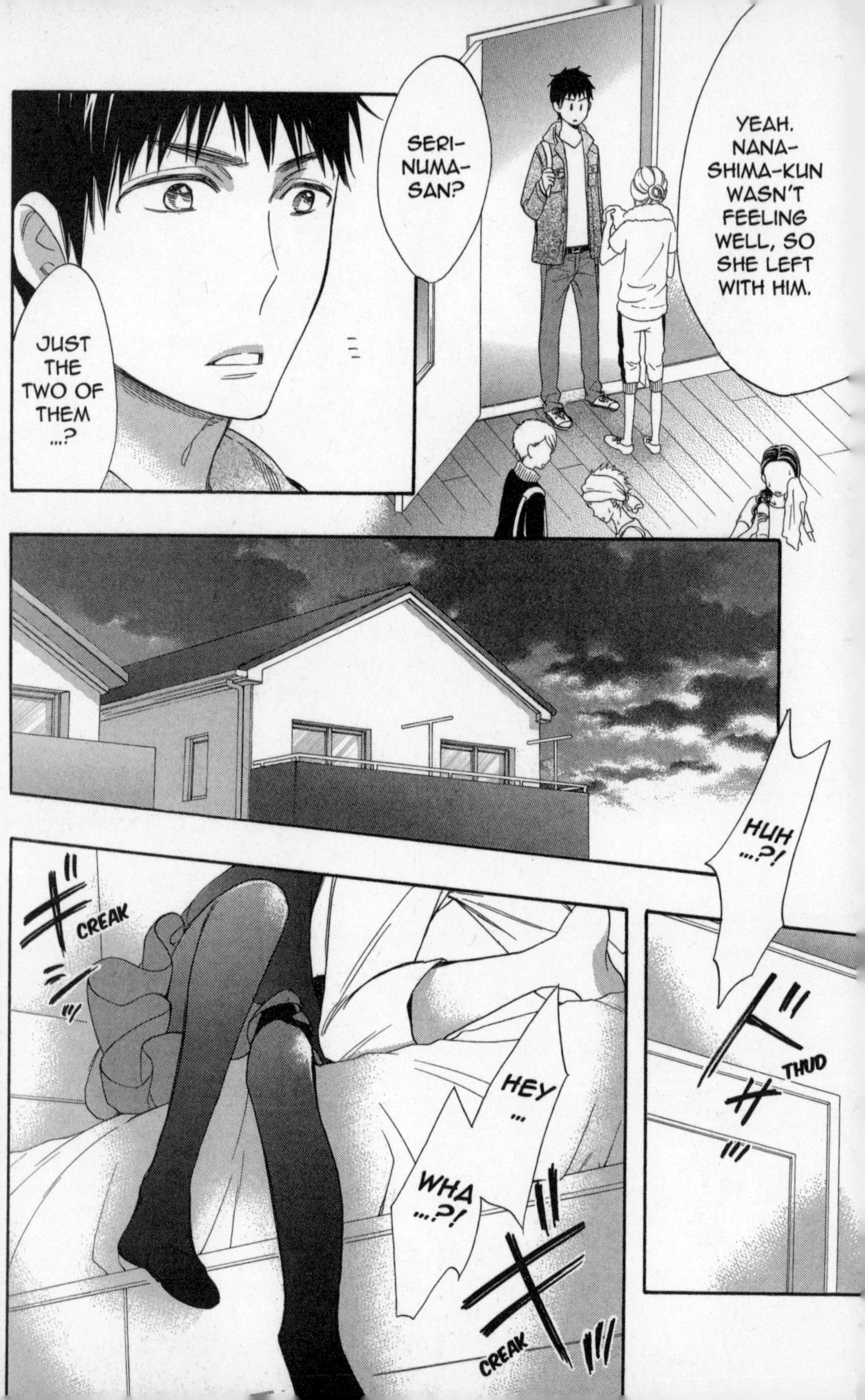
SERI-NUMA-SAN?
YEAH. NANA-SHIMA-KUN WASN'T FEELING WELL, SO SHE LEFT WITH HIM.
JUST THE TWO OF THEM ...?
HUH ...?!
THUD
CREAK
HEY ...
WHA ...?!
CREAK

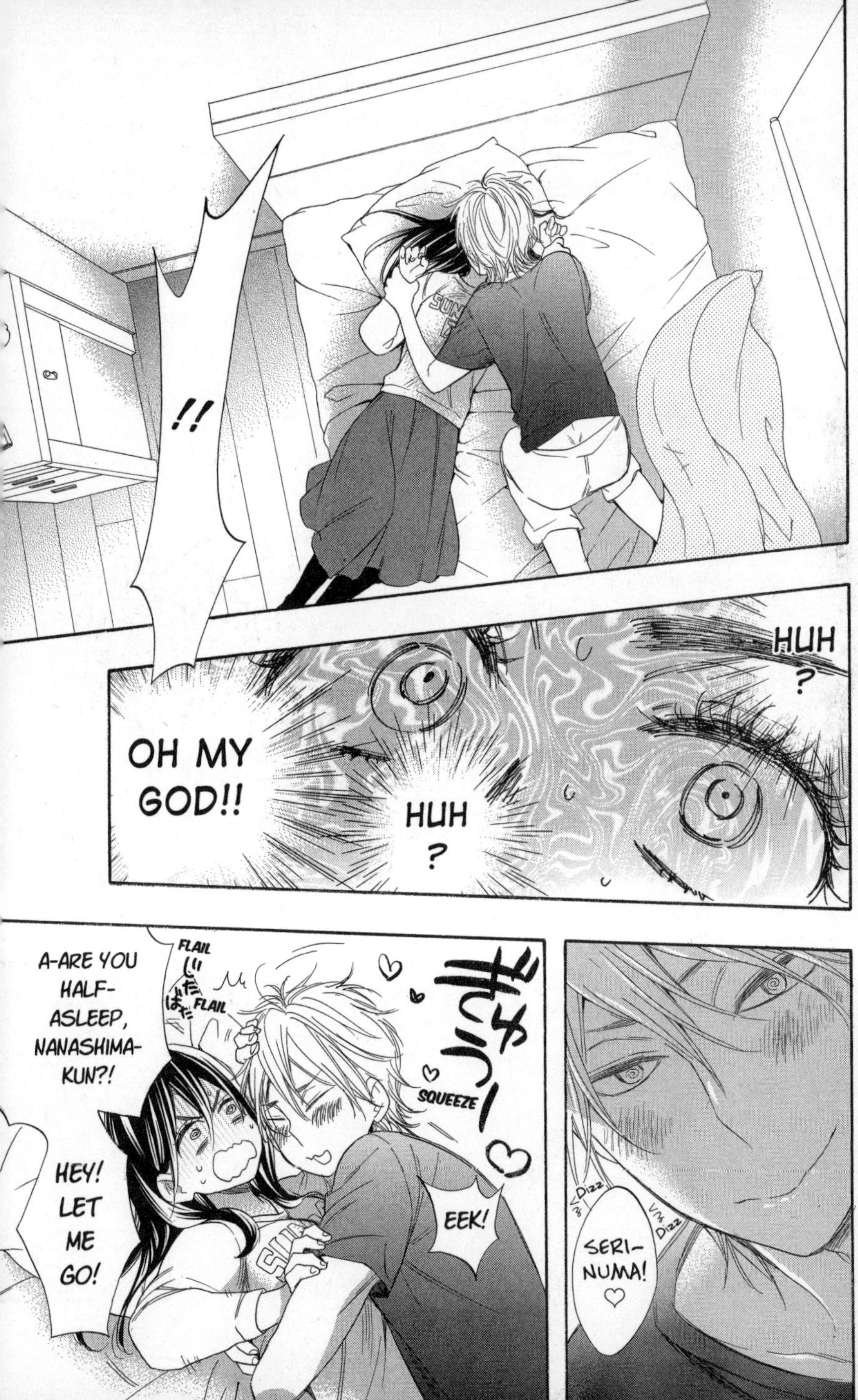
!!
HUH ?
HUH ?
OH MY GOD!!
Dizz Dizz
SERI-NUMA! ♡
SQUEEZE
EEK!
FLAIL FLAIL
A-ARE YOU HALF-ASLEEP, NANASHIMA-KUN?!
HEY! LET ME GO!

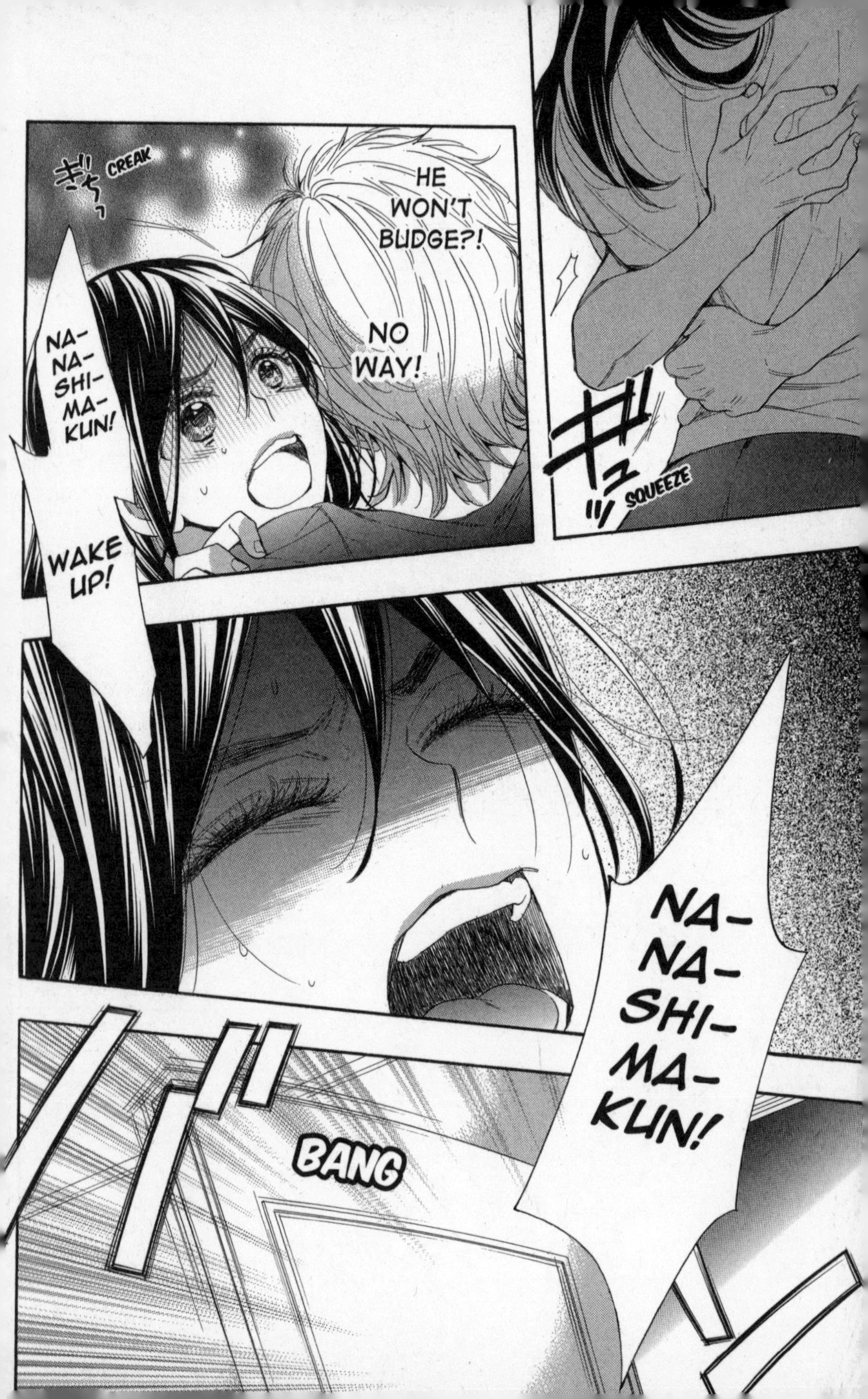
SQUEEZE
HE WON'T BUDGE?!
NO WAY!
CREAK
NA-NA-SHI-MA-KUN!
WAKE UP!
NA-NA-SHI-MA-KUN!
BANG

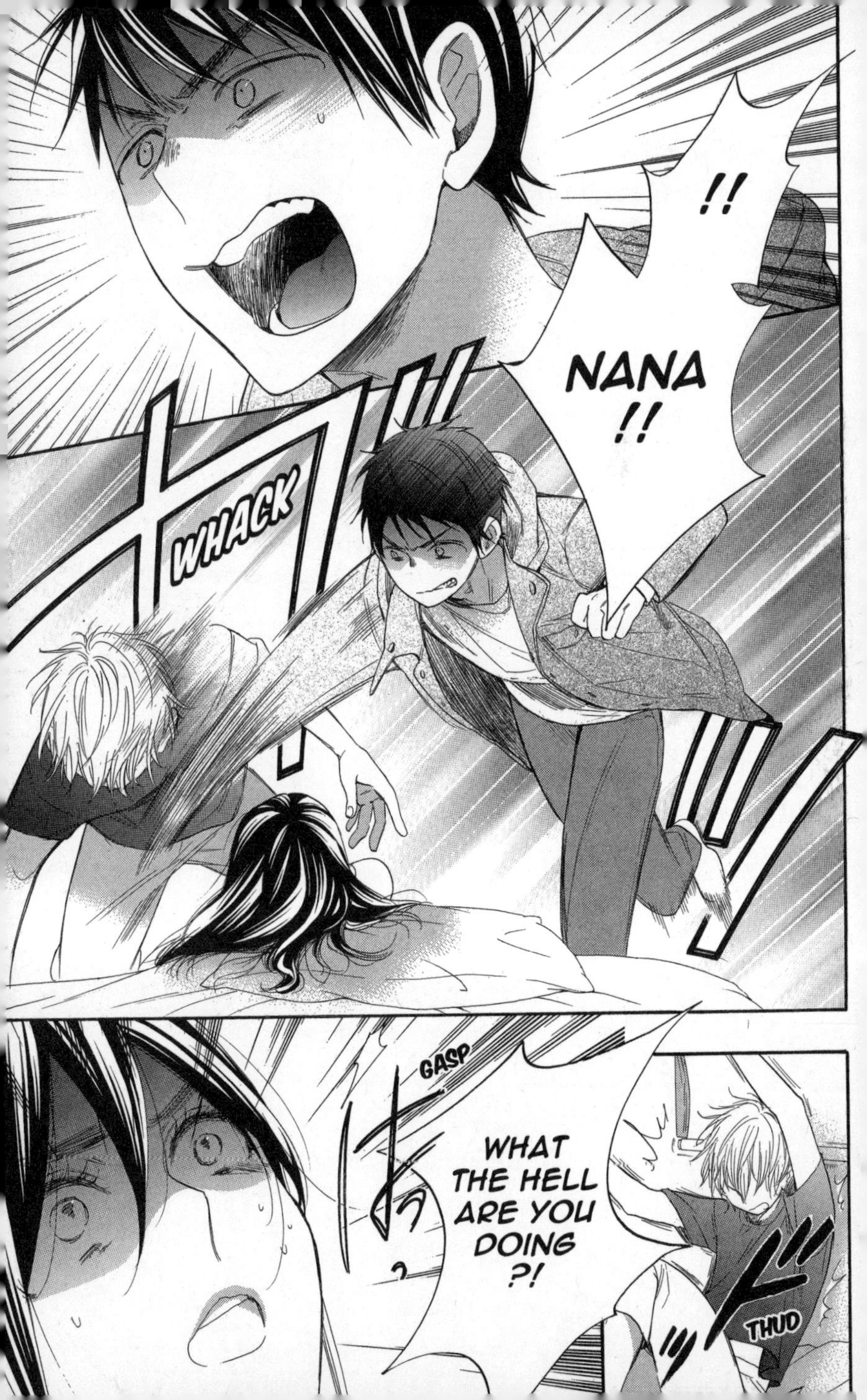
!!
NANA !!
WHACK
GASP
WHAT THE HELL ARE YOU DOING ?!
THUD

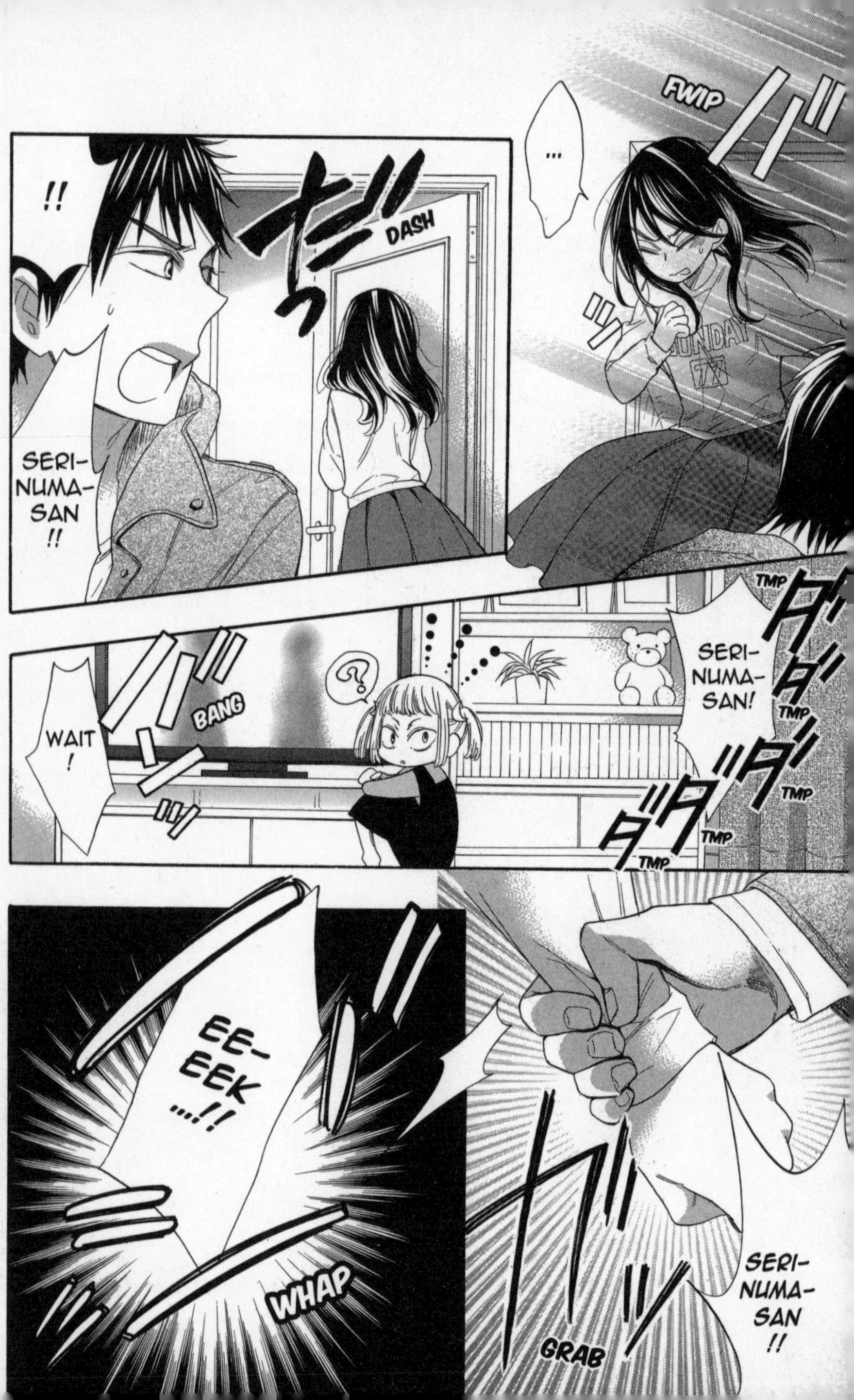
FWIP
...
!!
DASH
SERI-NUMA-SAN!!
TMP
SERI-NUMA-SAN!
TMP
TMP
TMP
TMP
?
BANG
WAIT!
SERI-NUMA-SAN!!
GRAB
EE-EEK...!!
WHAP

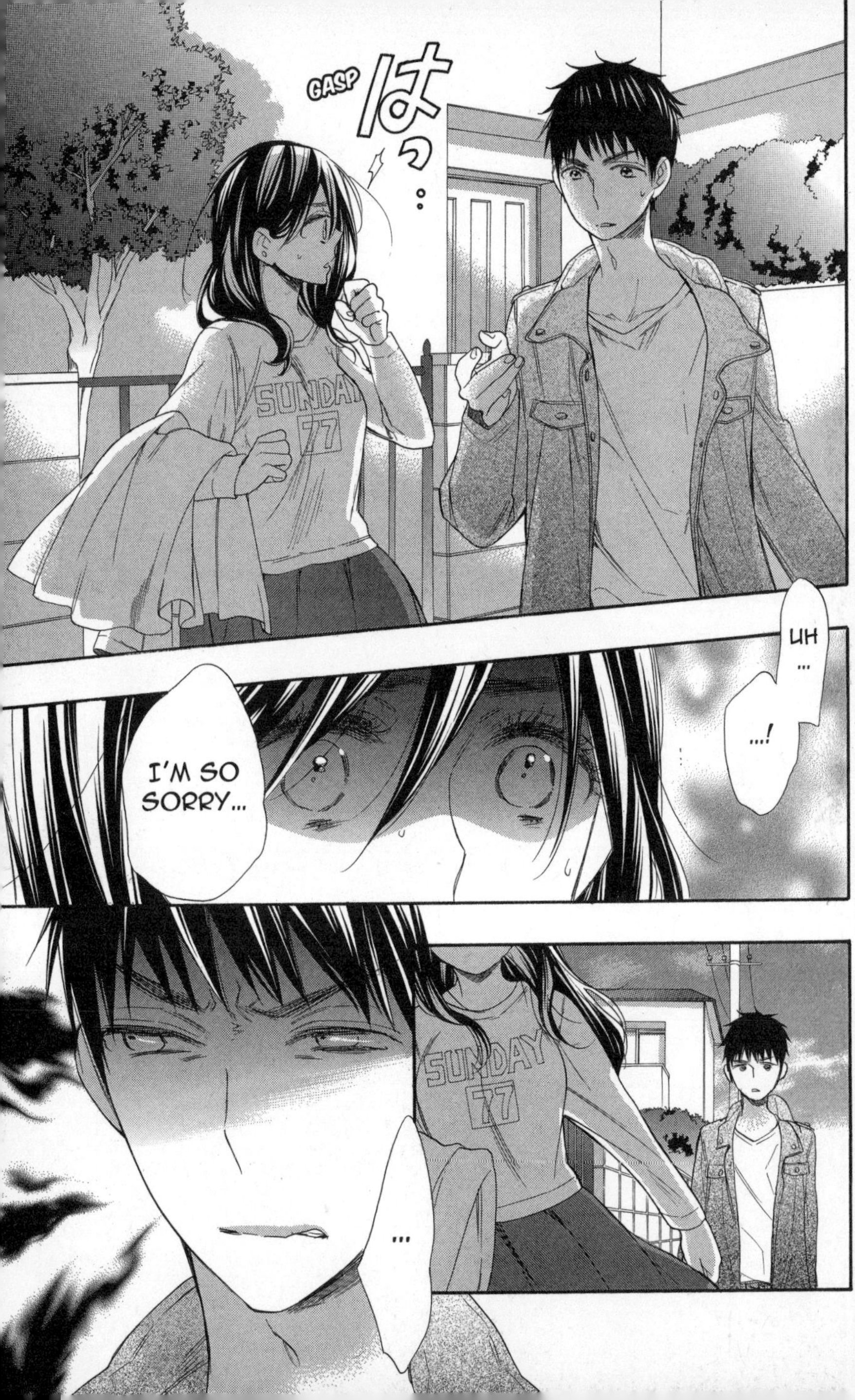
GASP
はっ
UH ...
...!
I'M SO SORRY...
...

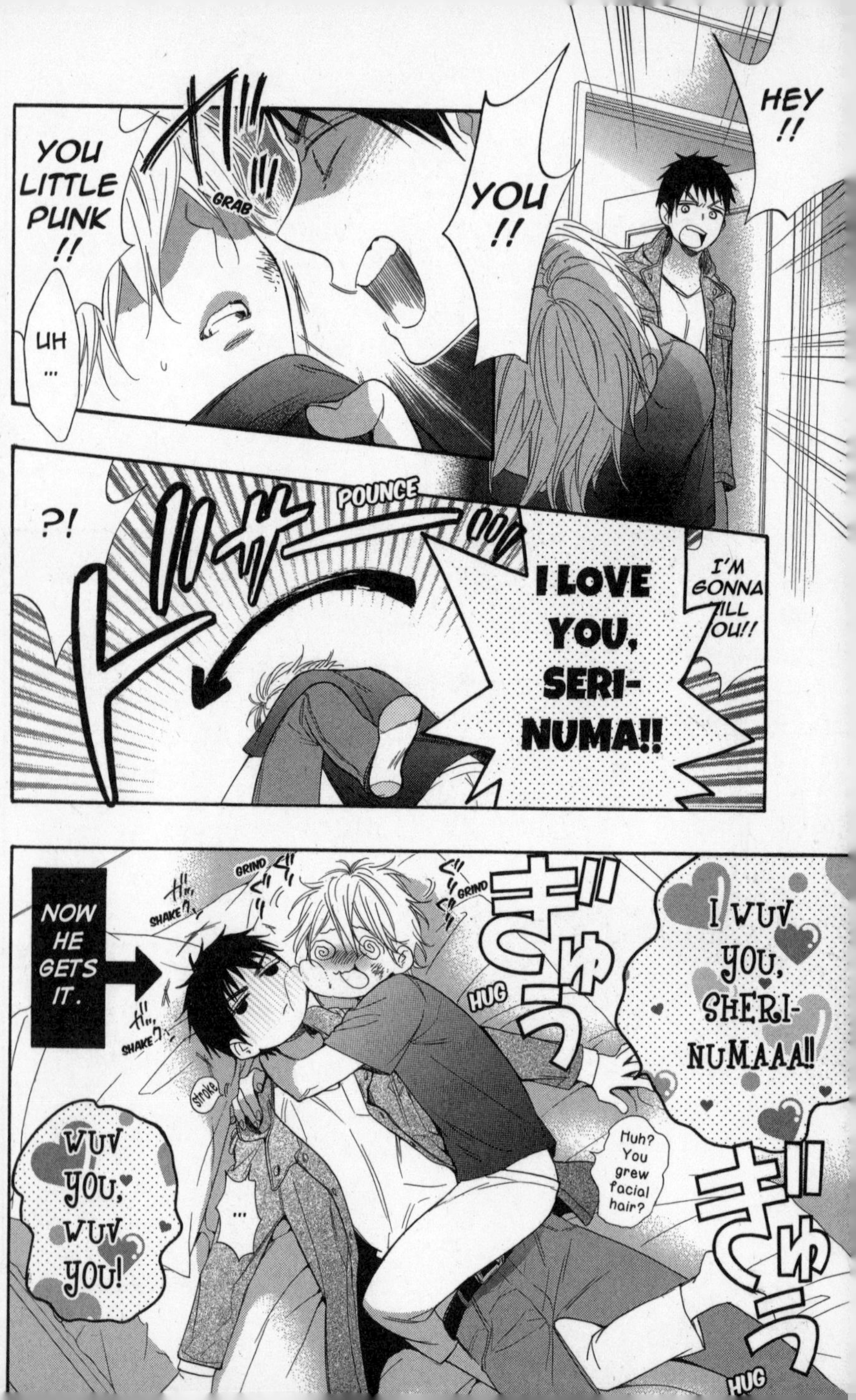
HEY!!
YOU!!
GRAB
YOU LITTLE PUNK!!
UH...
I'M GONNA ILL OU!!
I LOVE YOU, SERI-NUMA!!
POUNCE
?!
I WUV YOU, SHERI-NUMAAA!!
ぎゅう
HUG
ぎゅう
HUG
GRIND
GRIND
Huh? You grew facial hair?
...
NOW HE GETS IT.
SHAKE
SHAKE
stroke
WUV YOU, WUV YOU!

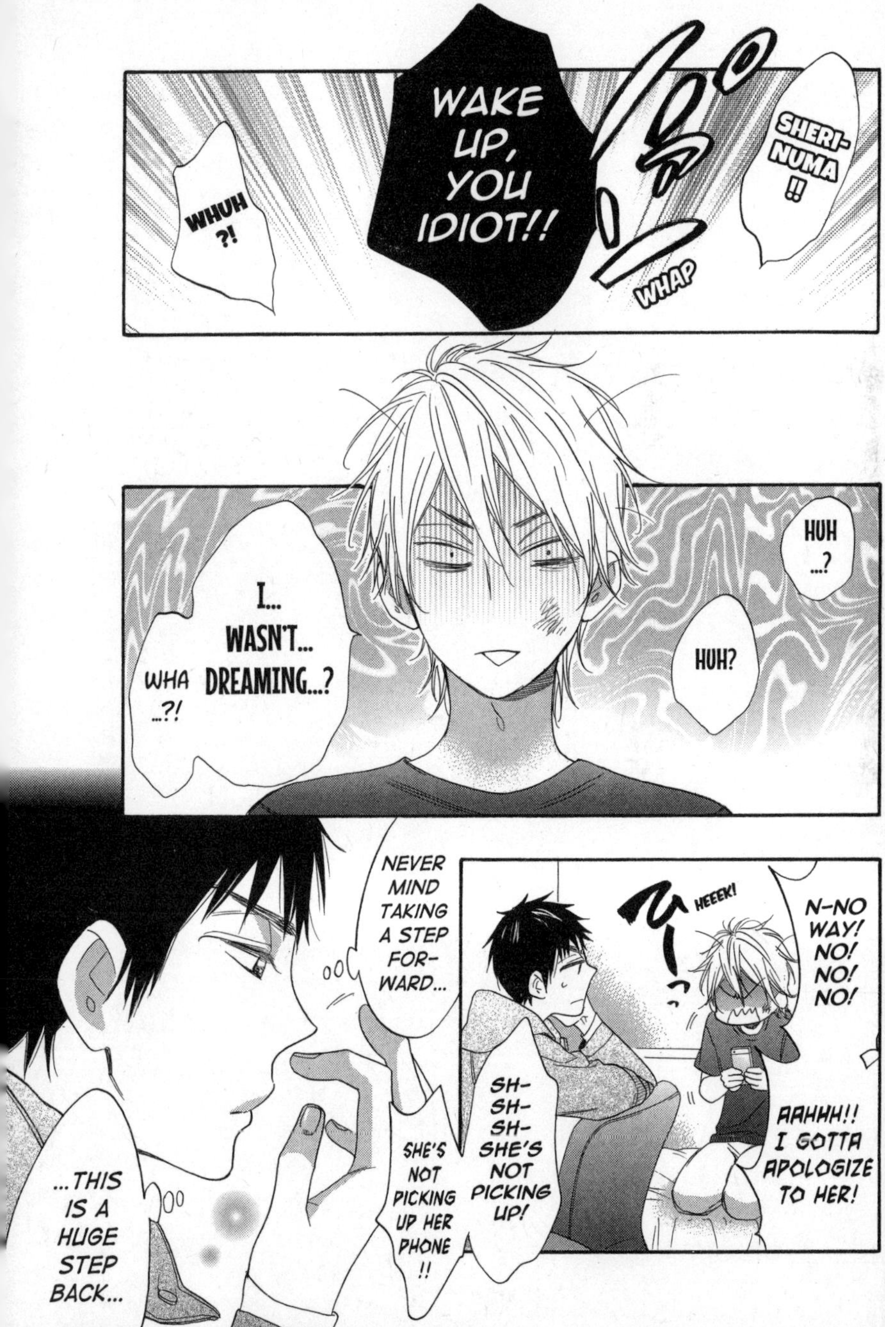
SHERI-NUMA!!
WHAP
WAKE UP, YOU IDIOT!!
WHUH?!
HUH...?
HUH?
I... WASN'T... DREAMING...?
WHA...?!
HEEEK!
N-NO WAY! NO! NO! NO!
AAHHH!! I GOTTA APOLOGIZE TO HER!
SH-SH-SH-SHE'S NOT PICKING UP!
SHE'S NOT PICKING UP HER PHONE!!
NEVER MIND TAKING A STEP FOR-WARD...
...THIS IS A HUGE STEP BACK...

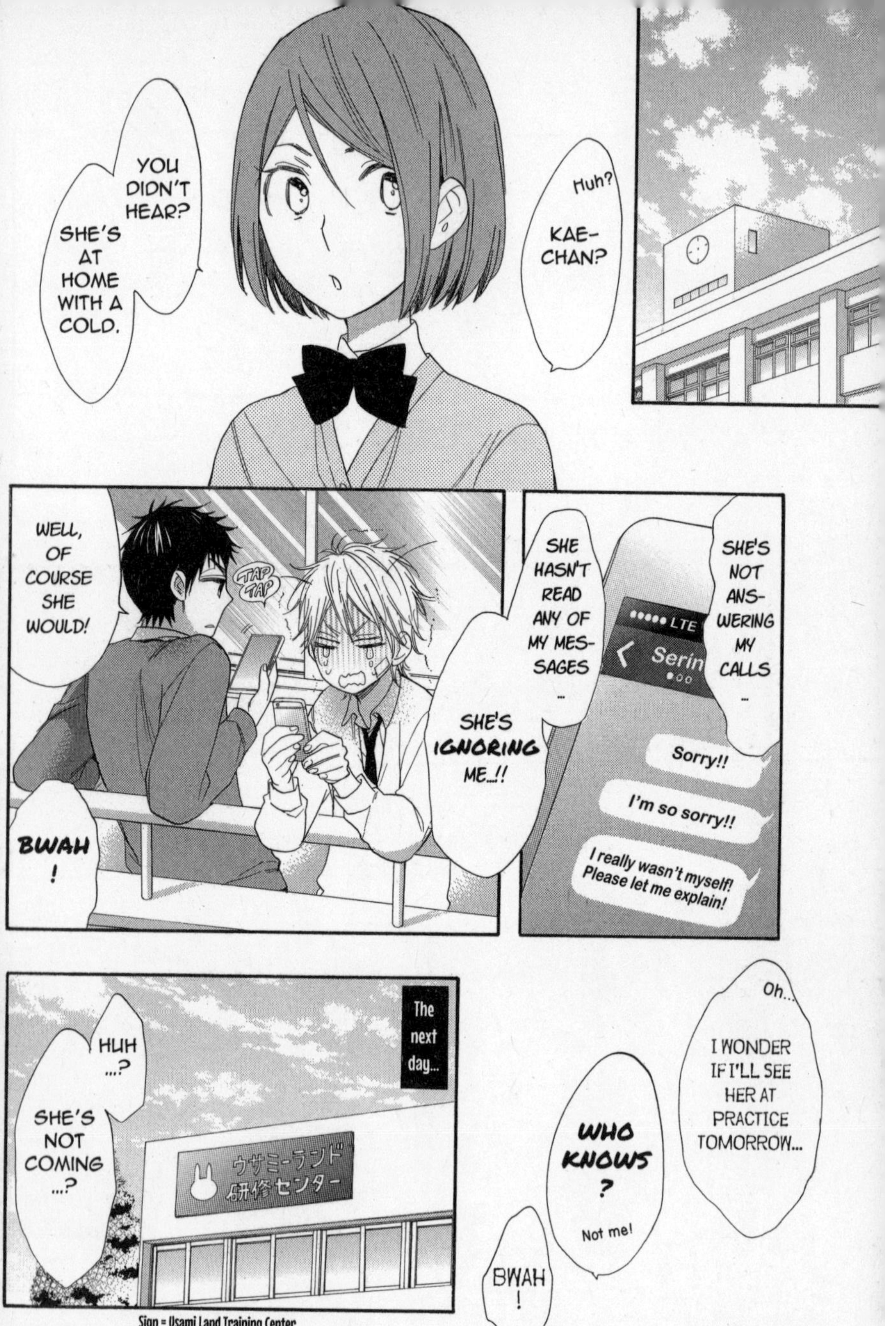
Huh?
KAE-CHAN?
YOU DIDN'T HEAR? SHE'S AT HOME WITH A COLD.
SHE'S NOT ANSWERING MY CALLS...
SHE HASN'T READ ANY OF MY MESSAGES...
LTE
Serin
Sorry!!
I'm so sorry!!
I really wasn't myself! Please let me explain!
SHE'S IGNORING ME...!!
TAP TAP
WELL, OF COURSE SHE WOULD!
BWAH!
Oh...
I WONDER IF I'LL SEE HER AT PRACTICE TOMORROW...
WHO KNOWS?
Not me!
BWAH!
The next day...
ウサミーランド
研修センター
HUH...?
SHE'S NOT COMING...?

Sign = Usami Land Training Center

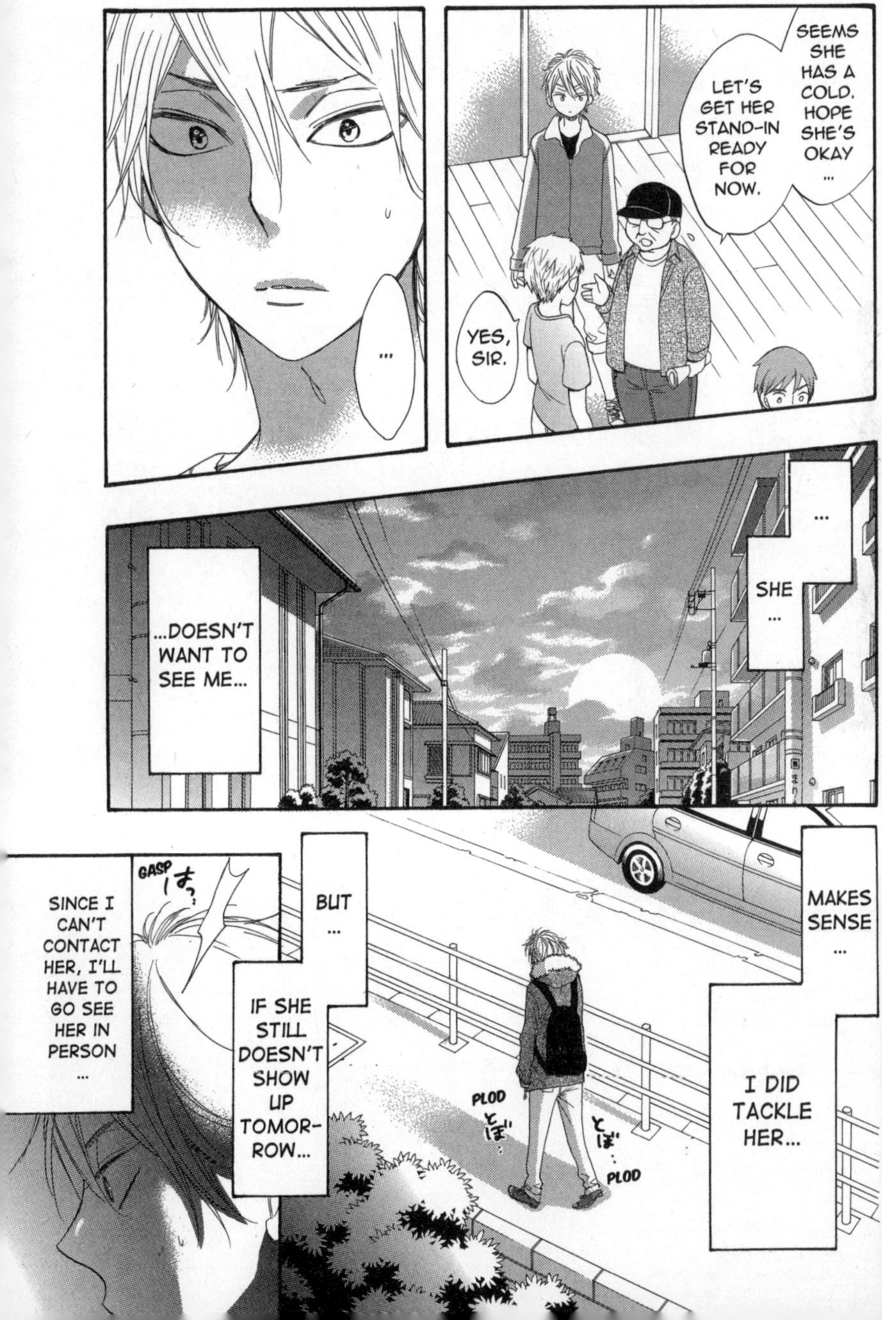
SEEMS SHE HAS A COLD. HOPE SHE'S OKAY ...
LET'S GET HER STAND-IN READY FOR NOW.
YES, SIR.
...
...
SHE ...
...DOESN'T WANT TO SEE ME...
MAKES SENSE ...
I DID TACKLE HER...
PLOD とぼ
とぼ... PLOD
BUT ...
IF SHE STILL DOESN'T SHOW UP TOMOR-ROW...
GASP はっ
SINCE I CAN'T CONTACT HER, I'LL HAVE TO GO SEE HER IN PERSON ...

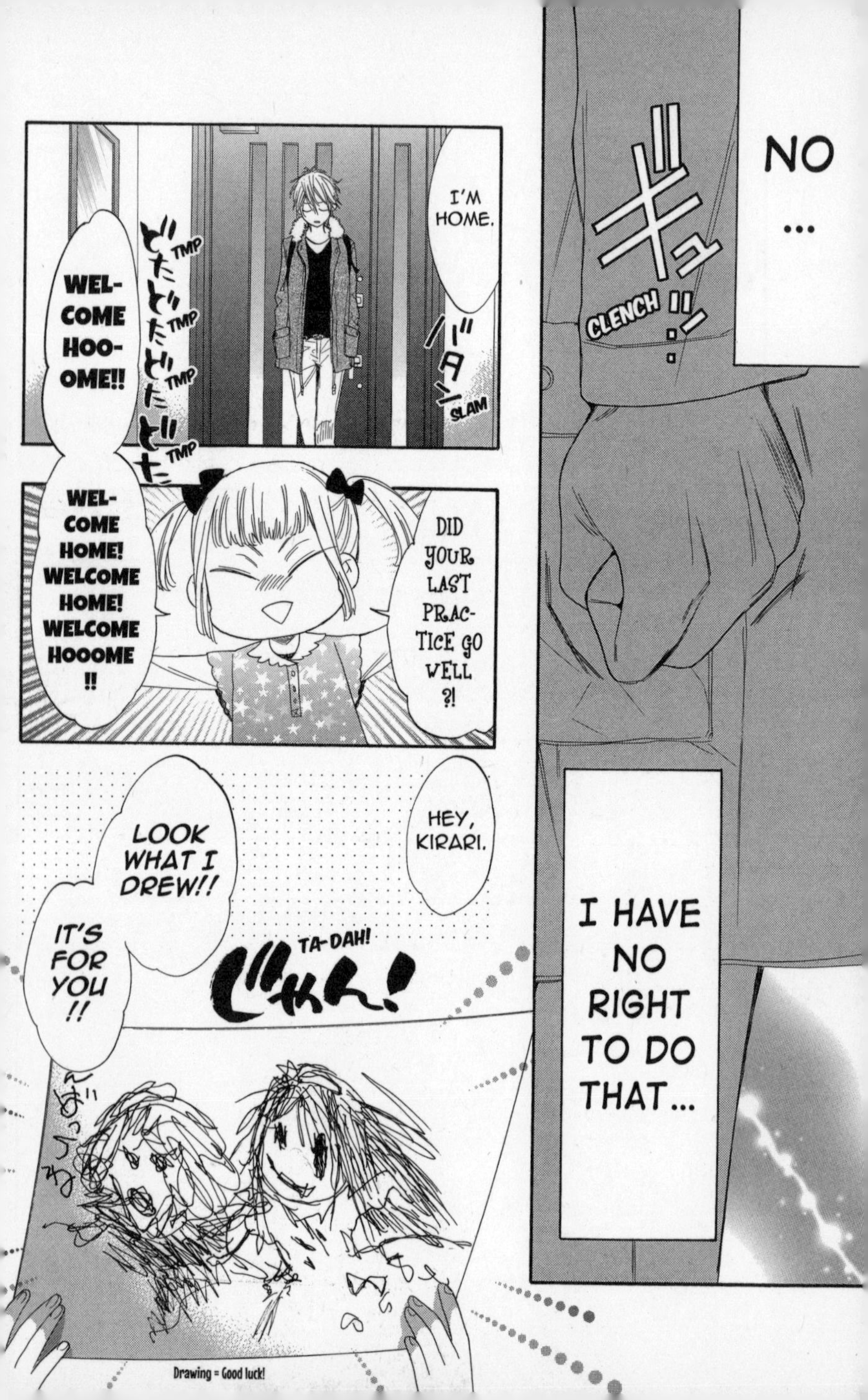
NO ...
CLENCH!!
I HAVE NO RIGHT TO DO THAT...
I'M HOME.
SLAM
TMP TMP TMP TMP
WEL-COME HOO-OME!!
DID YOUR LAST PRAC-TICE GO WELL ?!
WEL-COME HOME! WELCOME HOME! WELCOME HOOOME !!
HEY, KIRARI.
TA-DAH!
LOOK WHAT I DREW!!
IT'S FOR YOU !!
Drawing = Good luck!

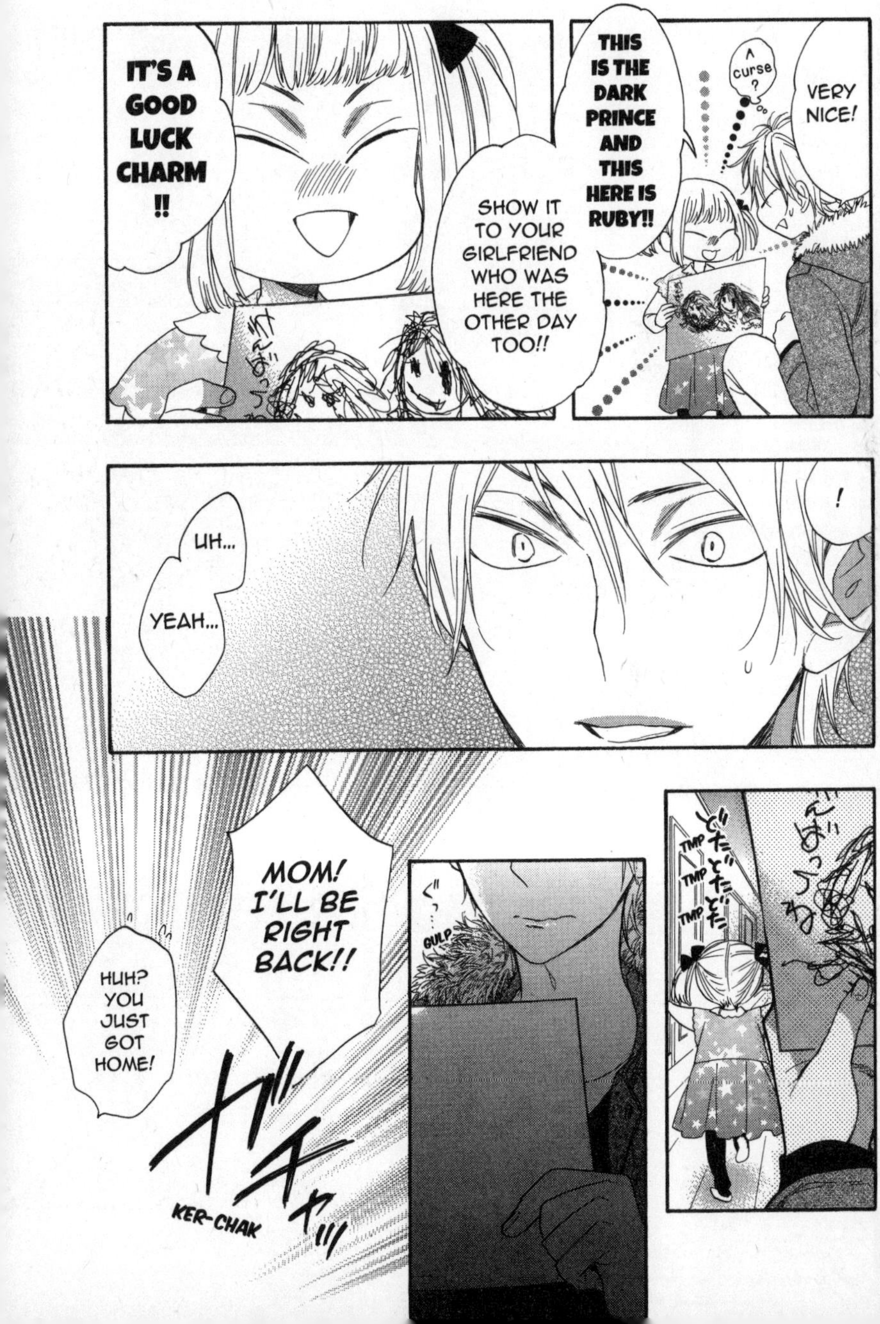
VERY NICE!
A curse?
THIS IS THE DARK PRINCE AND THIS HERE IS RUBY!!
SHOW IT TO YOUR GIRLFRIEND WHO WAS HERE THE OTHER DAY TOO!!
IT'S A GOOD LUCK CHARM !!
!
UH... YEAH...
TMP
TMP
TMP
GULP
MOM! I'LL BE RIGHT BACK!!
HUH? YOU JUST GOT HOME!
KER-CHAK

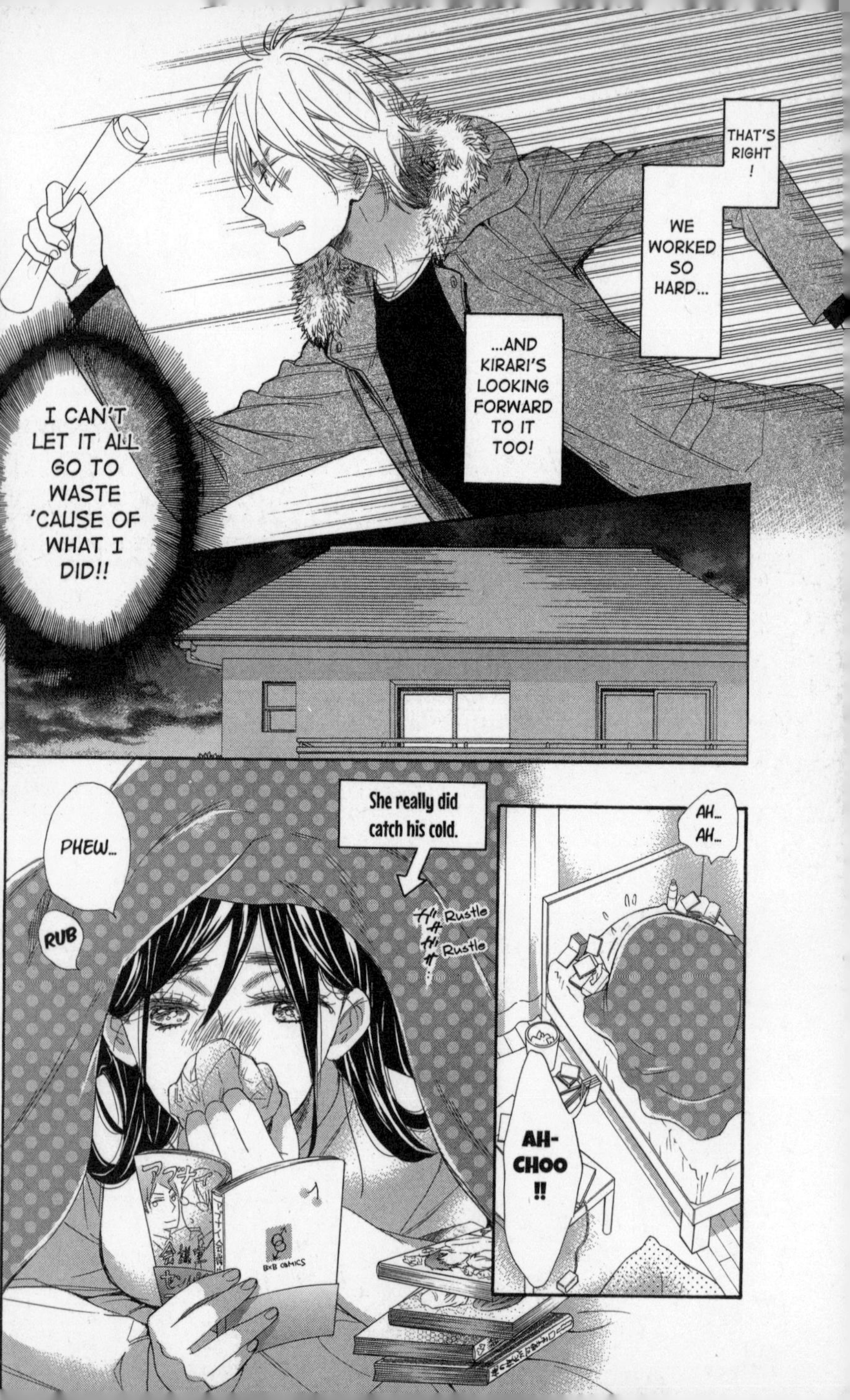
THAT'S RIGHT!
WE WORKED SO HARD...
...AND KIRARI'S LOOKING FORWARD TO IT TOO!
I CAN'T LET IT ALL GO TO WASTE 'CAUSE OF WHAT I DID!!
AH... AH...
AH-CHOO!!
She really did catch his cold.
Rustle
Rustle
PHEW...
RUB
BxB COMICS

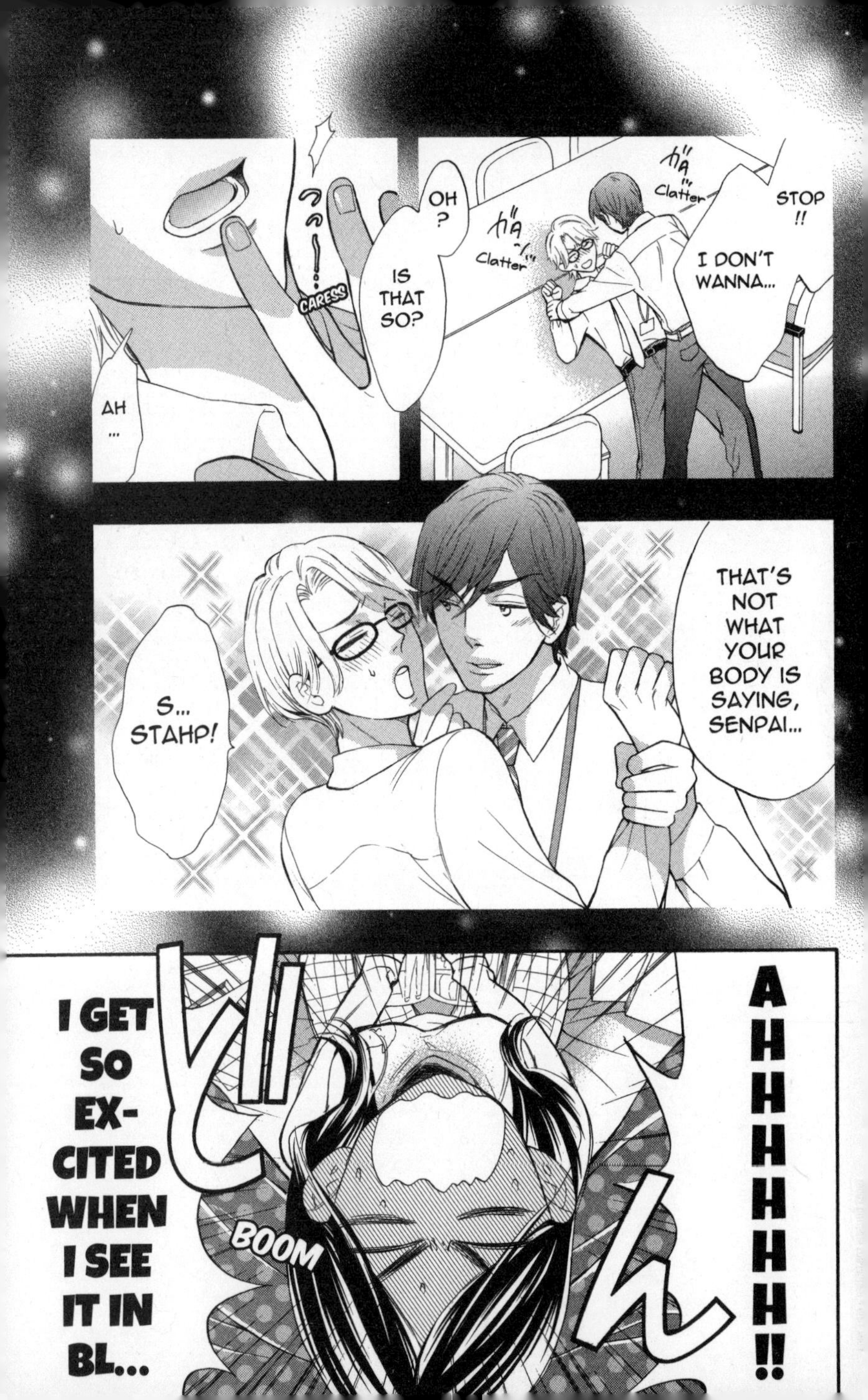
STOP!!
I DON'T WANNA...
Clatter
Clatter
OH? IS THAT SO?
CARESS
AH...
THAT'S NOT WHAT YOUR BODY IS SAYING, SENPAI...
S... STAHP!
AHHHHHHH!!
BOOM
I GET SO EX-CITED WHEN I SEE IT IN BL...

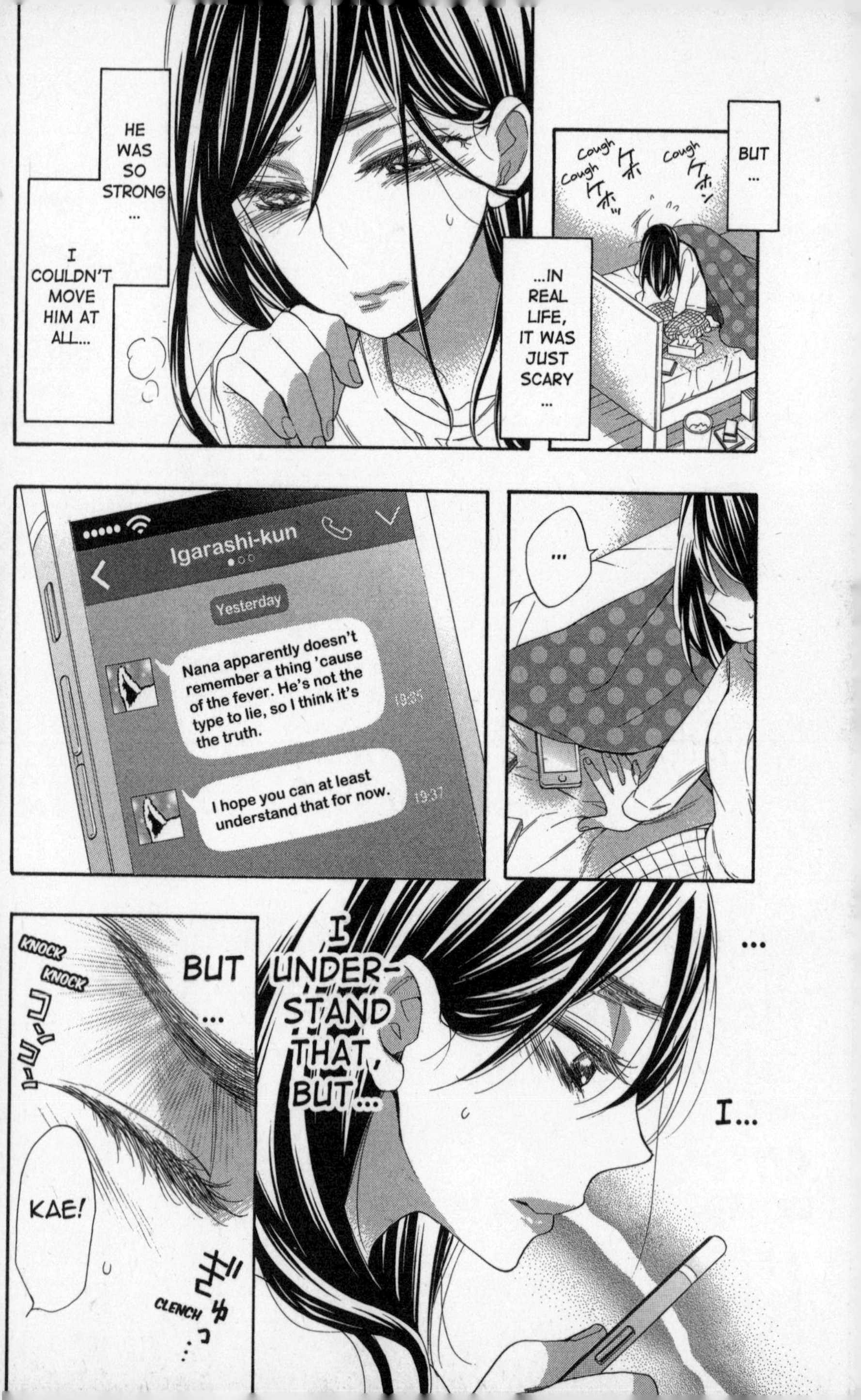
BUT ...
Cough Cough
Cough
...IN REAL LIFE, IT WAS JUST SCARY ...
HE WAS SO STRONG ...
I COULDN'T MOVE HIM AT ALL...
...
Igarashi-kun
Yesterday
Nana apparently doesn't remember a thing 'cause of the fever. He's not the type to lie, so I think it's the truth.
I hope you can at least understand that for now.
19:37
...
I UNDER-STAND THAT, BUT...
I...
BUT ...
KNOCK KNOCK
KAE!
CLENCH

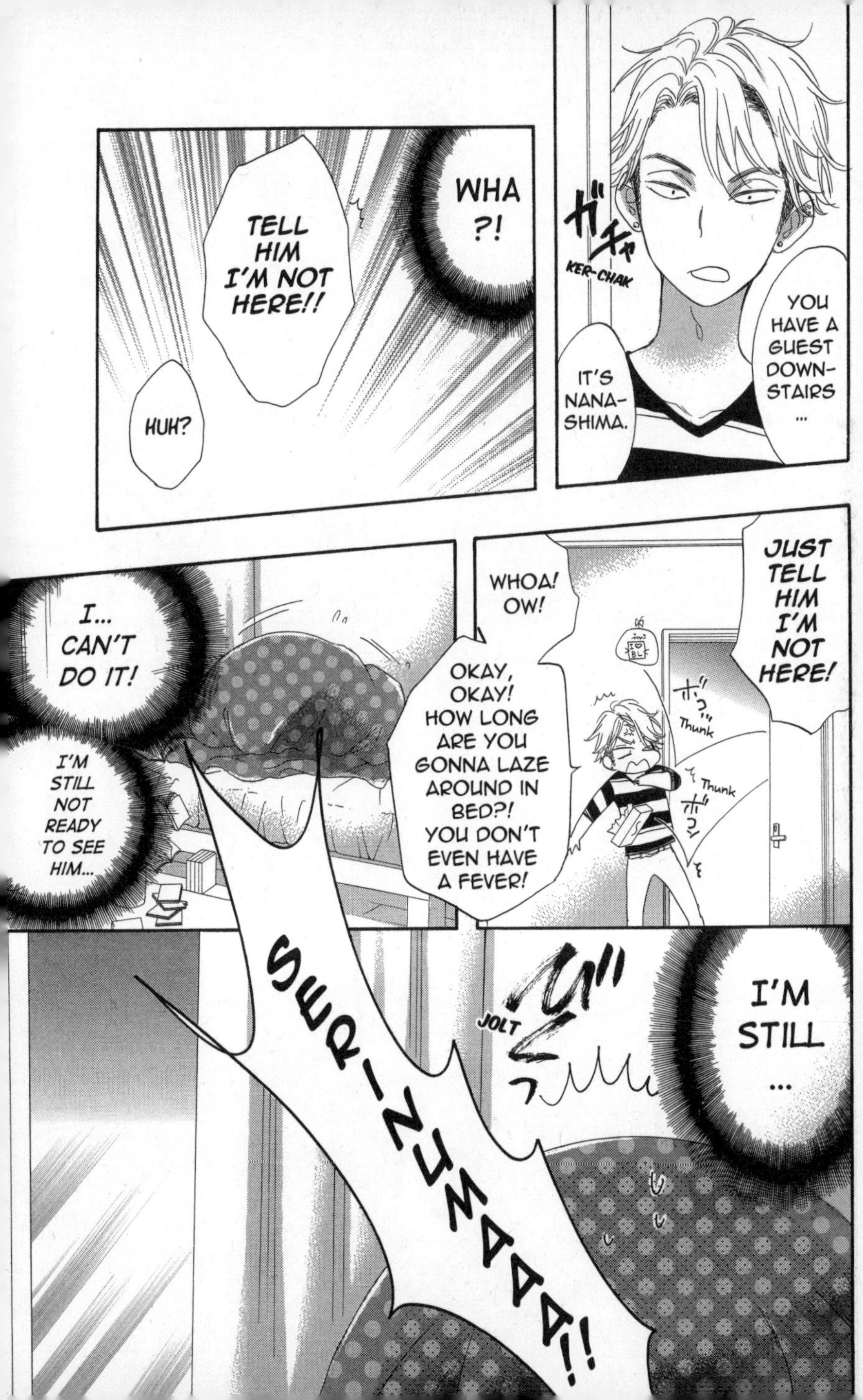
ガチャ
KER-CHAK
YOU HAVE A GUEST DOWNSTAIRS...
IT'S NANASHIMA.
WHA?!
TELL HIM I'M NOT HERE!!
HUH?
JUST TELL HIM I'M NOT HERE!
WHOA! OW!
Thunk
Thunk
OKAY, OKAY! HOW LONG ARE YOU GONNA LAZE AROUND IN BED?! YOU DON'T EVEN HAVE A FEVER!
I... CAN'T DO IT!
I'M STILL NOT READY TO SEE HIM...
I'M STILL...
JOLT
SERI-ZUMAAA!!

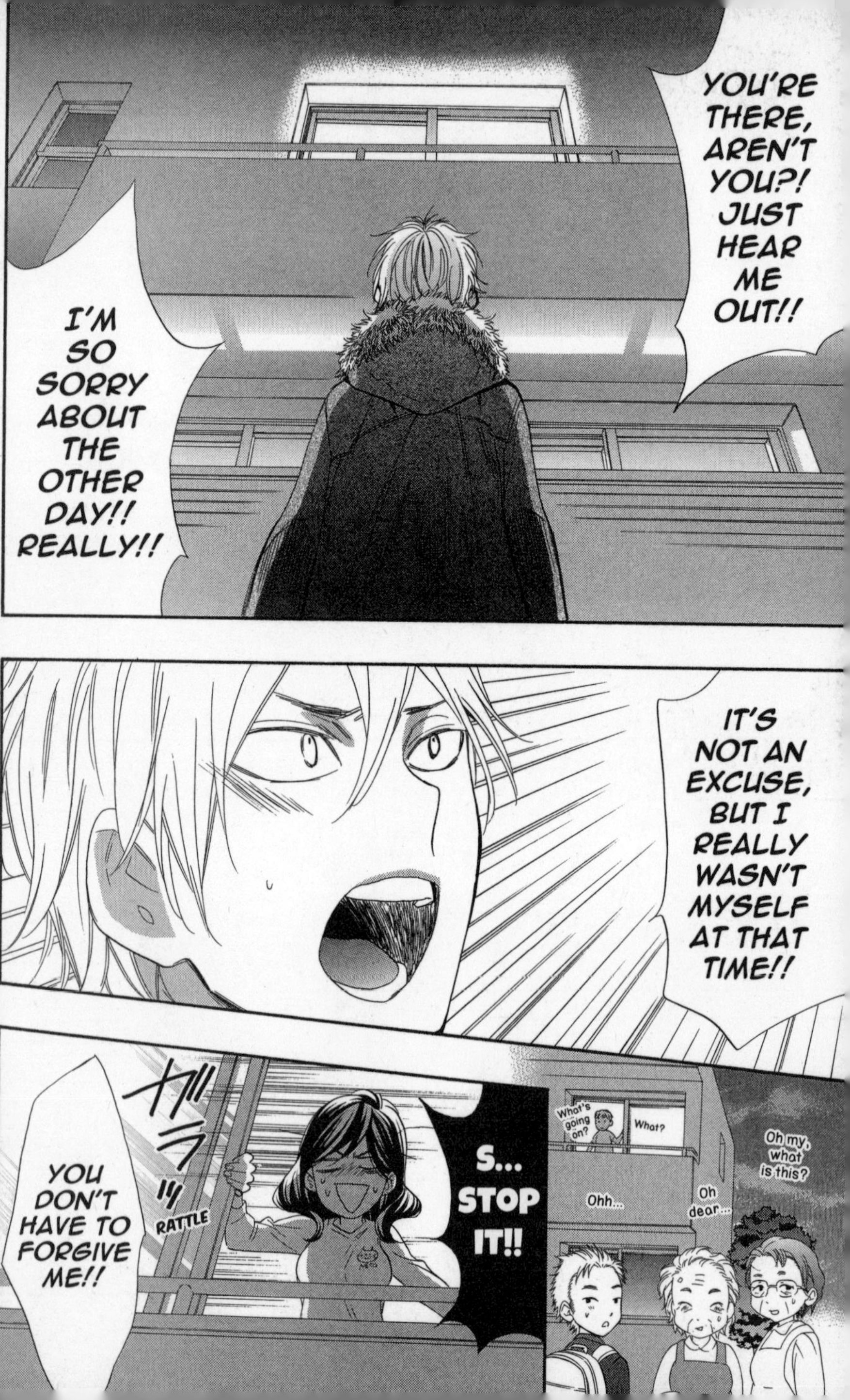
YOU'RE THERE, AREN'T YOU?! JUST HEAR ME OUT!!
I'M SO SORRY ABOUT THE OTHER DAY!! REALLY!!
IT'S NOT AN EXCUSE, BUT I REALLY WASN'T MYSELF AT THAT TIME!!
Oh my, what is this?
What?
What's going on?
Oh dear...
Ohh...
S... STOP IT!!
RATTLE
YOU DON'T HAVE TO FORGIVE ME!!

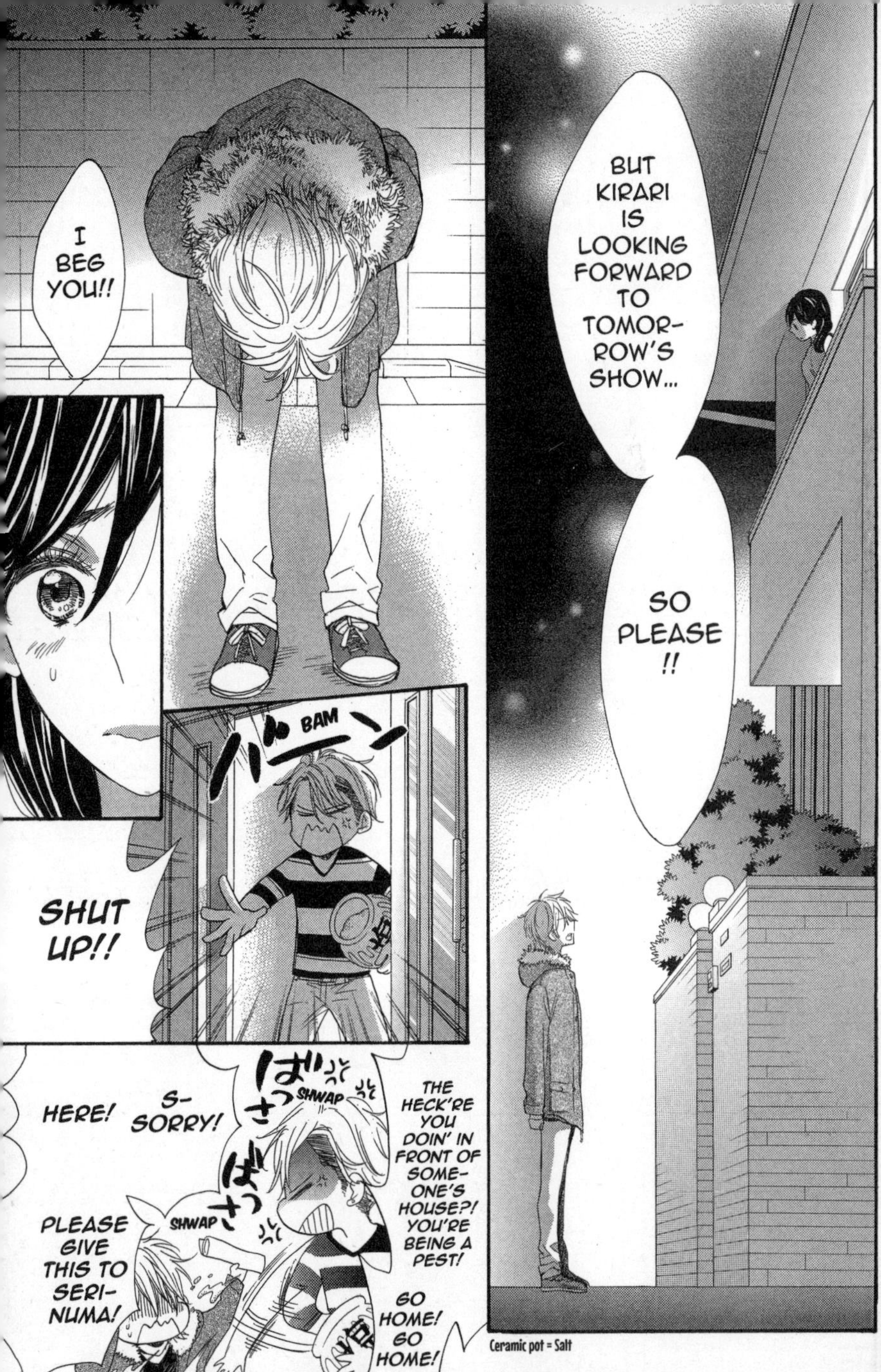
BUT KIRARI IS LOOKING FORWARD TO TOMORROW'S SHOW...
SO PLEASE!!
I BEG YOU!!
BAM
SHUT UP!!
THE HECK'RE YOU DOIN' IN FRONT OF SOMEONE'S HOUSE?! YOU'RE BEING A PEST!
SHWAP
S-SORRY!
HERE!
PLEASE GIVE THIS TO SERINUMA!
SHWAP
GO HOME! GO HOME!

Ceramic pot = Salt

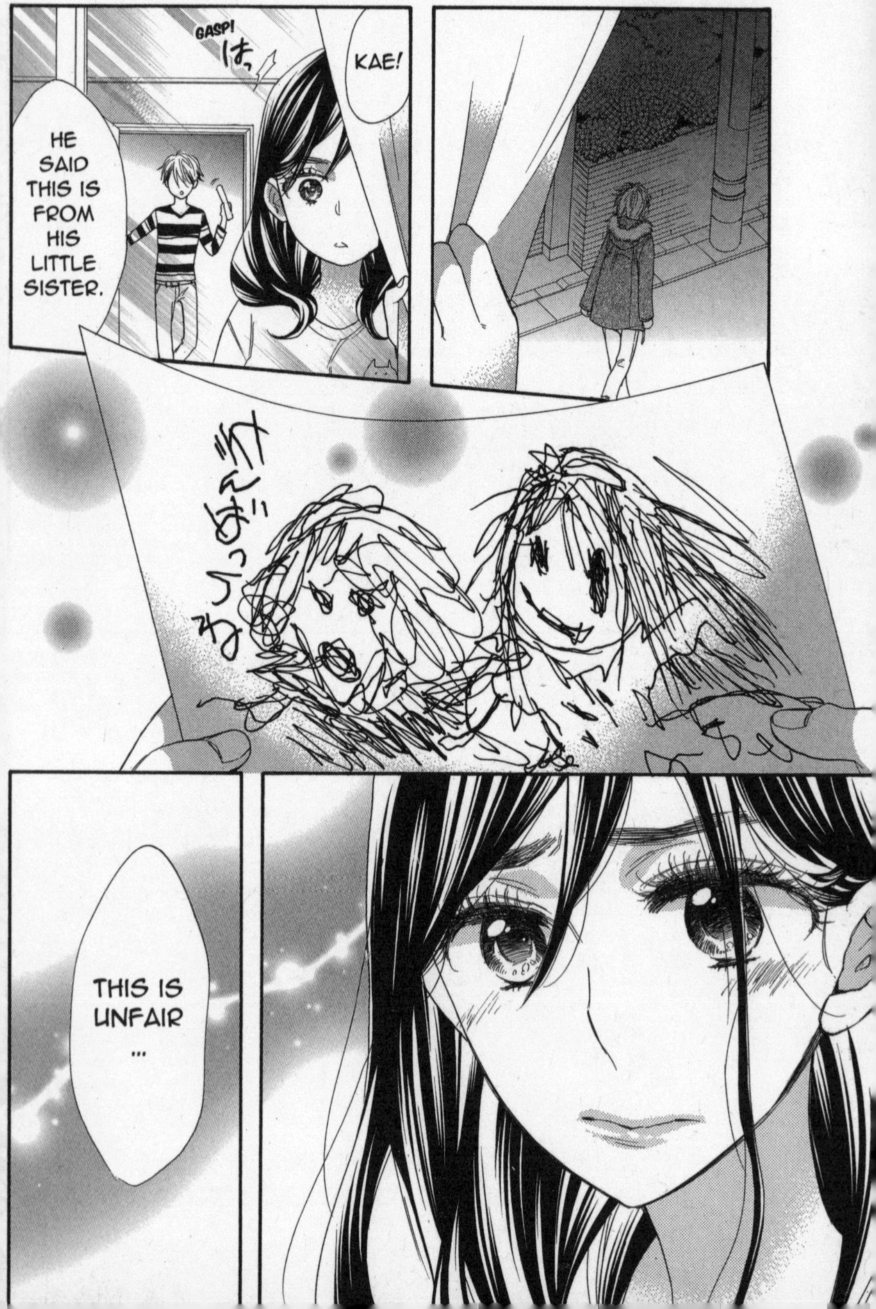
KAE!
GASP!
はっ
HE SAID THIS IS FROM HIS LITTLE SISTER.
THIS IS UNFAIR ...

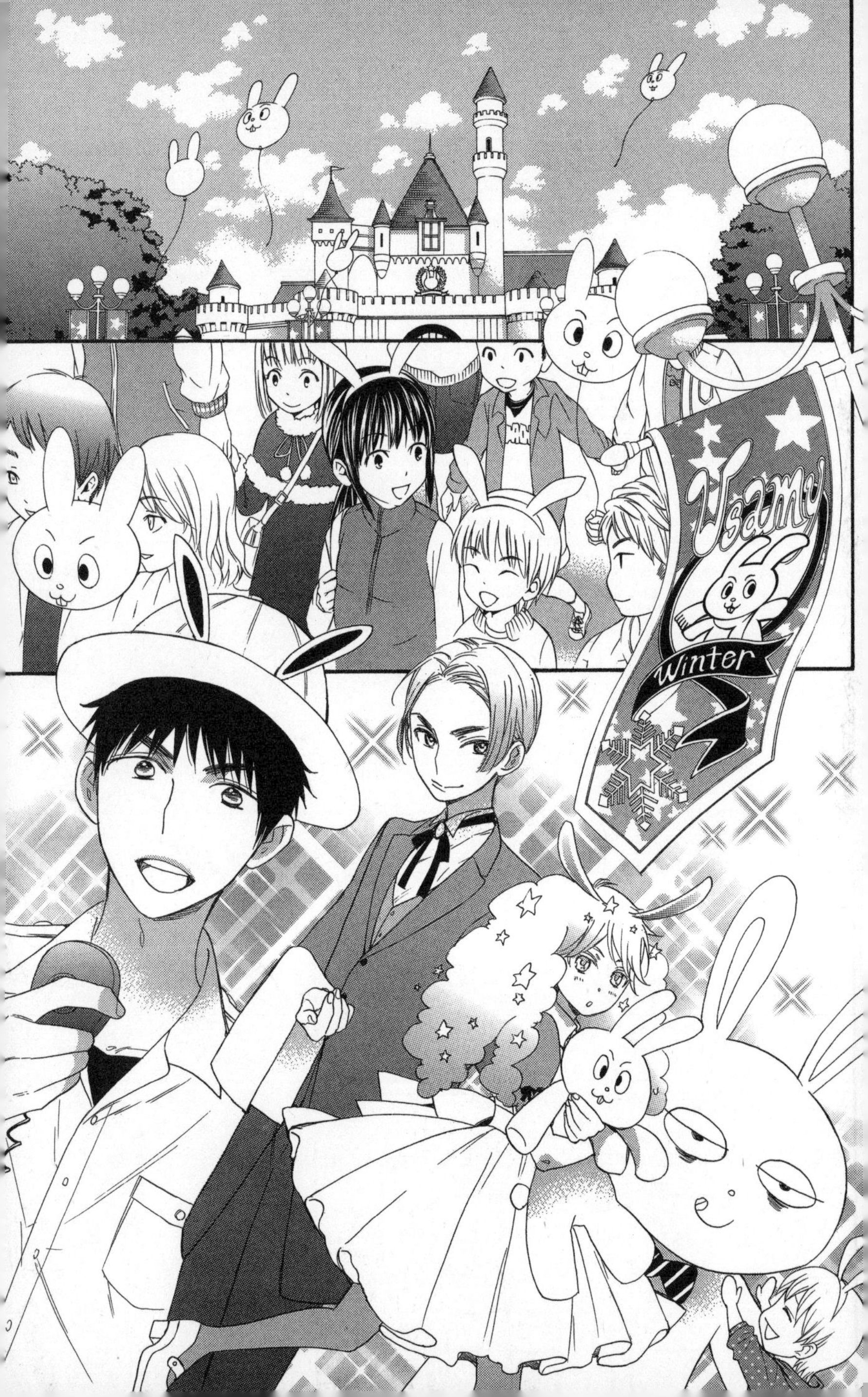
Usamy
Winter

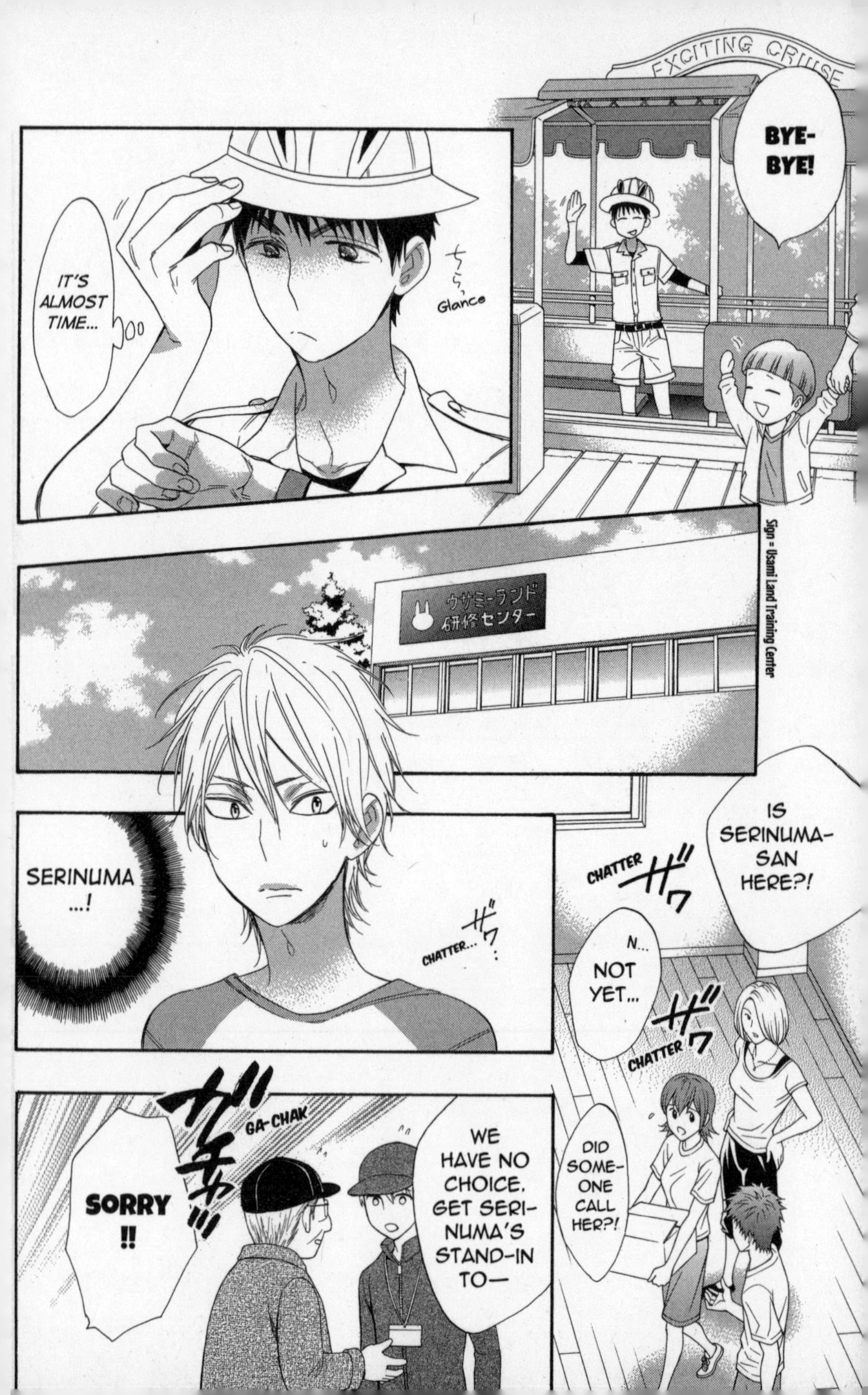
EXCITING CRUISE
BYE-BYE!
Glance
IT'S ALMOST TIME...
Sign = Usami Land Training Center
ウサミーランド 研修センター
IS SERINUMA-SAN HERE?!
CHATTER
N... NOT YET...
CHATTER
DID SOMEONE CALL HER?!
SERINUMA ...!
CHATTER...
WE HAVE NO CHOICE. GET SERINUMA'S STAND-IN TO—
GA-CHAK
SORRY!!

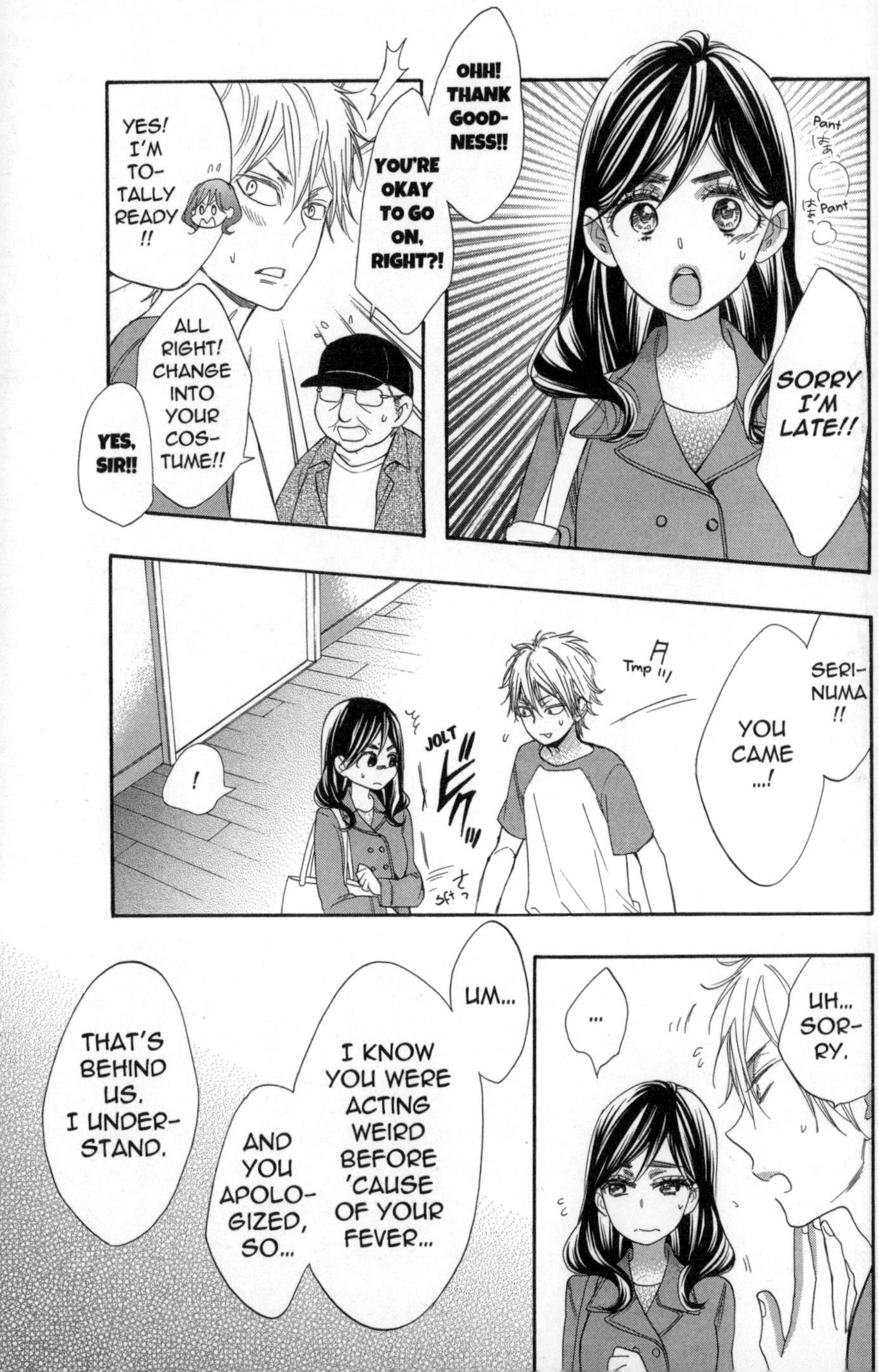
Pant
はぁ
Pant
はぁ
SORRY I'M LATE!!
OHH! THANK GOOD-NESS!!
YOU'RE OKAY TO GO ON, RIGHT?!
YES! I'M TO-TALLY READY!!
ALL RIGHT! CHANGE INTO YOUR COS-TUME!!
YES, SIR!!
SERI-NUMA!!
YOU CAME...!
Tmp
JOLT
!
Sft
UH... SOR-RY.
...
UM...
I KNOW YOU WERE ACTING WEIRD BEFORE 'CAUSE OF YOUR FEVER...
AND YOU APOLO-GIZED, SO...
THAT'S BEHIND US. I UNDER-STAND.

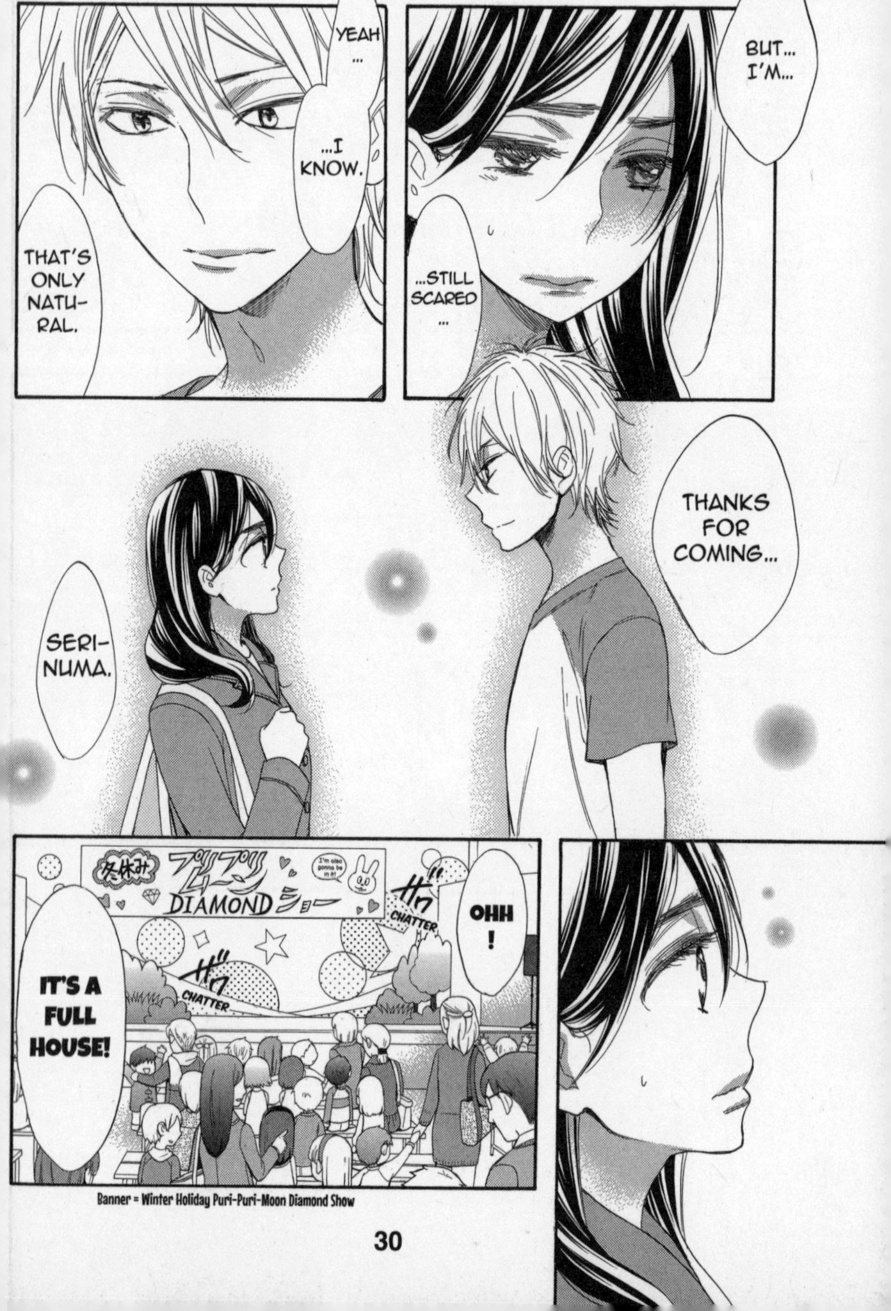
BUT... I'M...
...STILL SCARED...
YEAH...
...I KNOW.
THAT'S ONLY NATURAL.
THANKS FOR COMING...
SERI-NUMA.
OHH!
CHATTER
I'm also gonna be in it!
DIAMOND
CHATTER
IT'S A FULL HOUSE!
Banner = Winter Holiday Puri-Puri-Moon Diamond Show

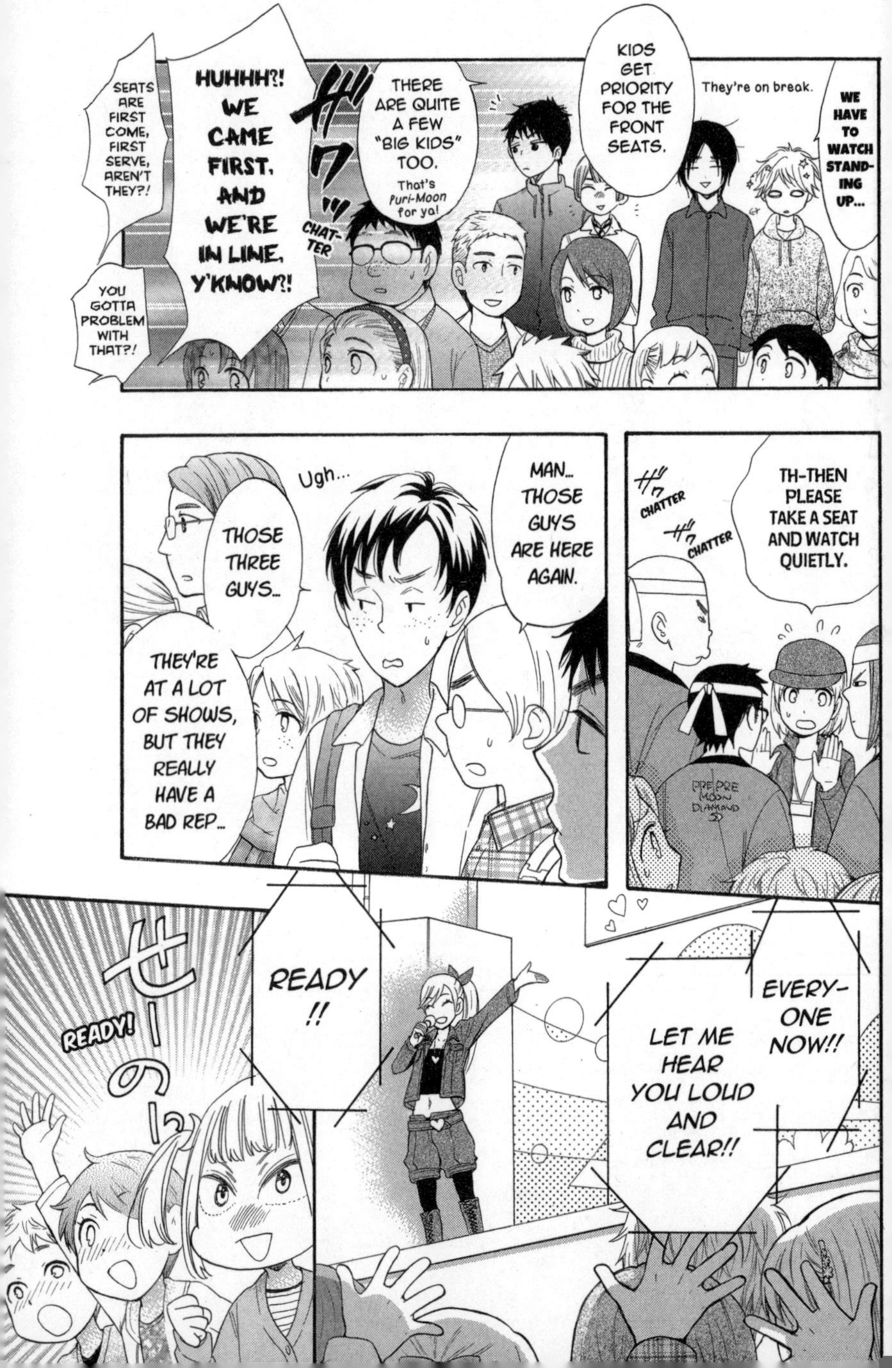
WE HAVE TO WATCH STANDING UP...
They're on break.
KIDS GET PRIORITY FOR THE FRONT SEATS.
THERE ARE QUITE A FEW "BIG KIDS" TOO.
That's Puri-Moon for ya!
ザワッ
CHAT-TER
HUHHH?! WE CAME FIRST, AND WE'RE IN LINE, Y'KNOW?!
SEATS ARE FIRST COME, FIRST SERVE, AREN'T THEY?!
YOU GOTTA PROBLEM WITH THAT?!
CHATTER
CHATTER
TH-THEN PLEASE TAKE A SEAT AND WATCH QUIETLY.
PRE PRE MOON DIAMOND
MAN... THOSE GUYS ARE HERE AGAIN.
Ugh...
THOSE THREE GUYS...
THEY'RE AT A LOT OF SHOWS, BUT THEY REALLY HAVE A BAD REP...
EVERY-ONE NOW!!
LET ME HEAR YOU LOUD AND CLEAR!!
READY !!
せーのっ
READY!

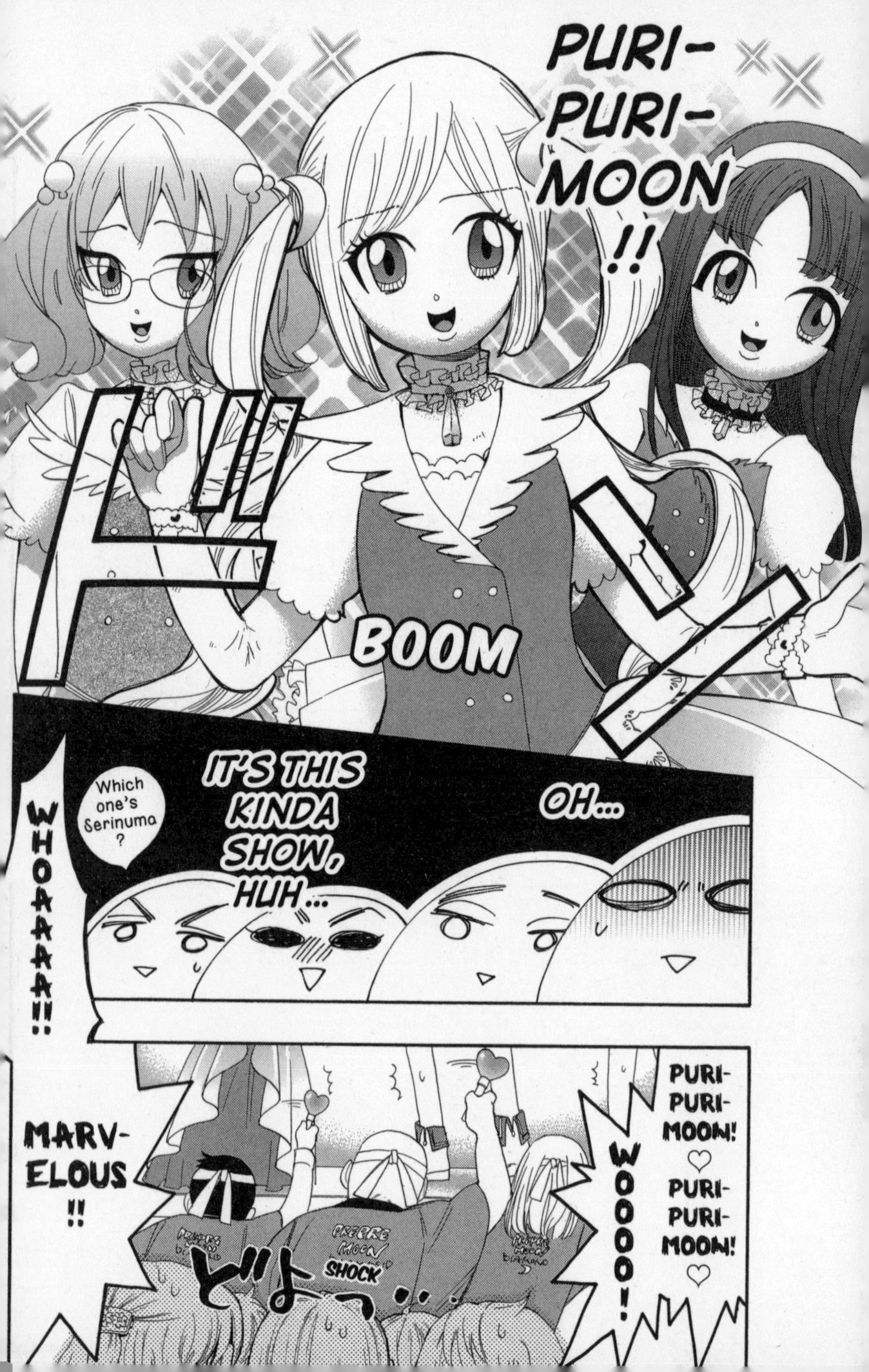

PURI-PURI-MOON!!
BOOM
OH...
IT'S THIS KINDA SHOW, HUH...
Which one's Serinuma?
WHOAAAAA!!
PURI-PURI-MOON! ♡ PURI-PURI-MOON! ♡
WOOOO!
MARV-ELOUS!!
SHOCK

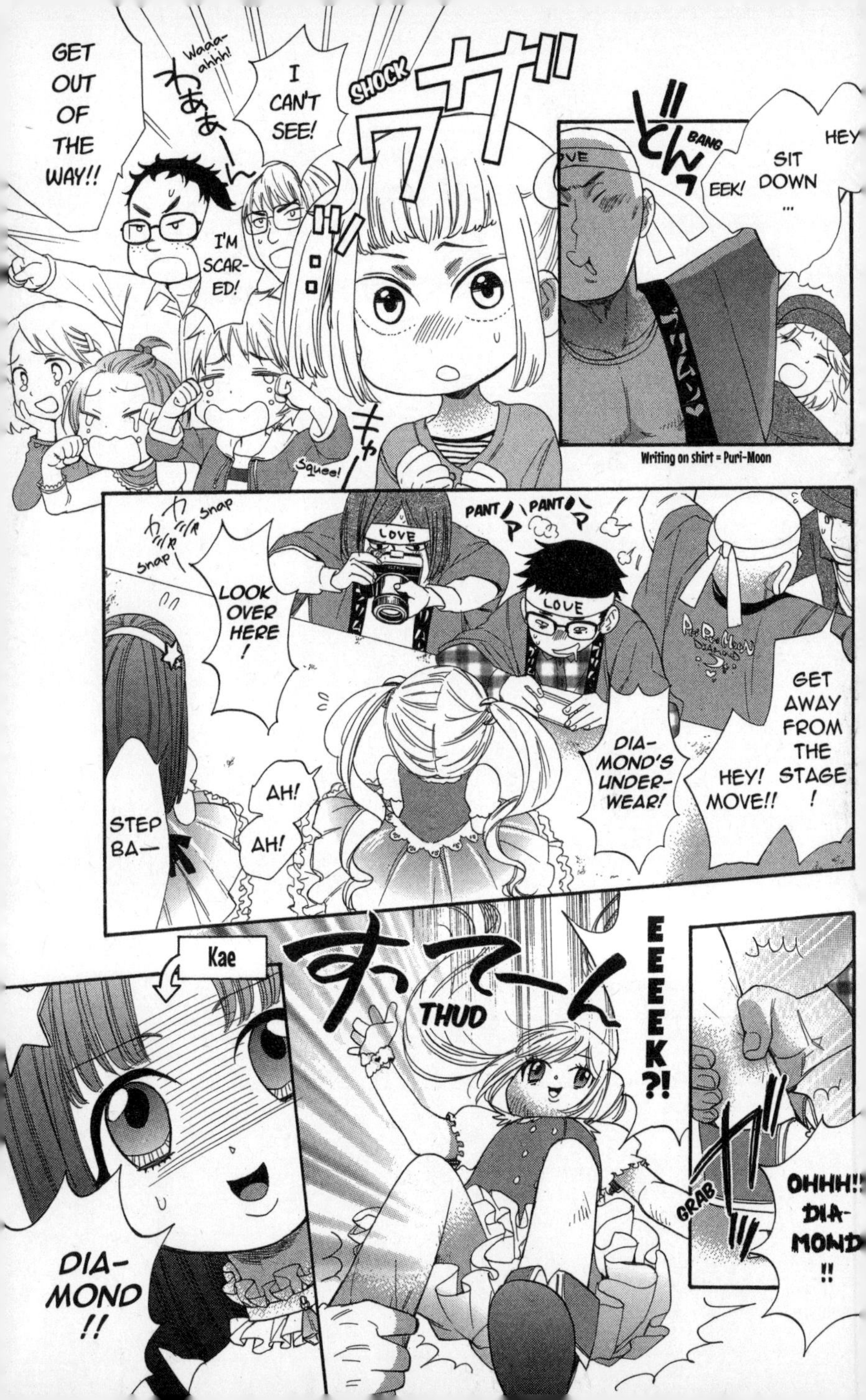
BANG
HEY SIT DOWN ...
EEK!
Writing on shirt = Puri-Moon
SHOCK
I CAN'T SEE!
Waaa-ahhh!
GET OUT OF THE WAY!!
I'M SCAR-ED!
Squee!
GET AWAY FROM THE STAGE!
HEY! MOVE!!
PANT PANT
DIA-MOND'S UNDER-WEAR!
LOVE
LOVE
Snap Snap
LOOK OVER HERE!
AH!
AH!
STEP BA—
OHHH!! DIA-MOND!!
GRAB
EEEEK?!
THUD
Kae
DIA-MOND!!

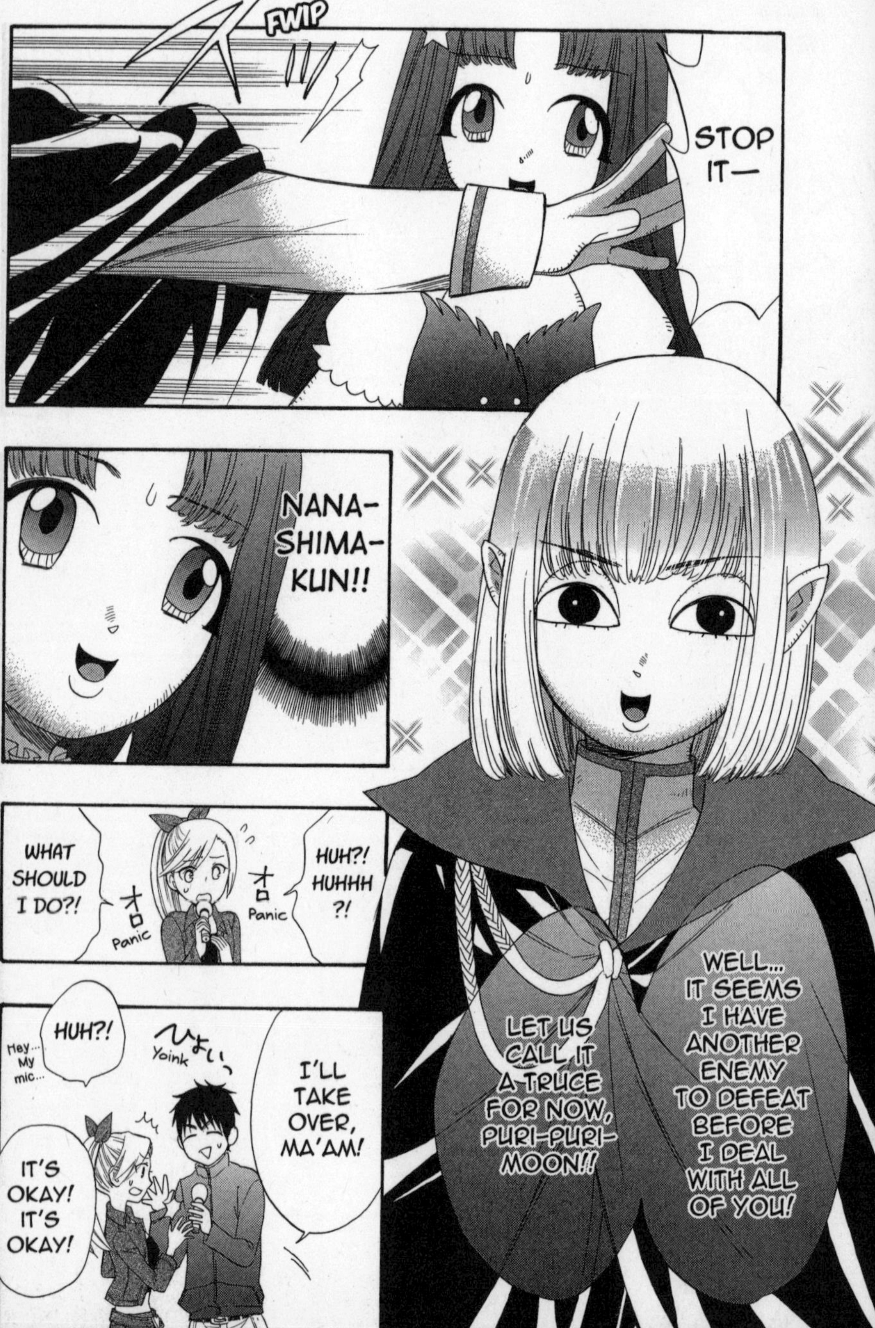
FWIP
STOP IT—
WELL... IT SEEMS I HAVE ANOTHER ENEMY TO DEFEAT BEFORE I DEAL WITH ALL OF YOU!
LET US CALL IT A TRUCE FOR NOW, PURI-PURI-MOON!!
NANA-SHIMA-KUN!!
HUH?! HUHHH ?!
オロ Panic
オロ Panic
WHAT SHOULD I DO?!
I'LL TAKE OVER, MA'AM!
ひょい Yoink
HUH?!
Hey... My mic...
IT'S OKAY! IT'S OKAY!

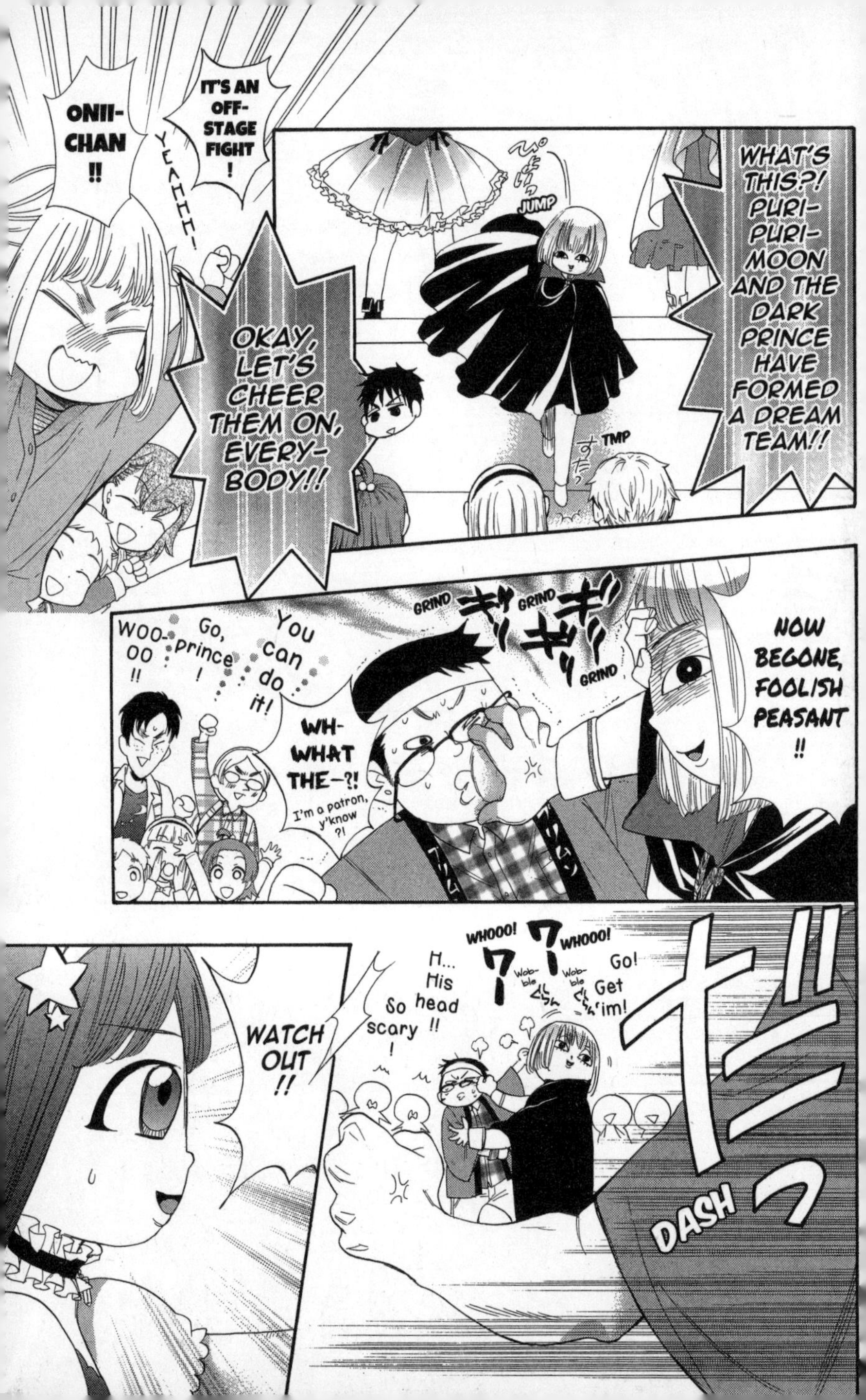
WHAT'S THIS?! PURI-PURI-MOON AND THE DARK PRINCE HAVE FORMED A DREAM TEAM!!
JUMP
TMP
OKAY, LET'S CHEER THEM ON, EVERY-BODY!!
IT'S AN OFF-STAGE FIGHT!
YEAHHH!
ONII-CHAN!!
GRIND GRIND GRIND
NOW BEGONE, FOOLISH PEASANT!!
WH-WHAT THE-?!
I'm a patron, y'know?!
You can do it!
Go, prince!
WOO-OO!!
DASH
WHOOO! WHOOO!
Go! Get 'im!
Wob-ble Wob-ble
H... His head!!
So scary!
WATCH OUT!!

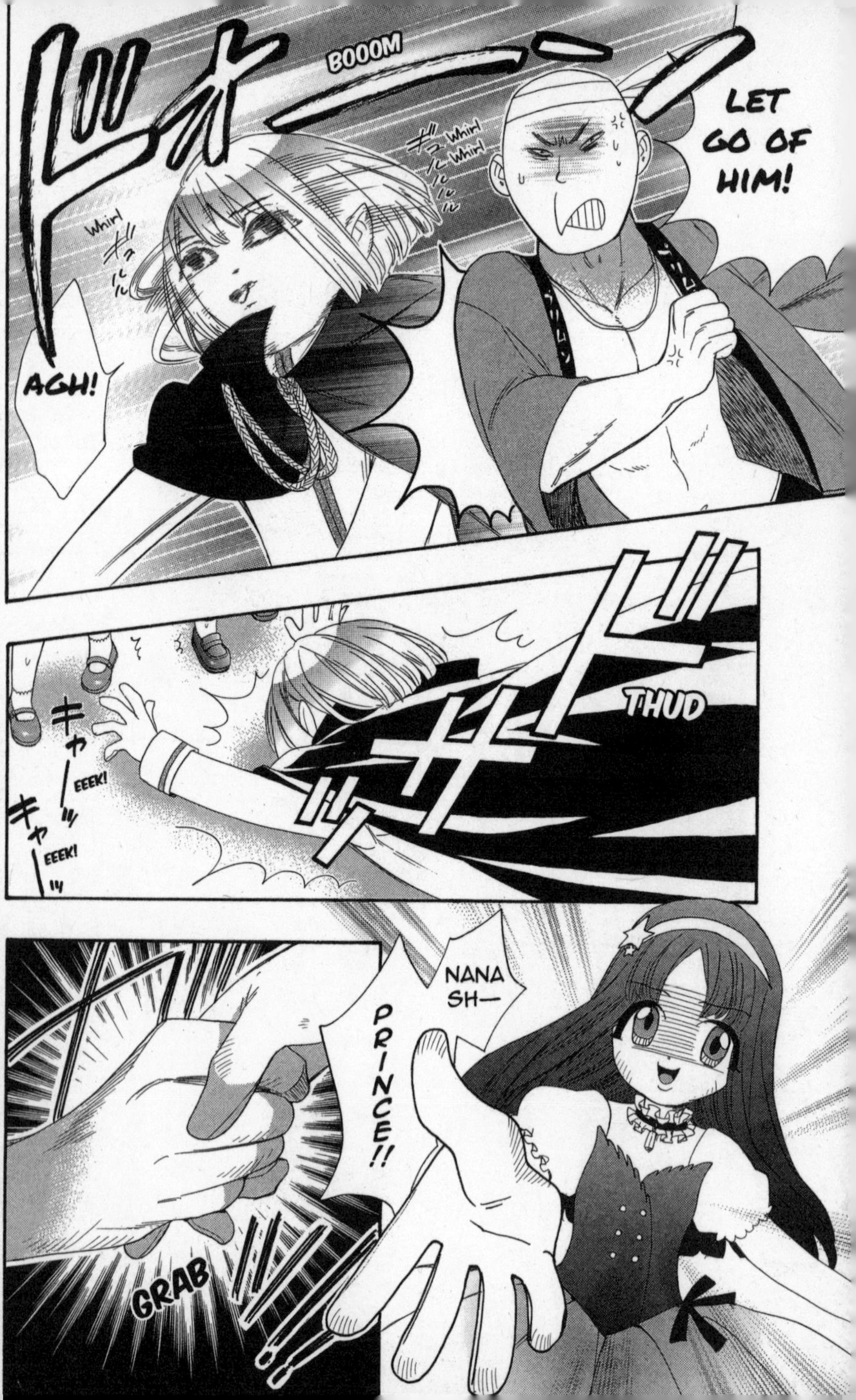
BOOOM
LET GO OF HIM!
Whirl Whirl
Whirl
AGH!
THUD
EEEK!
EEEK!
NANA SH—
PRINCE!!
GRAB

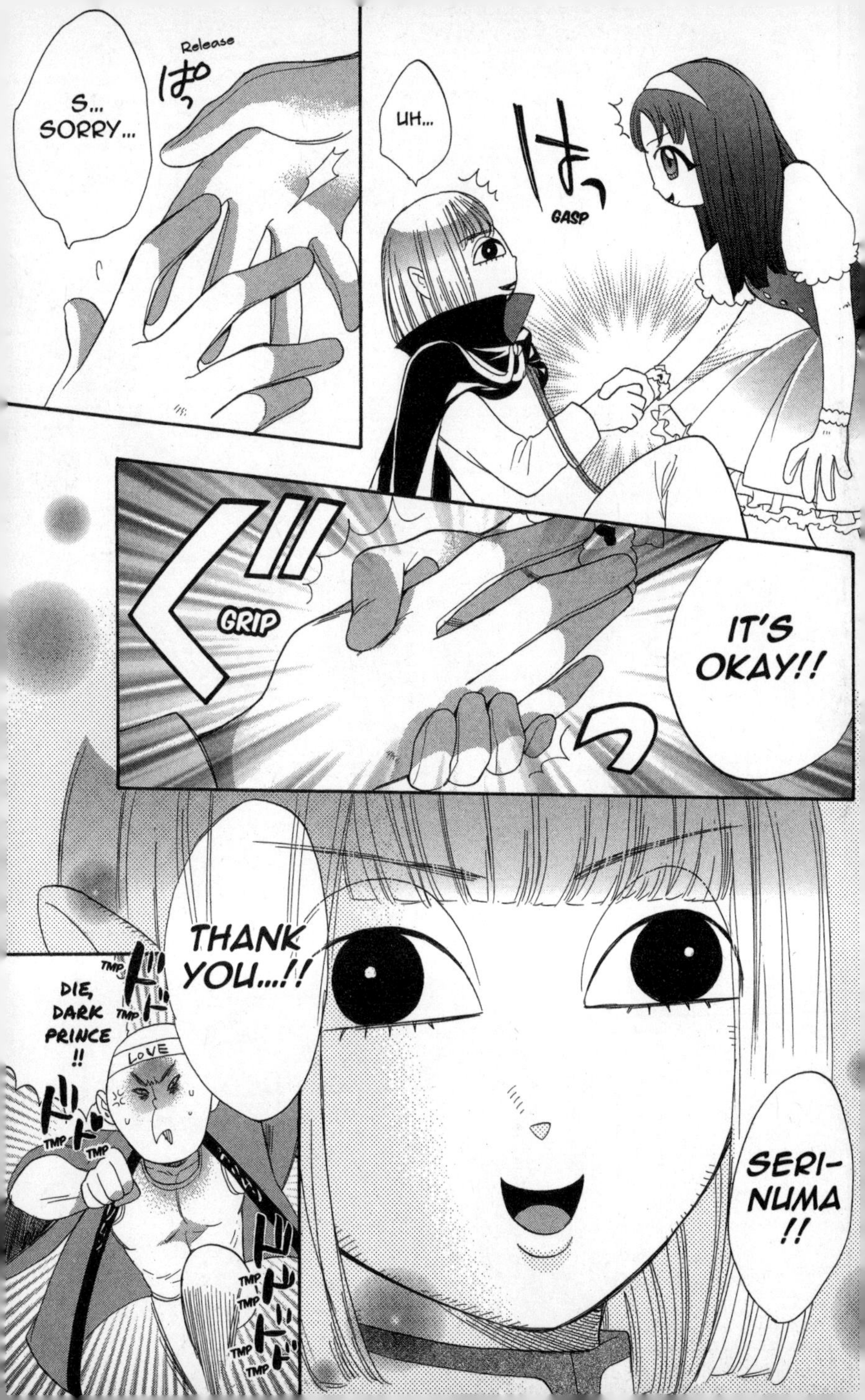
はっ
GASP
UH...
Release
ぱっ
S... SORRY...
IT'S OKAY!!
ぐっ
GRIP
SERI-NUMA!!
THANK YOU...!!
TMP
TMP
DIE, DARK PRINCE!!
LOVE
TMP
TMP
TMP
TMP
TMP
TMP

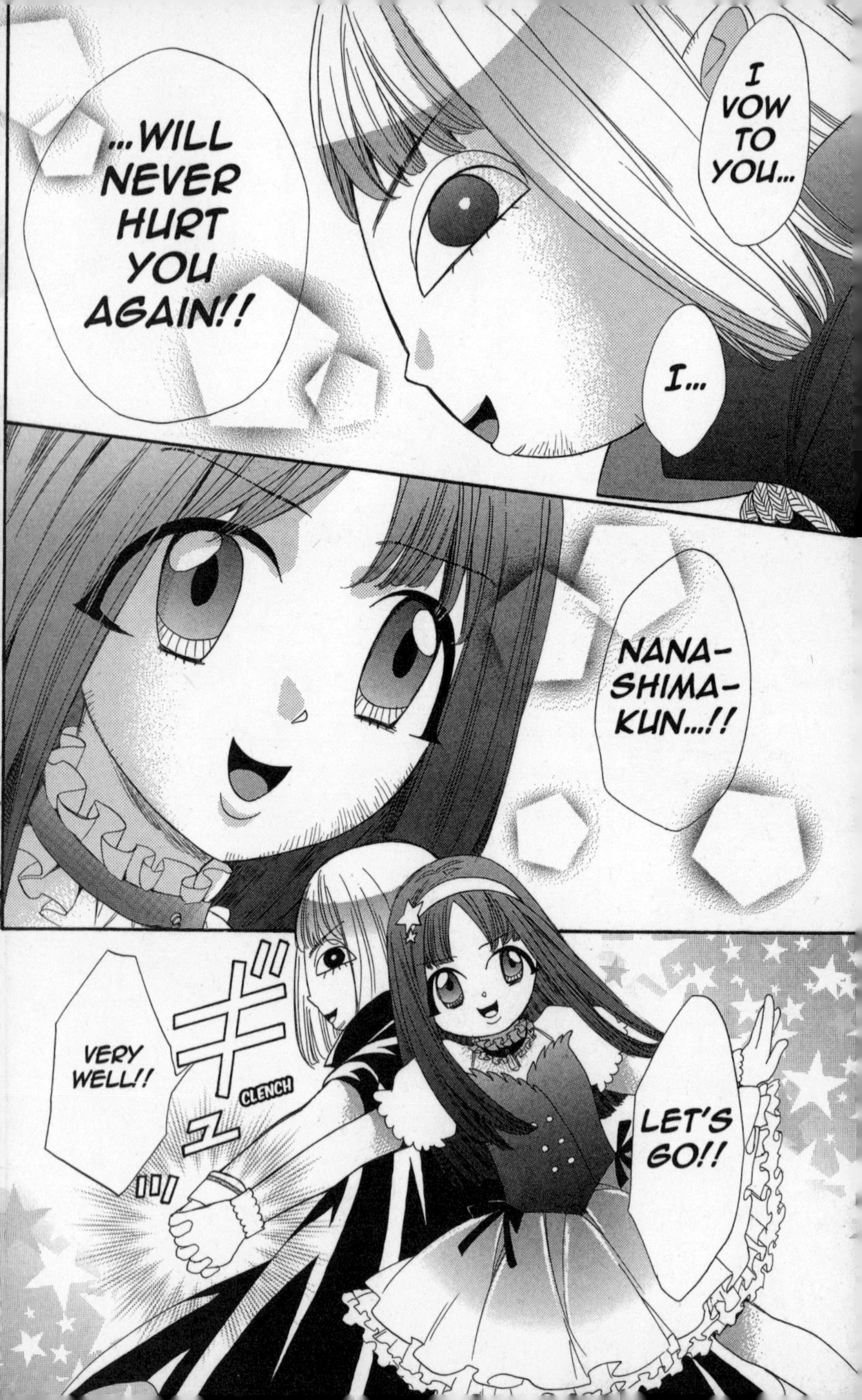
I VOW TO YOU...
I...
...WILL NEVER HURT YOU AGAIN!!
NANA-SHIMA-KUN...!!
LET'S GO!!
ギュッ
CLENCH
VERY WELL!!

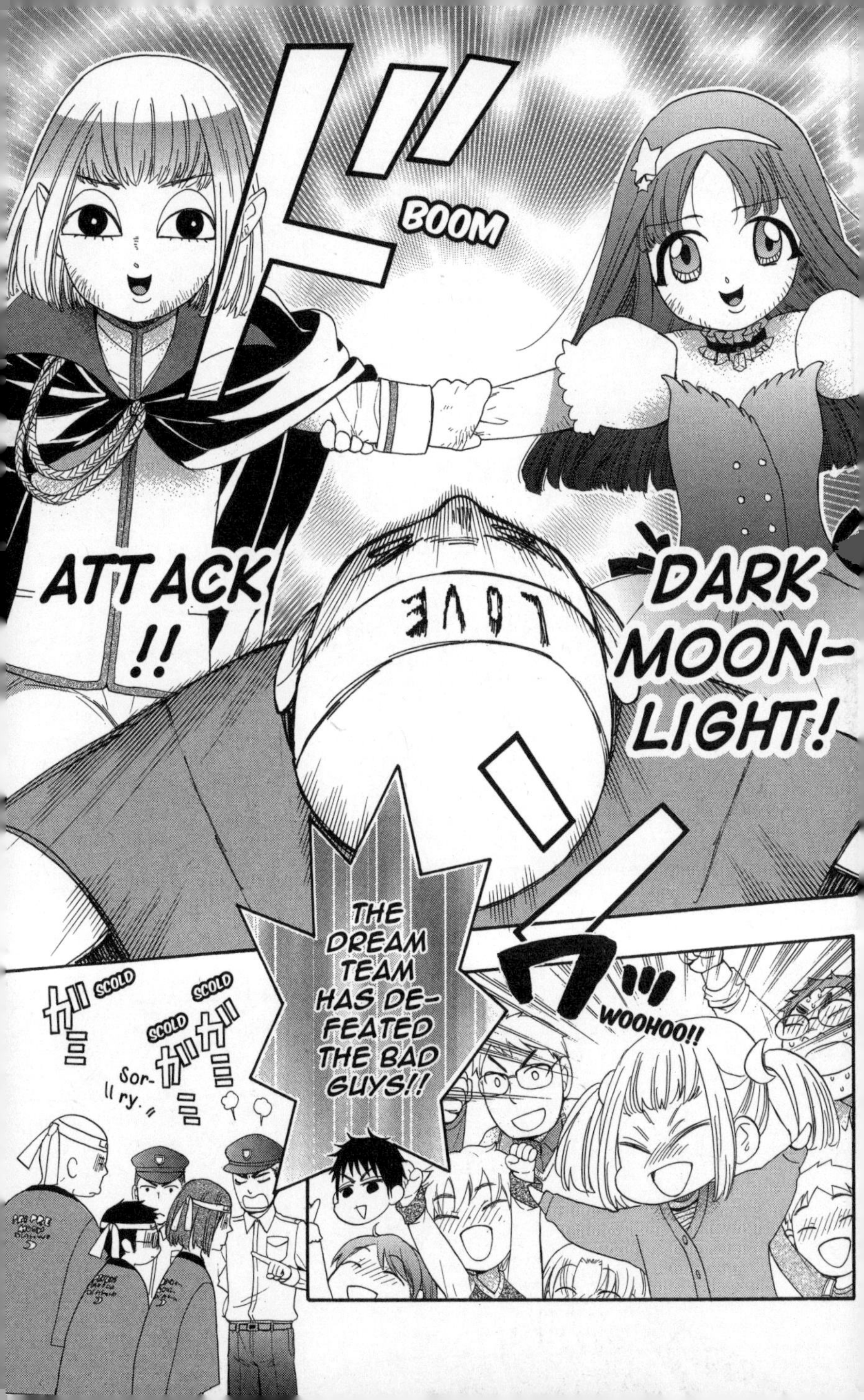
BOOM
DARK MOON-LIGHT!
ATTACK!!
THE DREAM TEAM HAS DE-FEATED THE BAD GUYS!!
WOOHOO!!
SCOLD
SCOLD
SCOLD
Sor- ry..

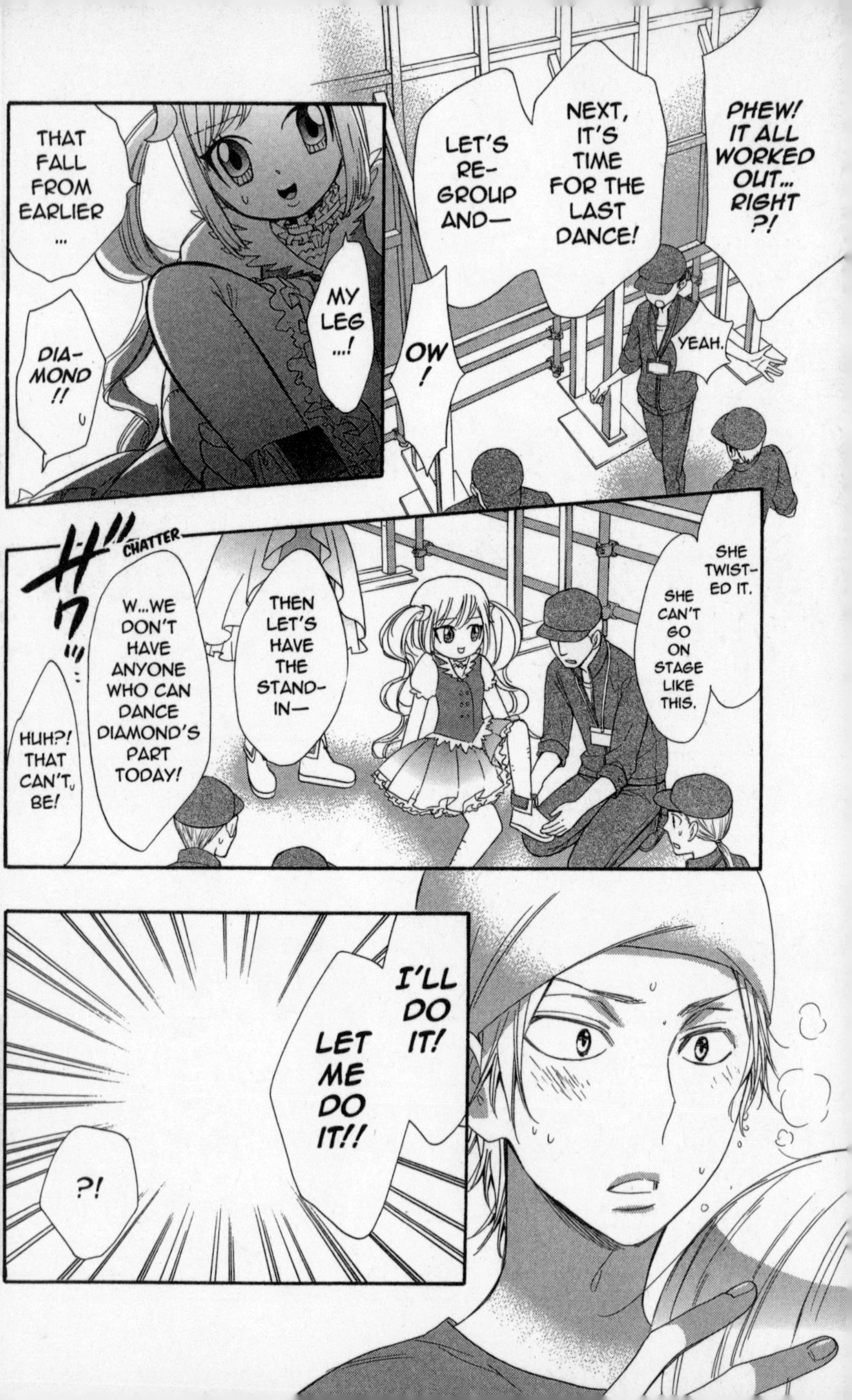
PHEW! IT ALL WORKED OUT... RIGHT?!
NEXT, IT'S TIME FOR THE LAST DANCE!
LET'S RE-GROUP AND—
YEAH.
OW!
MY LEG ...!
THAT FALL FROM EARLIER ...
DIAMOND!!
SHE TWISTED IT.
SHE CAN'T GO ON STAGE LIKE THIS.
THEN LET'S HAVE THE STAND-IN—
W...WE DON'T HAVE ANYONE WHO CAN DANCE DIAMOND'S PART TODAY!
CHATTER
HUH?! THAT CAN'T BE!
I'LL DO IT!
LET ME DO IT!!
?!

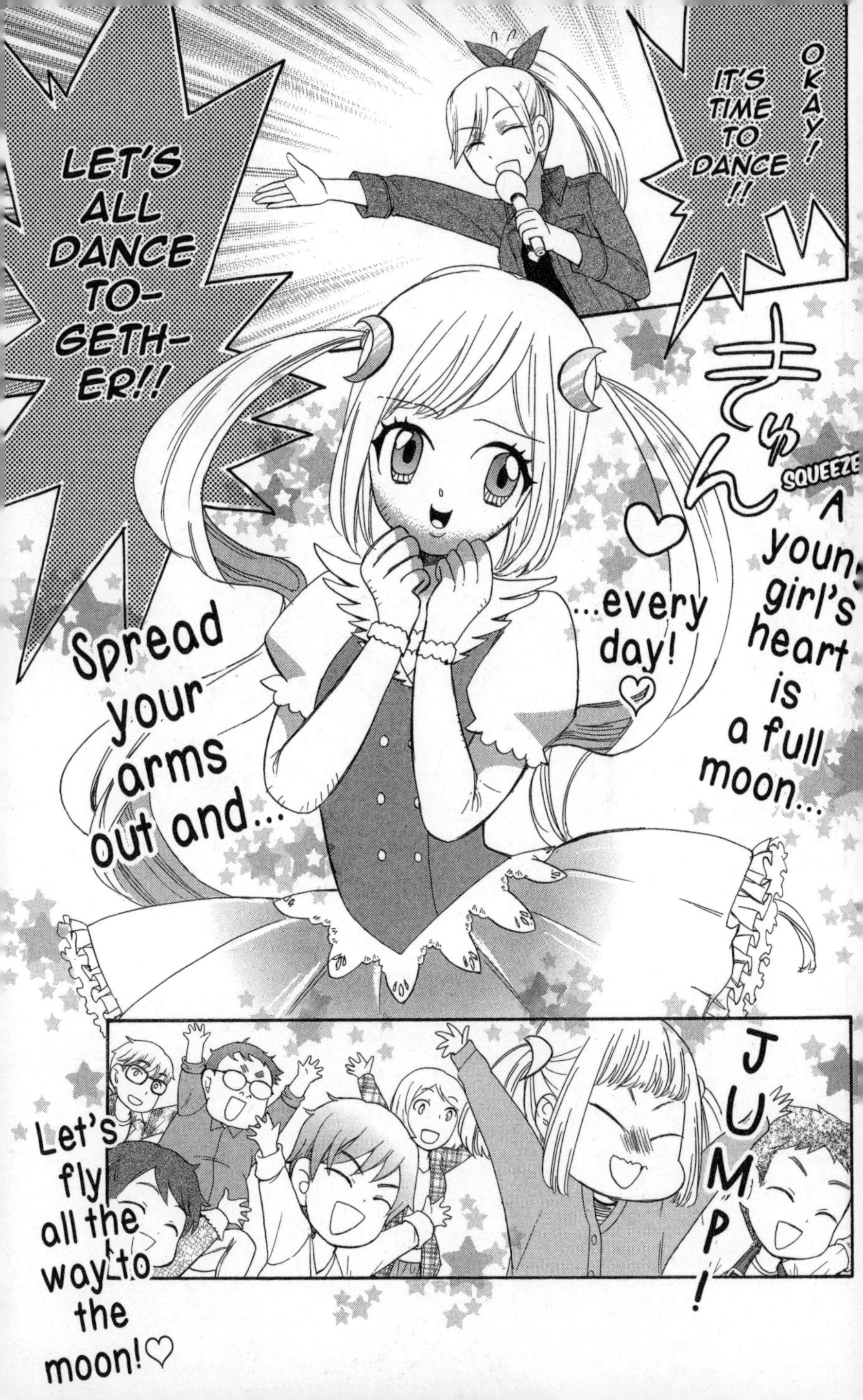
OKAY! IT'S TIME TO DANCE!!
LET'S ALL DANCE TO-GETH-ER!!
きゅん
SQUEEZE
A young girl's heart is a full moon...
...every day! ♡
Spread your arms out and...
JUMP!
Let's fly all the way to the moon! ♡

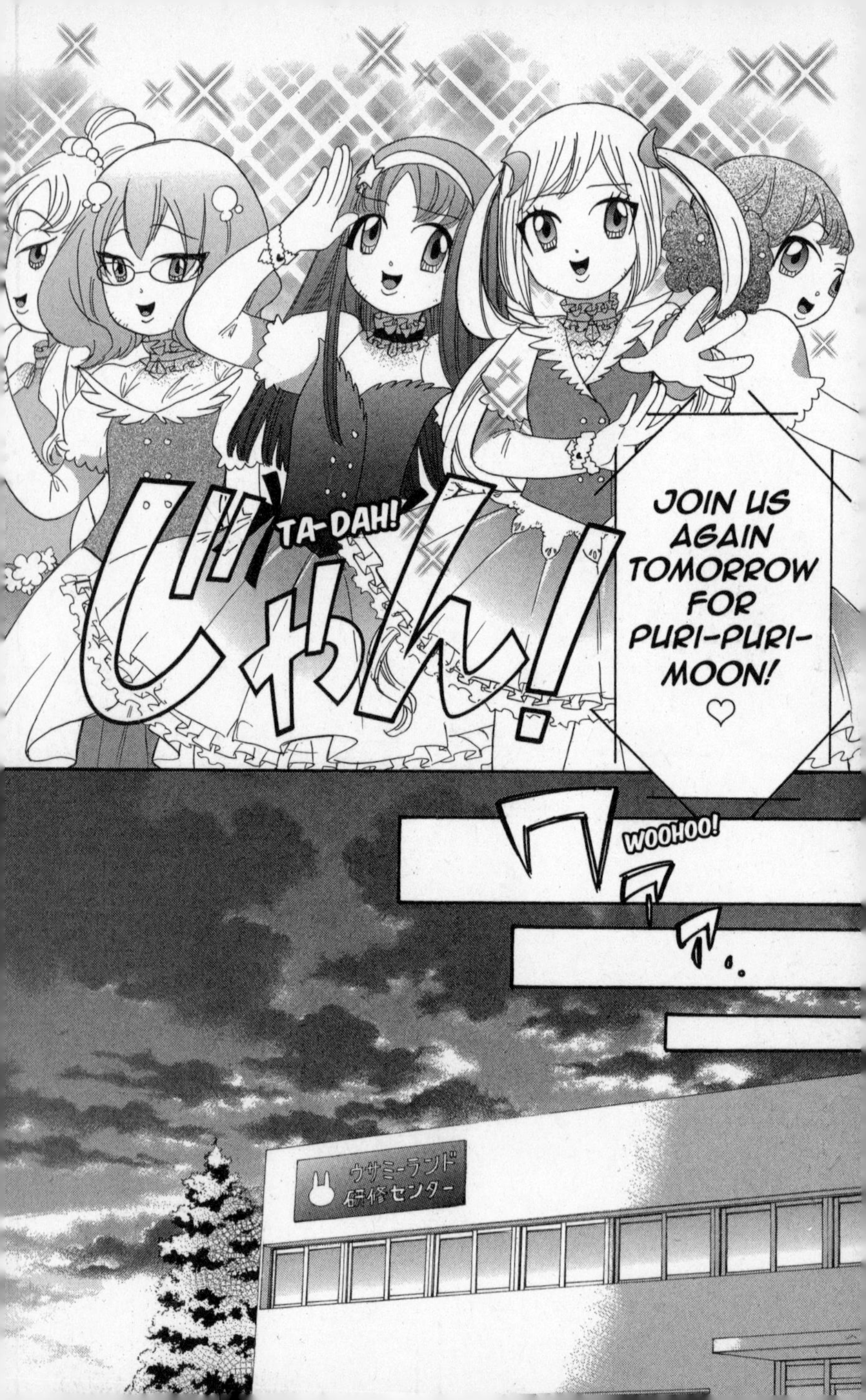
JOIN US AGAIN TOMORROW FOR PURI-PURI-MOON! ♡
じゃん!
TA-DAH!
WOOHOO!
ウサミーランド
研修センター

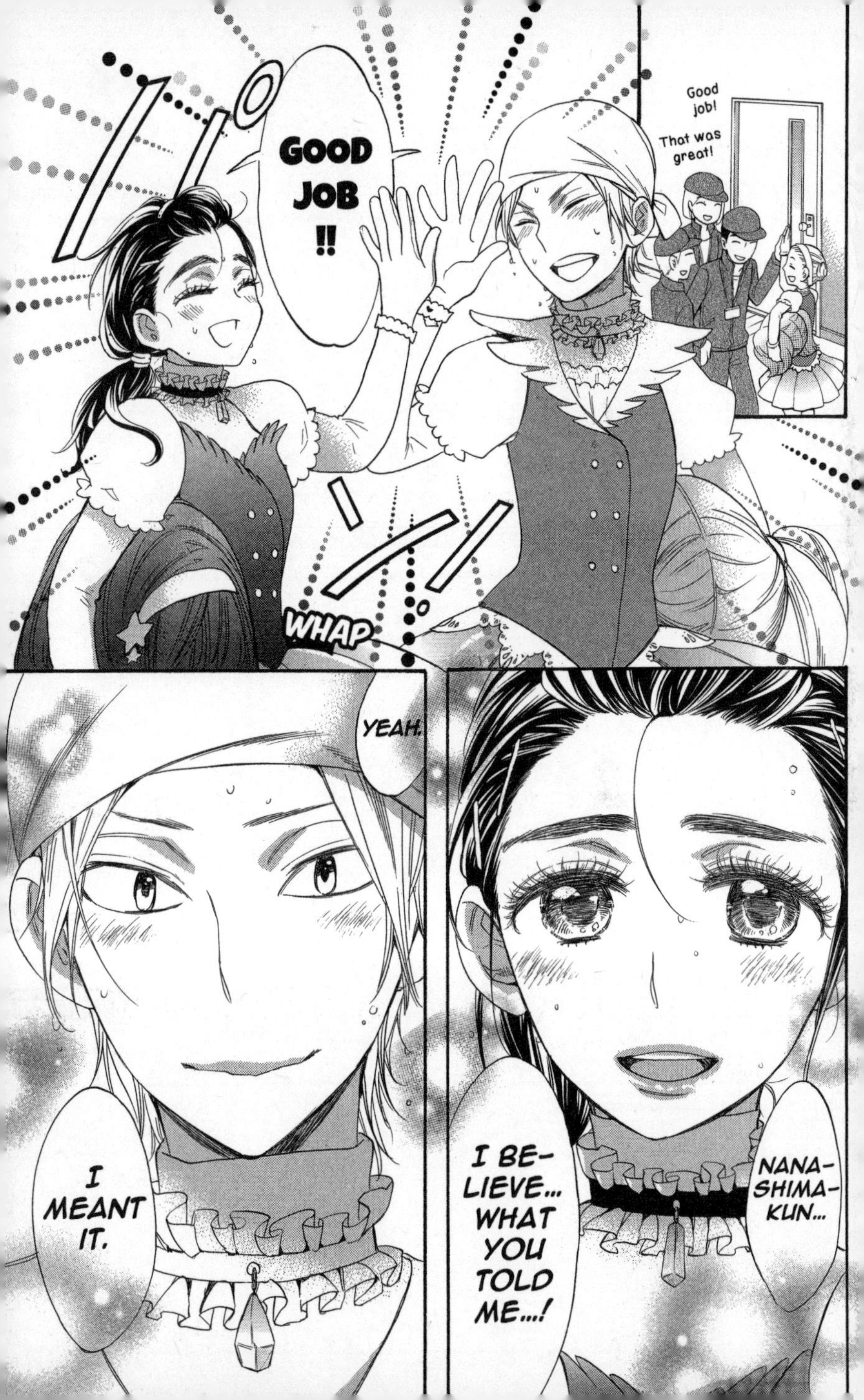
Good job!
That was great!
GOOD JOB!!
WHAP
NANA-SHIMA-KUN...
I BE-LIEVE... WHAT YOU TOLD ME...!
YEAH.
I MEANT IT.

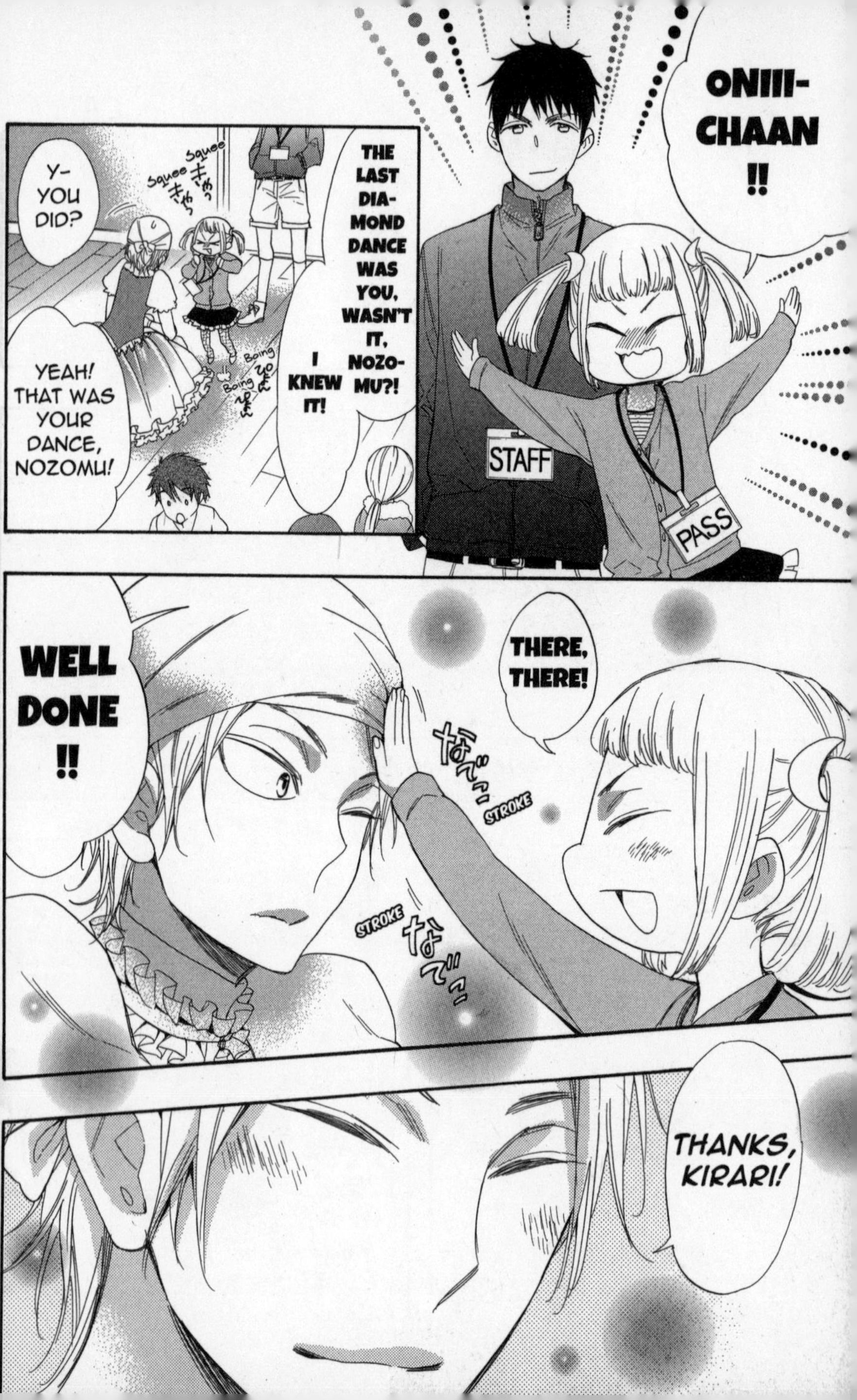
ONIII-CHAAN!!
STAFF
PASS
THE LAST DIAMOND DANCE WAS YOU, WASN'T IT, NOZOMU?!
I KNEW IT!
Squee Squee
Y-YOU DID?
Boing Boing
YEAH! THAT WAS YOUR DANCE, NOZOMU!
THERE, THERE!
STROKE
WELL DONE!!
STROKE
THANKS, KIRARI!

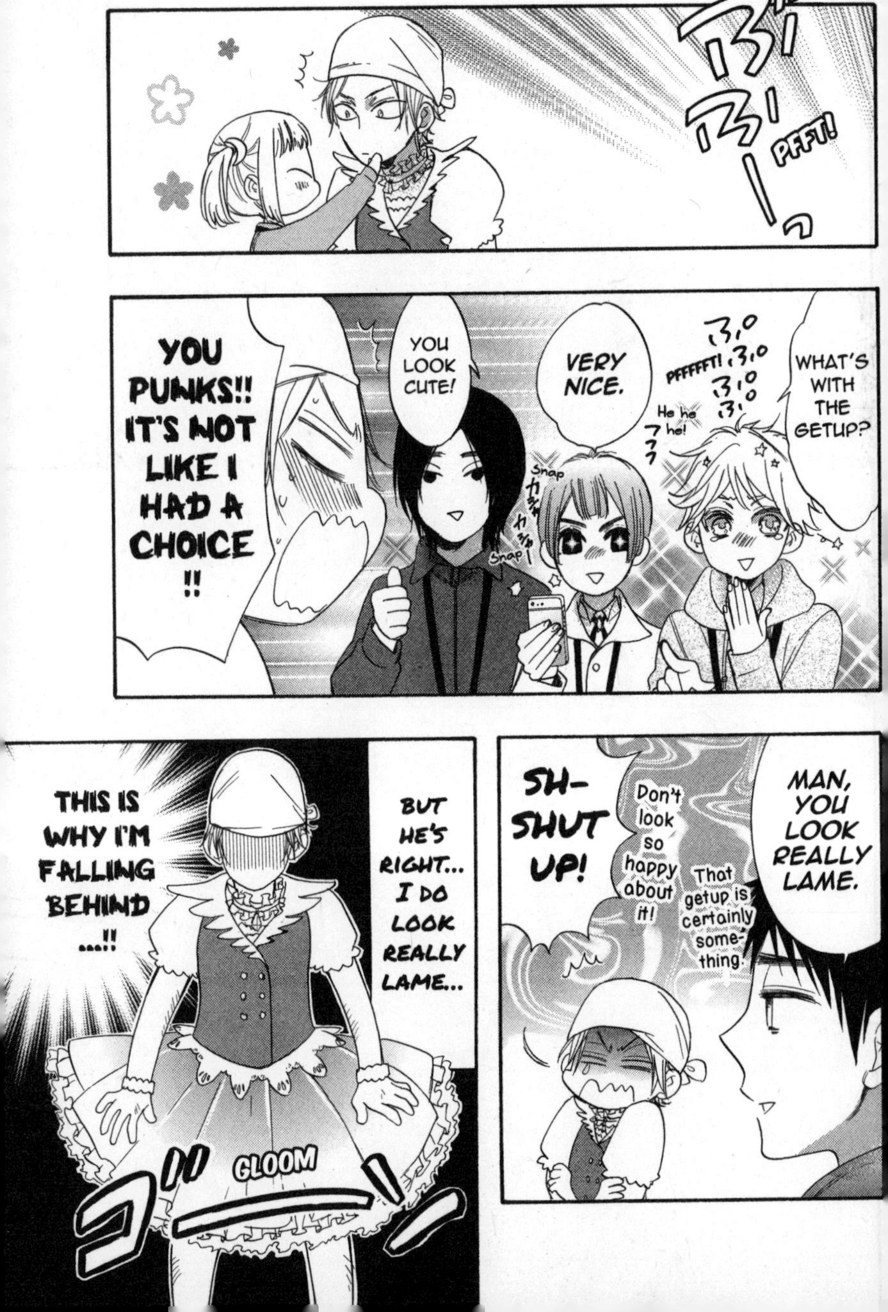
PFFT!
WHAT'S WITH THE GETUP?
PFFFFFT!
He he he!
VERY NICE.
Snap
Snap
YOU LOOK CUTE!
YOU PUNKS!! IT'S NOT LIKE I HAD A CHOICE!!
MAN, YOU LOOK REALLY LAME.
That getup is certainly some-thing.
Don't look so happy about it!
SH-SHUT UP!
BUT HE'S RIGHT... I DO LOOK REALLY LAME...
THIS IS WHY I'M FALLING BEHIND...!!
GLOOM

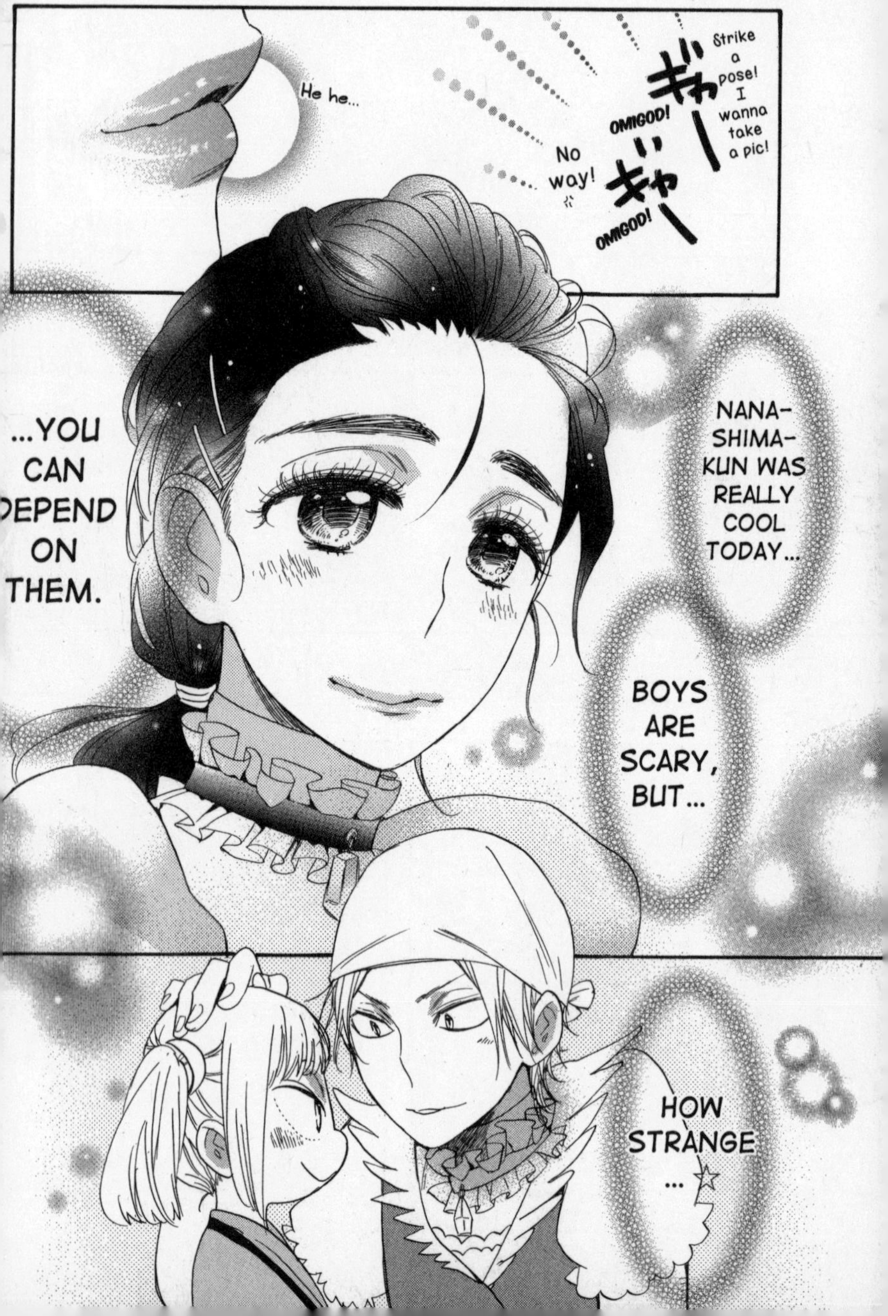
Strike a pose! I wanna take a pic!
ぎゃー
OMIGOD!
ぎゃー
OMIGOD!
No way!
He he...
NANA-SHIMA-KUN WAS REALLY COOL TODAY...
BOYS ARE SCARY, BUT...
...YOU CAN DEPEND ON THEM.
HOW STRANGE ...☆

#30 HIDEO'S RETURN

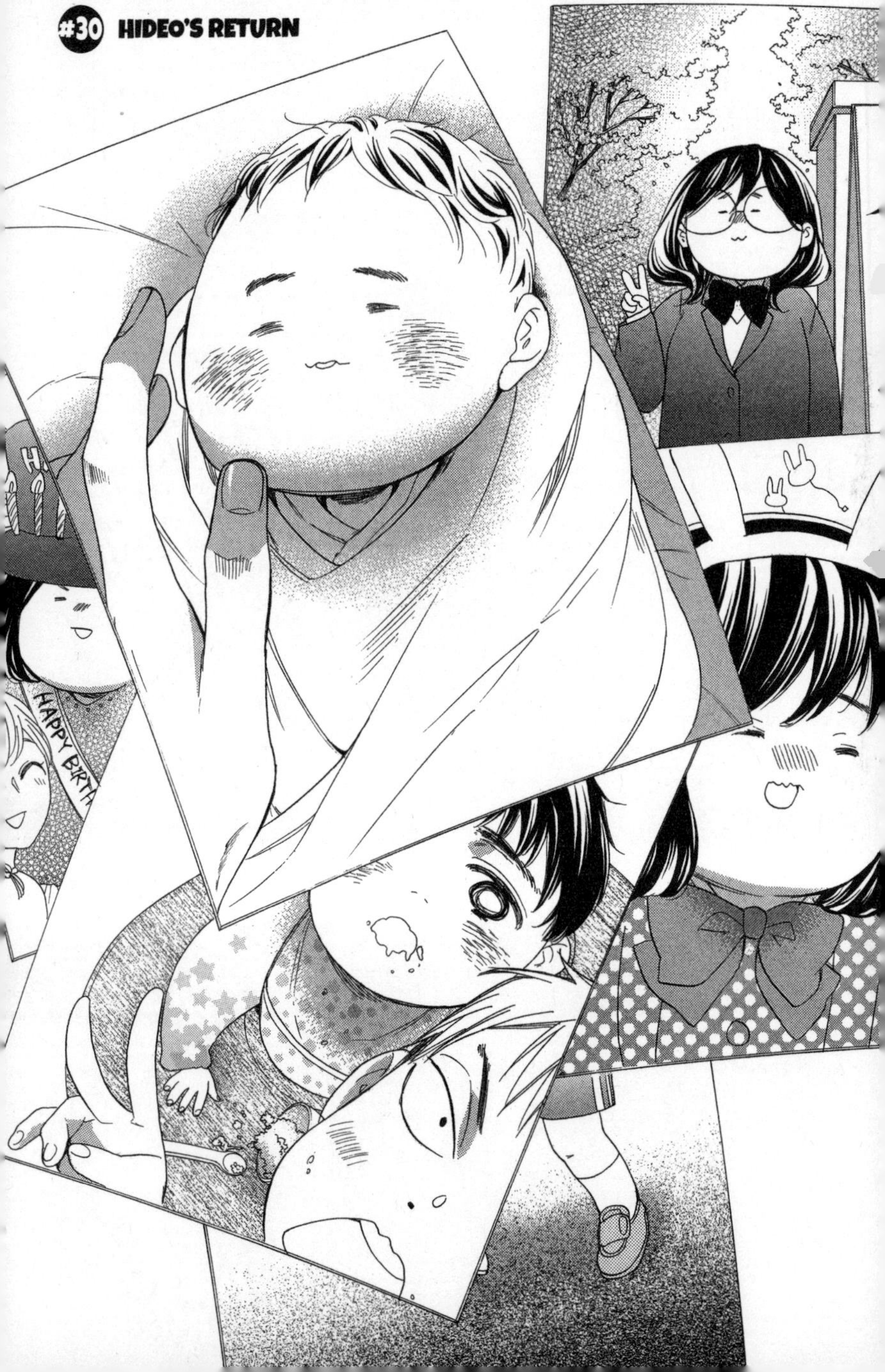
HAPPY BIRTH

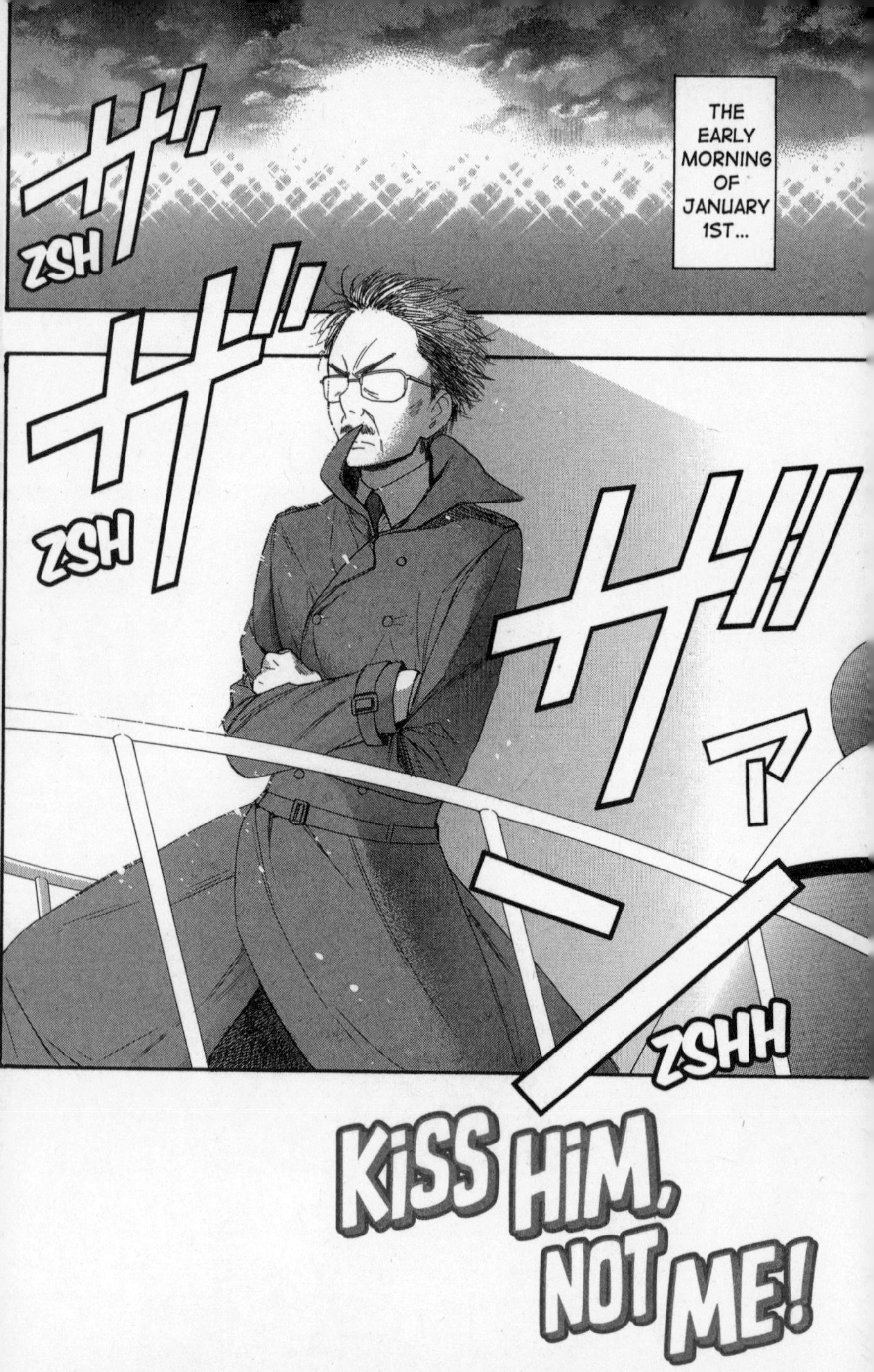
THE EARLY MORNING OF JANUARY 1ST...
ZSH
ZSH
ZSHH

KiSS HiM, NOT ME!

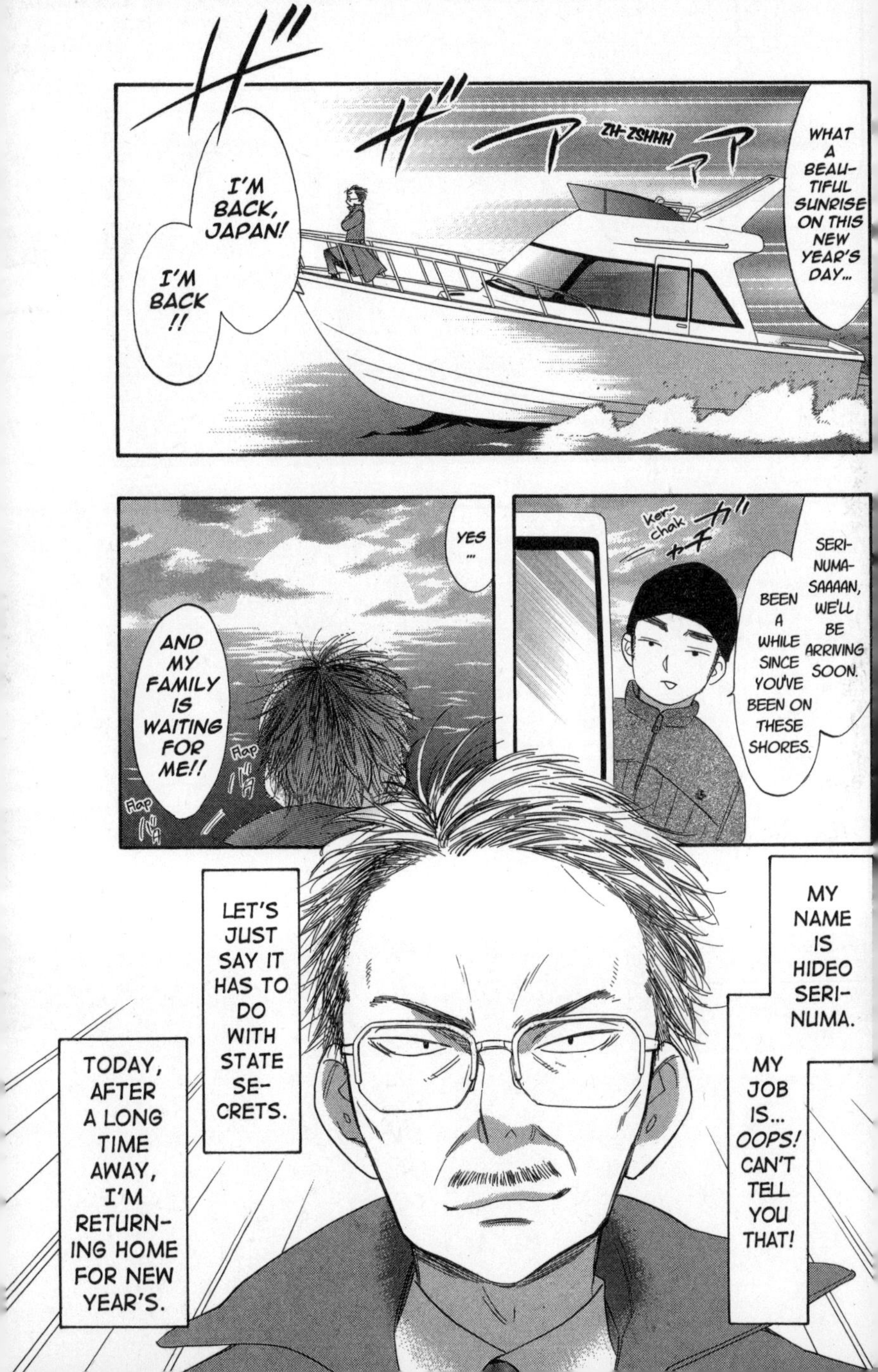

WHAT A BEAUTIFUL SUNRISE ON THIS NEW YEAR'S DAY...
ZH-ZSHHH
I'M BACK, JAPAN!
I'M BACK!!
ker-chak
SERINUMA-SAAAAN, WE'LL BE ARRIVING SOON.
BEEN A WHILE SINCE YOU'VE BEEN ON THESE SHORES.
YES ...
AND MY FAMILY IS WAITING FOR ME!!
Flap
Flap
MY NAME IS HIDEO SERINUMA.
MY JOB IS... OOPS! CAN'T TELL YOU THAT!
LET'S JUST SAY IT HAS TO DO WITH STATE SECRETS.
TODAY, AFTER A LONG TIME AWAY, I'M RETURNING HOME FOR NEW YEAR'S.

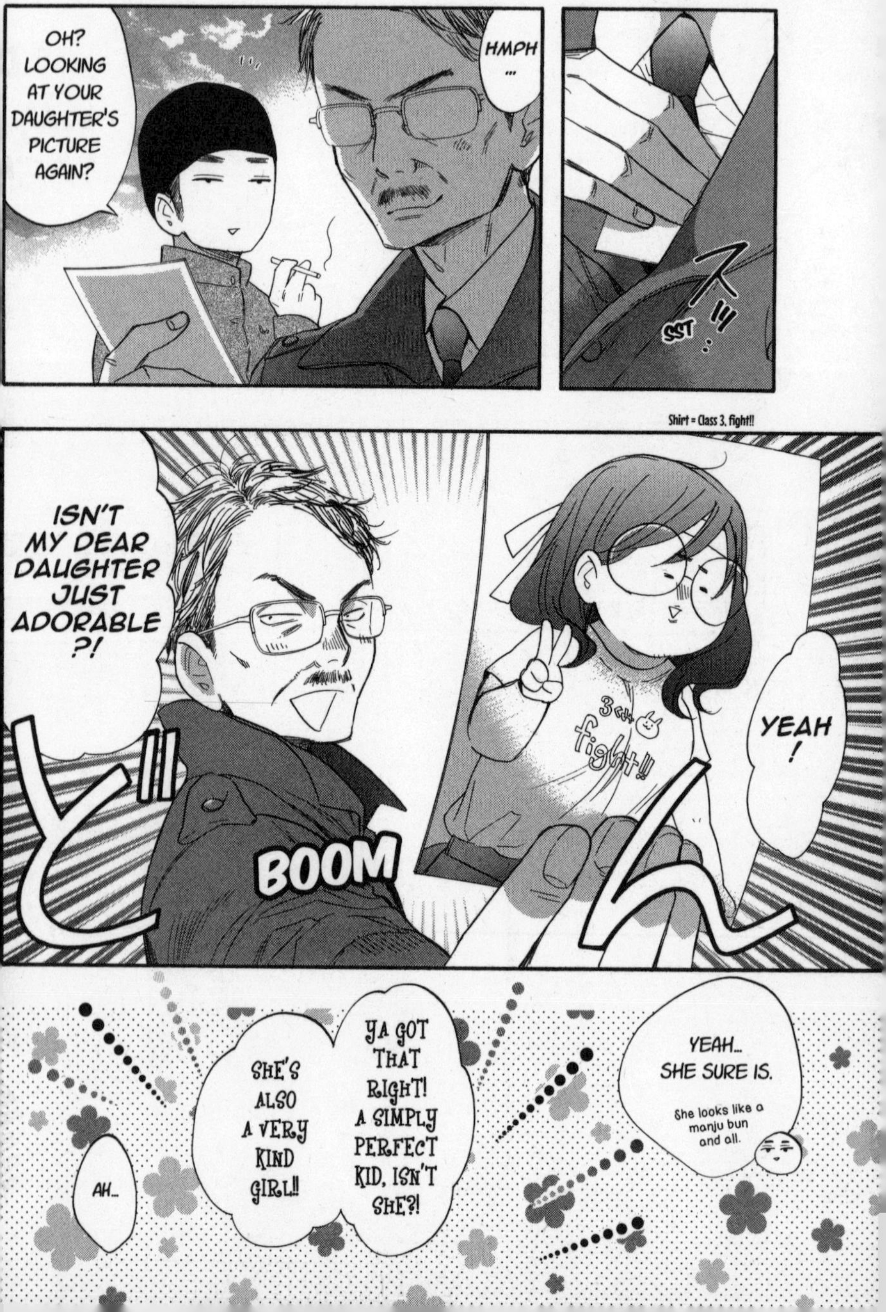
SST
HMPH...
OH? LOOKING AT YOUR DAUGHTER'S PICTURE AGAIN?
Shirt = Class 3, fight!!
3くみ fight!!
ISN'T MY DEAR DAUGHTER JUST ADORABLE?!
YEAH!
BOOM
YEAH... SHE SURE IS.
She looks like a manju bun and all.
YA GOT THAT RIGHT! A SIMPLY PERFECT KID, ISN'T SHE?!
SHE'S ALSO A VERY KIND GIRL!!
AH...

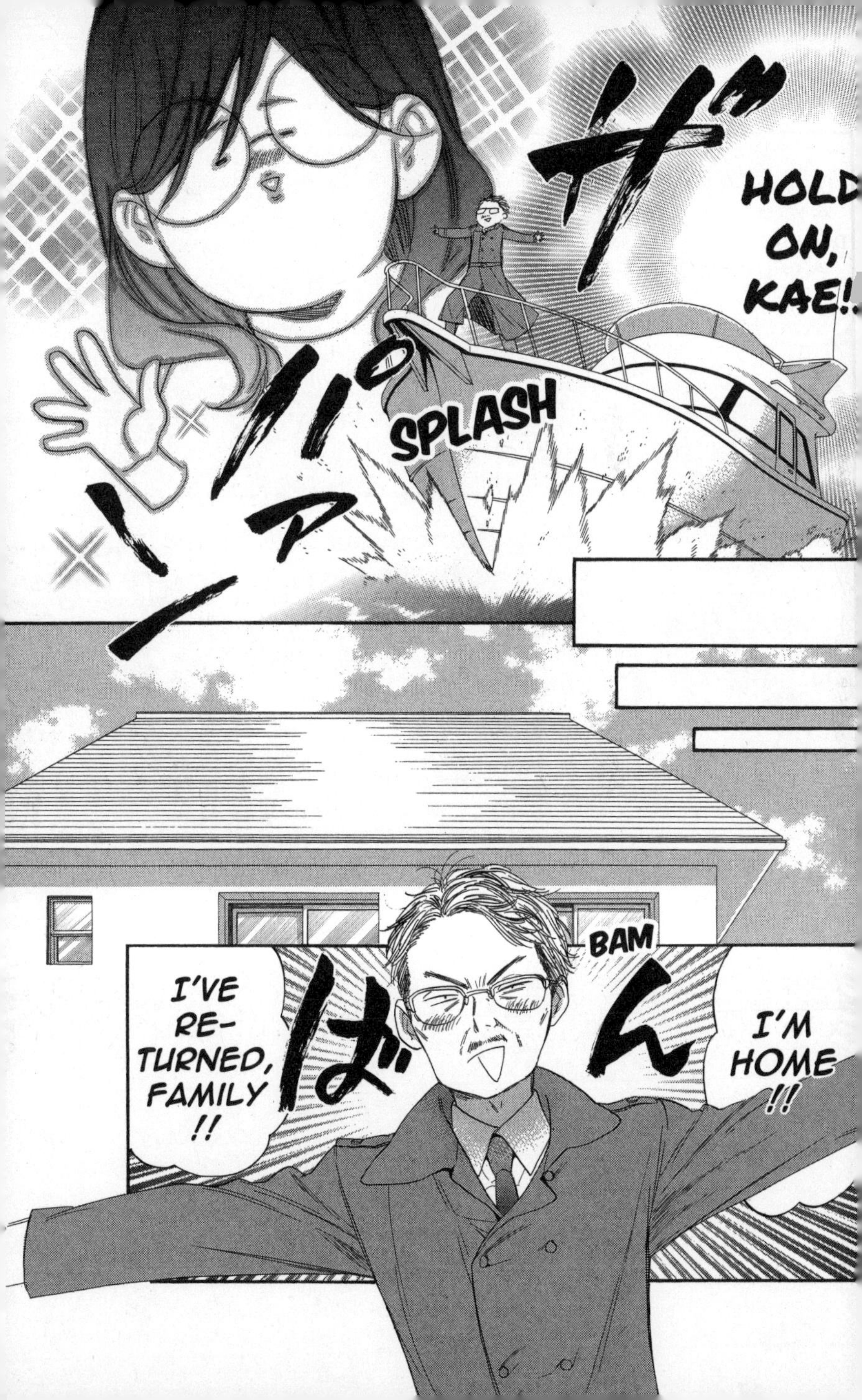
HOLD ON, KAE!..
SPLASH
BAM
ばん
I'M HOME!!
I'VE RE-TURNED, FAMILY!!

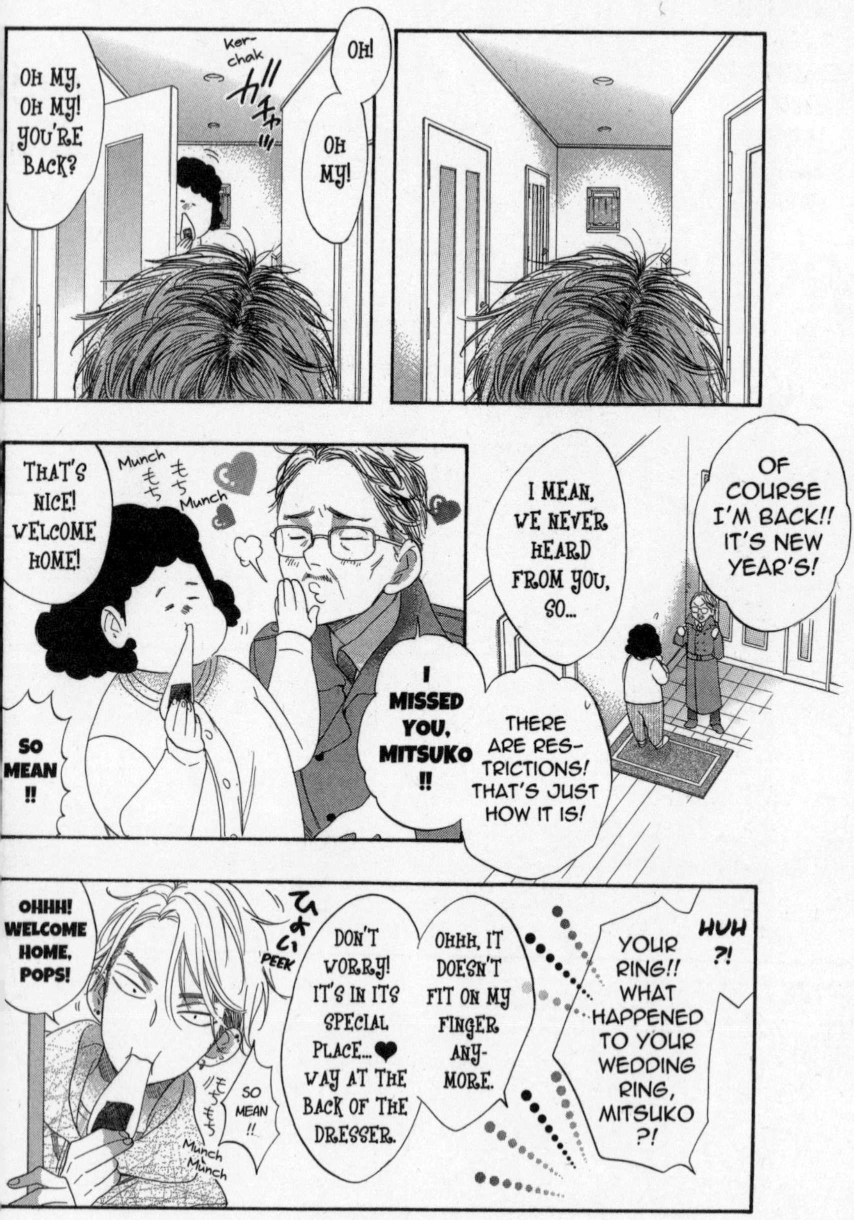
OH!
Ker-chak
カチャ
OH MY!
OH MY, OH MY! YOU'RE BACK?
OF COURSE I'M BACK!! IT'S NEW YEAR'S!
I MEAN, WE NEVER HEARD FROM YOU, SO...
THERE ARE RES-TRICTIONS! THAT'S JUST HOW IT IS!
I MISSED YOU, MITSUKO!!
Munch もち もち Munch
THAT'S NICE! WELCOME HOME!
SO MEAN!!
HUH?!
YOUR RING!! WHAT HAPPENED TO YOUR WEDDING RING, MITSUKO?!
OHHH, IT DOESN'T FIT ON MY FINGER ANY-MORE.
DON'T WORRY! IT'S IN ITS SPECIAL PLACE...❤ WAY AT THE BACK OF THE DRESSER.
ひょい PEEK
OHHH! WELCOME HOME, POPS!
SO MEAN!!
Munch Munch

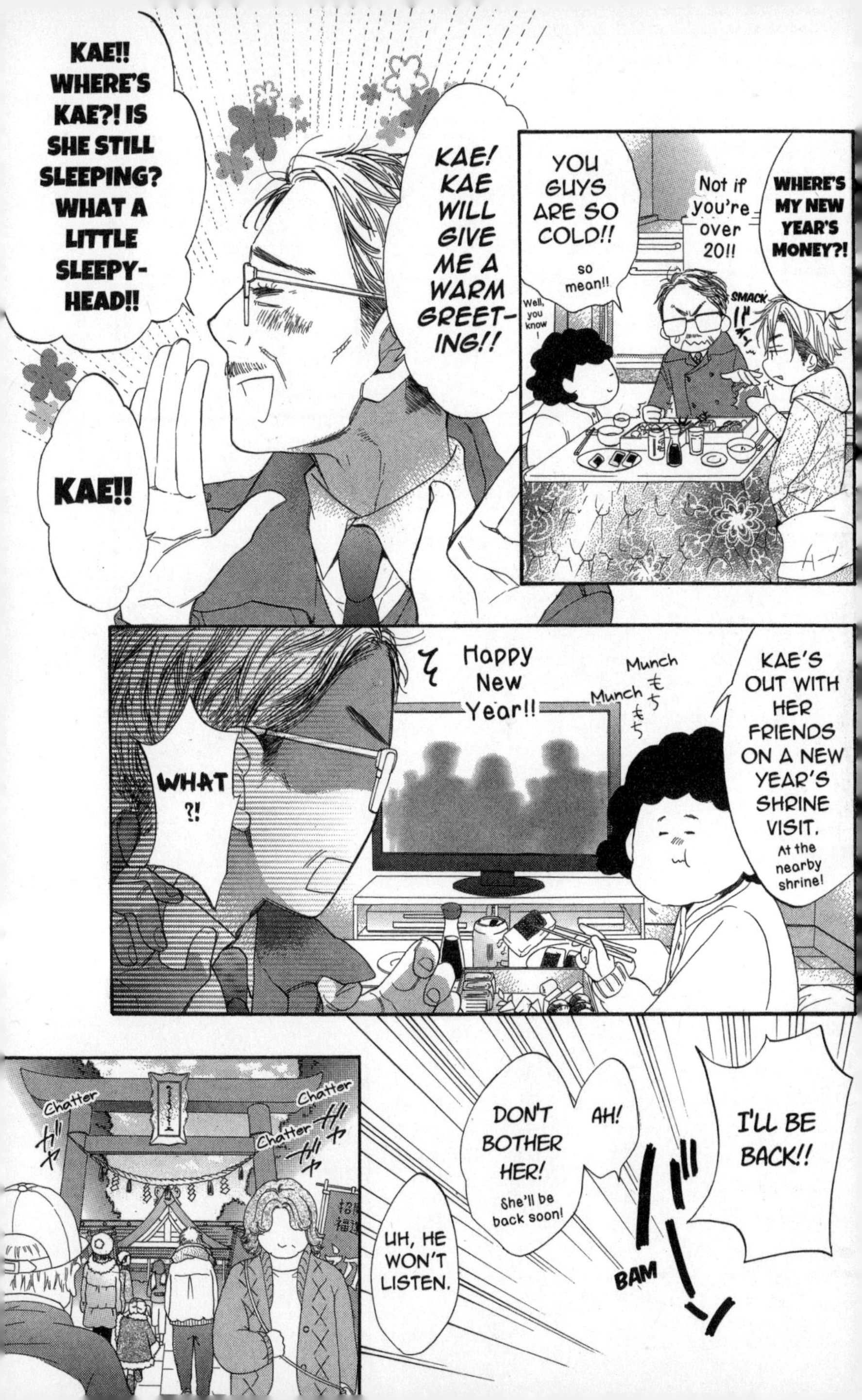
WHERE'S MY NEW YEAR'S MONEY?!
SMACK
Not if you're over 20!!
YOU GUYS ARE SO COLD!!
so mean!!
Well, you know!
KAE! KAE WILL GIVE ME A WARM GREETING!!
KAE!! WHERE'S KAE?! IS SHE STILL SLEEPING? WHAT A LITTLE SLEEPY-HEAD!!
KAE!!
KAE'S OUT WITH HER FRIENDS ON A NEW YEAR'S SHRINE VISIT.
At the nearby shrine!
Munch もち
Munch もち
Happy New Year!!
WHAT?!
I'LL BE BACK!!
BAM
AH!
DON'T BOTHER HER!
She'll be back soon!
UH, HE WON'T LISTEN.
Chatter
Chatter
Chatter

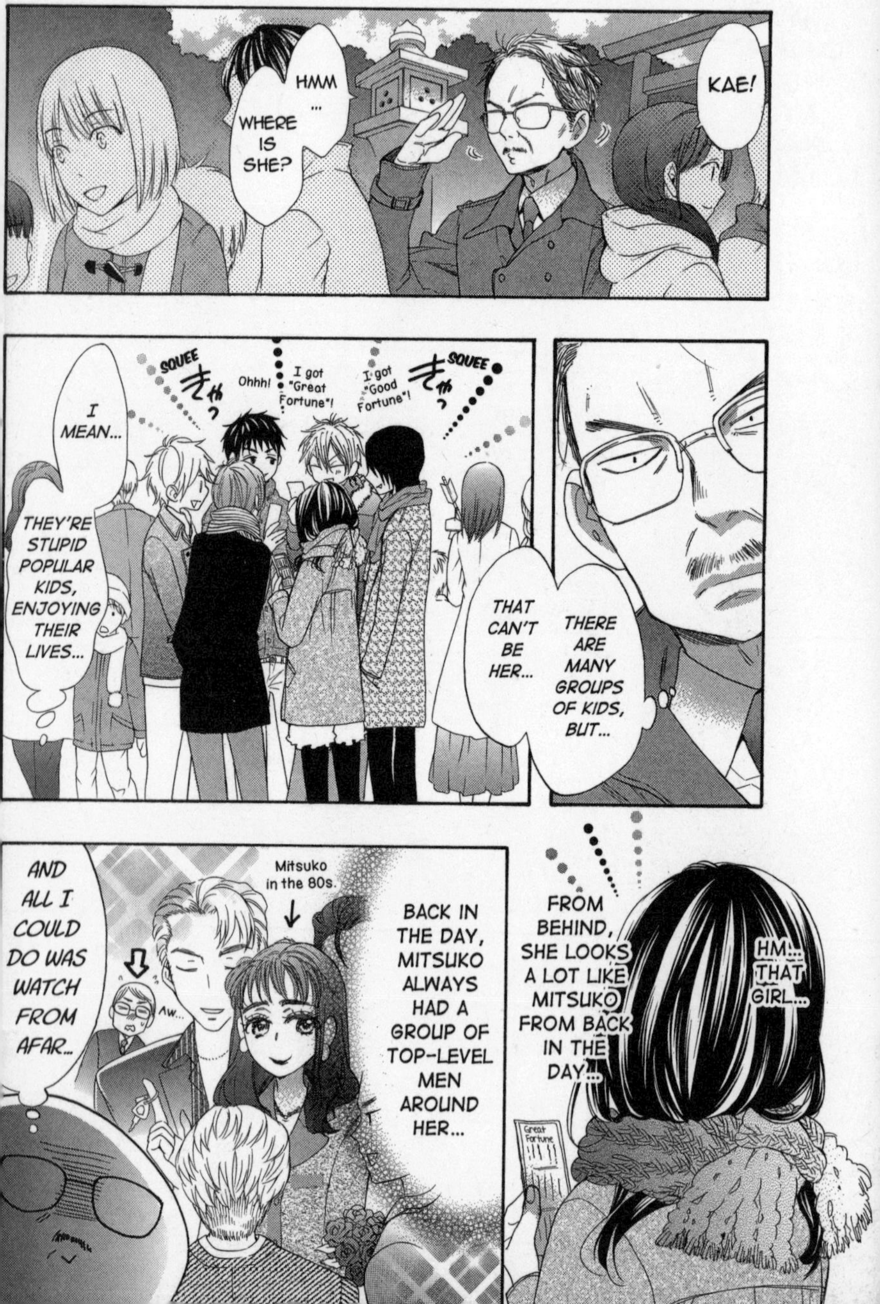
KAE!
HMM... WHERE IS SHE?
THERE ARE MANY GROUPS OF KIDS, BUT...
THAT CAN'T BE HER...
SQUEE
きゃっ
I got "Good Fortune"!
I got "Great Fortune"!
Ohhh!
SQUEE
きゃっ
I MEAN... THEY'RE STUPID POPULAR KIDS, ENJOYING THEIR LIVES...
HM... THAT GIRL...
FROM BEHIND, SHE LOOKS A LOT LIKE MITSUKO FROM BACK IN THE DAY...
Great Fortune
BACK IN THE DAY, MITSUKO ALWAYS HAD A GROUP OF TOP-LEVEL MEN AROUND HER...
Mitsuko in the 80s.
Aw...
AND ALL I COULD DO WAS WATCH FROM AFAR...

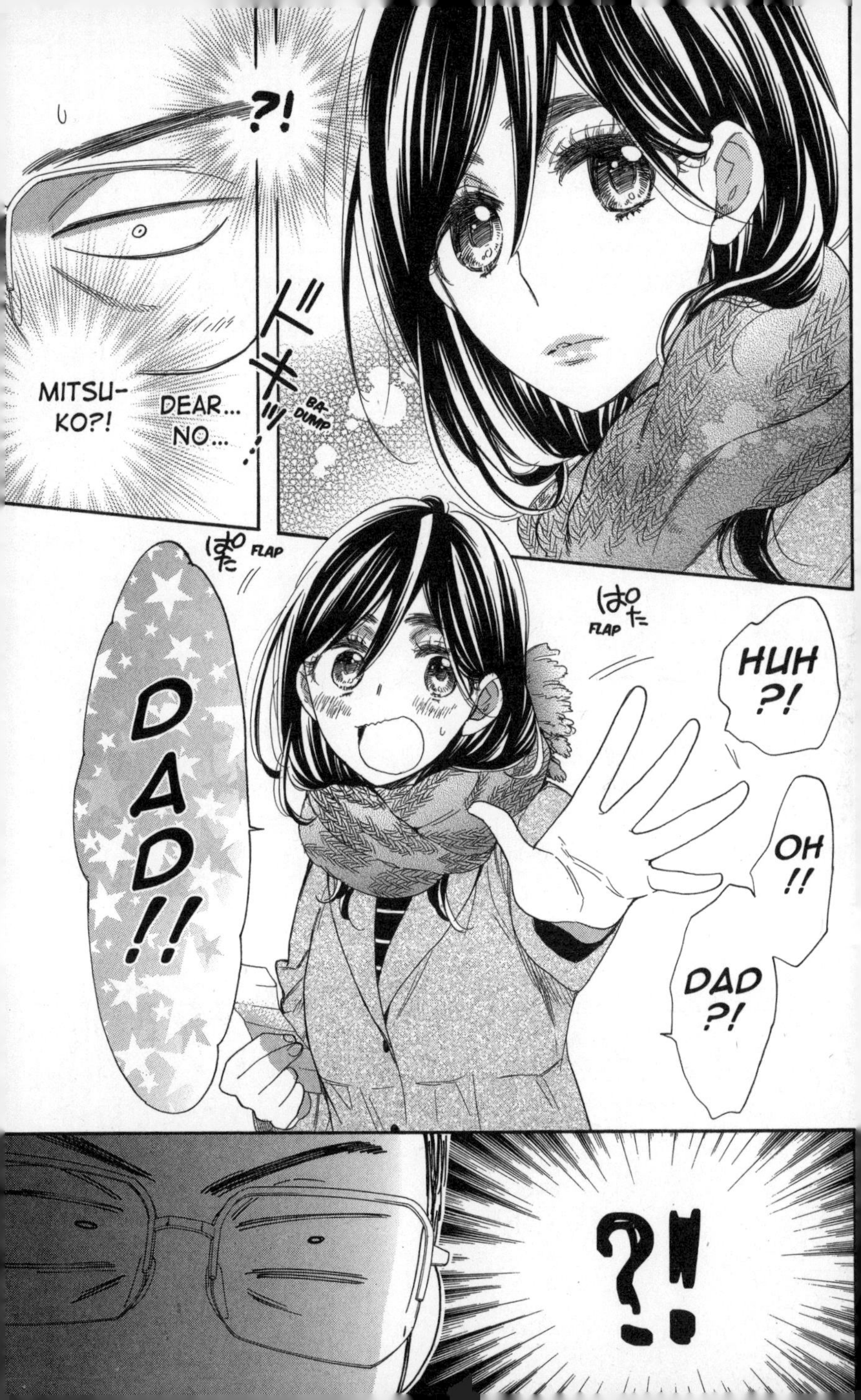
ドキ!!!
BA-DUMP
?!
DEAR...
NO...
MITSU-KO?!
ぱた
FLAP
HUH ?!
OH !!
DAD ?!
ぱた
FLAP
DAD!!
?!!

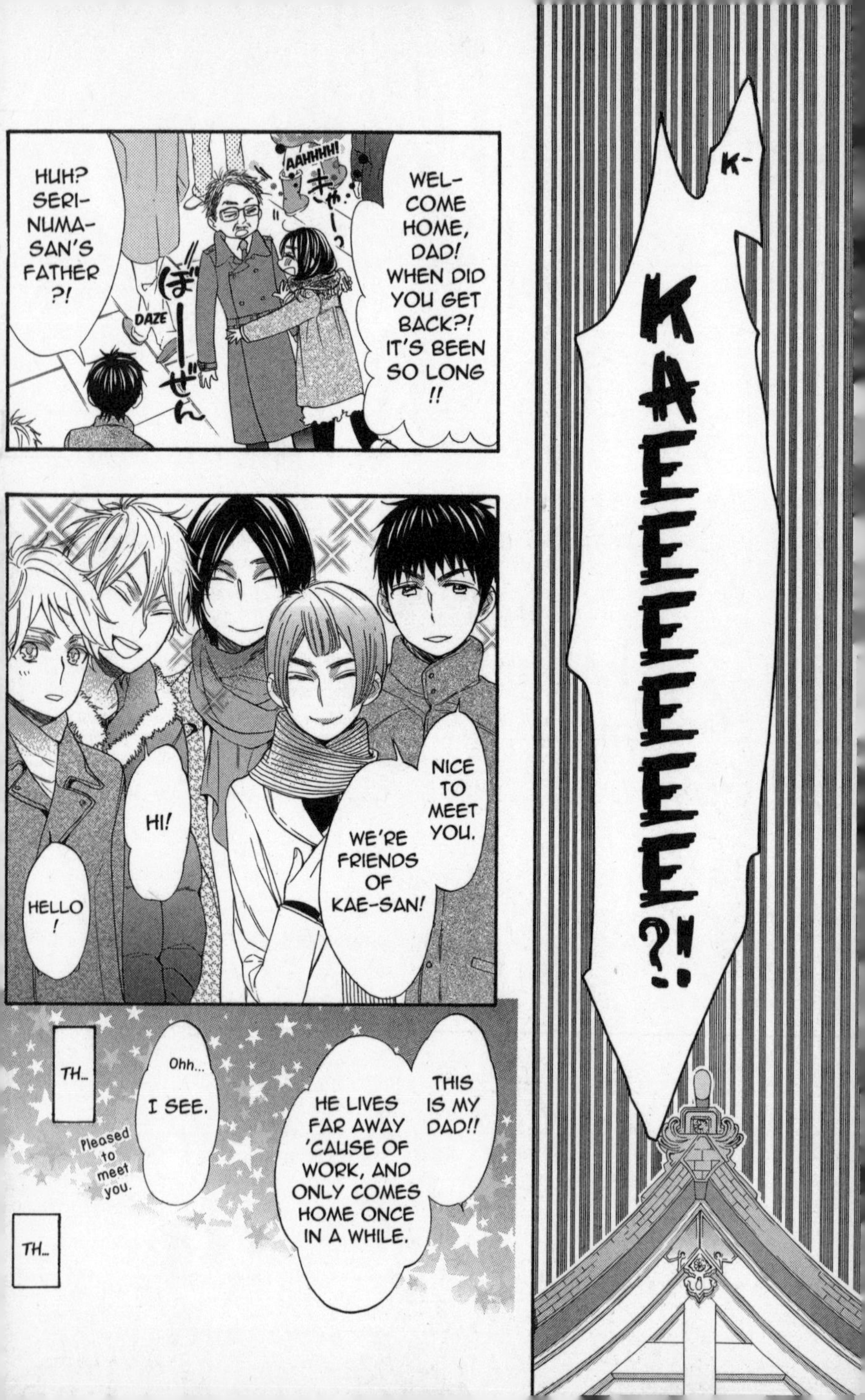
K-
KAEEEEEEE?!
WEL-COME HOME, DAD! WHEN DID YOU GET BACK?! IT'S BEEN SO LONG!!
AAHHHH!
きゃー
ぼーぜん
DAZE
HUH? SERI-NUMA-SAN'S FATHER?!
NICE TO MEET YOU.
WE'RE FRIENDS OF KAE-SAN!
HI!
HELLO!
THIS IS MY DAD!!
HE LIVES FAR AWAY 'CAUSE OF WORK, AND ONLY COMES HOME ONCE IN A WHILE.
Ohh...
I SEE.
Pleased to meet you.
TH...
TH...

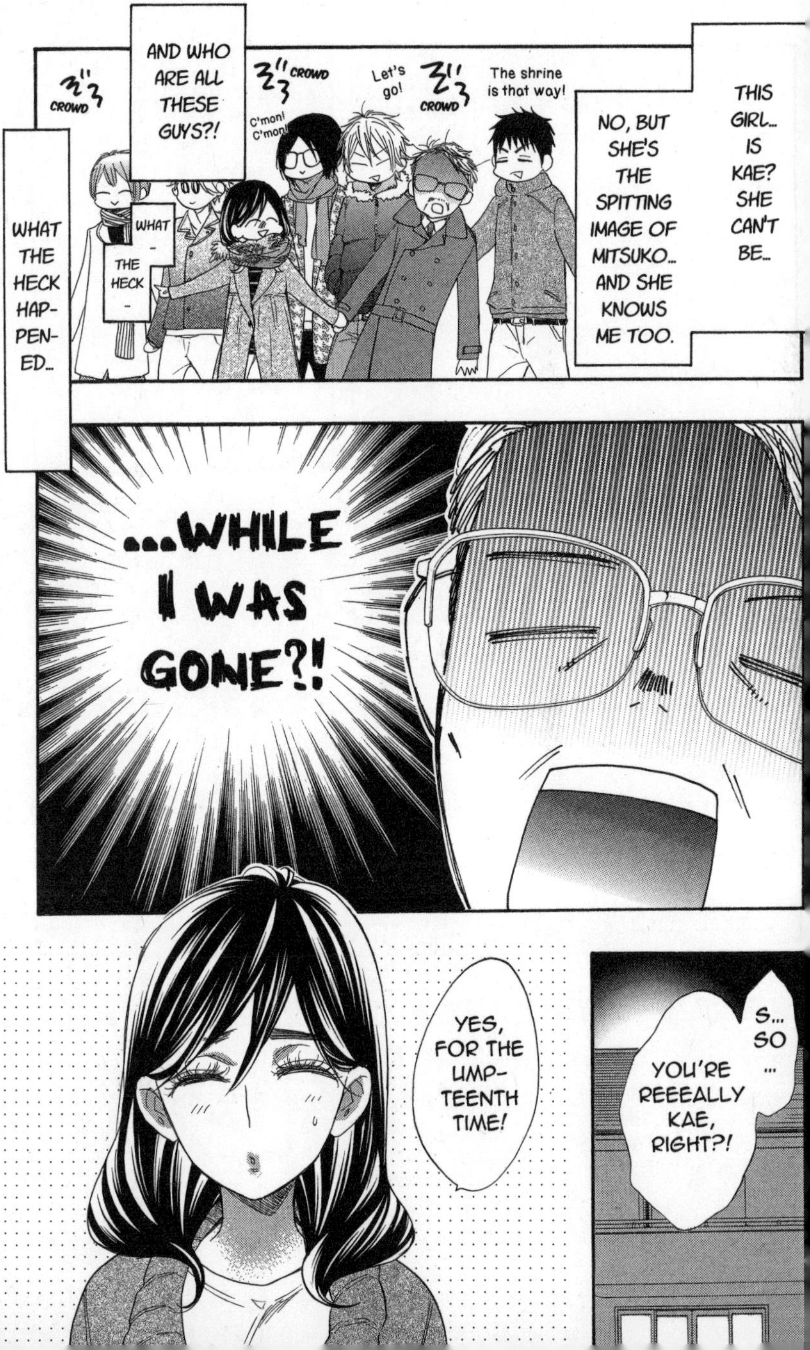
THIS GIRL... IS KAE? SHE CAN'T BE...
NO, BUT SHE'S THE SPITTING IMAGE OF MITSUKO... AND SHE KNOWS ME TOO.
The shrine is that way!
CROWD
Let's go!
CROWD
C'mon! C'mon!
AND WHO ARE ALL THESE GUYS?!
CROWD
WHAT - THE HECK -
WHAT THE HECK HAP-PEN-ED...
...WHILE I WAS GONE?!
S... SO ... YOU'RE REEEALLY KAE, RIGHT?!
YES, FOR THE UMP-TEENTH TIME!

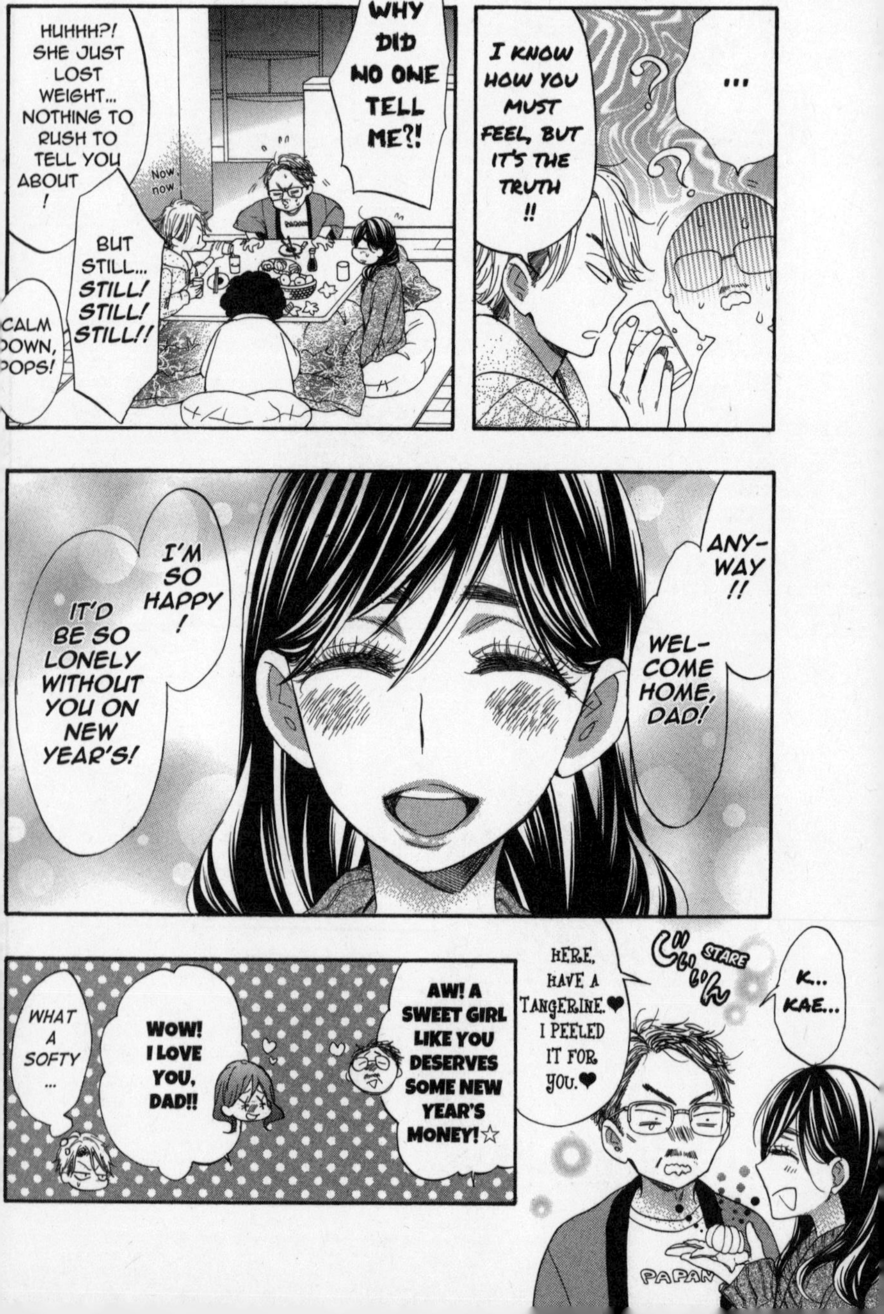
...
I KNOW HOW YOU MUST FEEL, BUT IT'S THE TRUTH!!
WHY DID NO ONE TELL ME?!
HUHHH?! SHE JUST LOST WEIGHT... NOTHING TO RUSH TO TELL YOU ABOUT!
Now, now
BUT STILL... STILL! STILL! STILL!!
CALM DOWN, POPS!
ANYWAY!!
WELCOME HOME, DAD!
I'M SO HAPPY!
IT'D BE SO LONELY WITHOUT YOU ON NEW YEAR'S!
K.. KAE...
STARE
HERE, HAVE A TANGERINE.❤ I PEELED IT FOR YOU.❤
PAPAN
AW! A SWEET GIRL LIKE YOU DESERVES SOME NEW YEAR'S MONEY!☆
WOW! I LOVE YOU, DAD!!
WHAT A SOFTY...

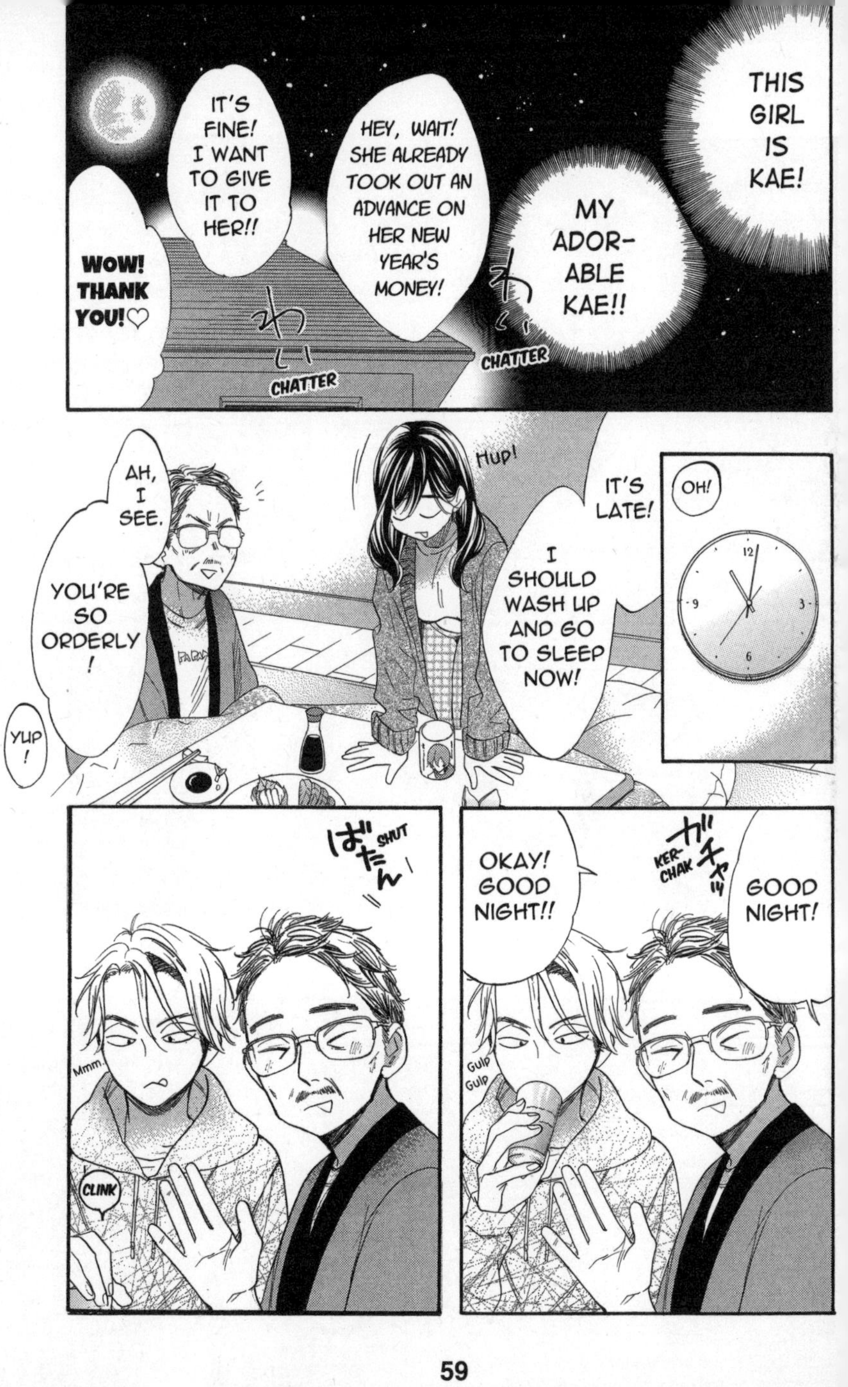
THIS GIRL IS KAE!
MY ADORABLE KAE!!
CHATTER
HEY, WAIT! SHE ALREADY TOOK OUT AN ADVANCE ON HER NEW YEAR'S MONEY!
IT'S FINE! I WANT TO GIVE IT TO HER!!
CHATTER
WOW! THANK YOU!♡
OH!
IT'S LATE!
I SHOULD WASH UP AND GO TO SLEEP NOW!
Hup!
AH, I SEE.
YOU'RE SO ORDERLY!
YUP!
GOOD NIGHT!
KER-CHAK
OKAY! GOOD NIGHT!!
Gulp Gulp
SHUT
Mmm.
CLINK

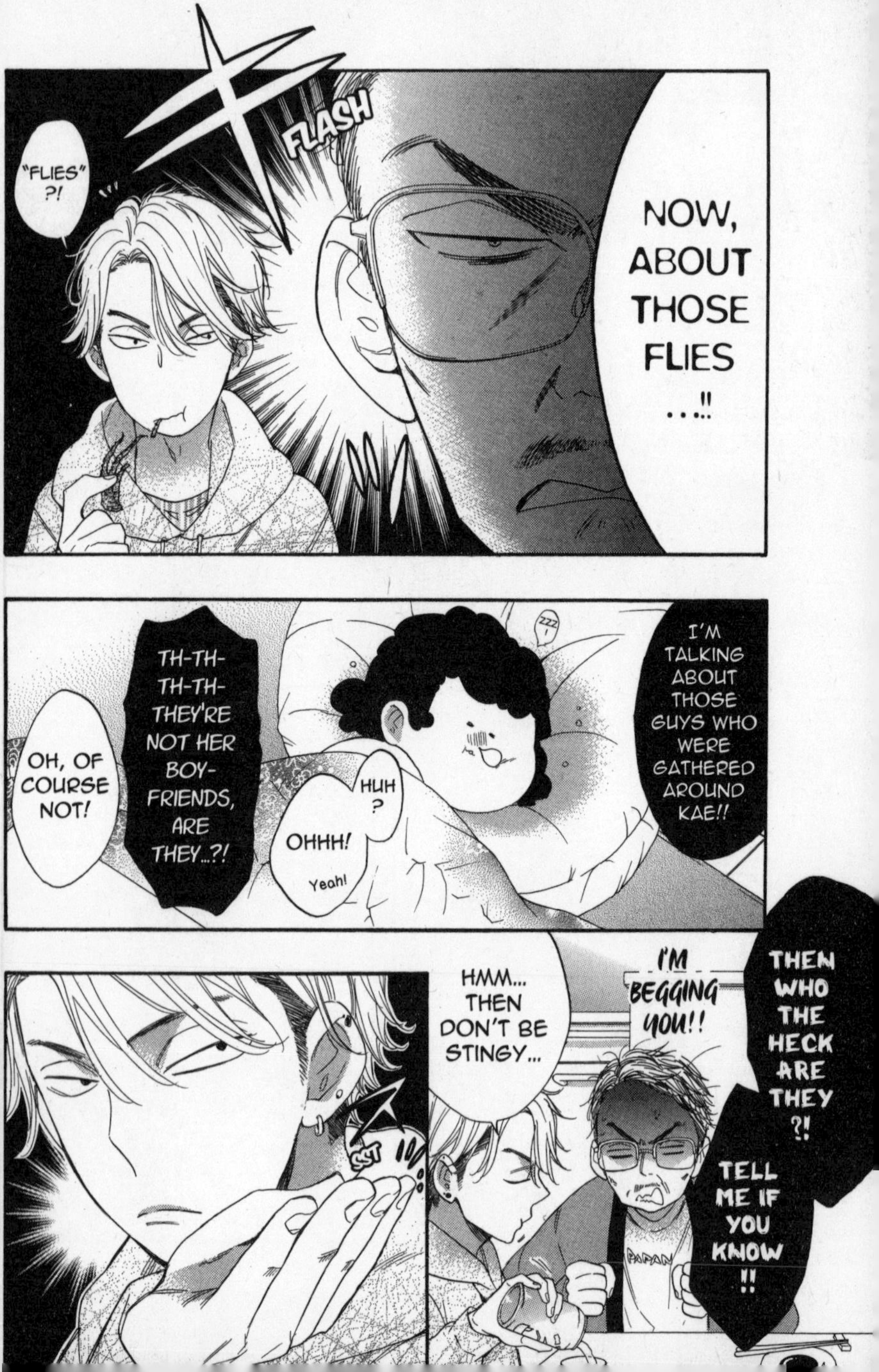
NOW, ABOUT THOSE FLIES ...!!
FLASH
"FLIES" ?!
I'M TALKING ABOUT THOSE GUYS WHO WERE GATHERED AROUND KAE!!
HUH ?
OHHH!
Yeah!
TH-TH-TH-TH-THEY'RE NOT HER BOY-FRIENDS, ARE THEY...?!
OH, OF COURSE NOT!
THEN WHO THE HECK ARE THEY ?!
TELL ME IF YOU KNOW !!
I'M BEGGING YOU!!
HMM... THEN DON'T BE STINGY...
SST

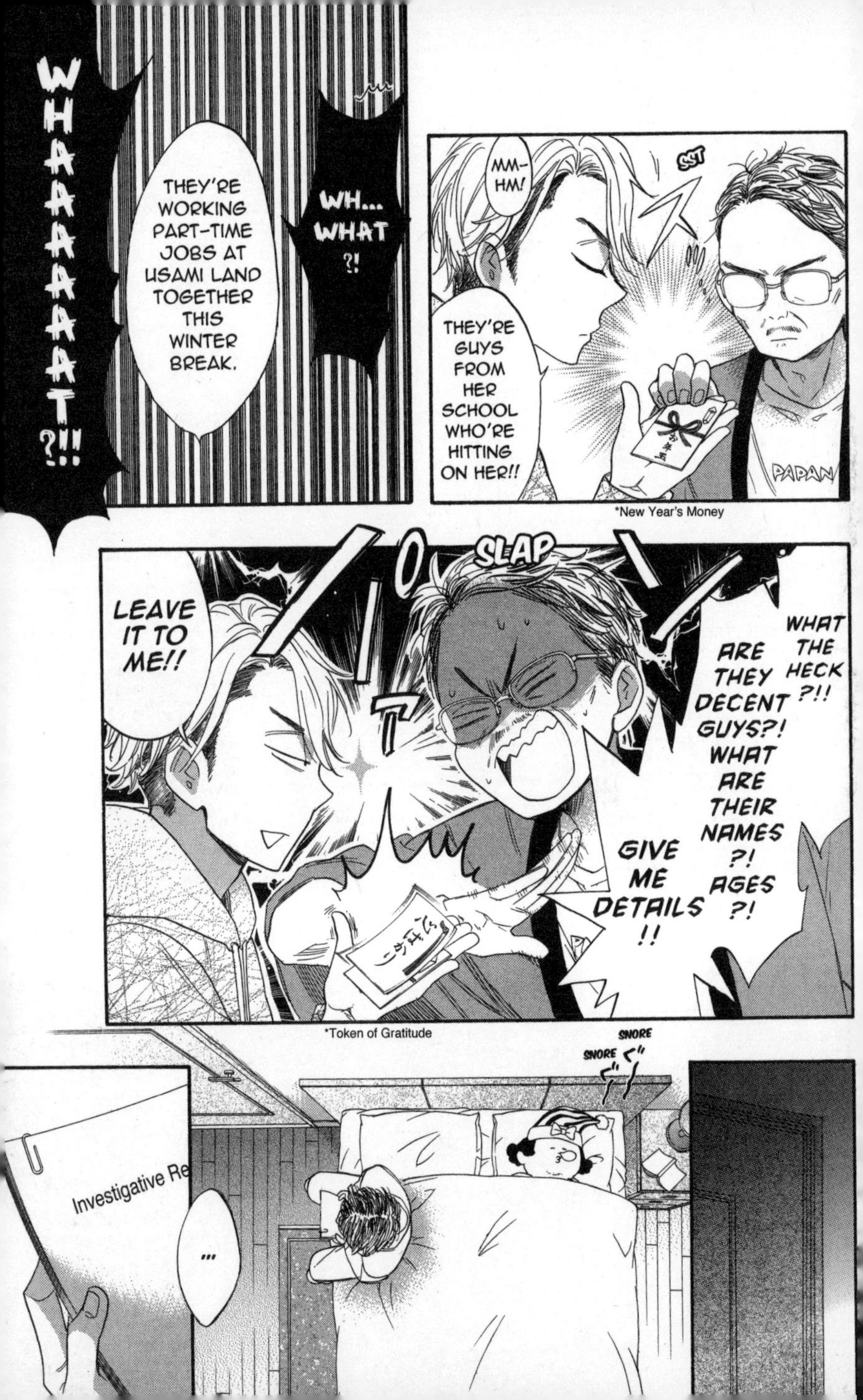
MM-HM!
SST
THEY'RE GUYS FROM HER SCHOOL WHO'RE HITTING ON HER!!
PAPAN
*New Year's Money
THEY'RE WORKING PART-TIME JOBS AT USAMI LAND TOGETHER THIS WINTER BREAK.
WH... WHAT ?!
WHAAAAAAAT ?!!
SLAP
WHAT THE HECK ?!!
ARE THEY DECENT GUYS?! WHAT ARE THEIR NAMES ?! AGES ?!
GIVE ME DETAILS !!
LEAVE IT TO ME!!
*Token of Gratitude
SNORE
SNORE
Investigative Re
...

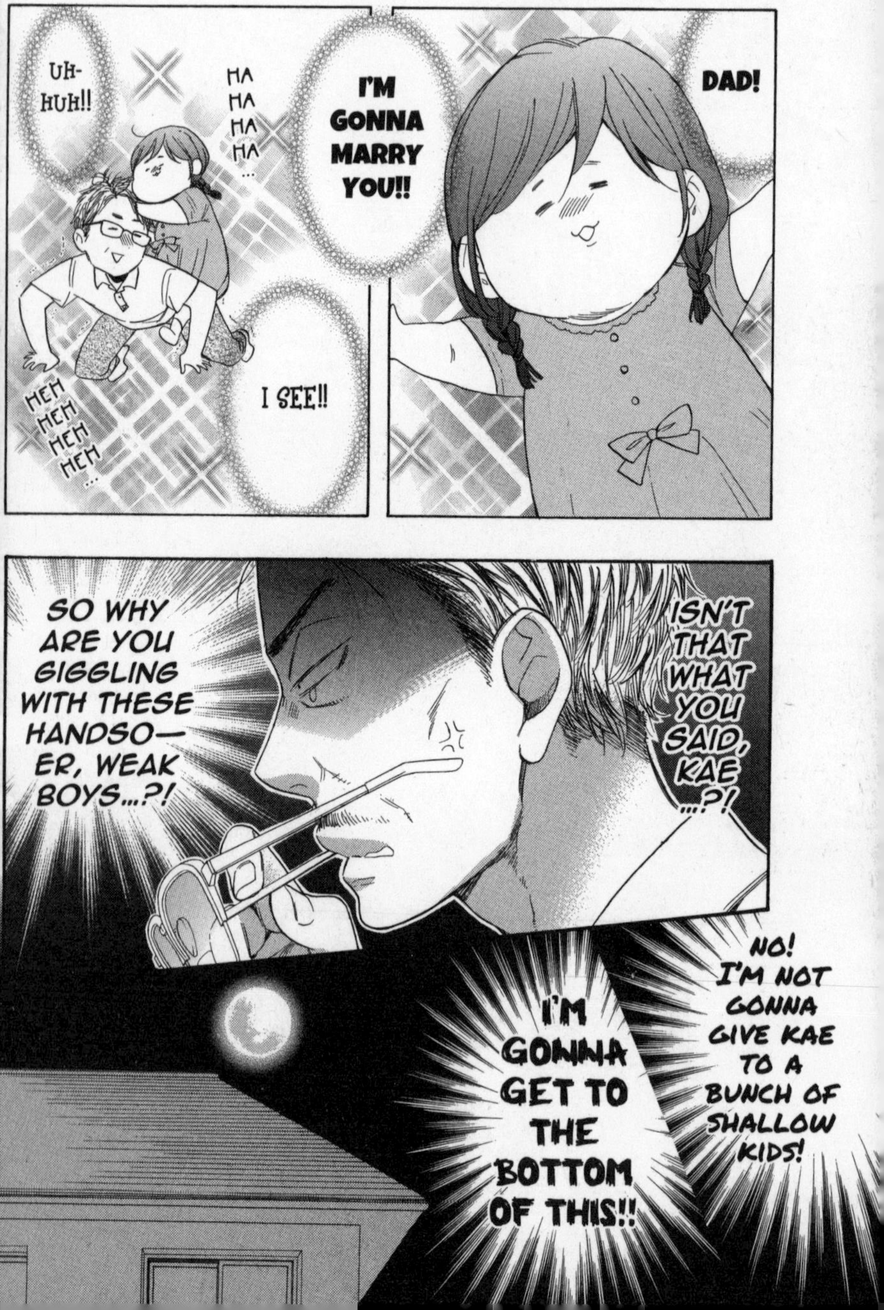
DAD!
I'M GONNA MARRY YOU!!
HA HA HA HA ...
UH-HUH!!
I SEE!!
HEH HEH HEH HEH ...
ISN'T THAT WHAT YOU SAID, KAE ...?!
SO WHY ARE YOU GIGGLING WITH THESE HANDSO— ER, WEAK BOYS...?!
NO! I'M NOT GONNA GIVE KAE TO A BUNCH OF SHALLOW KIDS!
I'M GONNA GET TO THE BOTTOM OF THIS!!

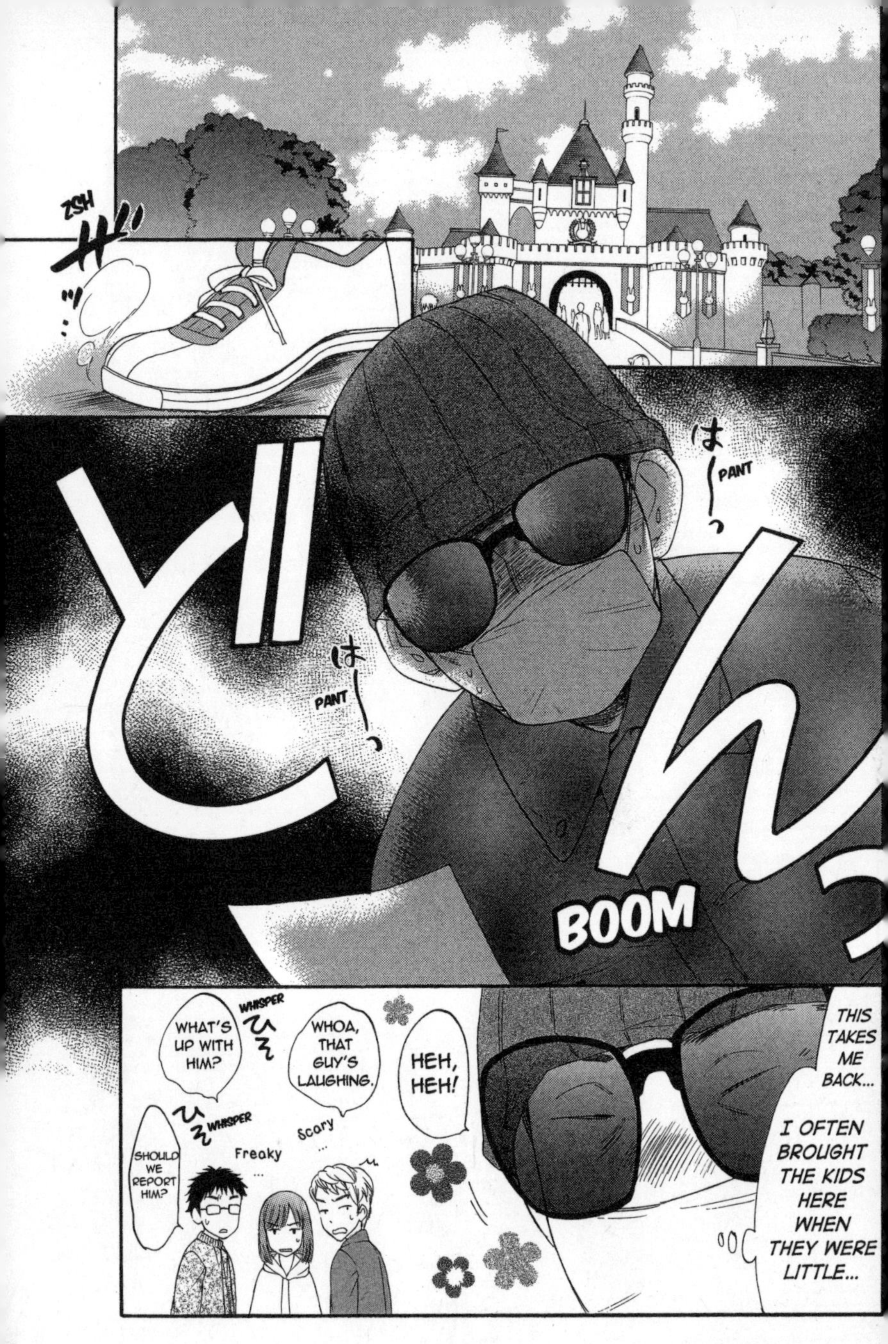
ZSH
ザッ
はーっ
PANT
はーっ
PANT
どーんっ
BOOM
THIS TAKES ME BACK...
I OFTEN BROUGHT THE KIDS HERE WHEN THEY WERE LITTLE...
HEH, HEH!
WHOA, THAT GUY'S LAUGHING.
WHISPER
ひそ
WHAT'S UP WITH HIM?
ひそ
WHISPER
Scary ...
Freaky ...
SHOULD WE REPORT HIM?

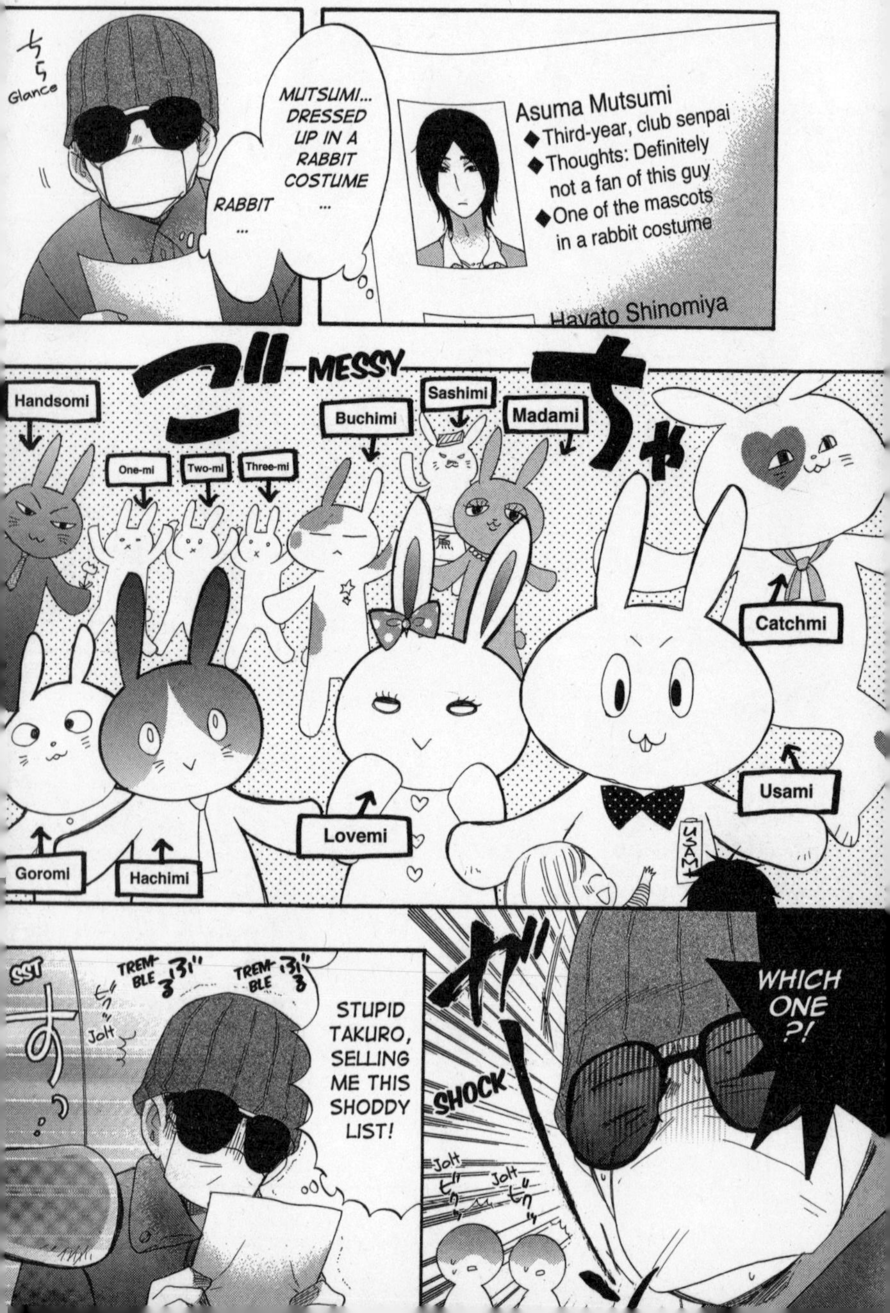
Asuma Mutsumi
◆Third-year, club senpai
◆Thoughts: Definitely not a fan of this guy
◆One of the mascots in a rabbit costume
Hayato Shinomiya
Glance
MUTSUMI... DRESSED UP IN A RABBIT COSTUME ...
RABBIT ...
Catchmi
Madami
Sashimi
Buchimi
MESSY
Three-mi
Two-mi
One-mi
Handsomi
Usami
USAMI
Lovemi
Hachimi
Gorom
WHICH ONE ?!
SHOCK
Jolt
Jolt
TREMBLE
TREMBLE
SST
Jolt
STUPID TAKURO, SELLING ME THIS SHODDY LIST!

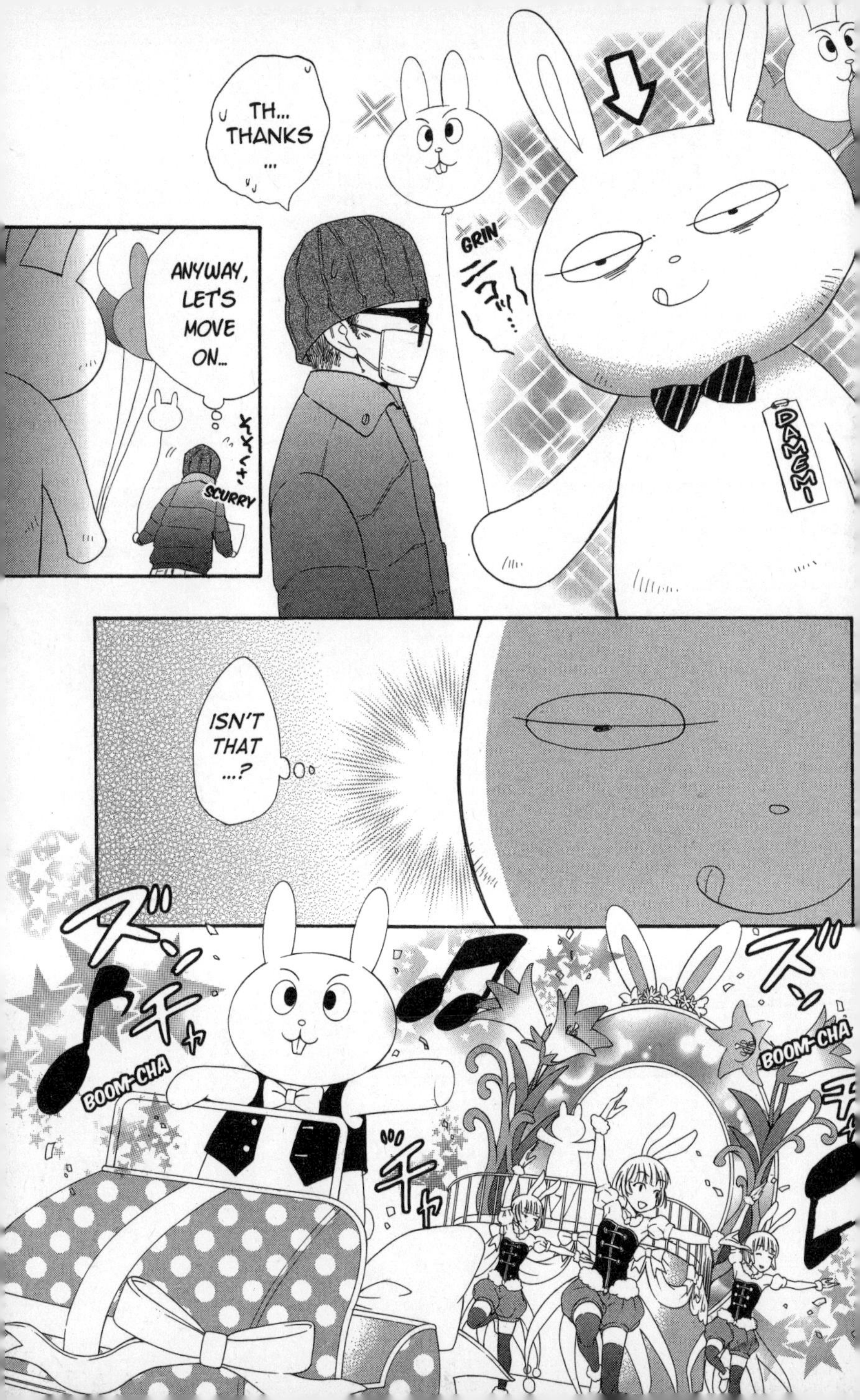
TH... THANKS ...
GRIN
ANYWAY, LET'S MOVE ON...
SCURRY
ISN'T THAT ...?
BOOM-CHA
BOOM-CHA

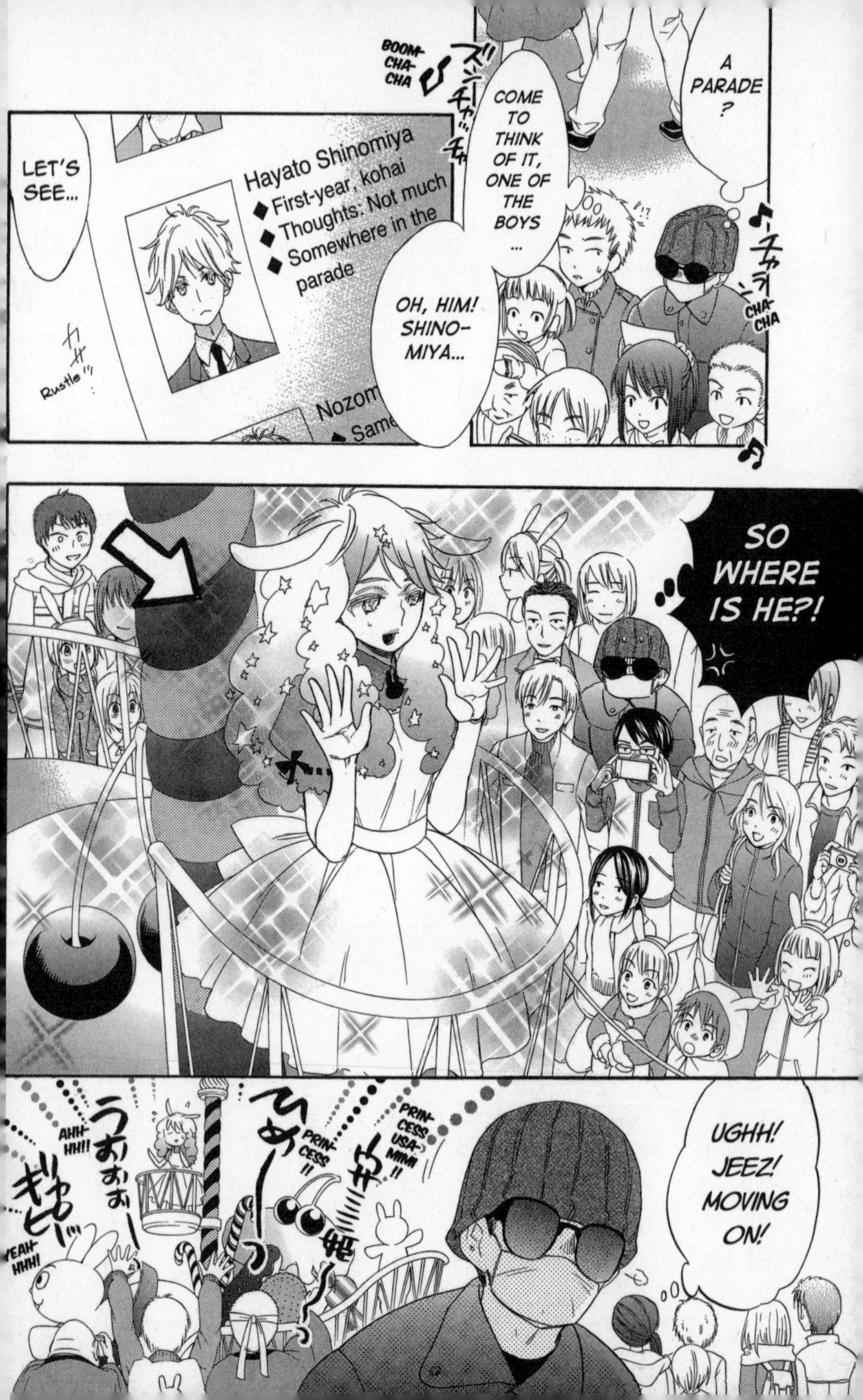

A PARADE?
BOOM-CHA-CHA
COME TO THINK OF IT, ONE OF THE BOYS...
OH, HIM! SHINOMIYA...
CHA-CHA
LET'S SEE...
Hayato Shinomiya
◆ First-year, kohai
◆ Thoughts: Not much
◆ Somewhere in the parade
Rustle
SO WHERE IS HE?!
UGHH! JEEZ! MOVING ON!
PRINCESS USA-MIMI!!
PRINCESS!!
AHHHH!!
YEAHHHH!!

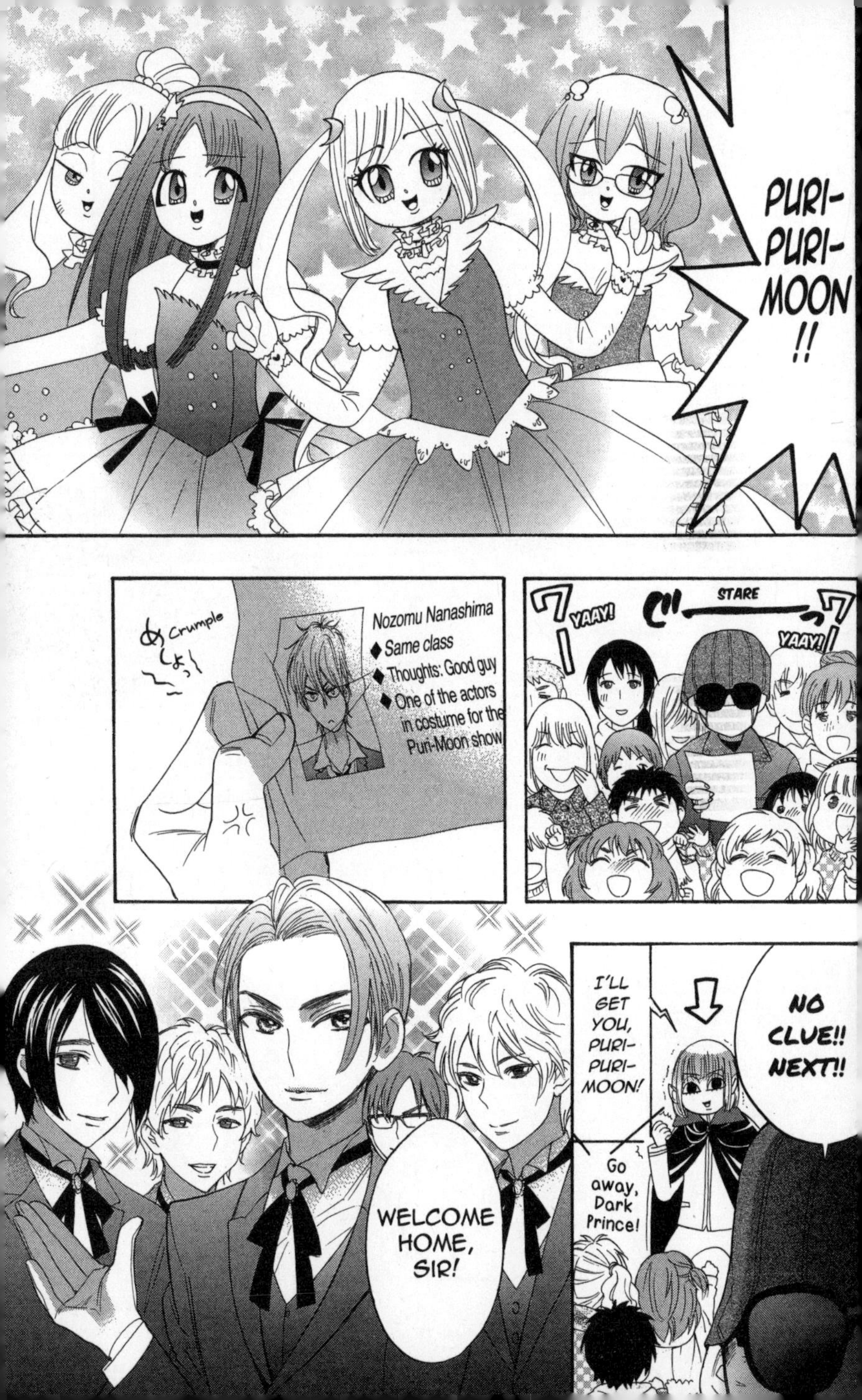
PURI-PURI-MOON!!
STARE
YAAY!
YAAY!
Crumple
Nozomu Nanashima
◆ Same class
◆ Thoughts: Good guy
◆ One of the actors in costume for the Puri-Moon show
NO CLUE!! NEXT!!
I'LL GET YOU, PURI-PURI-MOON!
Go away, Dark Prince!
WELCOME HOME, SIR!

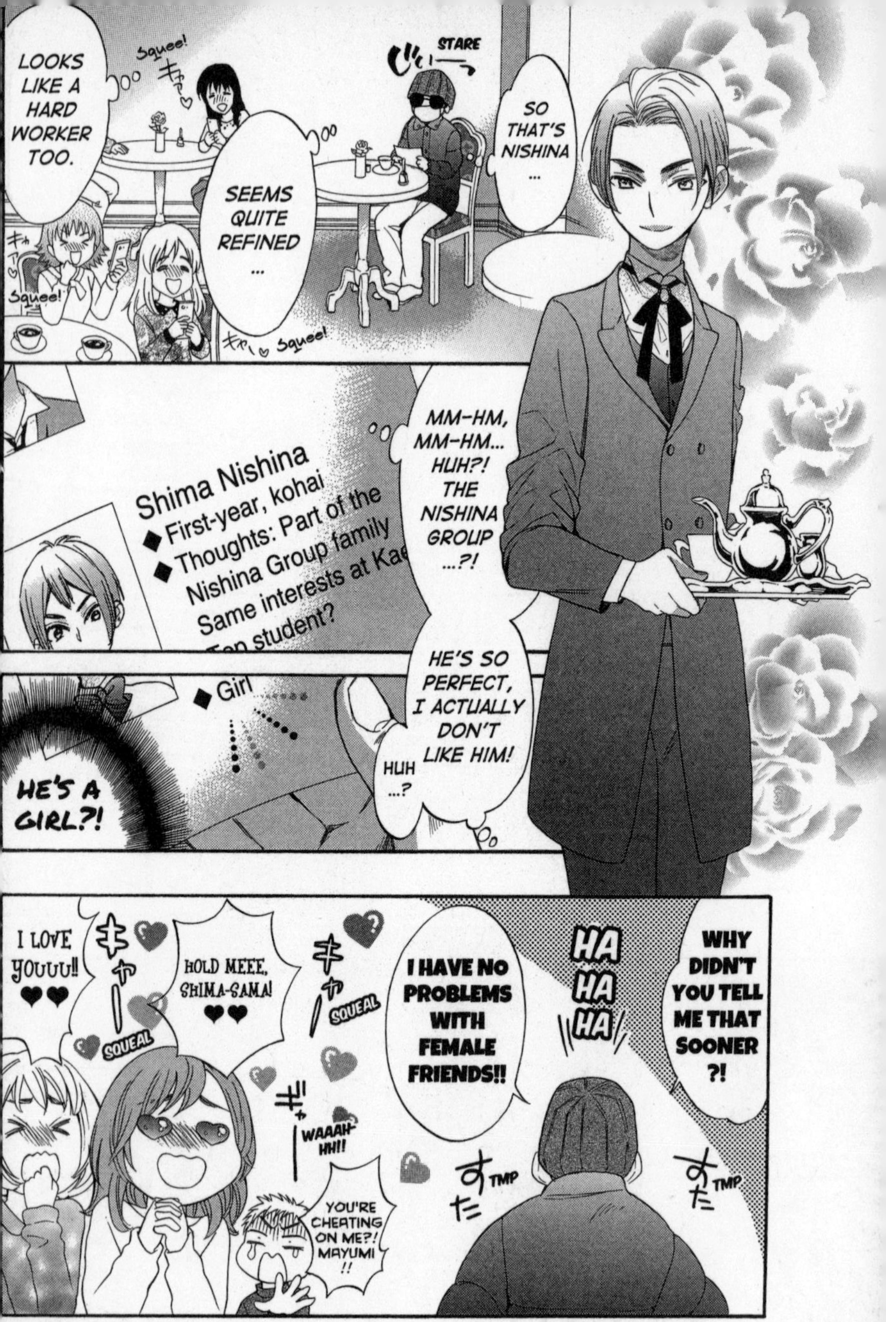
STARE
SO THAT'S NISHINA...
SEEMS QUITE REFINED...
LOOKS LIKE A HARD WORKER TOO.
Squee!
Squee!
Squee!
MM-HM, MM-HM... HUH?! THE NISHINA GROUP ...?!
Shima Nishina
◆ First-year, kohai
◆ Thoughts: Part of the Nishina Group family
Same interests at Kae
Ten student?
HE'S SO PERFECT, I ACTUALLY DON'T LIKE HIM!
HUH ...?
◆ Girl
HE'S A GIRL?!
WHY DIDN'T YOU TELL ME THAT SOONER ?!
HA HA HA
TMP
TMP
I HAVE NO PROBLEMS WITH FEMALE FRIENDS!!
WAAAHHH!!
YOU'RE CHEATING ON ME?! MAYUMI !!
SQUEAL
HOLD MEEE, SHIMA-SAMA! ❤❤
SQUEAL
I LOVE YOUUU!! ❤❤

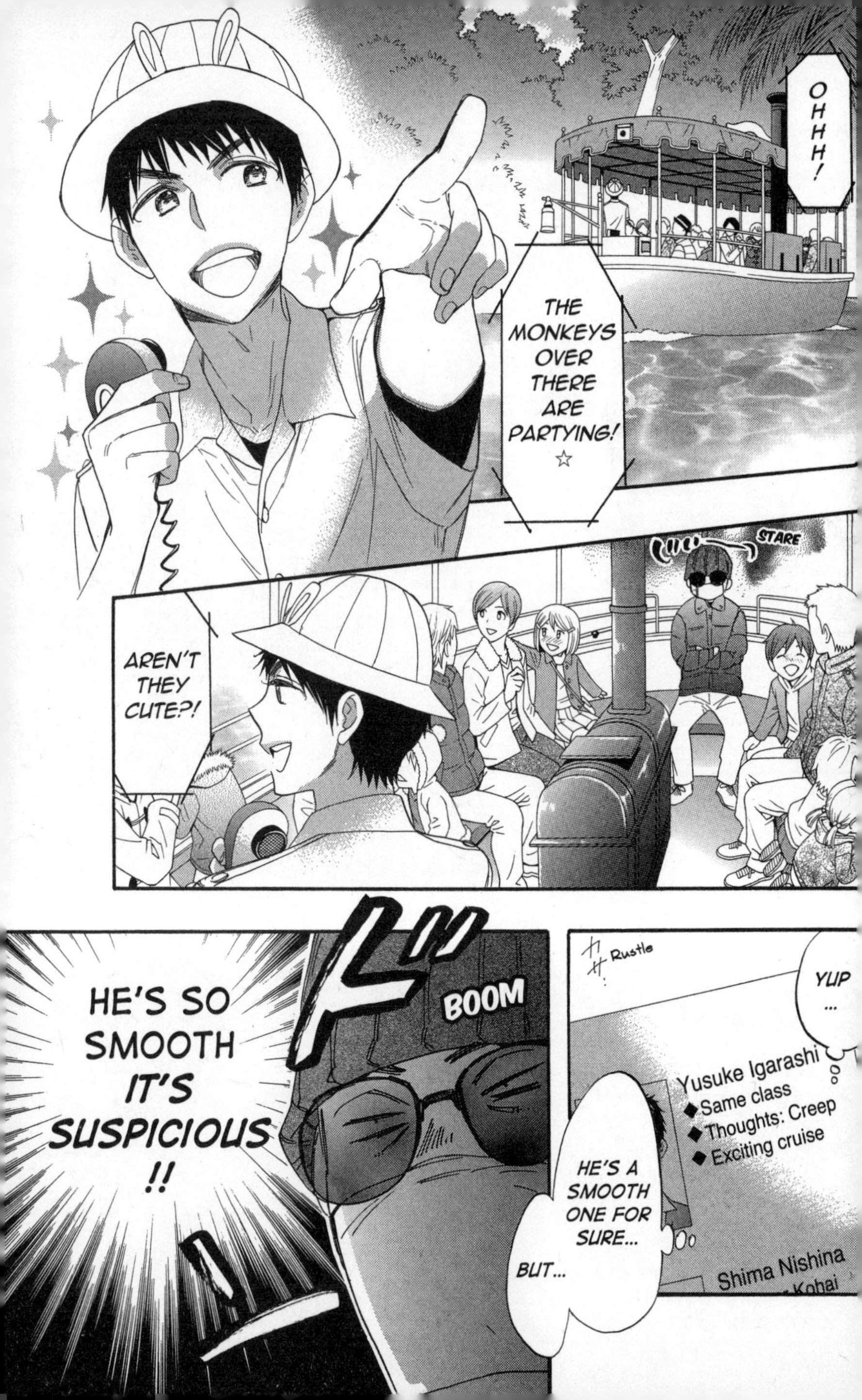
OHHH!
THE MONKEYS OVER THERE ARE PARTYING! ☆
STARE
AREN'T THEY CUTE?!
Rustle
YUP...
Yusuke Igarashi
◆ Same class
◆ Thoughts: Creep
◆ Exciting cruise
HE'S A SMOOTH ONE FOR SURE...
BUT...
Shima Nishina
Kohai
BOOM
HE'S SO SMOOTH IT'S SUSPICIOUS!!

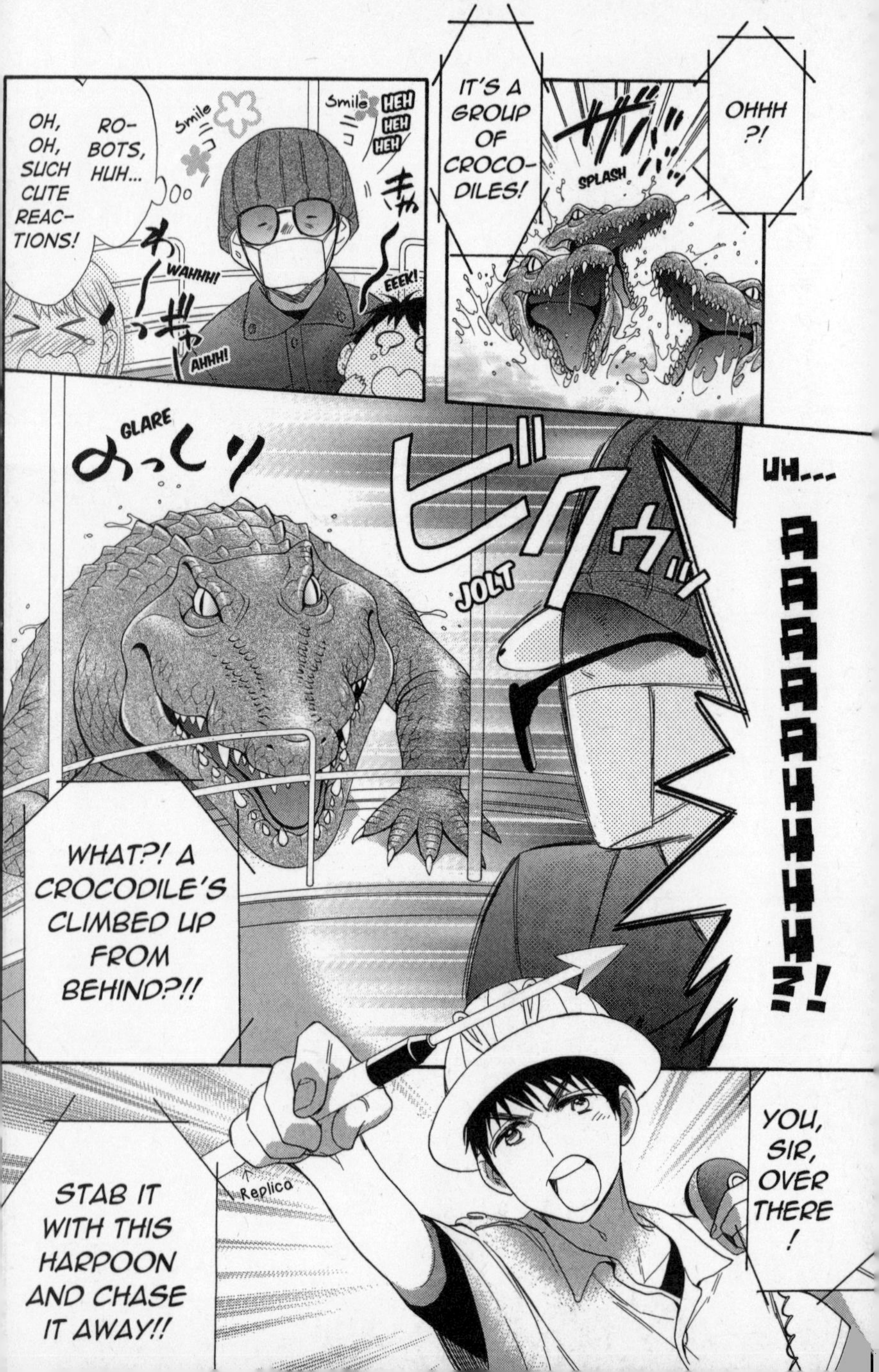
OHHH ?!
IT'S A GROUP OF CROCODILES!
SPLASH
HEH HEH HEH
Smile
Smile
ROBOTS, HUH...
OH, OH, SUCH CUTE REACTIONS!
EEEK!
WAHHH!
AHHH!
UH... AAAAAAAHHHHH?!
JOLT
GLARE
WHAT?! A CROCODILE'S CLIMBED UP FROM BEHIND?!!
YOU, SIR, OVER THERE!
Replica
STAB IT WITH THIS HARPOON AND CHASE IT AWAY!!

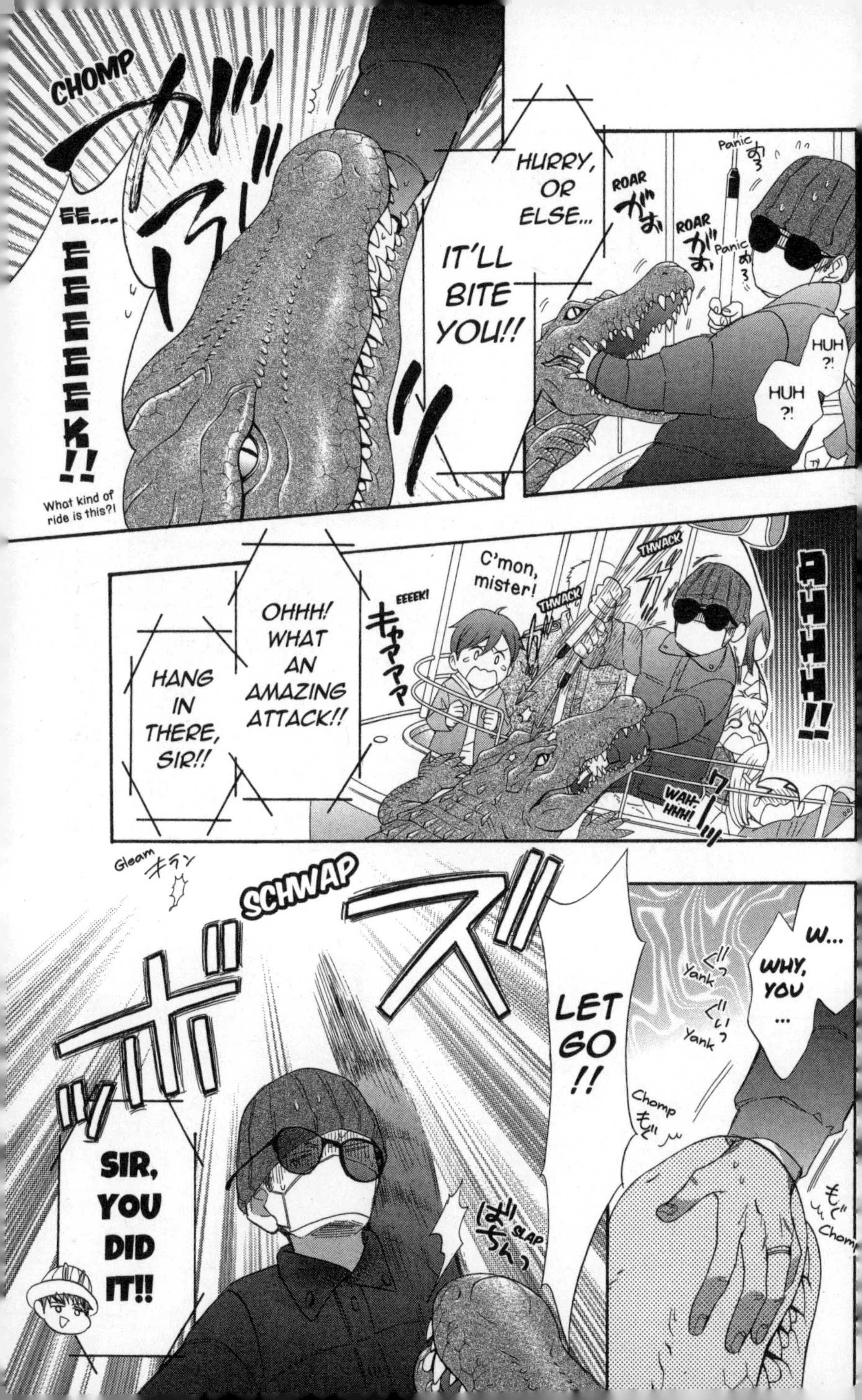
Panic
ROAR
ROAR
Panic
HURRY, OR ELSE...
IT'LL BITE YOU!!
HUH?!
HUH?!
CHOMP
EE... EEEEEEK!!
What kind of ride is this?!
AHHH!!
THWACK
C'mon, mister!
THWACK
EEEEK!
WAH-HHH!
OHHH! WHAT AN AMAZING ATTACK!!
HANG IN THERE, SIR!!
W... WHY, YOU...
Yank
Yank
LET GO!!
Chomp
Chomp
Gleam
SCHWAP
SLAP
SIR, YOU DID IT!!

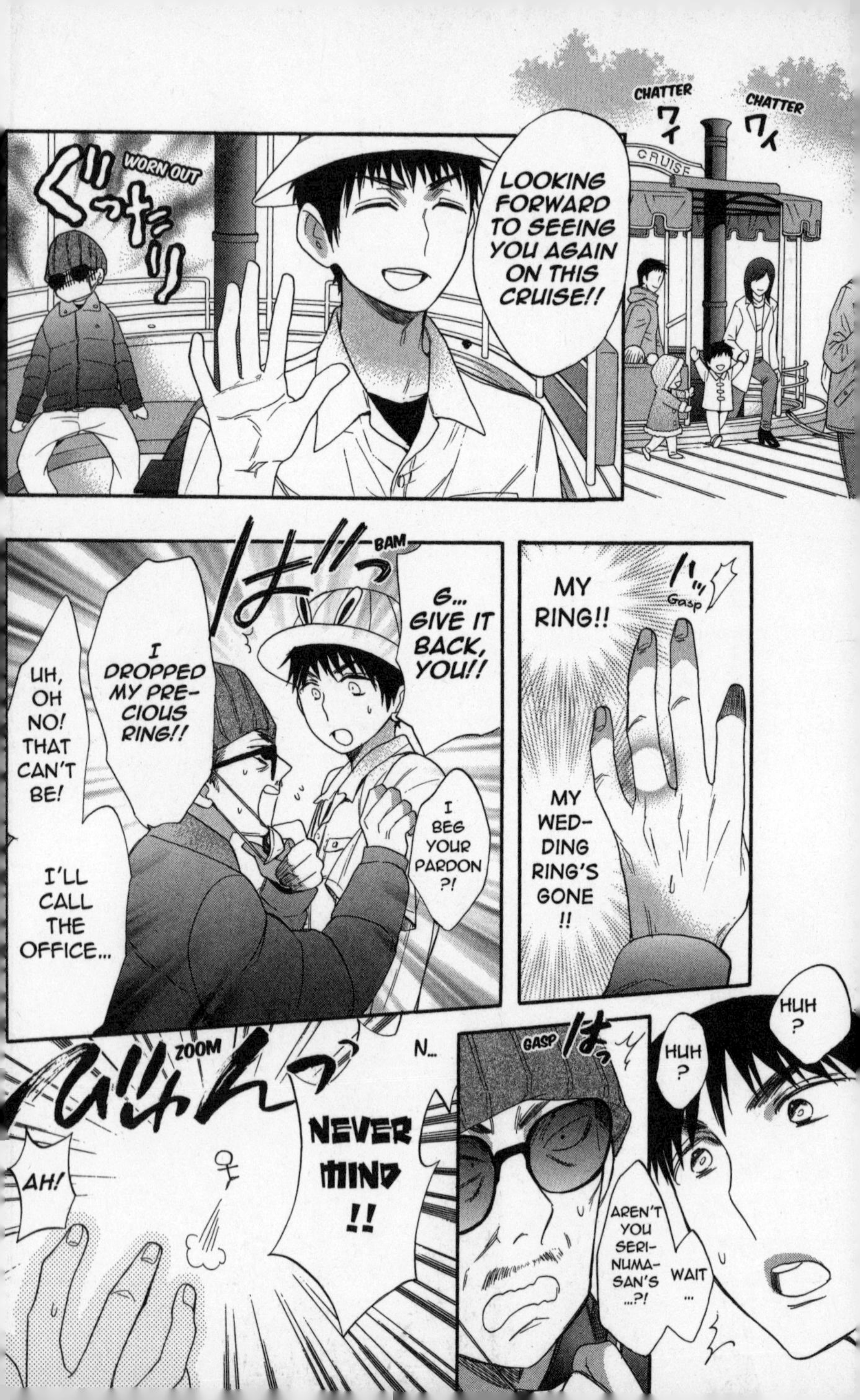

CHATTER
ワイ
CHATTER
ワイ
CRUISE
LOOKING FORWARD TO SEEING YOU AGAIN ON THIS CRUISE!!
WORN OUT
ぐったり
MY RING!!
バッ
Gasp
MY WEDDING RING'S GONE !!
ばっ
BAM
G... GIVE IT BACK, YOU!!
I DROPPED MY PRECIOUS RING!!
UH, OH NO! THAT CAN'T BE!
I BEG YOUR PARDON ?!
I'LL CALL THE OFFICE...
HUH ?
HUH ?
GASP
は
WAIT ...
AREN'T YOU SERINUMA-SAN'S ...?!
N...
ZOOM
ひゅんっ
NEVER MIND !!
AH!

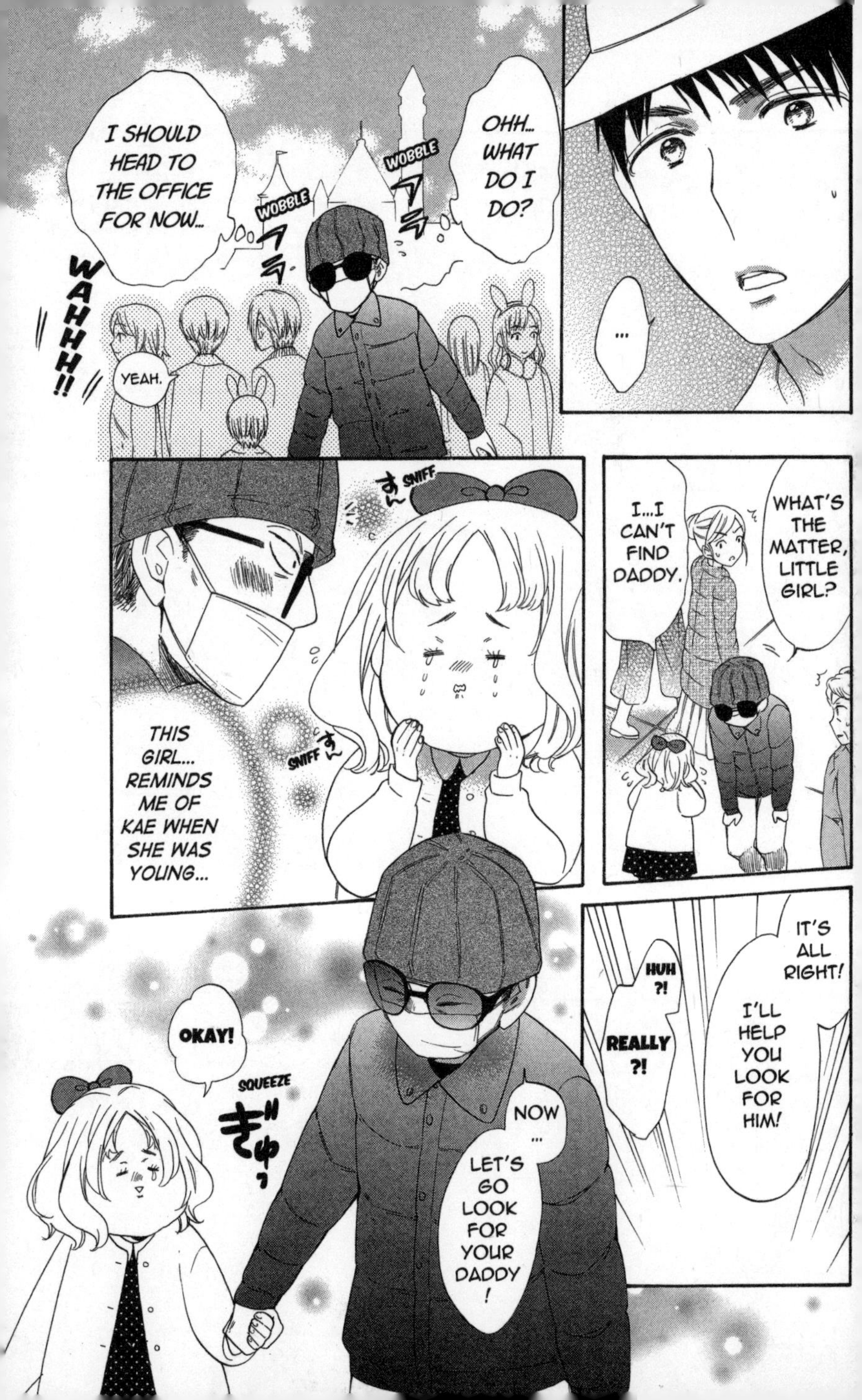
...
OHH... WHAT DO I DO?
WOBBLE
WOBBLE
I SHOULD HEAD TO THE OFFICE FOR NOW...
WAHHHH!!
YEAH.
WHAT'S THE MATTER, LITTLE GIRL?
I...I CAN'T FIND DADDY.
すん SNIFF
THIS GIRL... REMINDS ME OF KAE WHEN SHE WAS YOUNG...
SNIFF すん
IT'S ALL RIGHT! I'LL HELP YOU LOOK FOR HIM!
HUH?! REALLY?!
NOW... LET'S GO LOOK FOR YOUR DADDY!
SQUEEZE
OKAY!

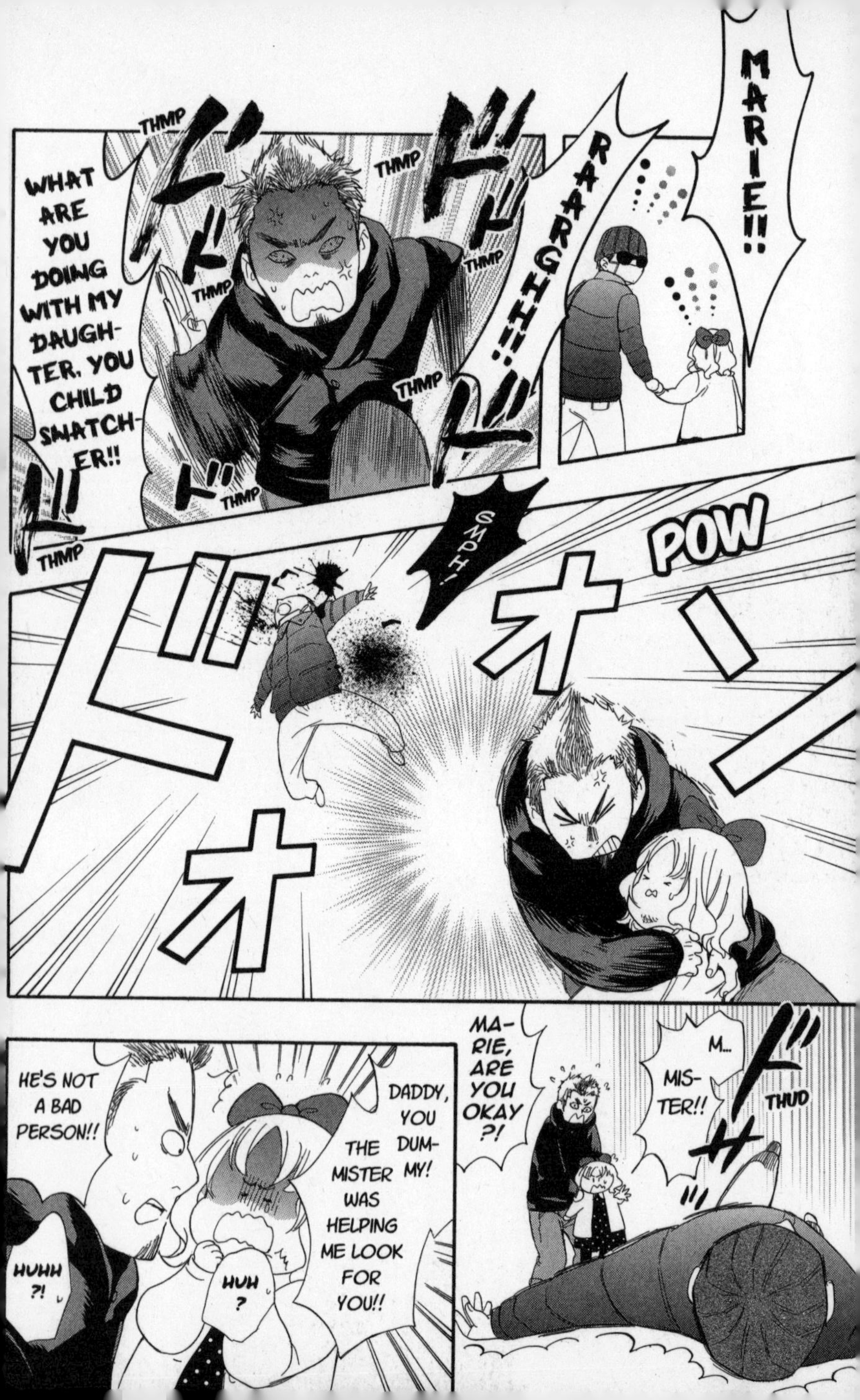

MARIE!!
RAARGHHH!!!
THMP
THMP
THMP
THMP
THMP
THMP
THMP
WHAT ARE YOU DOING WITH MY DAUGH-TER, YOU CHILD SNATCH-ER!!
GMPH!
POW
M... MIS-TER!!
THUD
MA-RIE, ARE YOU OKAY?!
DADDY, YOU DUM-MY! THE MISTER WAS HELPING ME LOOK FOR YOU!!
HUH?
HE'S NOT A BAD PERSON!!
HUHH?!

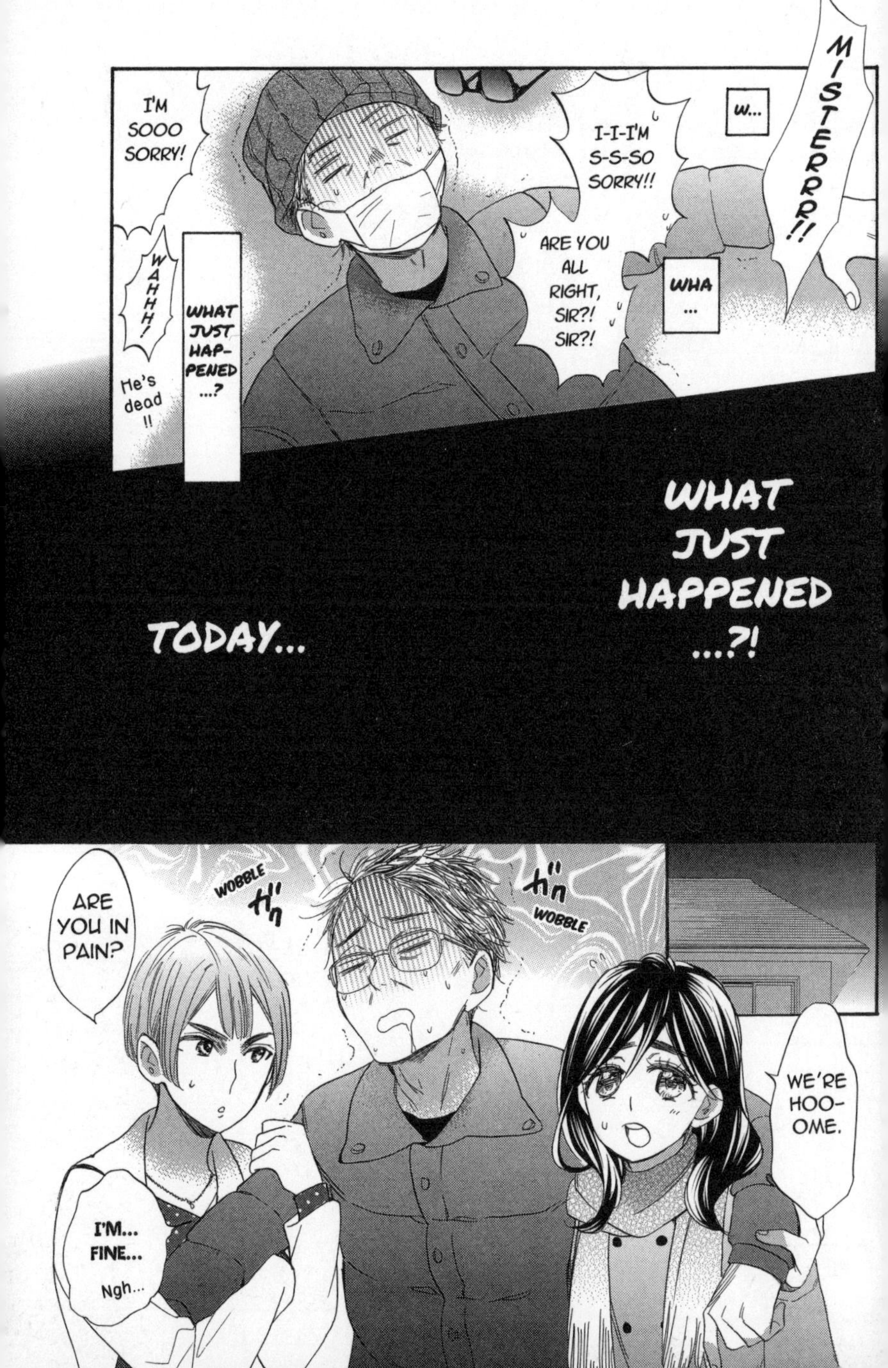
MISTERRR!!
W...
WHA...
I-I-I'M S-S-SO SORRY!!
ARE YOU ALL RIGHT, SIR?! SIR?!
I'M SOOO SORRY!
WAHHH!
He's dead !!
WHAT JUST HAP-PENED ...?
WHAT JUST HAPPENED ...?!
TODAY...
WE'RE HOO-OME.
WOBBLE
WOBBLE
ARE YOU IN PAIN?
I'M... FINE...
Ngh...

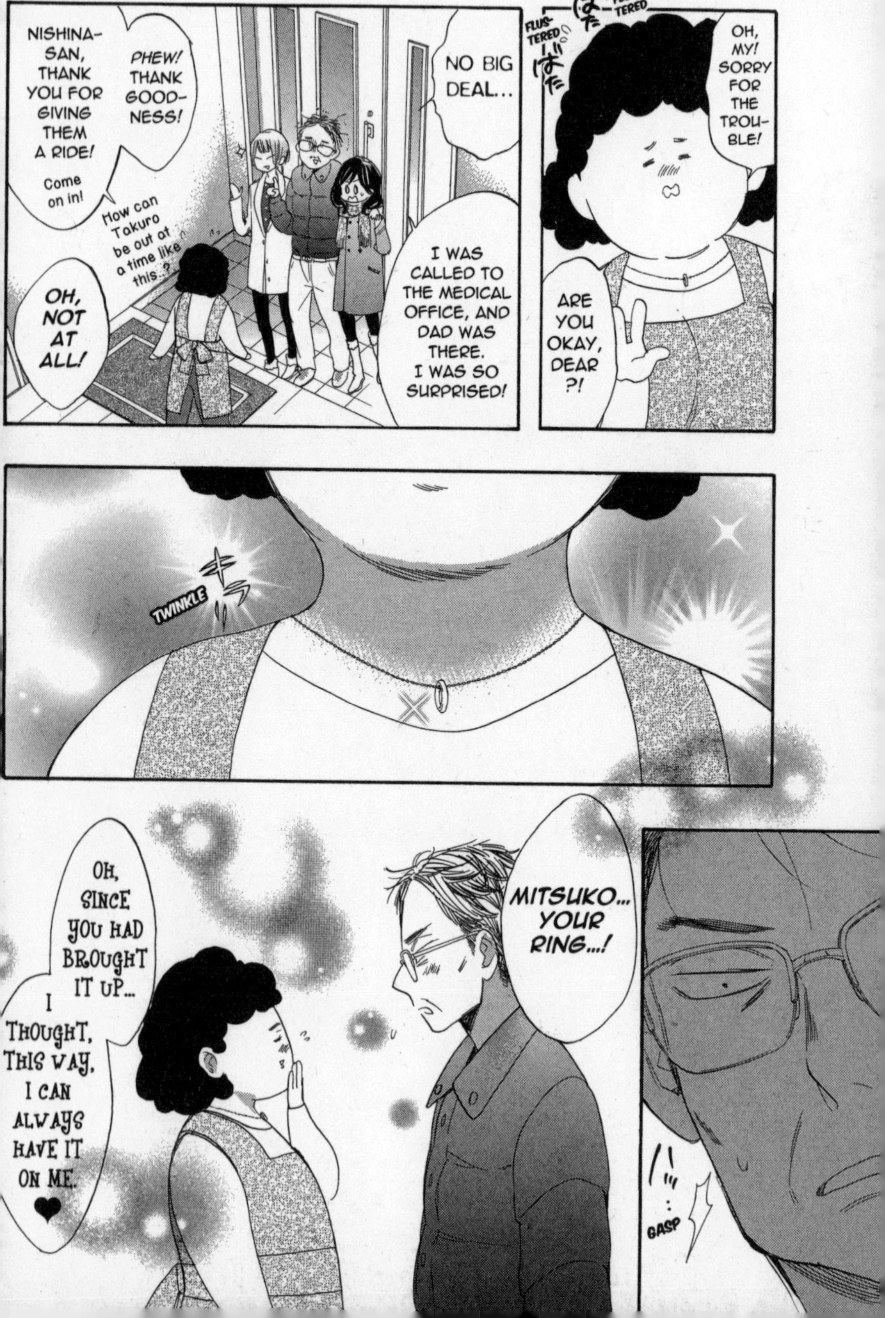
FLUSTERED
FLUSTERED
OH, MY! SORRY FOR THE TROUBLE!
ARE YOU OKAY, DEAR?!
NO BIG DEAL...
I WAS CALLED TO THE MEDICAL OFFICE, AND DAD WAS THERE. I WAS SO SURPRISED!
PHEW! THANK GOODNESS!
NISHINA-SAN, THANK YOU FOR GIVING THEM A RIDE!
Come on in!
How can Takuro be out at a time like this..?
OH, NOT AT ALL!
TWINKLE
GASP
MITSUKO... YOUR RING...!
OH, SINCE YOU HAD BROUGHT IT UP...
I THOUGHT, THIS WAY, I CAN ALWAYS HAVE IT ON ME. ♥

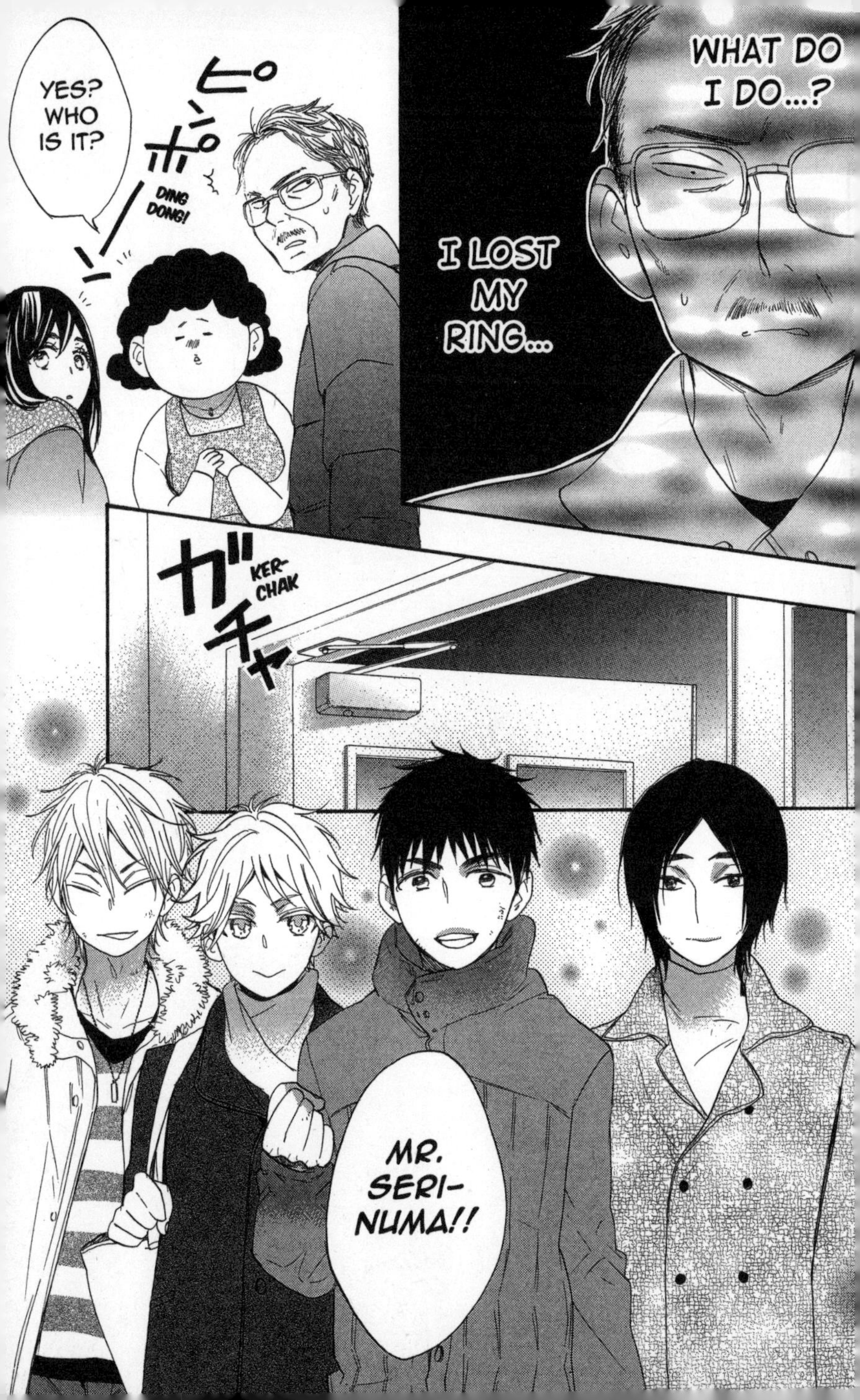
WHAT DO I DO...?
I LOST MY RING...
YES? WHO IS IT?
ピンポーン
DING DONG!
ガチャ
KER-CHAK
MR. SERI-NUMA!!

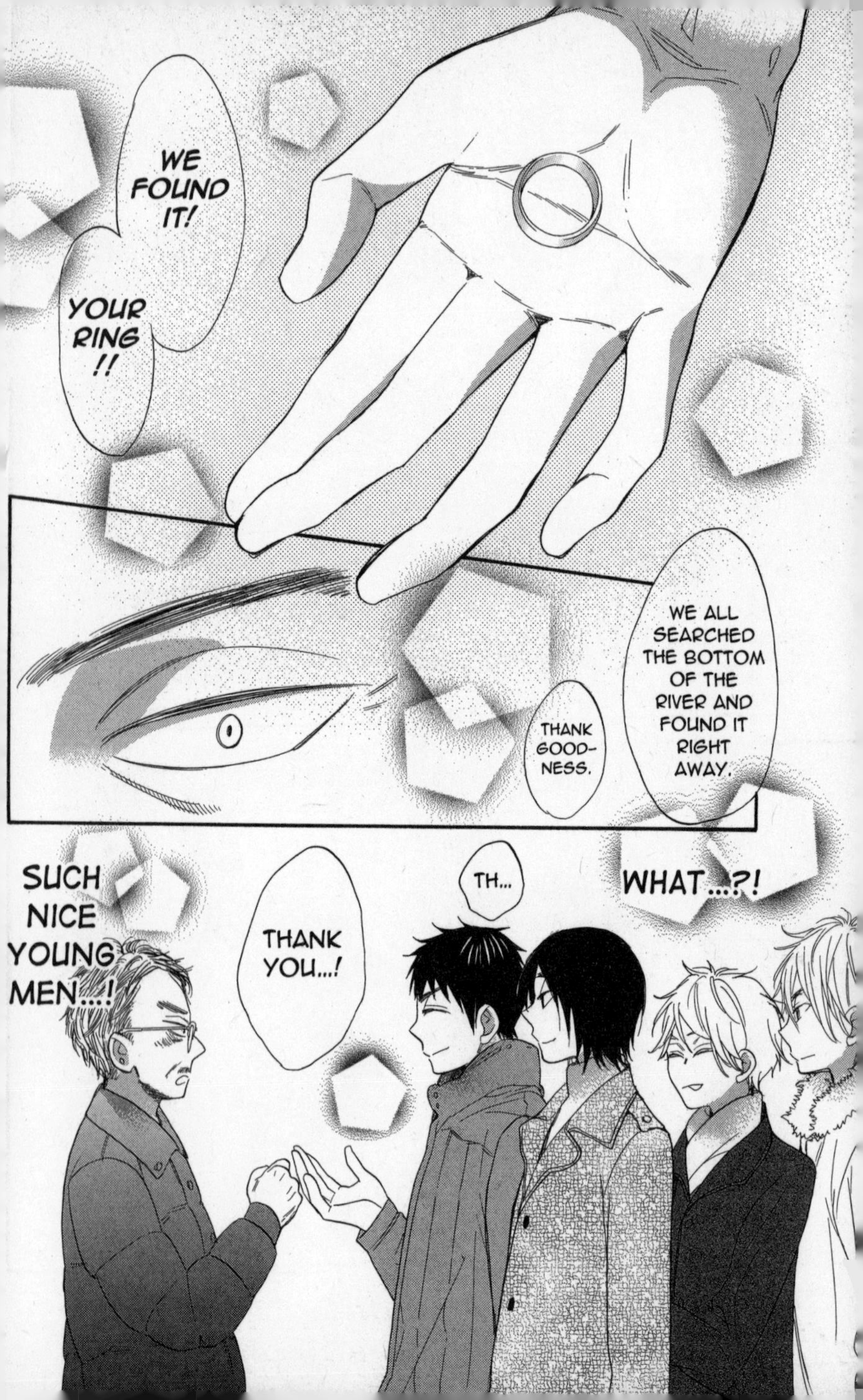
WE FOUND IT!
YOUR RING!!
WE ALL SEARCHED THE BOTTOM OF THE RIVER AND FOUND IT RIGHT AWAY.
THANK GOODNESS.
WHAT...?!
TH...
THANK YOU...!
SUCH NICE YOUNG MEN...!

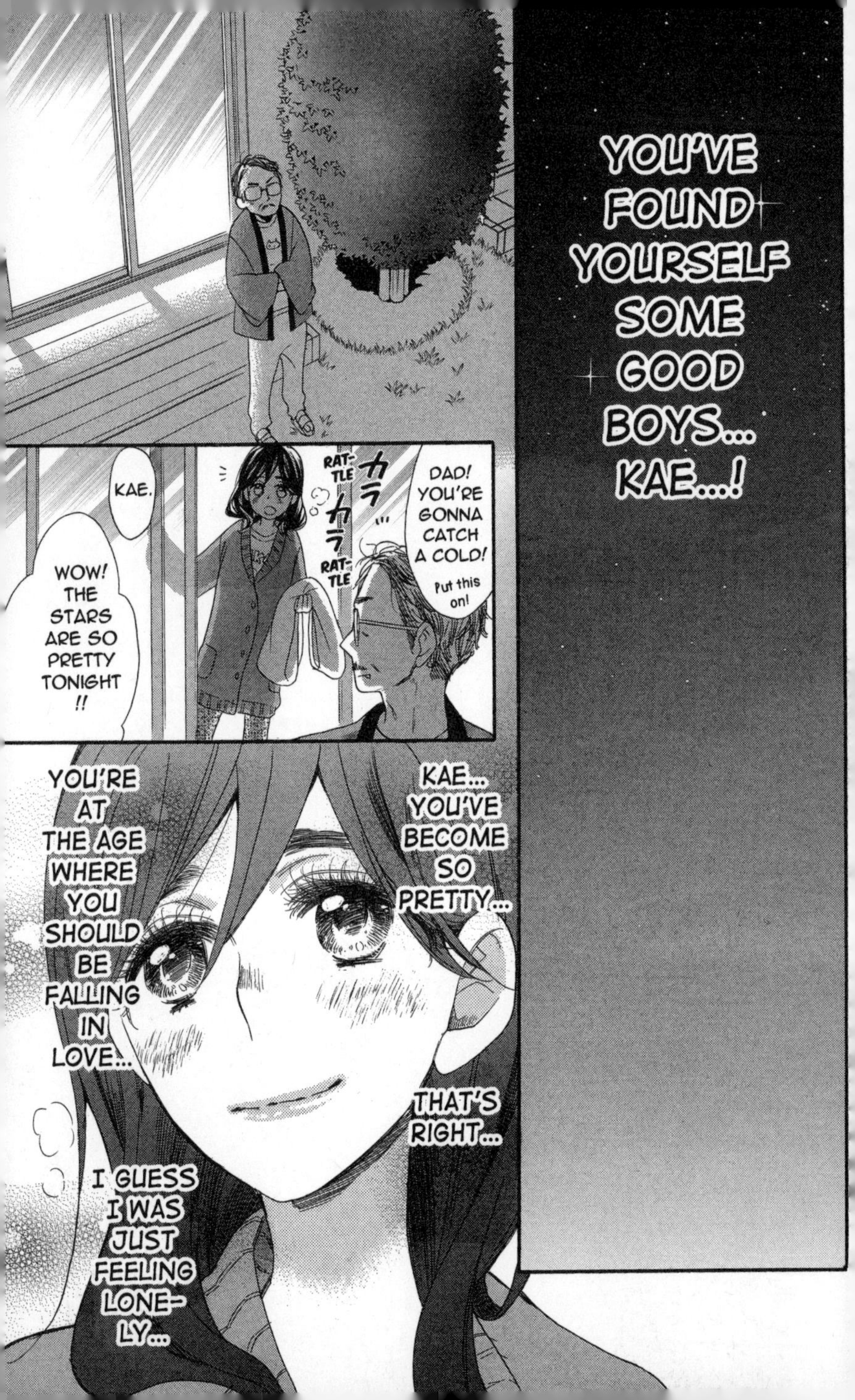
YOU'VE FOUND YOURSELF SOME GOOD BOYS... KAE...!
RAT-TLE カラ
DAD! YOU'RE GONNA CATCH A COLD!
Put this on!
RAT-TLE カラ
KAE.
WOW! THE STARS ARE SO PRETTY TONIGHT !!
KAE... YOU'VE BECOME SO PRETTY...
YOU'RE AT THE AGE WHERE YOU SHOULD BE FALLING IN LOVE...
THAT'S RIGHT...
I GUESS I WAS JUST FEELING LONE-LY...

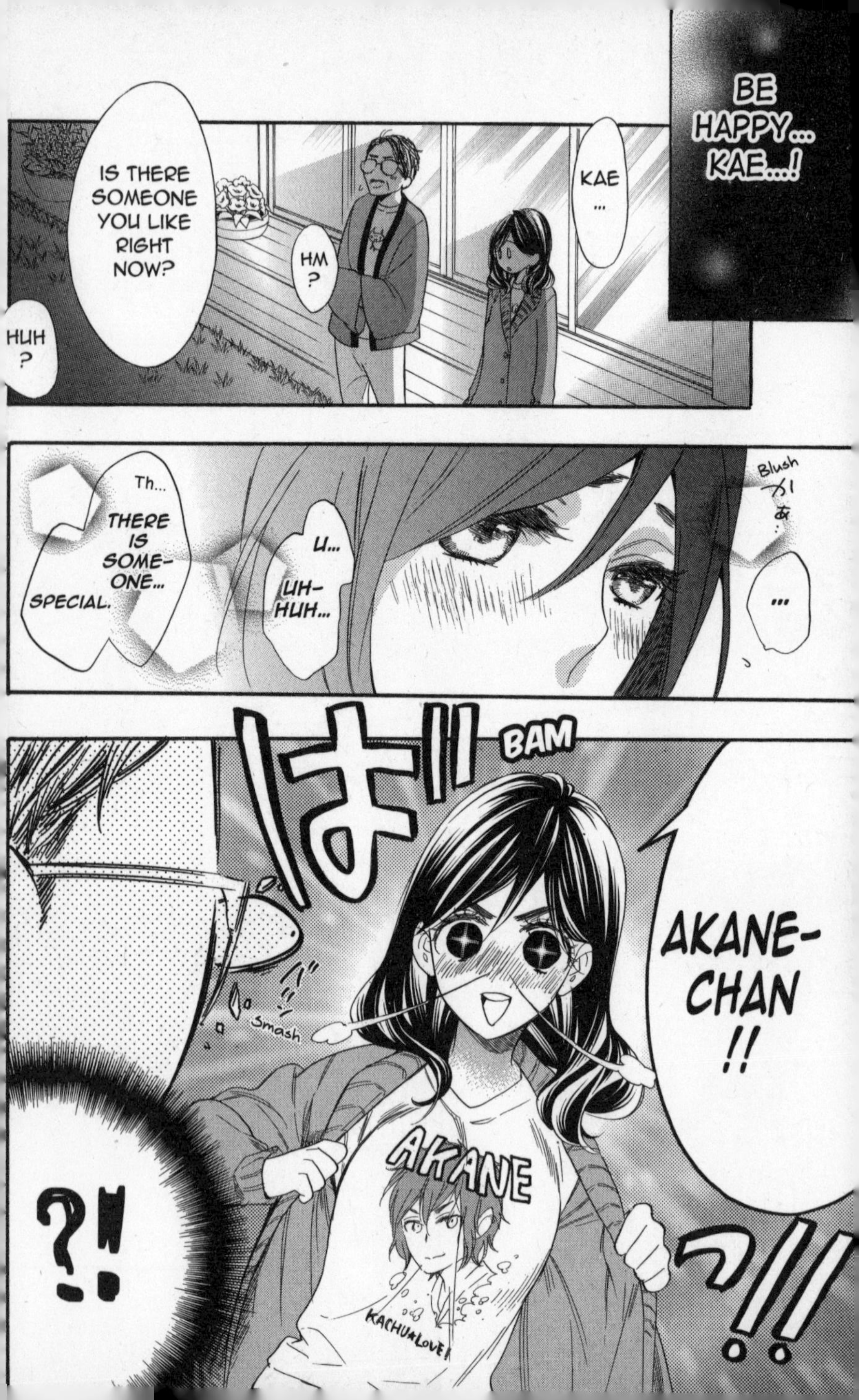
BE HAPPY... KAE...!
KAE ...
HM ?
IS THERE SOMEONE YOU LIKE RIGHT NOW?
HUH ?
Blush
...
U...
UH-HUH...
Th...
THERE IS SOME-ONE... SPECIAL.
BAM
は!!
AKANE-CHAN !!
っ!!
AKANE
KACHU★LOVE!
Smash
?!

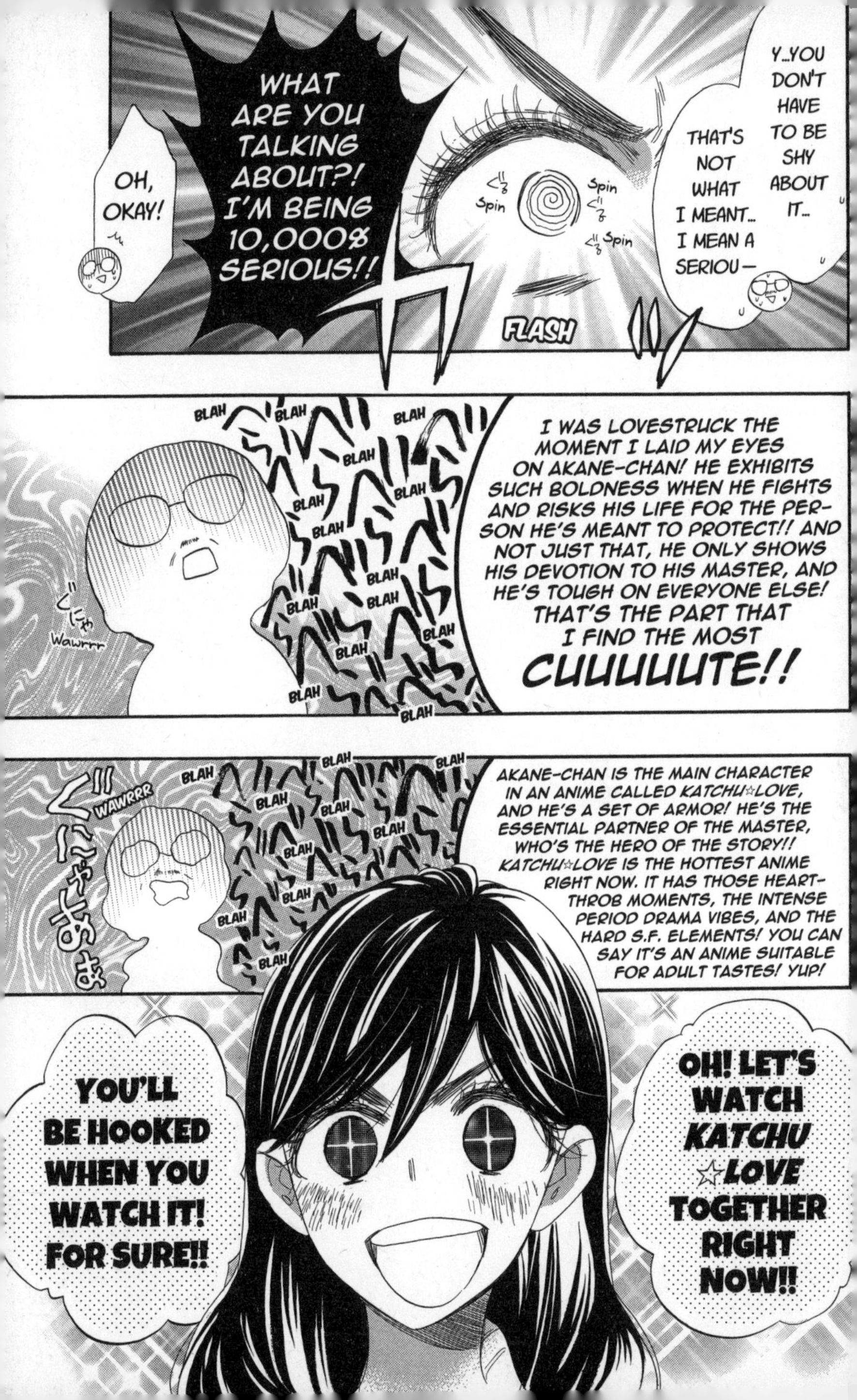

Y...YOU DON'T HAVE TO BE SHY ABOUT IT...
THAT'S NOT WHAT I MEANT... I MEAN A SERIOU—
Spin Spin Spin
FLASH
WHAT ARE YOU TALKING ABOUT?! I'M BEING 10,000% SERIOUS!!
OH, OKAY!
I WAS LOVESTRUCK THE MOMENT I LAID MY EYES ON AKANE-CHAN! HE EXHIBITS SUCH BOLDNESS WHEN HE FIGHTS AND RISKS HIS LIFE FOR THE PERSON HE'S MEANT TO PROTECT!! AND NOT JUST THAT, HE ONLY SHOWS HIS DEVOTION TO HIS MASTER, AND HE'S TOUGH ON EVERYONE ELSE! THAT'S THE PART THAT I FIND THE MOST CUUUUUTE!!
BLAH BLAH BLAH
Wawrrr
AKANE-CHAN IS THE MAIN CHARACTER IN AN ANIME CALLED KATCHU☆LOVE, AND HE'S A SET OF ARMOR! HE'S THE ESSENTIAL PARTNER OF THE MASTER, WHO'S THE HERO OF THE STORY!! KATCHU☆LOVE IS THE HOTTEST ANIME RIGHT NOW. IT HAS THOSE HEART-THROB MOMENTS, THE INTENSE PERIOD DRAMA VIBES, AND THE HARD S.F. ELEMENTS! YOU CAN SAY IT'S AN ANIME SUITABLE FOR ADULT TASTES! YUP!
BLAH BLAH BLAH
WAWRRR
OH! LET'S WATCH KATCHU☆LOVE TOGETHER RIGHT NOW!!
YOU'LL BE HOOKED WHEN YOU WATCH IT! FOR SURE!!

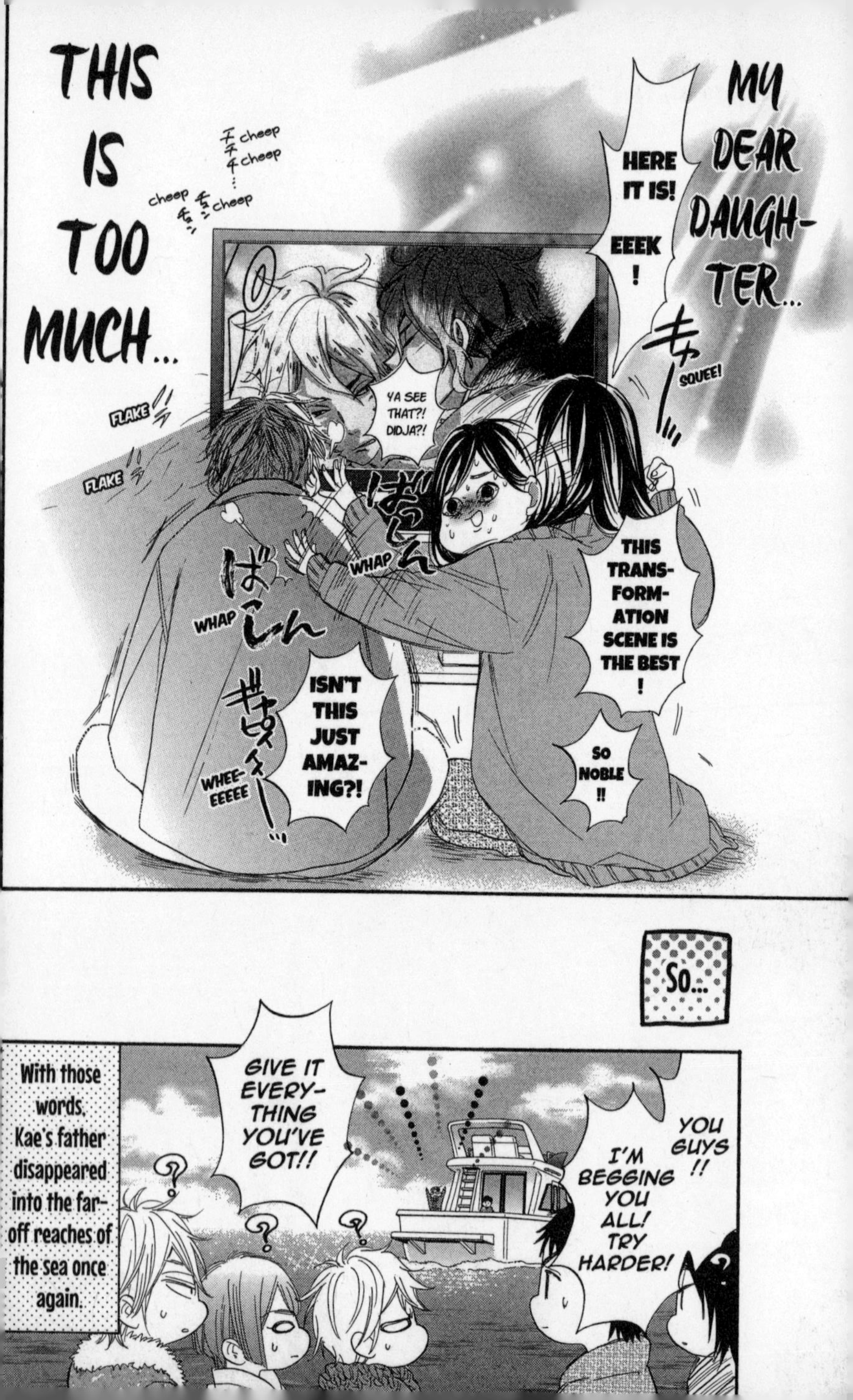

MY DEAR DAUGHTER...
HERE IT IS! EEEK!
SQUEE!
THIS IS TOO MUCH...
cheep cheep cheep cheep
YA SEE THAT?! DIDJA?!
FLAKE
FLAKE
THIS TRANSFORMATION SCENE IS THE BEST!
WHAP
SO NOBLE!!
WHAP
ISN'T THIS JUST AMAZING?!
WHEE-EEEEE
So...
YOU GUYS!!
I'M BEGGING YOU ALL! TRY HARDER!
GIVE IT EVERYTHING YOU'VE GOT!!
With those words, Kae's father disappeared into the far-off reaches of the sea once again.

#31 I CAN'T BE WITH YOU, SENPAI

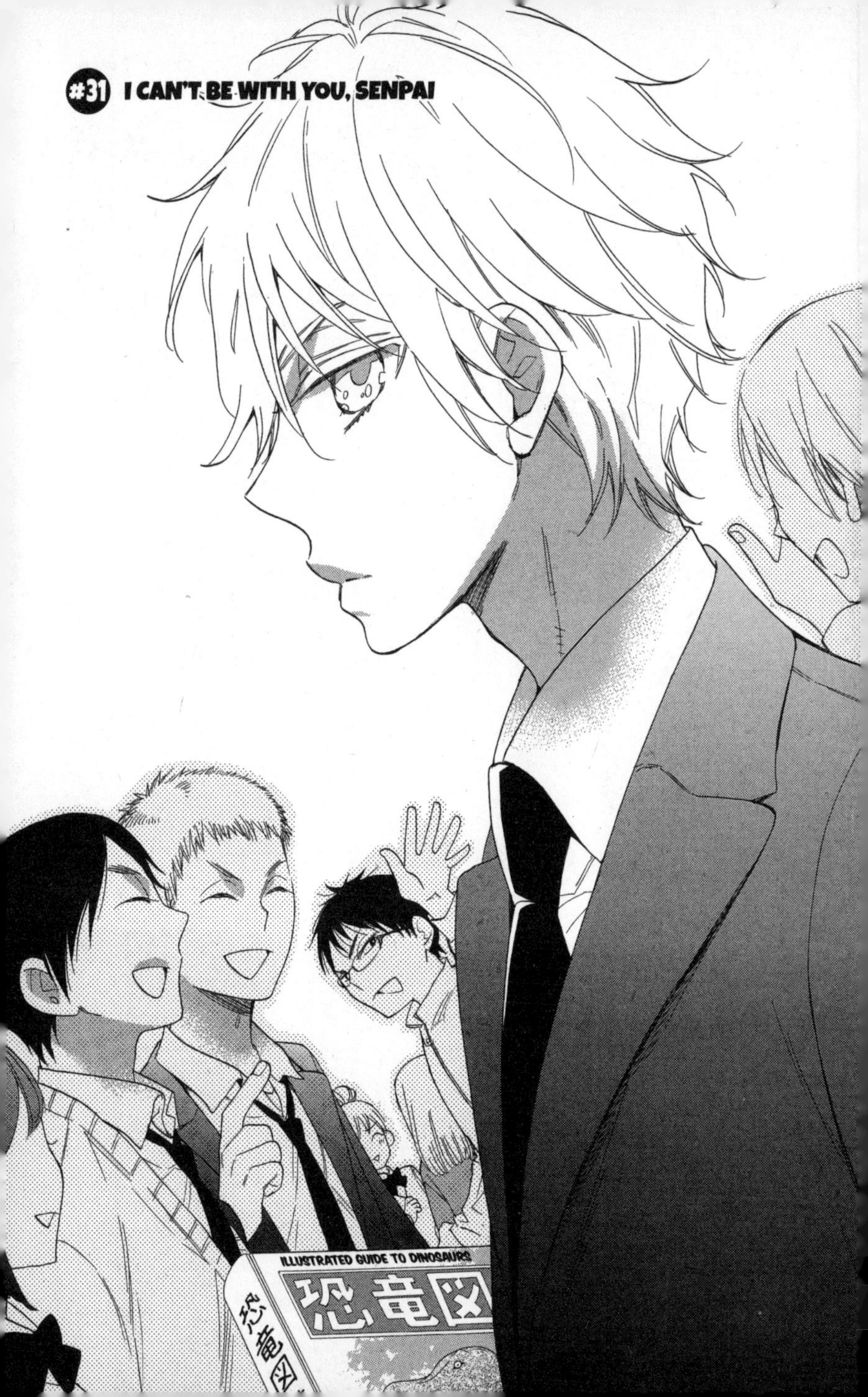
ILLUSTRATED GUIDE TO DINOSAURS
恐竜図
恐竜図

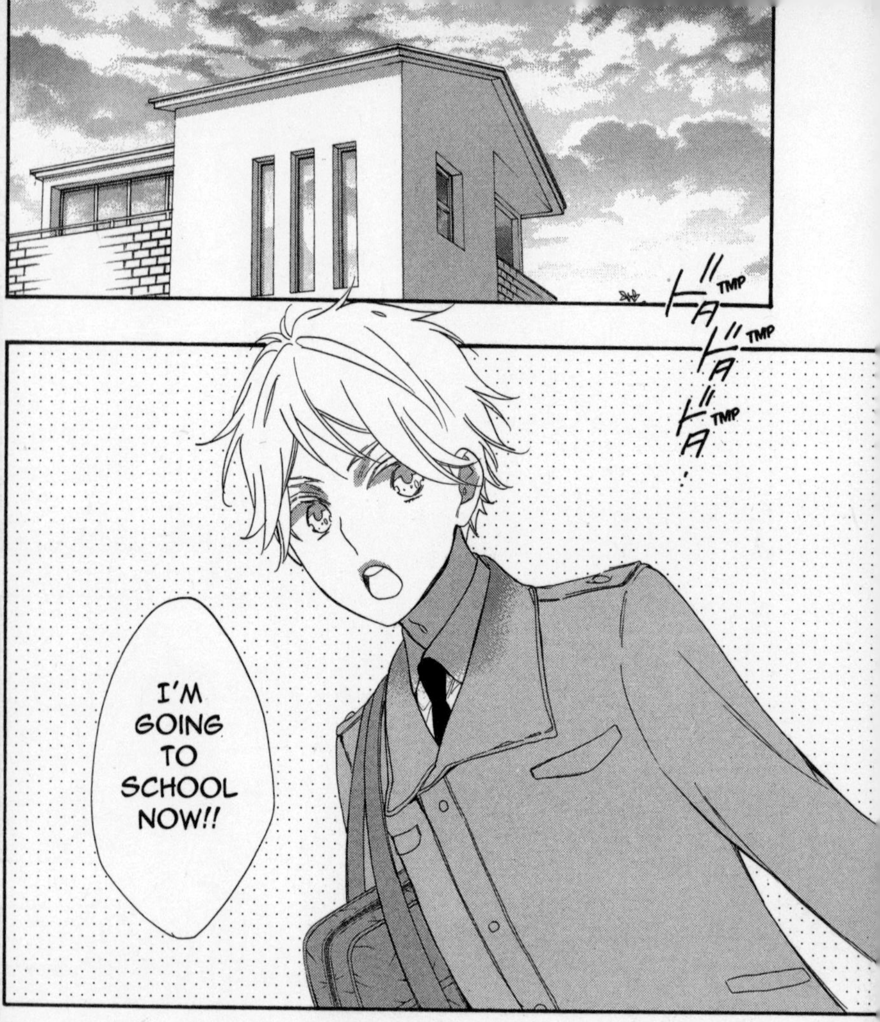
TMP
TMP
TMP
I'M GOING TO SCHOOL NOW!!

KiSS HiM, NOT ME!

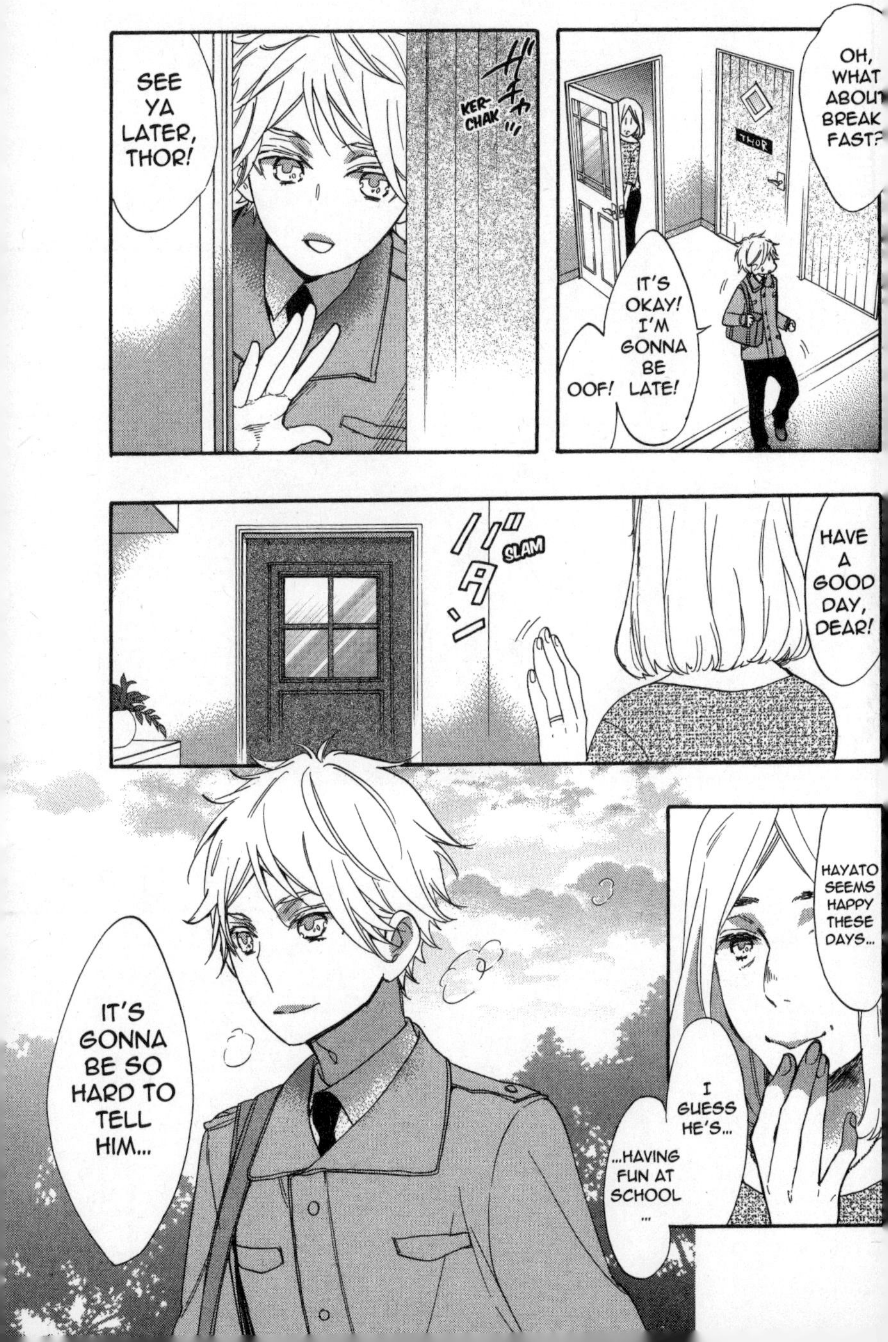
OH, WHAT ABOUT BREAKFAST?
THOR
IT'S OKAY! I'M GONNA BE LATE!
OOF!
KER-CHAK
SEE YA LATER, THOR!
HAVE A GOOD DAY, DEAR!
SLAM
HAYATO SEEMS HAPPY THESE DAYS...
I GUESS HE'S...
...HAVING FUN AT SCHOOL ...
IT'S GONNA BE SO HARD TO TELL HIM...

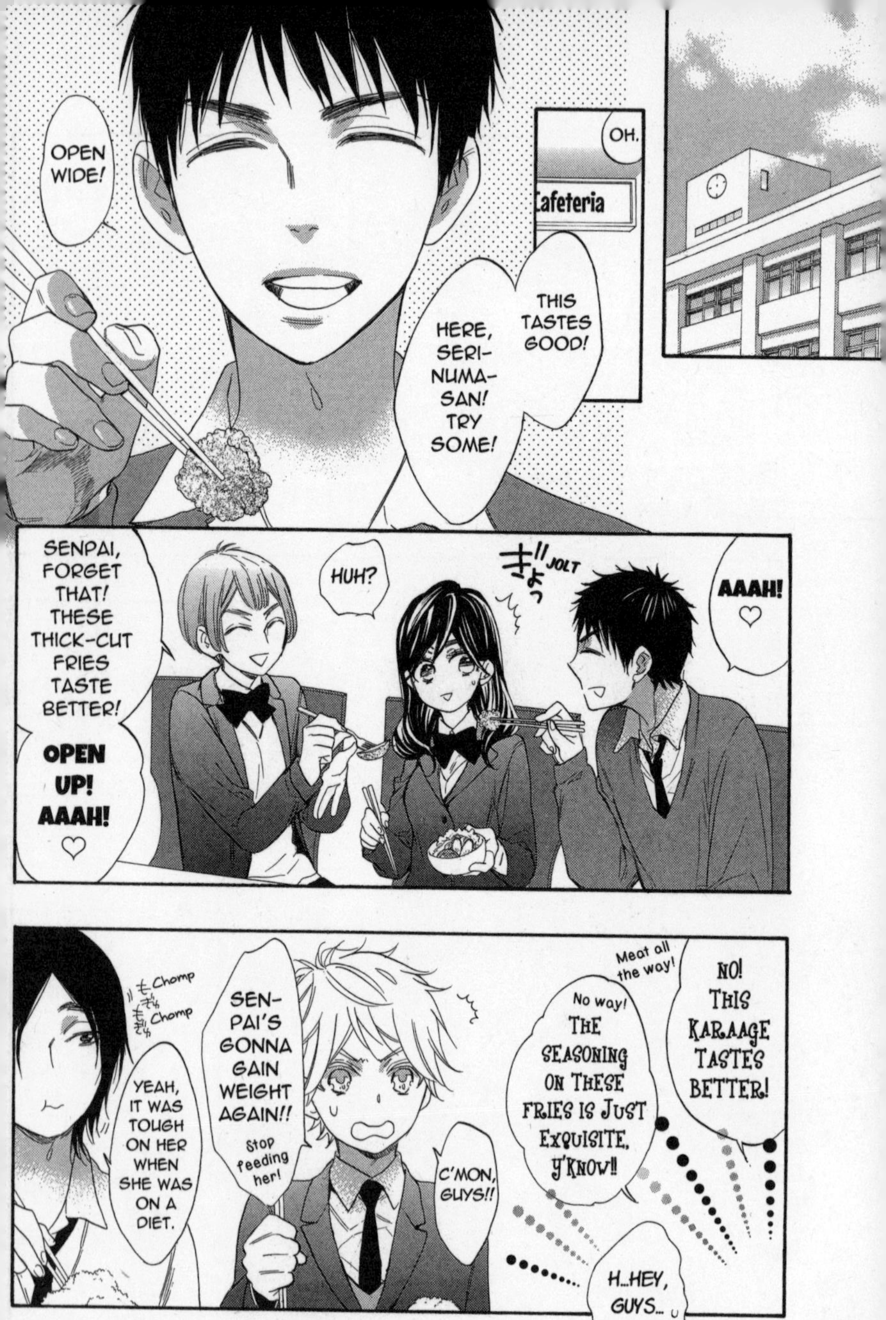
Cafeteria
OH.
THIS TASTES GOOD!
HERE, SERI-NUMA-SAN! TRY SOME!
OPEN WIDE!
AAAH! ♡
JOLT
HUH?
SENPAI, FORGET THAT! THESE THICK-CUT FRIES TASTE BETTER!
OPEN UP! AAAH! ♡
NO! THIS KARAAGE TASTES BETTER!
Meat all the way!
No way! THE SEASONING ON THESE FRIES IS JUST EXQUISITE, Y'KNOW!!
H...HEY, GUYS...
C'MON, GUYS!!
SEN-PAI'S GONNA GAIN WEIGHT AGAIN!!
Stop feeding her!
Chomp
Chomp
YEAH, IT WAS TOUGH ON HER WHEN SHE WAS ON A DIET.

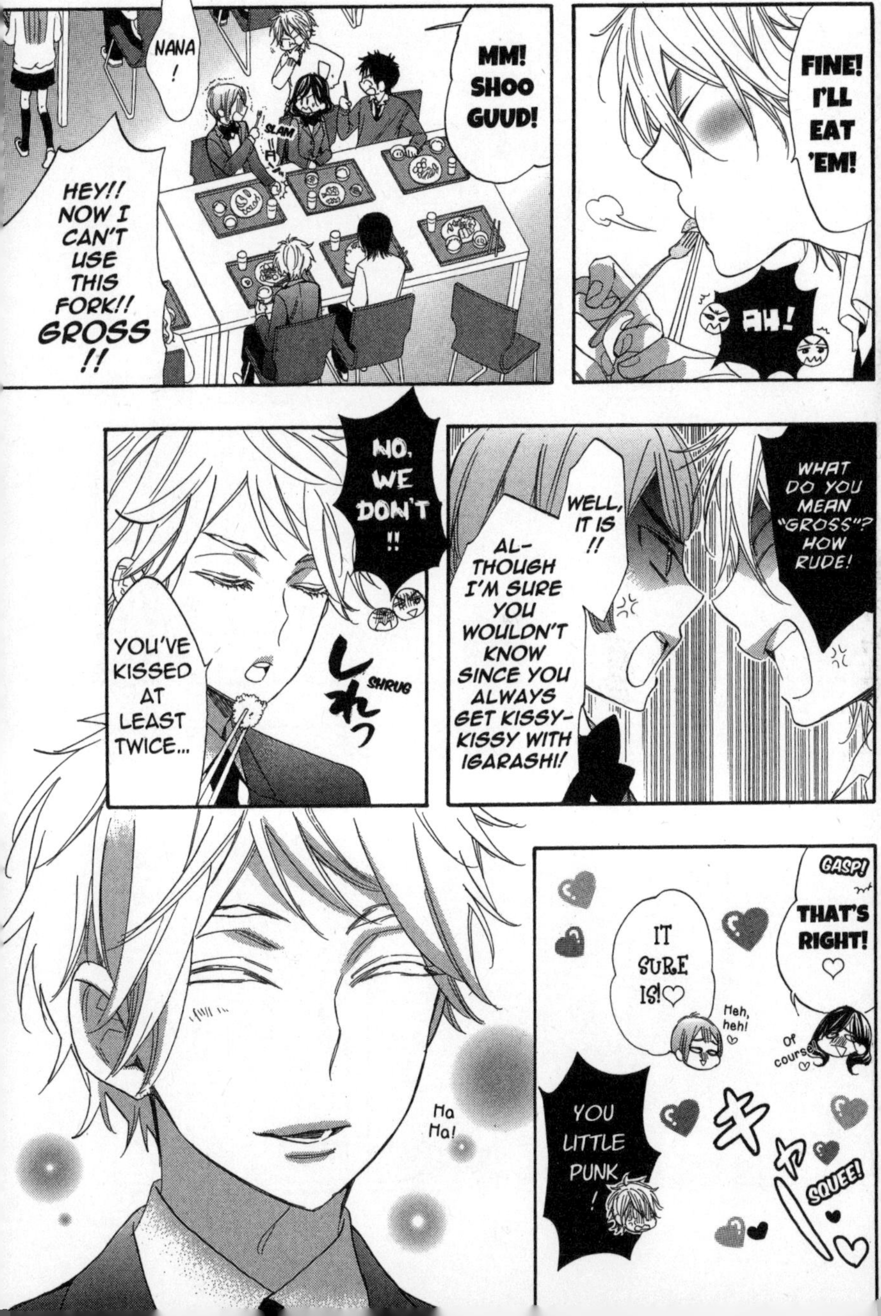
FINE! I'LL EAT 'EM!
AH!
MM! SHOO GUUD!
NANA!
SLAM
HEY!! NOW I CAN'T USE THIS FORK!! GROSS!!
WHAT DO YOU MEAN "GROSS"? HOW RUDE!
WELL, IT IS!!
AL-THOUGH I'M SURE YOU WOULDN'T KNOW SINCE YOU ALWAYS GET KISSY-KISSY WITH IGARASHI!
NO, WE DON'T!!
SHRUG
YOU'VE KISSED AT LEAST TWICE...
GASP!
THAT'S RIGHT! ♡
IT SURE IS!♡
Heh, heh! ♡
Of course
YOU LITTLE PUNK!
SQUEE!
Ha Ha!

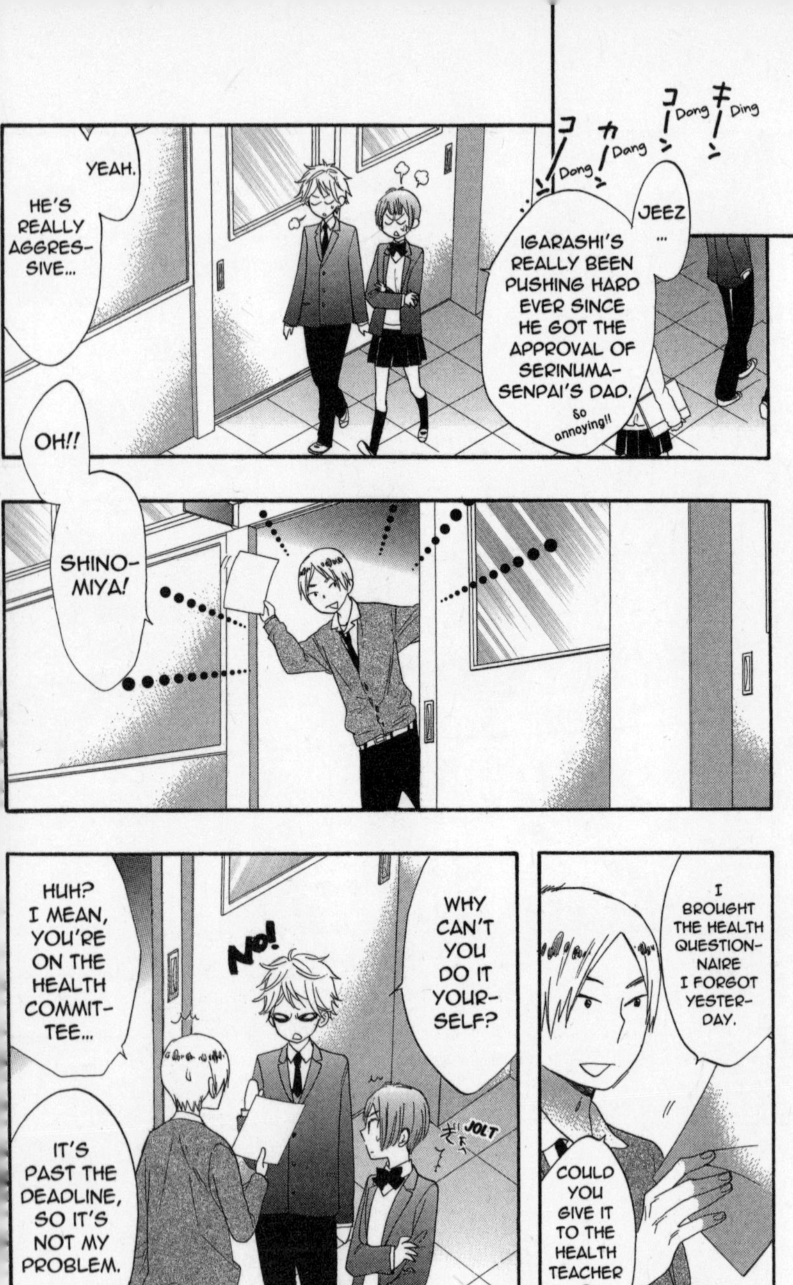
キーン Ding
コーン Dong
カーン Dang
コーン Dong
JEEZ ...
IGARASHI'S REALLY BEEN PUSHING HARD EVER SINCE HE GOT THE APPROVAL OF SERINUMA-SENPAI'S DAD.
So annoying!!
YEAH.
HE'S REALLY AGGRES-SIVE...
OH!!
SHINO-MIYA!
I BROUGHT THE HEALTH QUESTION-NAIRE I FORGOT YESTER-DAY.
COULD YOU GIVE IT TO THE HEALTH TEACHER ?
WHY CAN'T YOU DO IT YOUR-SELF?
NO!
HUH? I MEAN, YOU'RE ON THE HEALTH COMMIT-TEE...
JOLT
IT'S PAST THE DEADLINE, SO IT'S NOT MY PROBLEM.

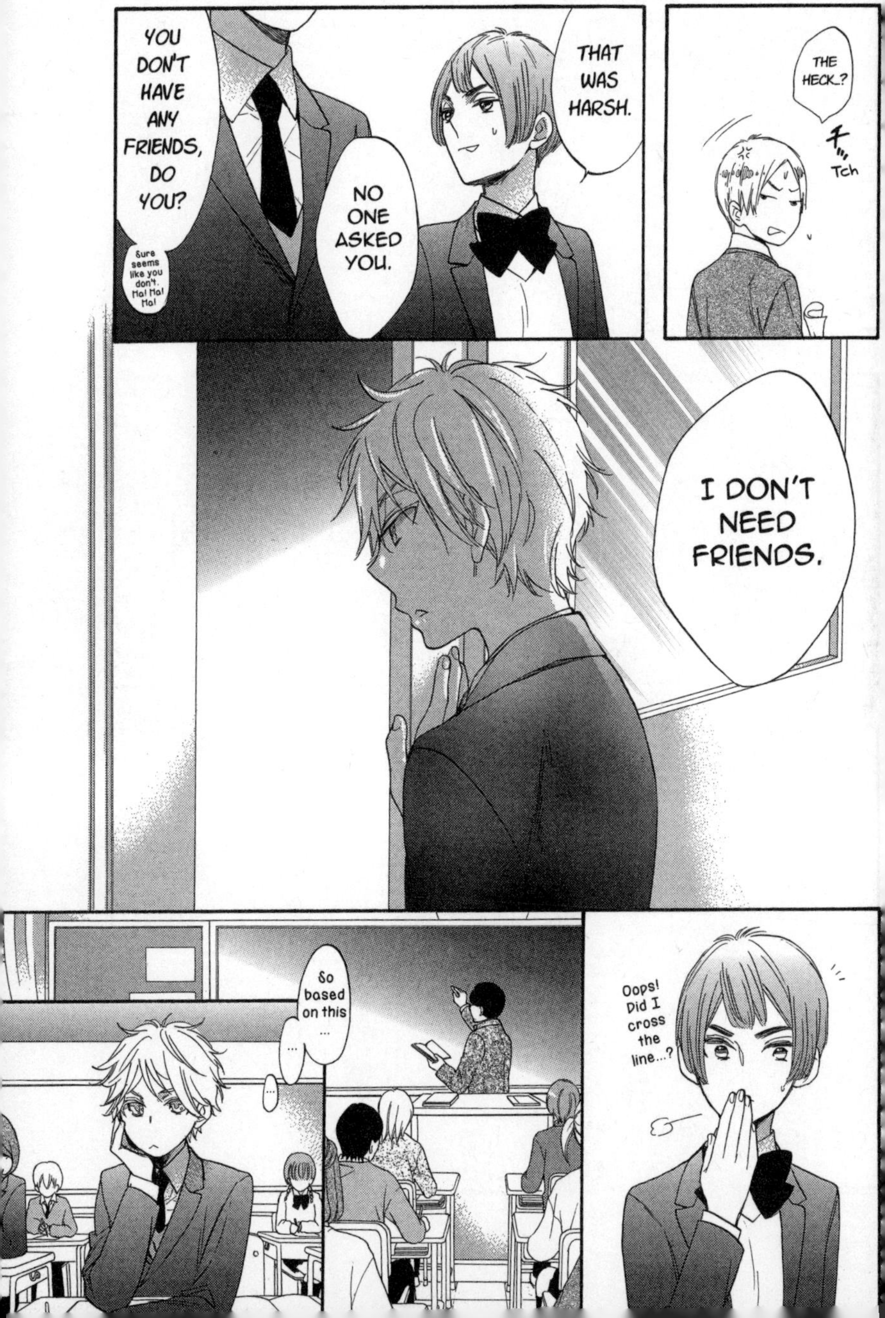
THE HECK..?
チ
Tch
THAT WAS HARSH.
NO ONE ASKED YOU.
YOU DON'T HAVE ANY FRIENDS, DO YOU?
Sure seems like you don't. Ha! Ha! Ha!
I DON'T NEED FRIENDS.
Oops! Did I cross the line...?
So based on this ...
...
...

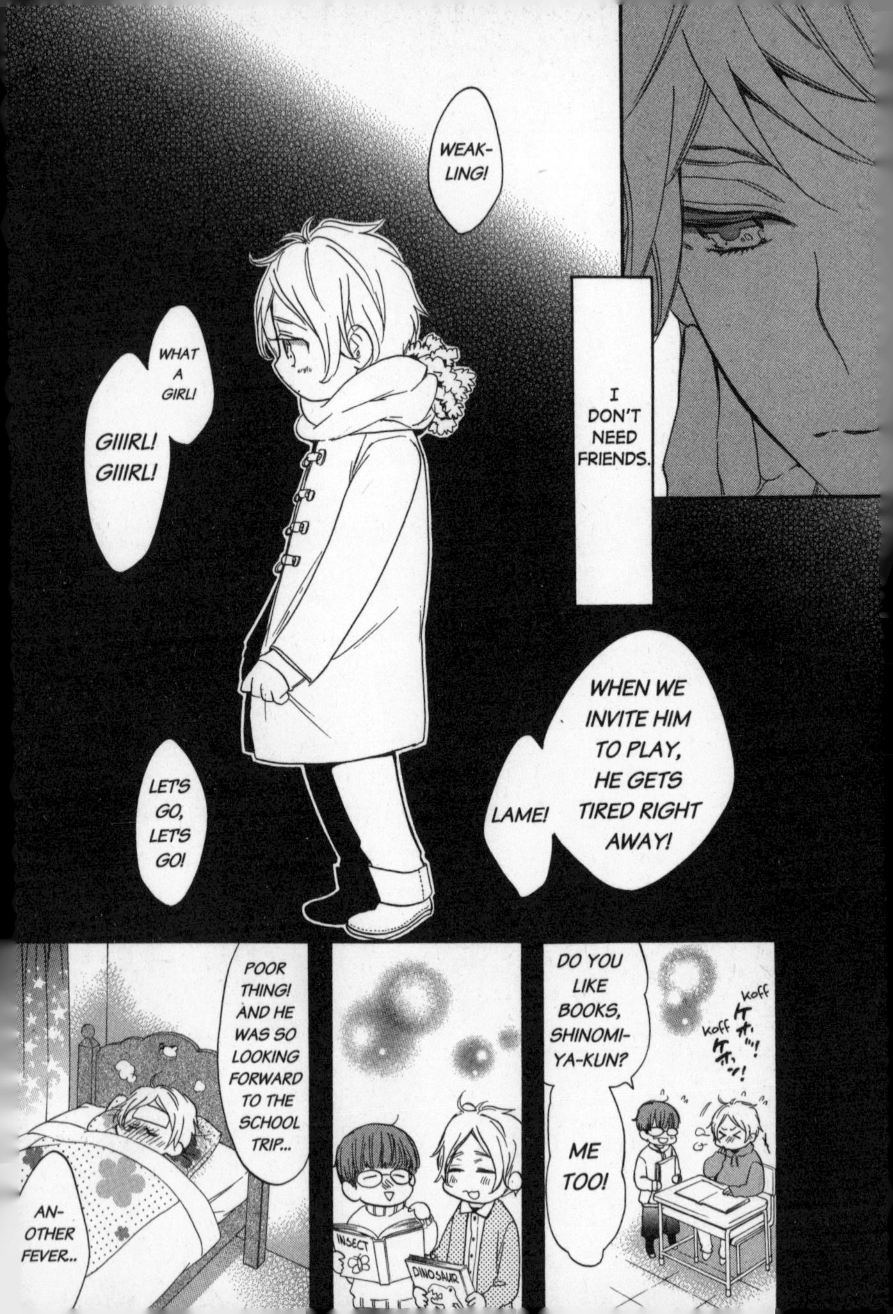
I DON'T NEED FRIENDS.
WEAK-LING!
WHEN WE INVITE HIM TO PLAY, HE GETS TIRED RIGHT AWAY!
LAME!
WHAT A GIRL!
GIIIRL! GIIIRL!
LET'S GO, LET'S GO!
DO YOU LIKE BOOKS, SHINOMI-YA-KUN?
koff
koff
ME TOO!
INSECT
DINOSAUR
POOR THING! AND HE WAS SO LOOKING FORWARD TO THE SCHOOL TRIP...
AN-OTHER FEVER...

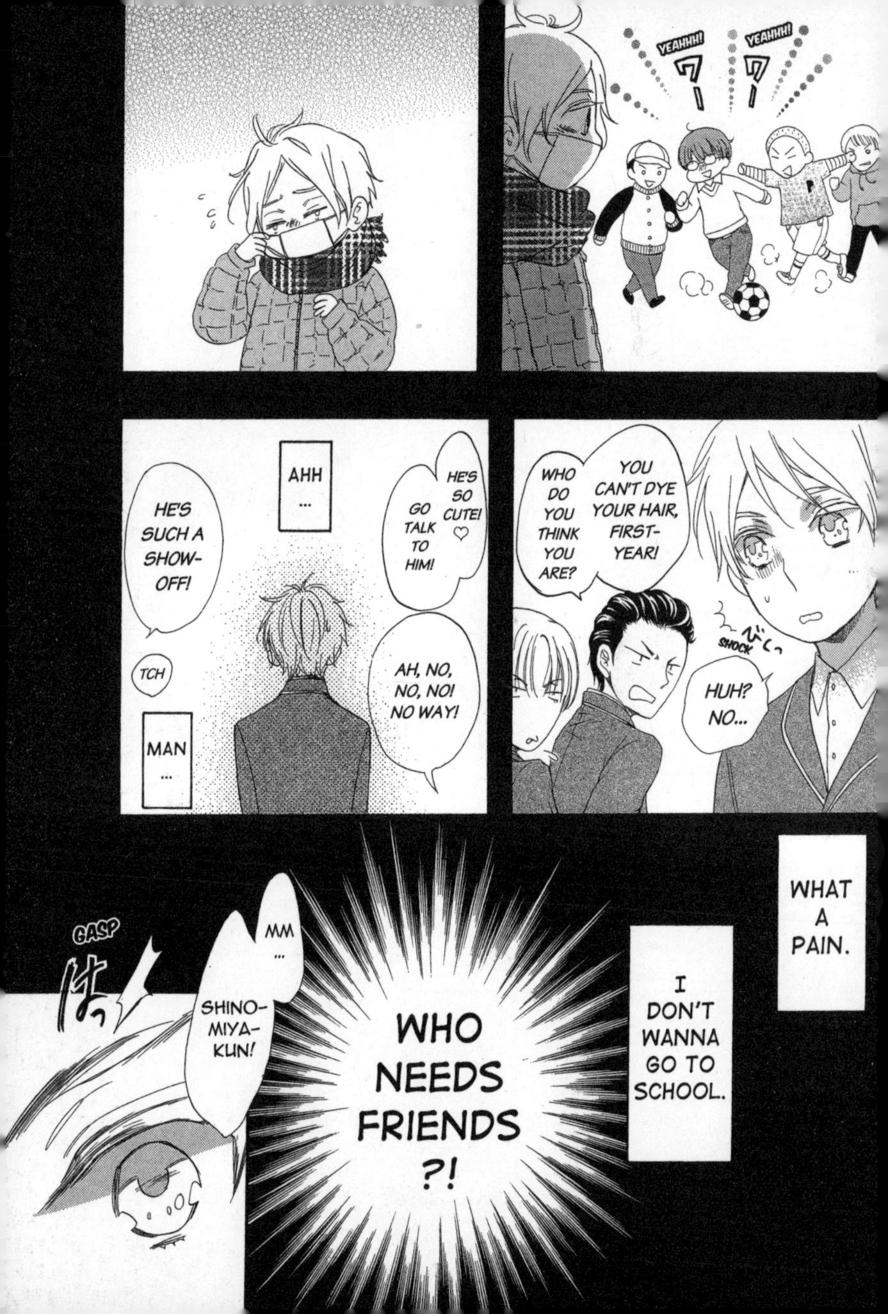
YEAHHH!
YEAHHH!
YOU CAN'T DYE YOUR HAIR, FIRST-YEAR!
WHO DO YOU THINK YOU ARE?
SHOCK
HUH? NO...
HE'S SO CUTE! ♡
GO TALK TO HIM!
AHH ...
HE'S SUCH A SHOW-OFF!
AH, NO, NO, NO! NO WAY!
TCH
MAN ...
WHAT A PAIN.
I DON'T WANNA GO TO SCHOOL.
WHO NEEDS FRIENDS ?!
MM ... SHINO-MIYA-KUN!
GASP

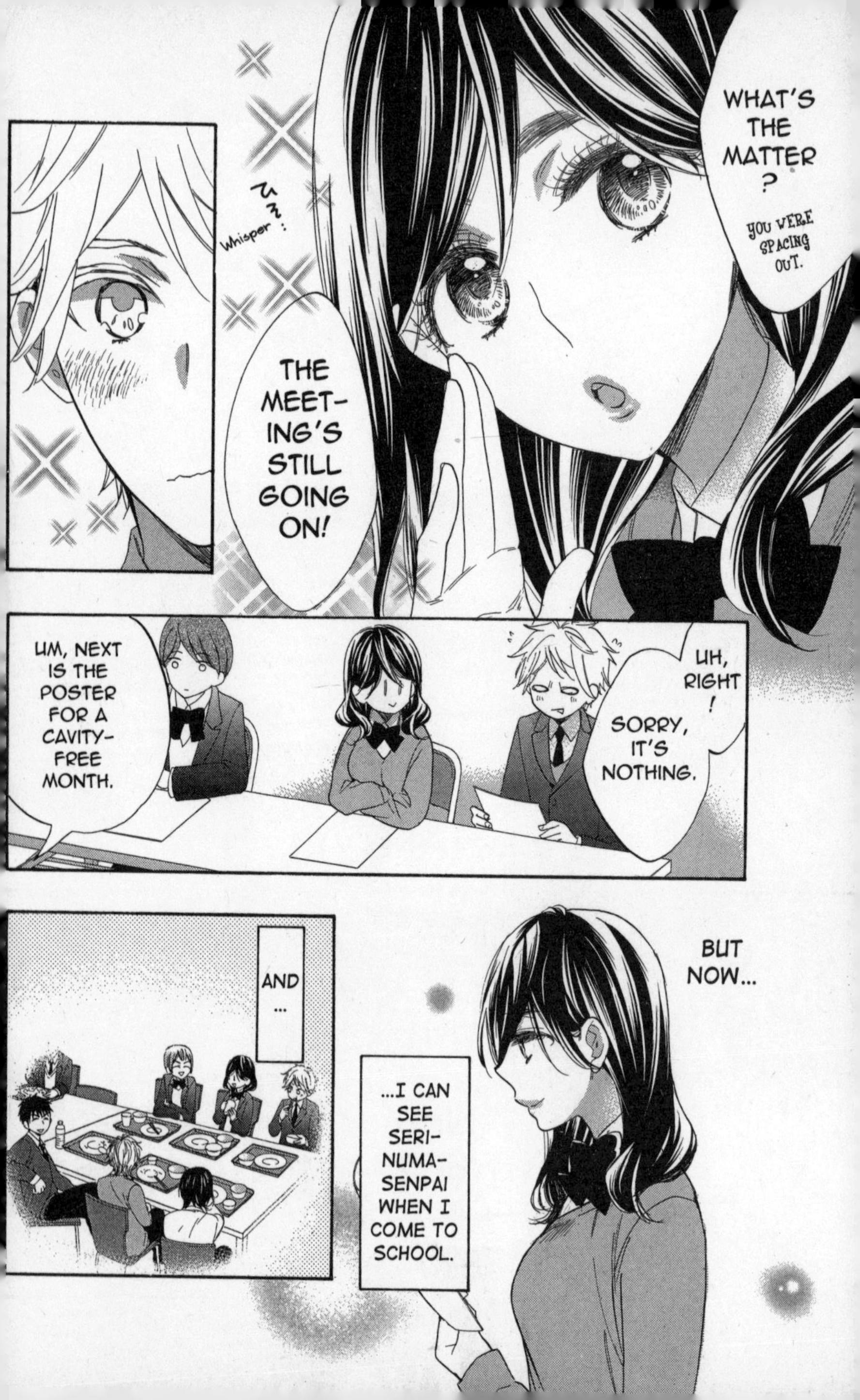
WHAT'S THE MATTER?
YOU WERE SPACING OUT.
THE MEETING'S STILL GOING ON!
Whisper
UH, RIGHT! SORRY, IT'S NOTHING.
UM, NEXT IS THE POSTER FOR A CAVITY-FREE MONTH.
BUT NOW...
...I CAN SEE SERINUMA-SENPAI WHEN I COME TO SCHOOL.
AND ...

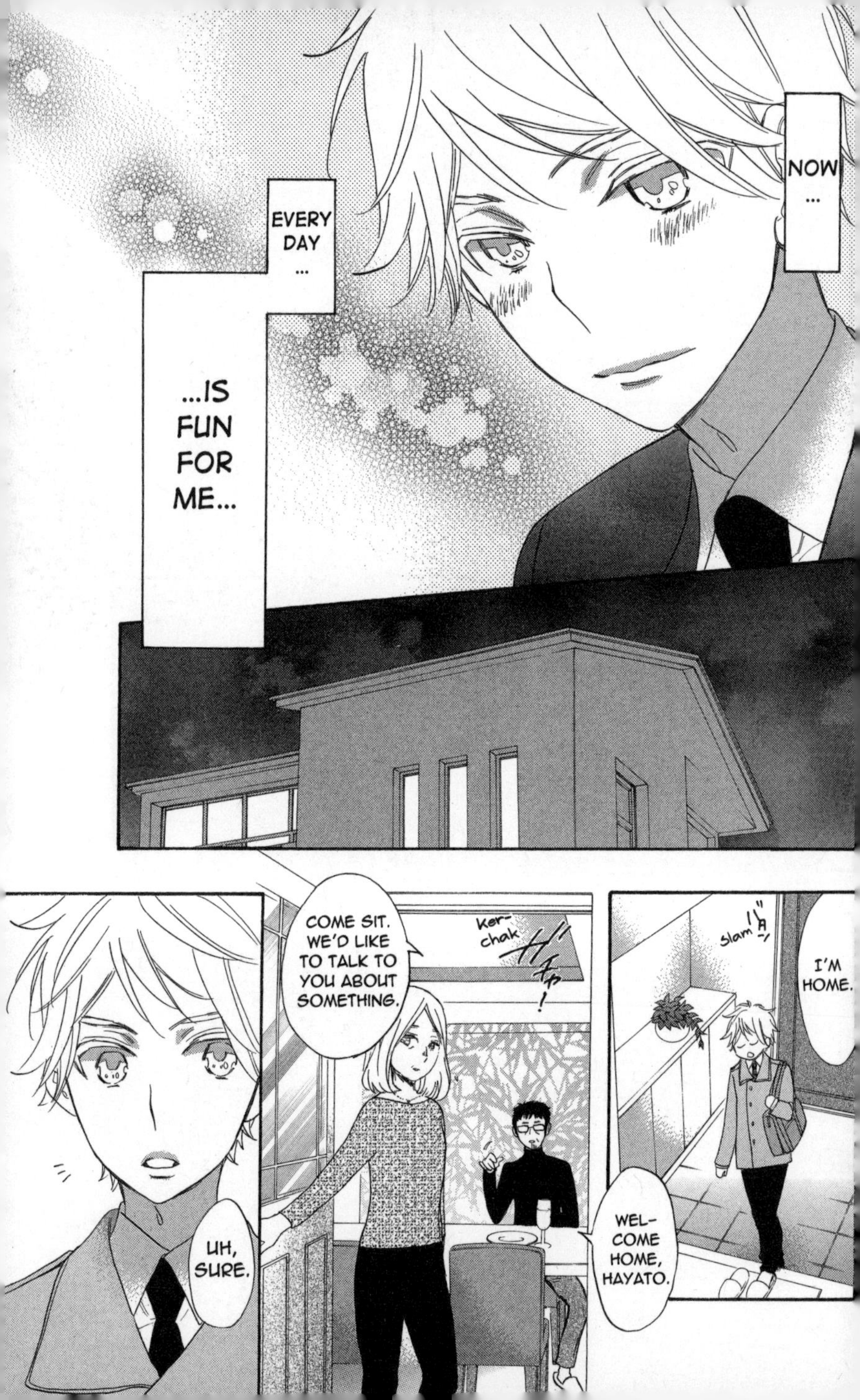
NOW...
EVERY DAY...
...IS FUN FOR ME...
Slam
I'M HOME.
Ker-chak
WEL-COME HOME, HAYATO.
COME SIT. WE'D LIKE TO TALK TO YOU ABOUT SOMETHING.
UH, SURE.

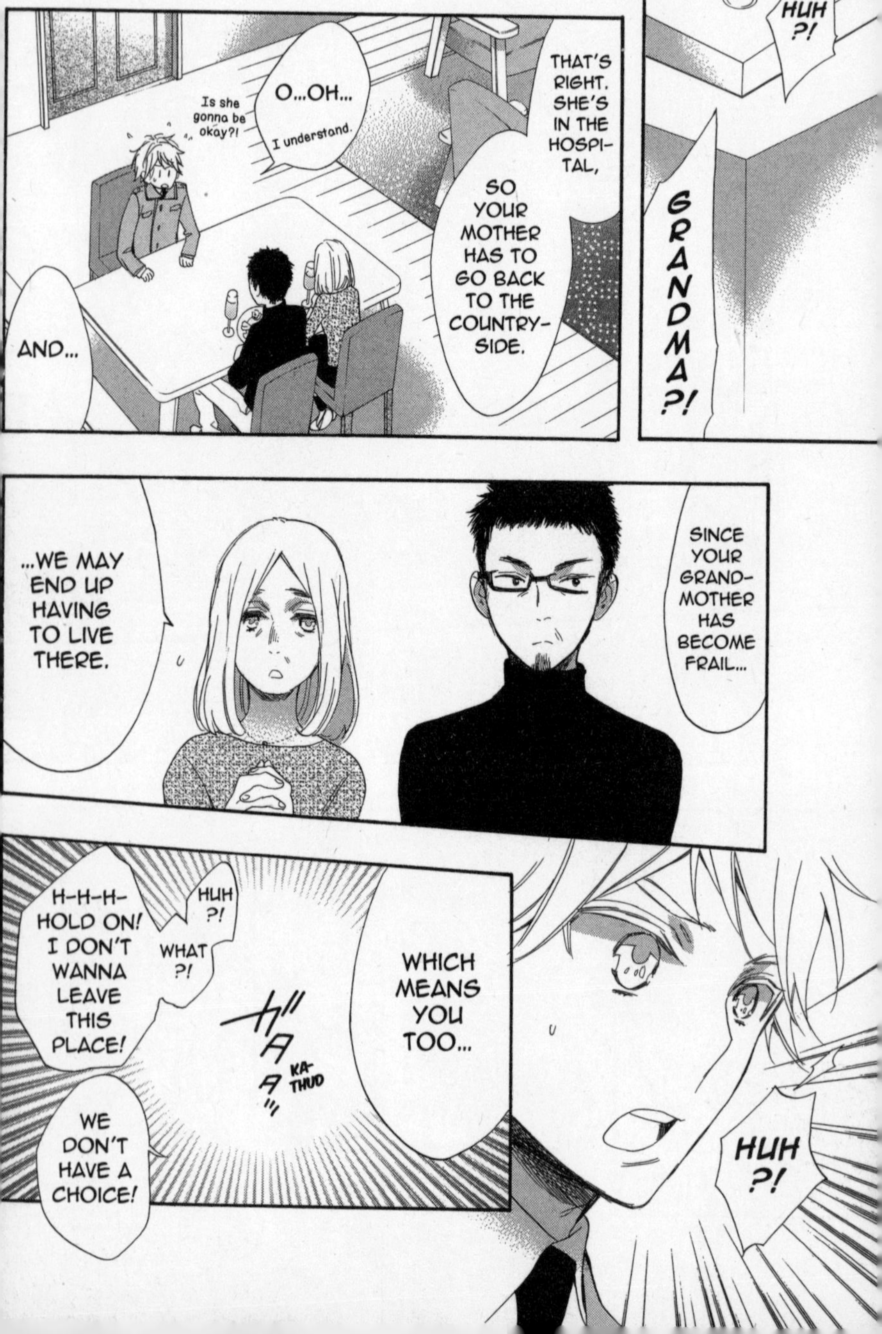

HUH ?!
GRANDMA?!
THAT'S RIGHT. SHE'S IN THE HOSPITAL,
SO YOUR MOTHER HAS TO GO BACK TO THE COUNTRYSIDE.
O...OH...
I understand.
Is she gonna be okay?!
AND...
SINCE YOUR GRANDMOTHER HAS BECOME FRAIL...
...WE MAY END UP HAVING TO LIVE THERE.
WHICH MEANS YOU TOO...
HUH ?!
HUH ?!
WHAT ?!
H-H-H-HOLD ON! I DON'T WANNA LEAVE THIS PLACE!
KA-THUD
WE DON'T HAVE A CHOICE!

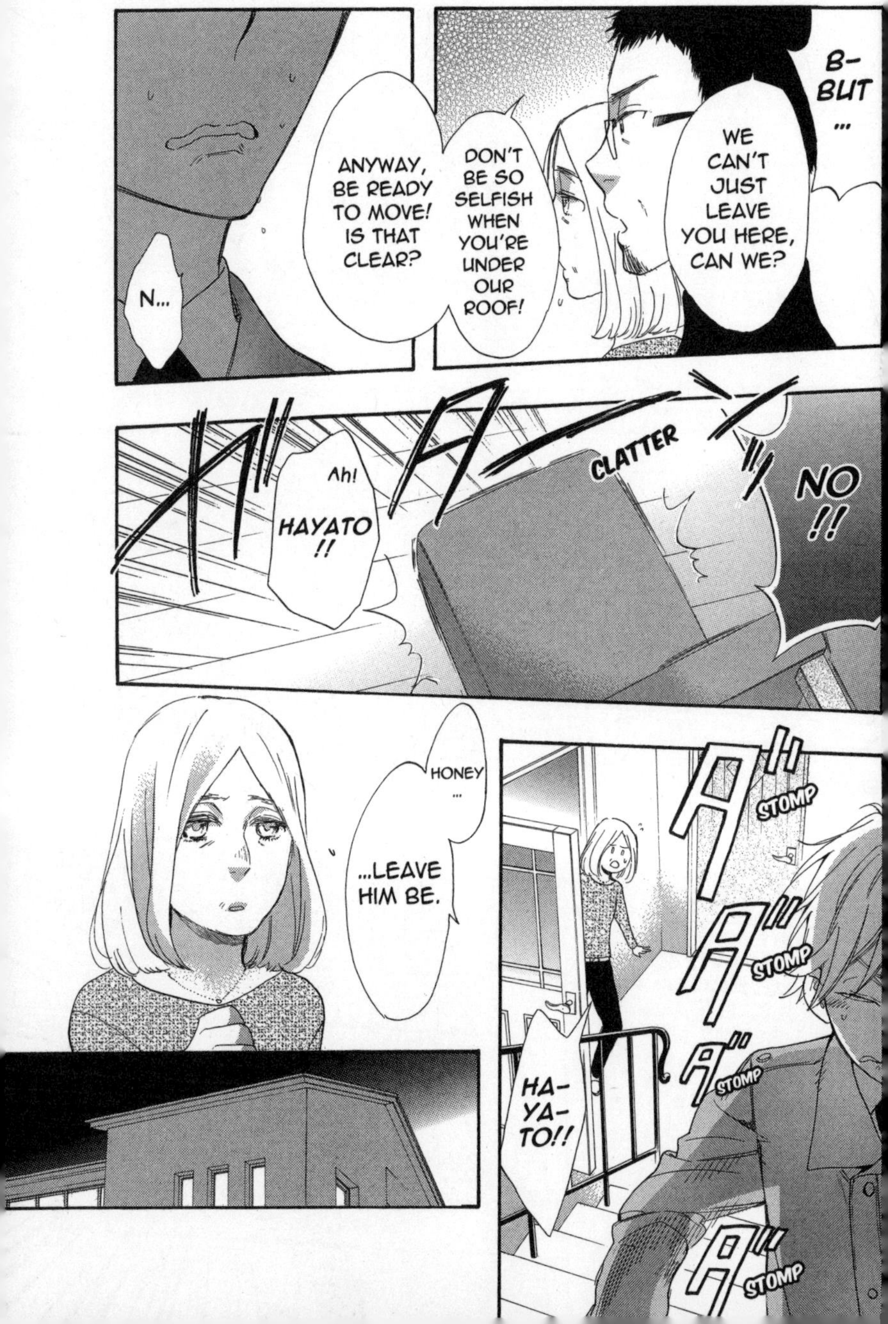
B-BUT...
WE CAN'T JUST LEAVE YOU HERE, CAN WE?
DON'T BE SO SELFISH WHEN YOU'RE UNDER OUR ROOF!
ANYWAY, BE READY TO MOVE! IS THAT CLEAR?
N...
CLATTER
NO!!
Ah!
HAYATO!!
STOMP
STOMP
STOMP
STOMP
HA-YA-TO!!
HONEY...
...LEAVE HIM BE.

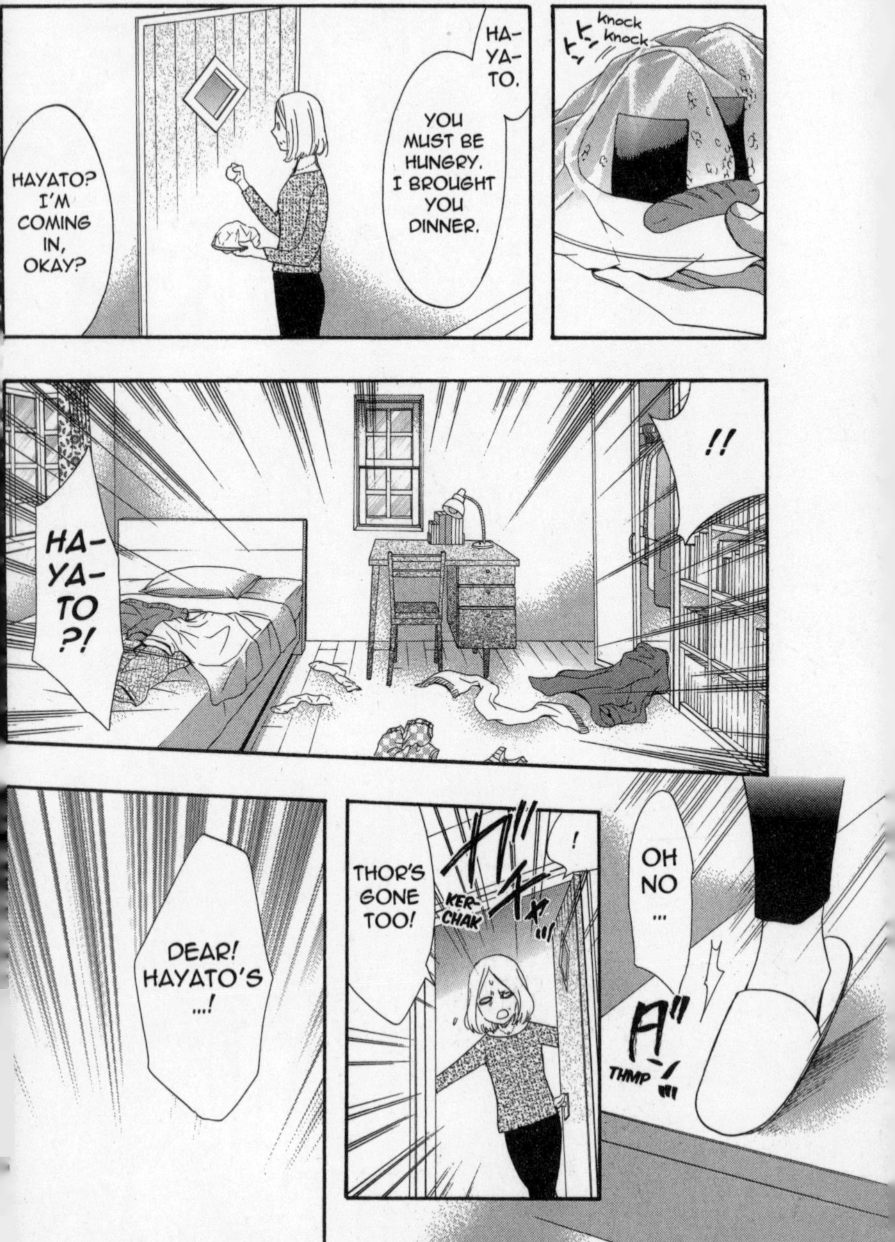
knock knock
HA-YA-TO.
YOU MUST BE HUNGRY. I BROUGHT YOU DINNER.
HAYATO? I'M COMING IN, OKAY?
!!
HA-YA-TO?!
OH NO ...
THMP
!
KER-CHAK
THOR'S GONE TOO!
DEAR! HAYATO'S ...!

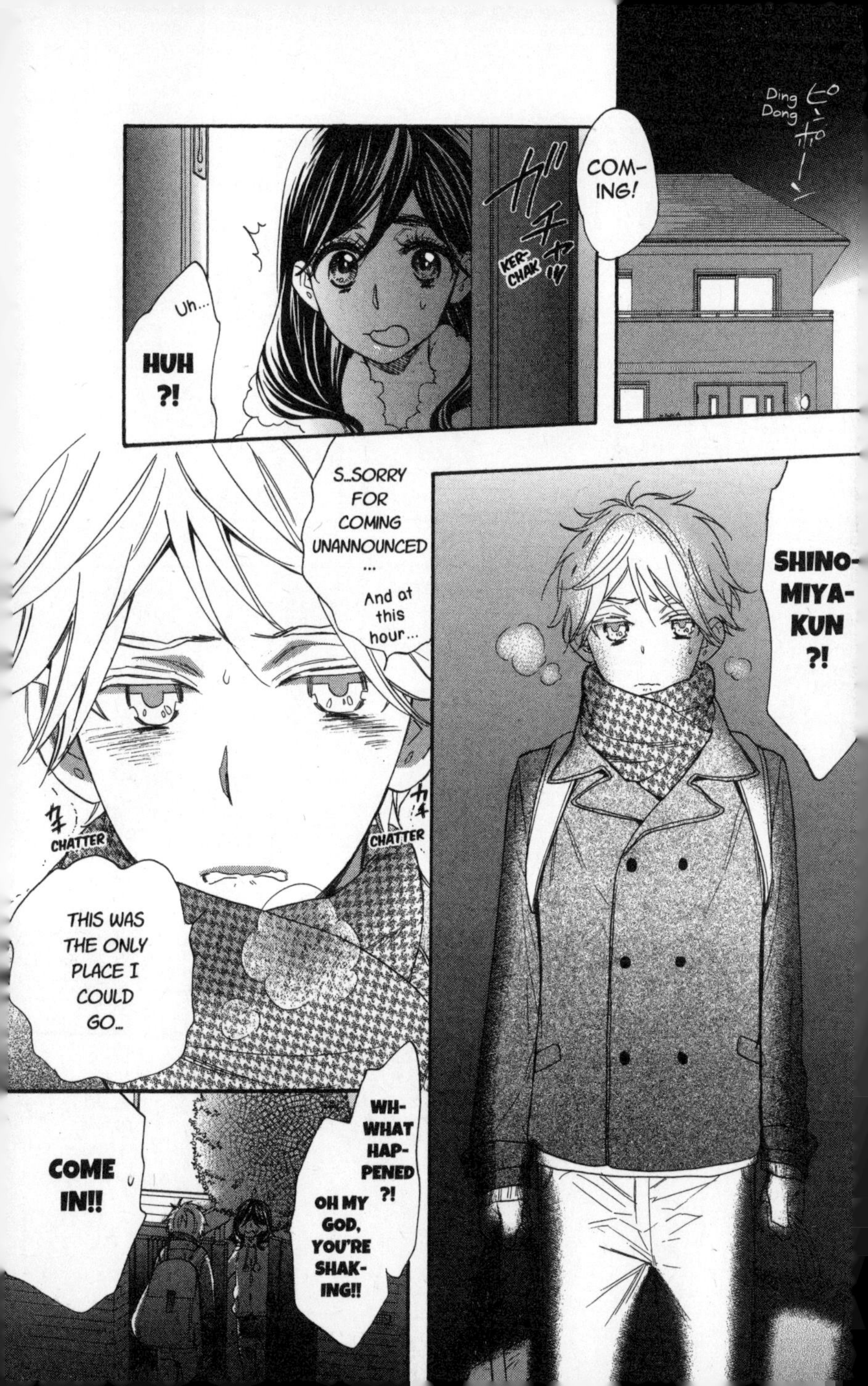
Ding Dong
COM-ING!
KER-CHAK
Uh...
HUH ?!
SHINO-MIYA-KUN ?!
S..SORRY FOR COMING UNANNOUNCED ...
And at this hour...
CHATTER
CHATTER
THIS WAS THE ONLY PLACE I COULD GO...
WH-WHAT HAP-PENED ?!
OH MY GOD, YOU'RE SHAK-ING!!
COME IN!!

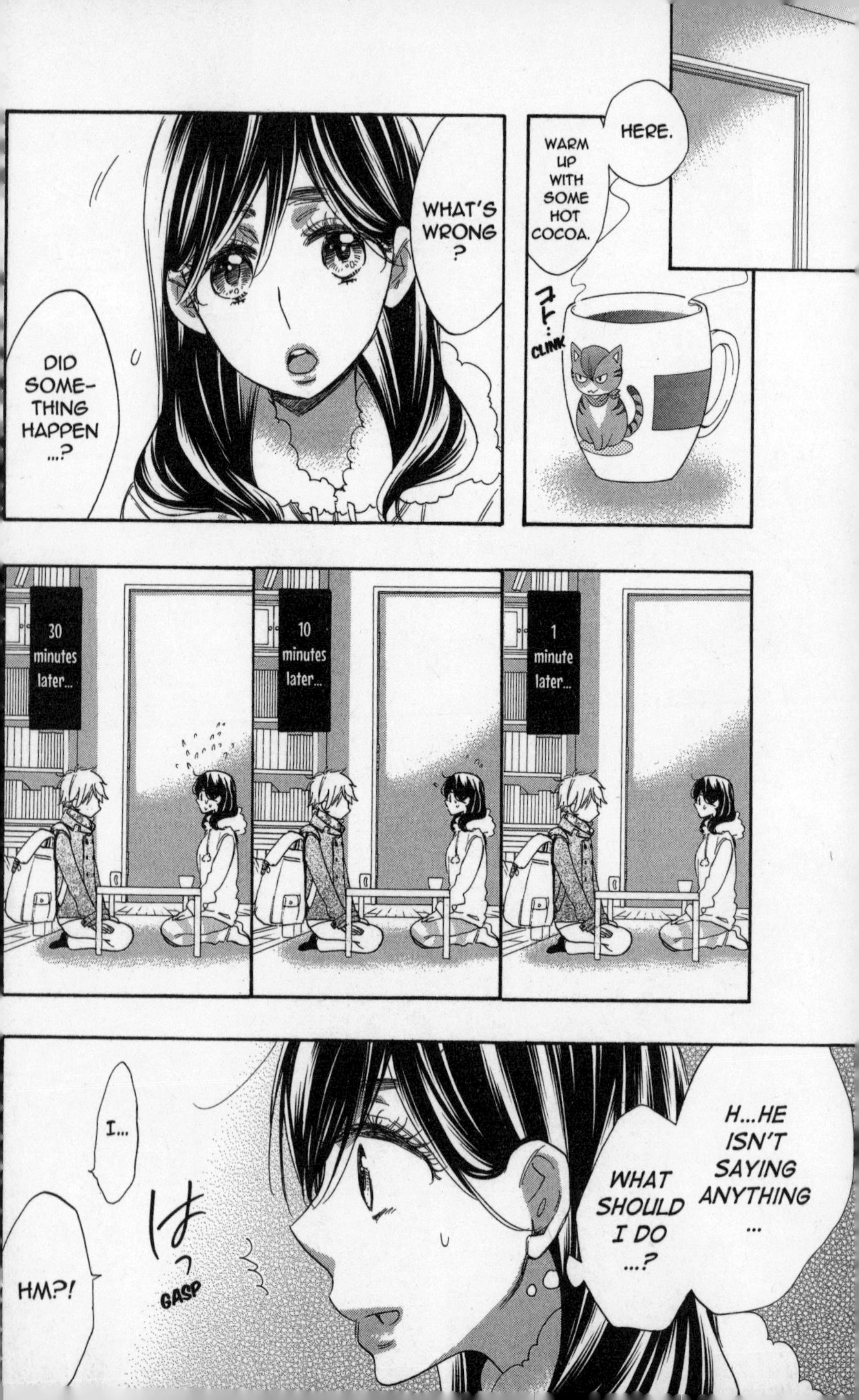
HERE.
WARM UP WITH SOME HOT COCOA.
コト… CLINK
WHAT'S WRONG?
DID SOMETHING HAPPEN...?
1 minute later...
10 minutes later...
30 minutes later...
H...HE ISN'T SAYING ANYTHING...
WHAT SHOULD I DO...?
はっ GASP
I...
HM?!

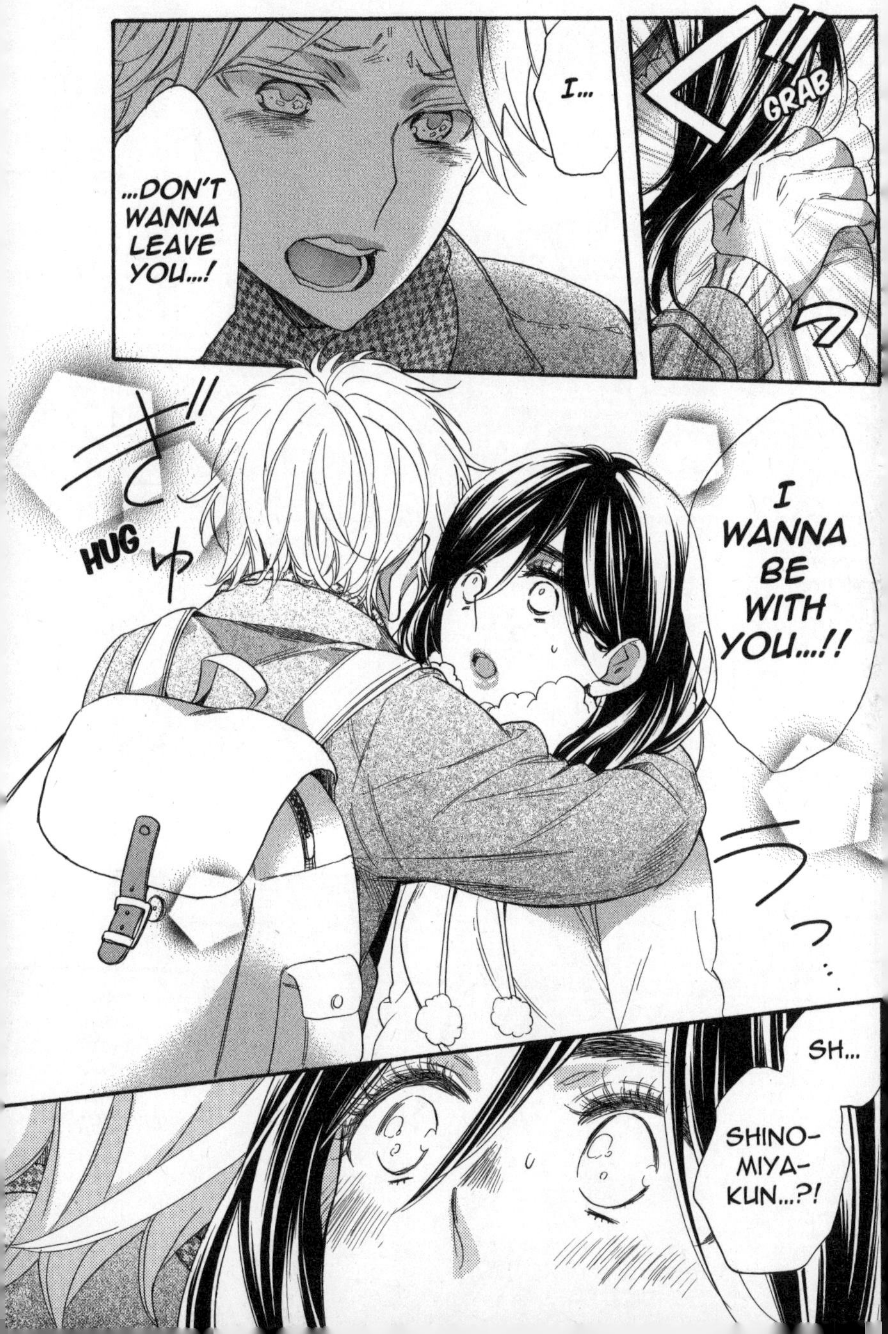
GRAB
I...
...DON'T WANNA LEAVE YOU...!
I WANNA BE WITH YOU...!!
HUG
SH...
SHINO-MIYA-KUN...?!

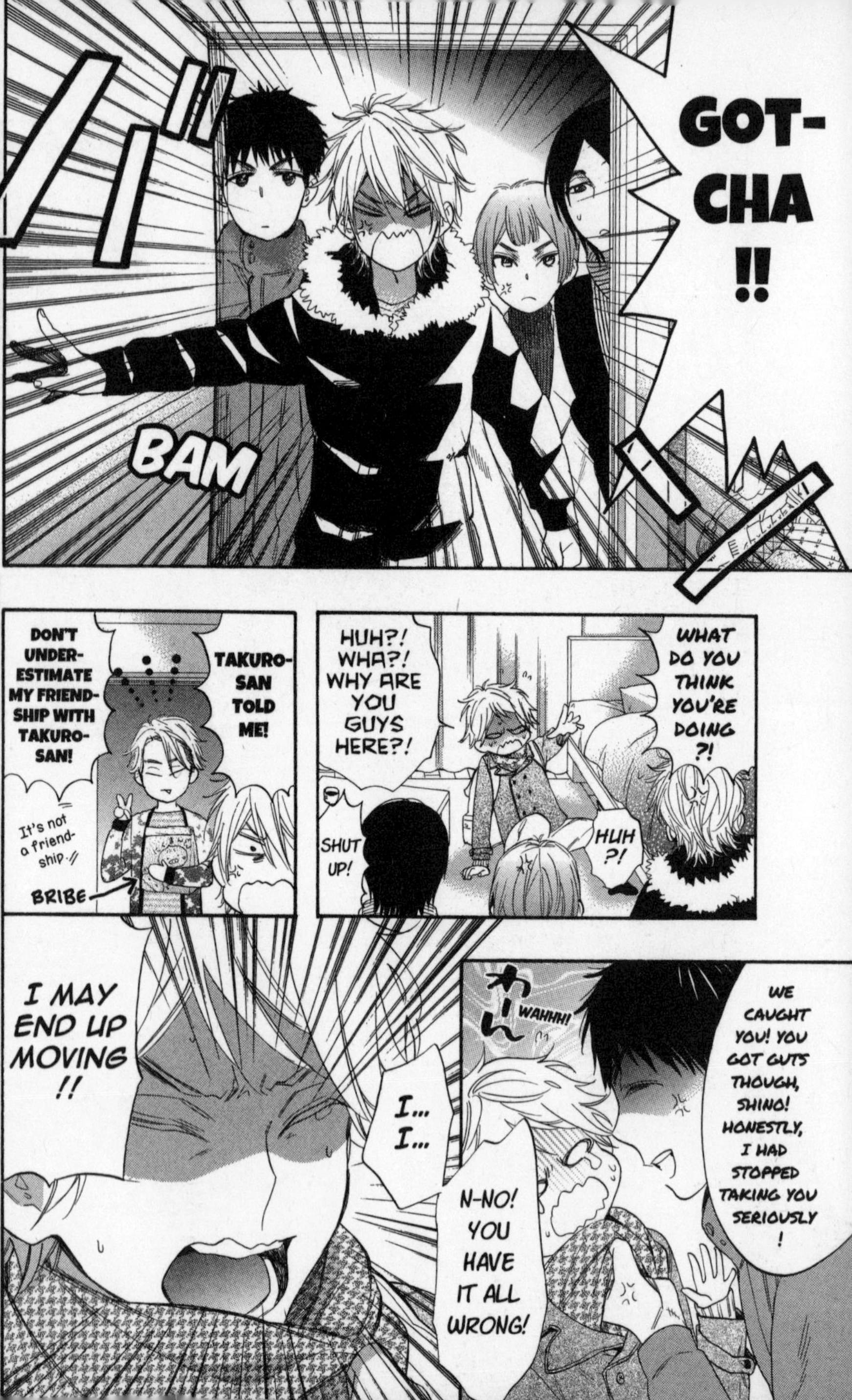
GOT-CHA!!
BAM
WHAT DO YOU THINK YOU'RE DOING?!
HUH?! WHA?! WHY ARE YOU GUYS HERE?!
HUH?!
SHUT UP!
TAKURO-SAN TOLD ME!
DON'T UNDER-ESTIMATE MY FRIEND-SHIP WITH TAKURO-SAN!
It's not a friend-ship.//
BRIBE
WE CAUGHT YOU! YOU GOT GUTS THOUGH, SHINO! HONESTLY, I HAD STOPPED TAKING YOU SERIOUSLY!
WAHHH!
N-NO! YOU HAVE IT ALL WRONG!
I... I...
I MAY END UP MOVING!!

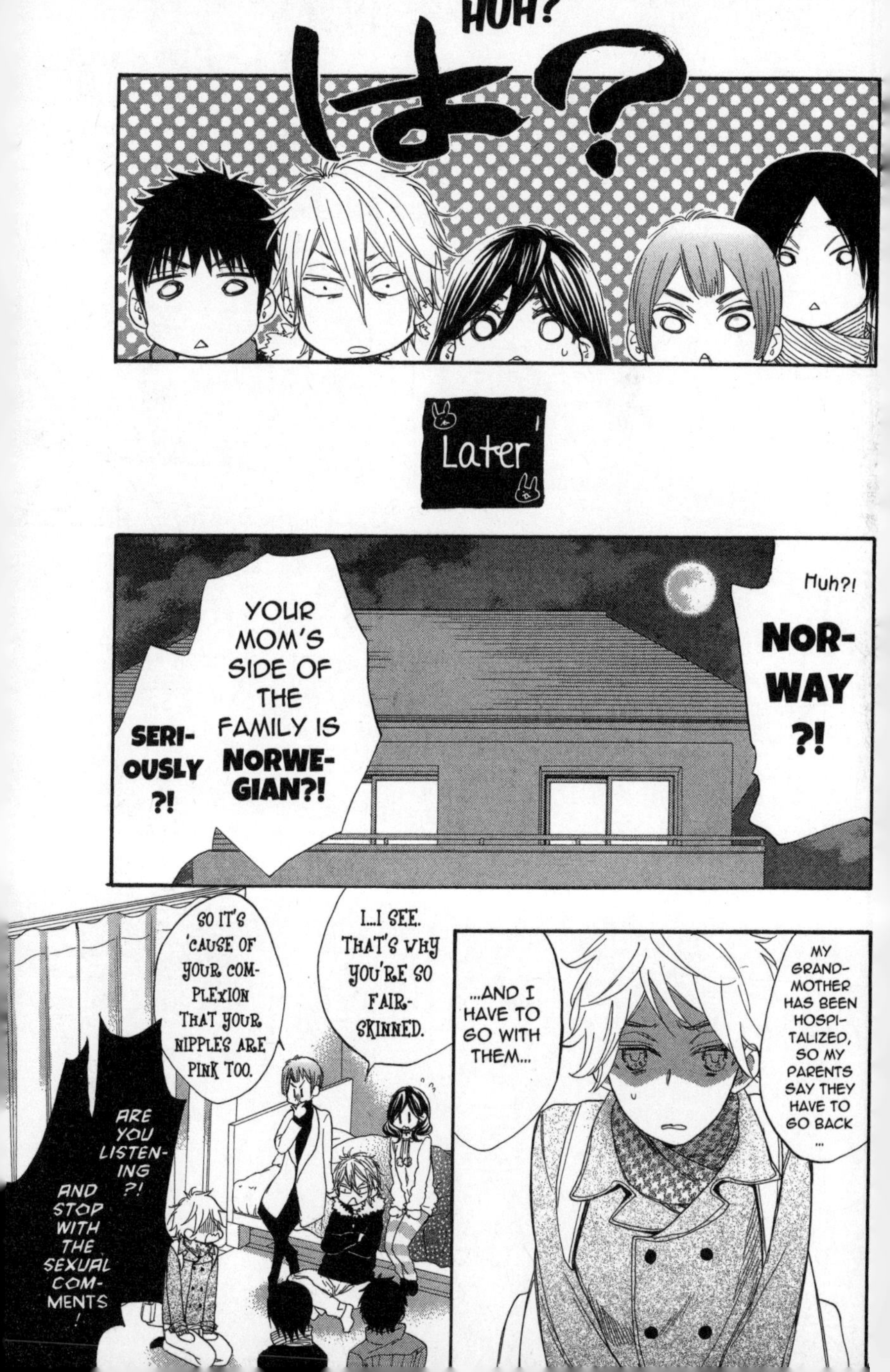
は？
HUH?
Later
Huh?!
NORWAY?!
YOUR MOM'S SIDE OF THE FAMILY IS NORWEGIAN?!
SERIOUSLY?!
MY GRANDMOTHER HAS BEEN HOSPITALIZED, SO MY PARENTS SAY THEY HAVE TO GO BACK...
...AND I HAVE TO GO WITH THEM...
I...I SEE. THAT'S WHY YOU'RE SO FAIR-SKINNED.
SO IT'S 'CAUSE OF YOUR COMPLEXION THAT YOUR NIPPLES ARE PINK TOO.
ARE YOU LISTENING?!
AND STOP WITH THE SEXUAL COMMENTS!

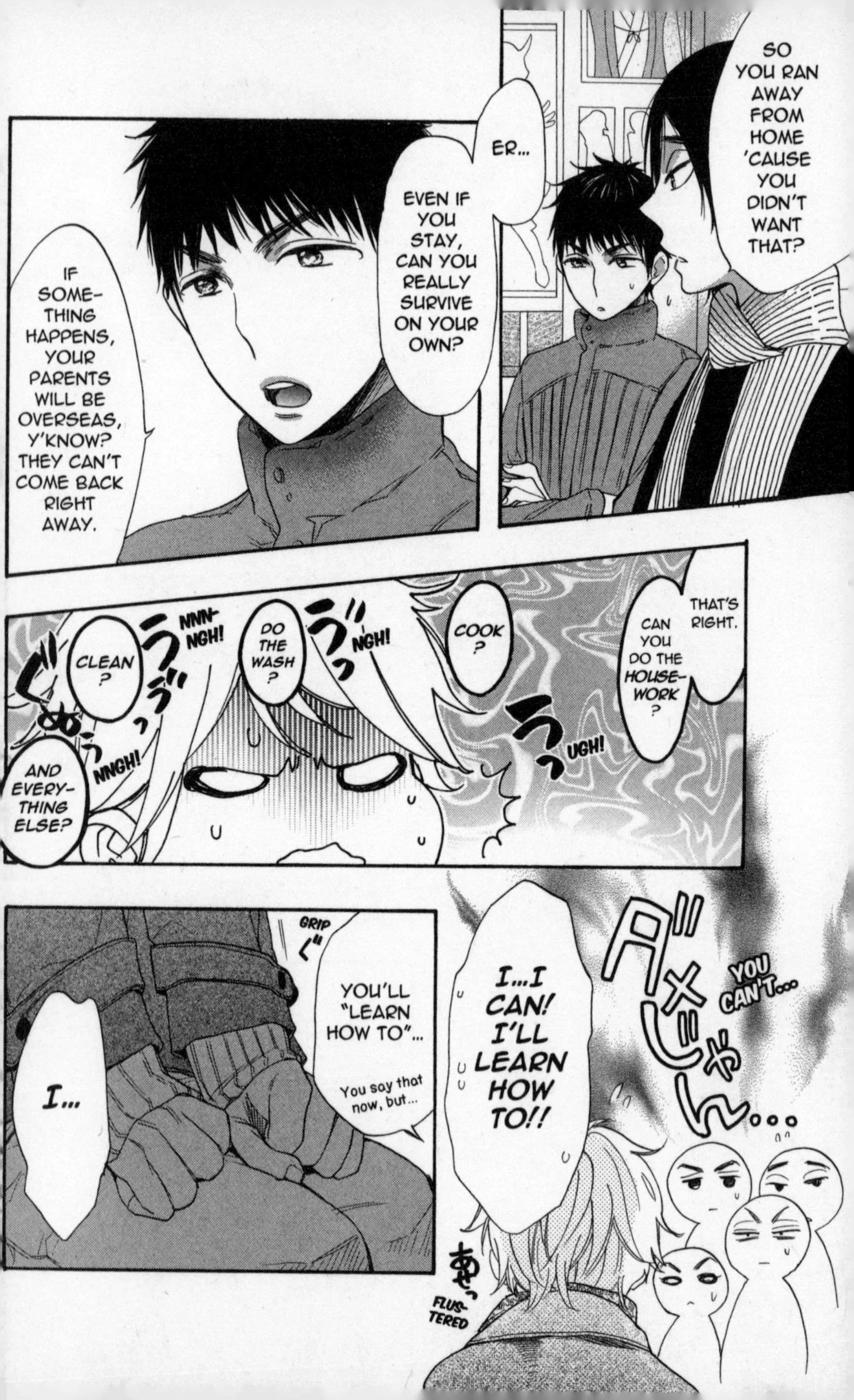

SO YOU RAN AWAY FROM HOME 'CAUSE YOU DIDN'T WANT THAT?
ER...
EVEN IF YOU STAY, CAN YOU REALLY SURVIVE ON YOUR OWN?
IF SOMETHING HAPPENS, YOUR PARENTS WILL BE OVERSEAS, Y'KNOW? THEY CAN'T COME BACK RIGHT AWAY.
THAT'S RIGHT.
CAN YOU DO THE HOUSEWORK?
UGH!
COOK?
NGH!
DO THE WASH?
NNN-NGH!
CLEAN?
NNGH!
AND EVERYTHING ELSE?
YOU CAN'T...
I...I CAN! I'LL LEARN HOW TO!!
FLUSTERED
GRIP
YOU'LL "LEARN HOW TO"...
You say that now, but...
I...

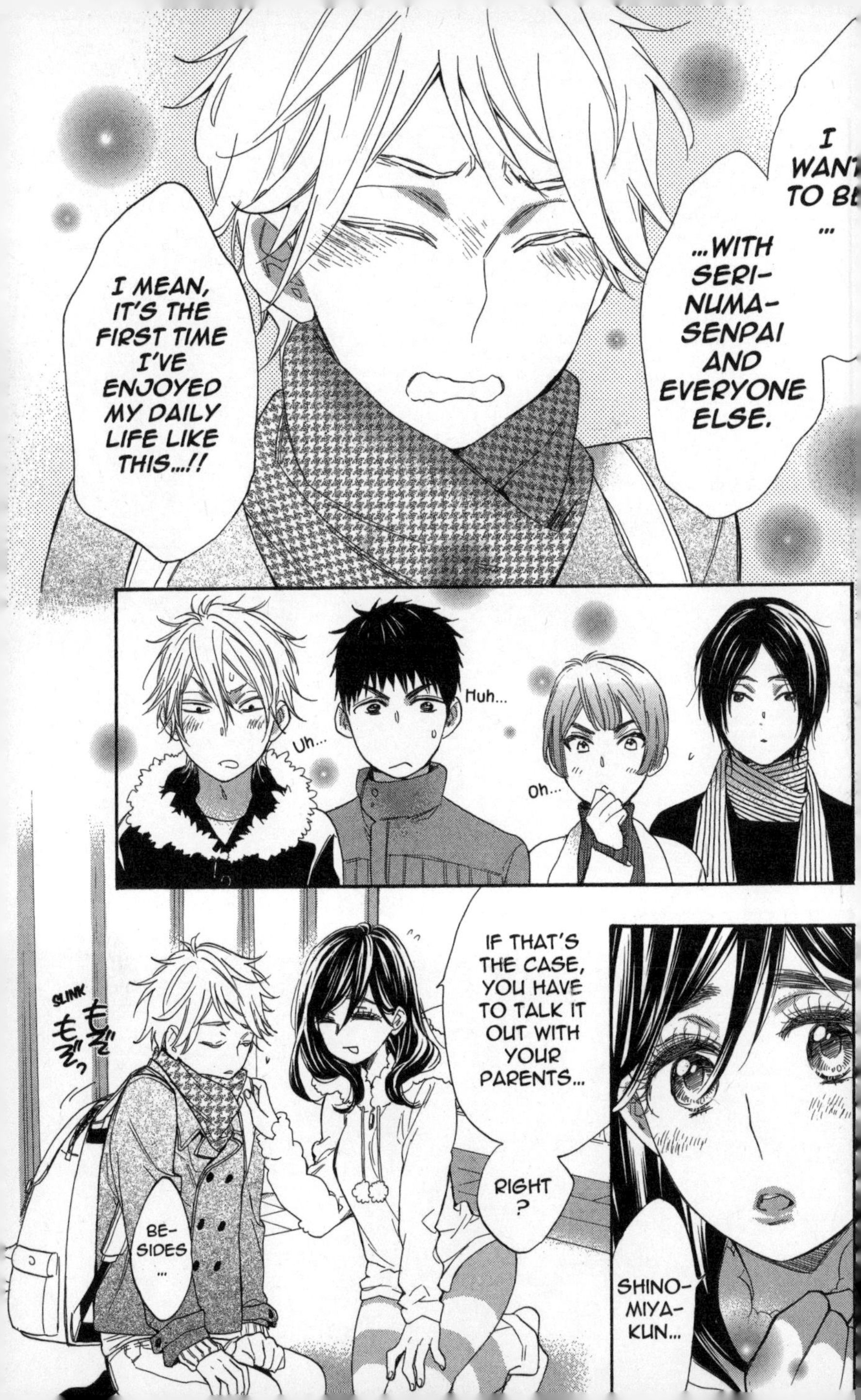
I WANT TO BE ...
...WITH SERI-NUMA-SENPAI AND EVERYONE ELSE.
I MEAN, IT'S THE FIRST TIME I'VE ENJOYED MY DAILY LIFE LIKE THIS...!!
Oh...
Huh...
Uh...
SHINO-MIYA-KUN...
IF THAT'S THE CASE, YOU HAVE TO TALK IT OUT WITH YOUR PARENTS...
RIGHT?
BE-SIDES ...
SLINK

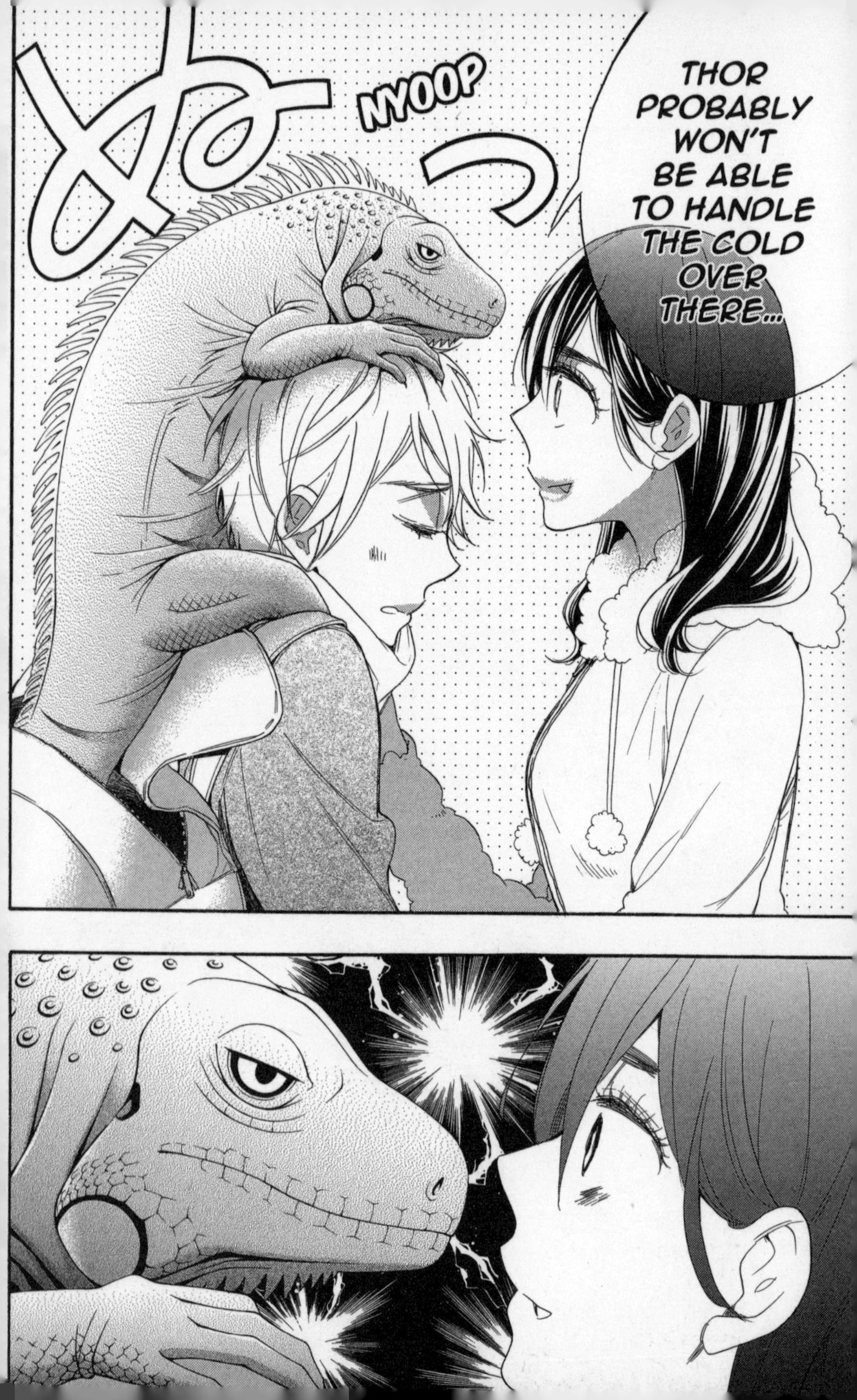
THOR PROBABLY WON'T BE ABLE TO HANDLE THE COLD OVER THERE...
NYOOP
ぬっ

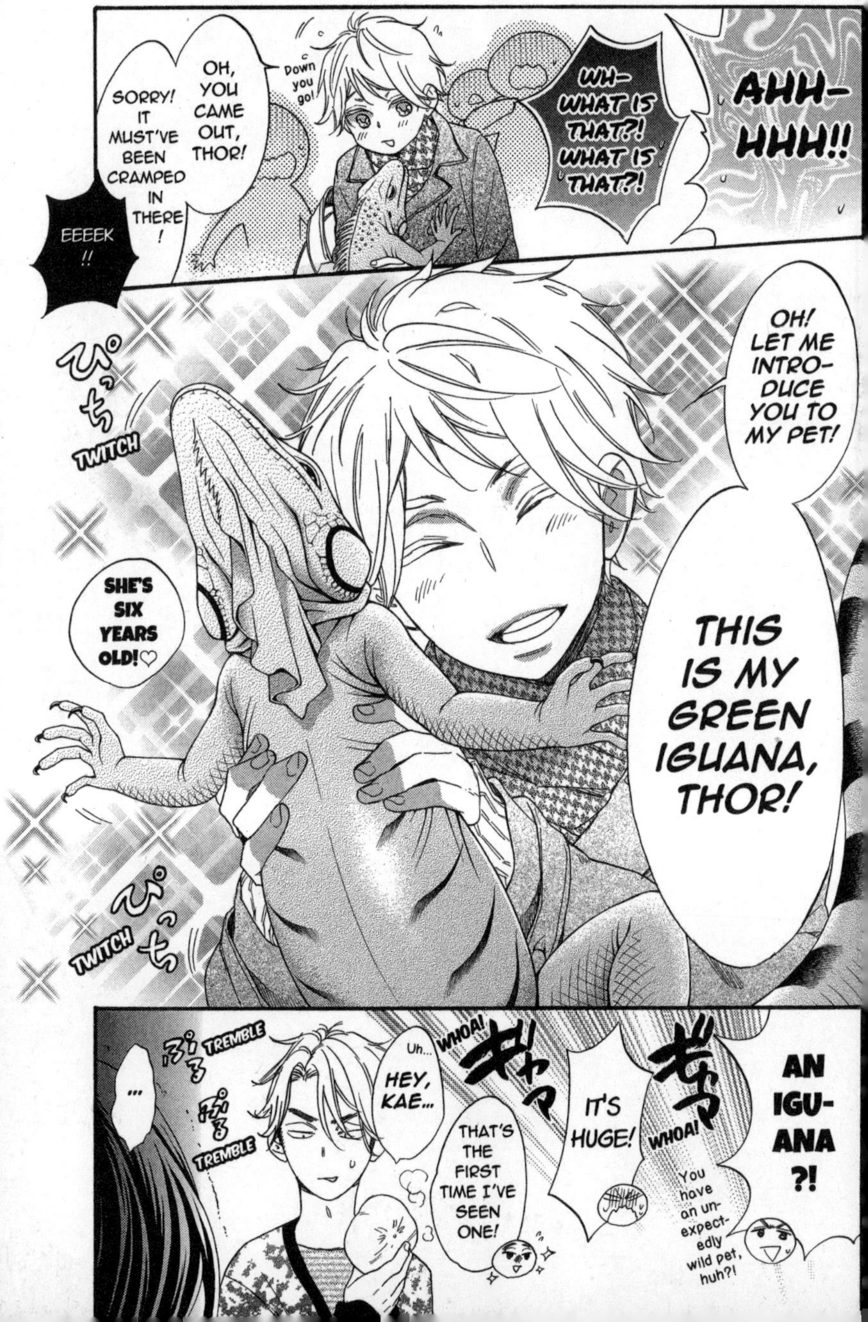
AHH-HHH!!
WH-WHAT IS THAT?! WHAT IS THAT?!
Down you go!
OH, YOU CAME OUT, THOR!
SORRY! IT MUST'VE BEEN CRAMPED IN THERE!
EEEEK!!
OH! LET ME INTRODUCE YOU TO MY PET!
THIS IS MY GREEN IGUANA, THOR!
SHE'S SIX YEARS OLD!♡
TWITCH
TWITCH
AN IGUANA?!
WHOA!
You have an unexpectedly wild pet, huh?!
IT'S HUGE!
WHOA!
Uh...
HEY, KAE...
THAT'S THE FIRST TIME I'VE SEEN ONE!
TREMBLE
TREMBLE
...

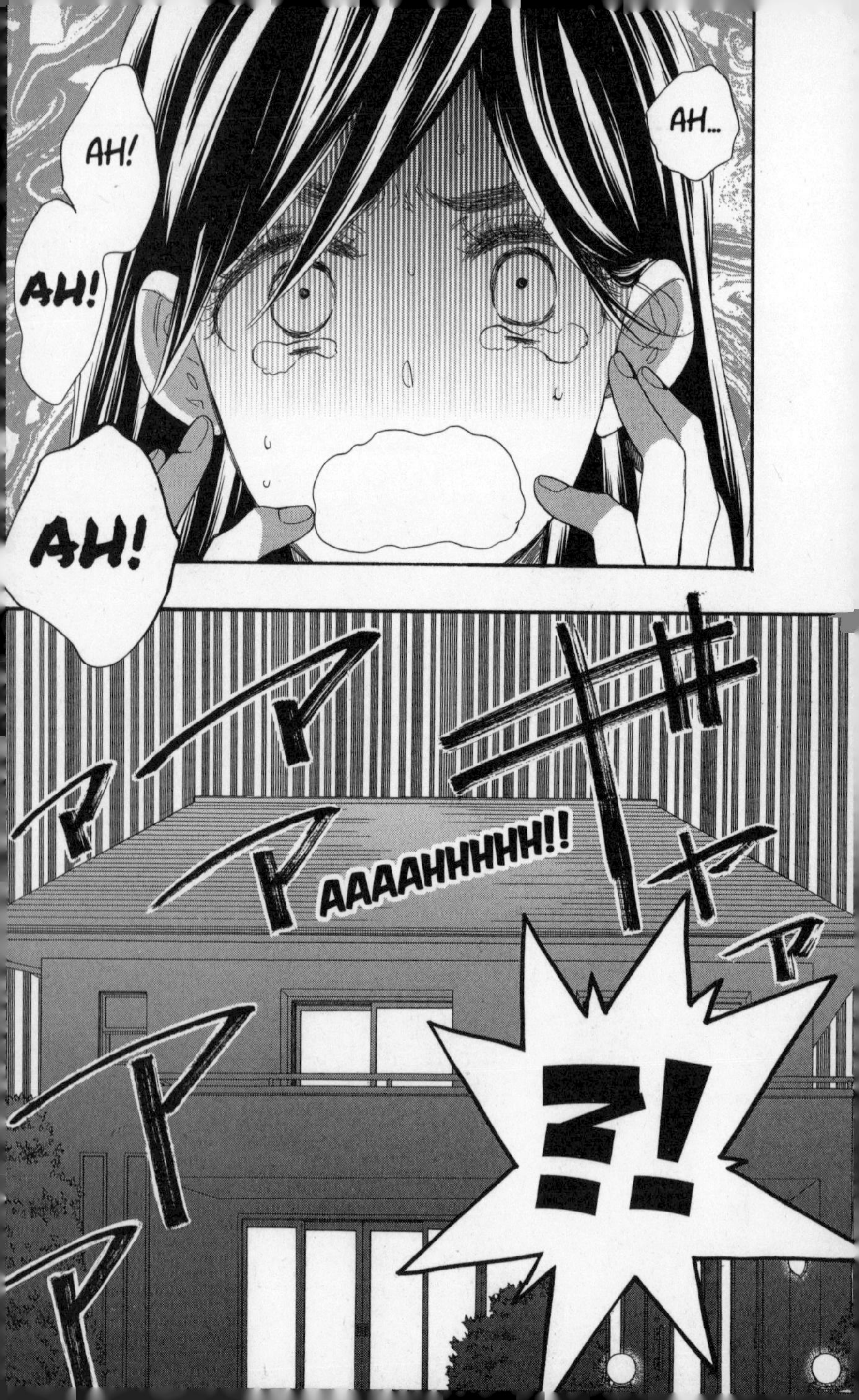

AH...
AH!
AH!
AH!
AAAAHHHHH!!
?!

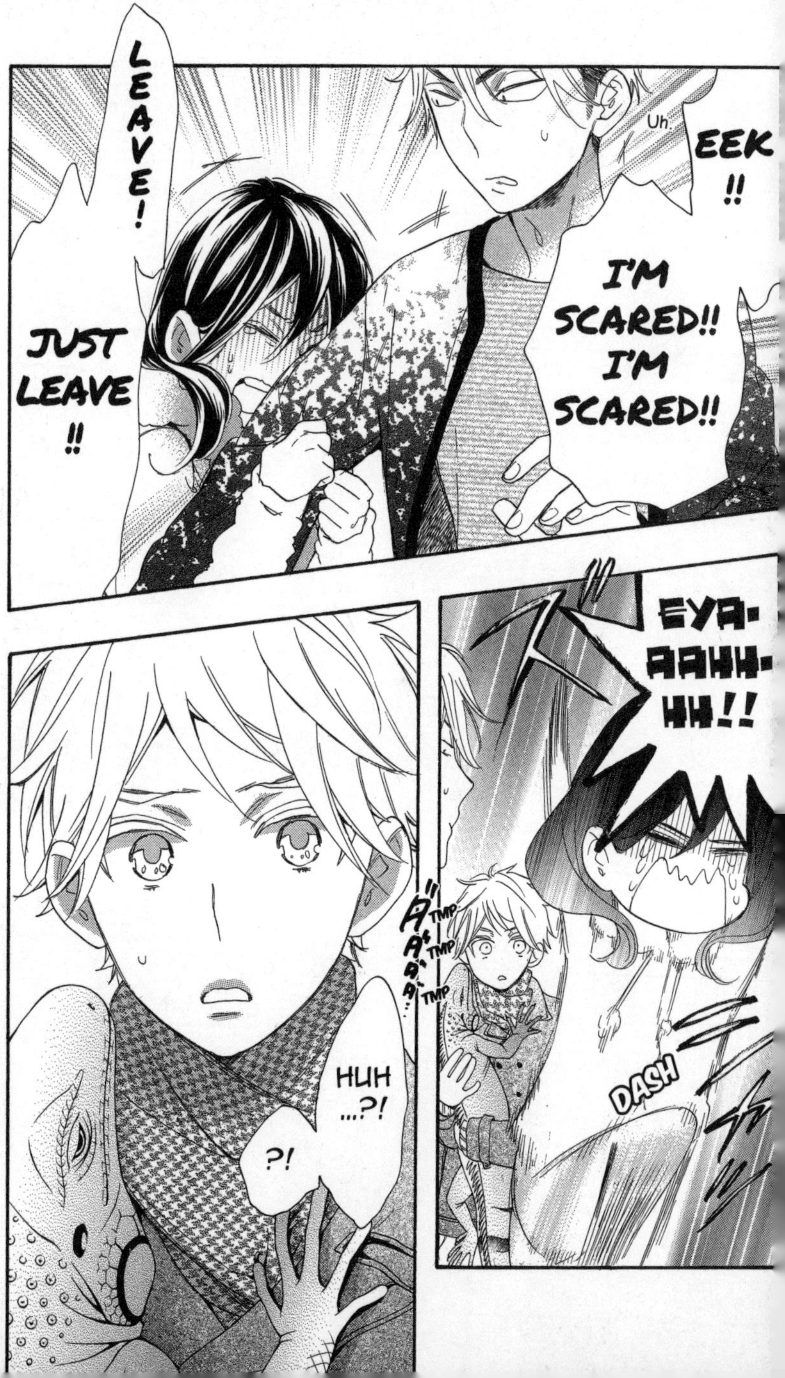

Uh.
EEK!!
I'M SCARED!! I'M SCARED!!
LEAVE!
JUST LEAVE!!
EYA-AAHH-HH!!
DASH
TMP TMP TMP
HUH ...?!
?!

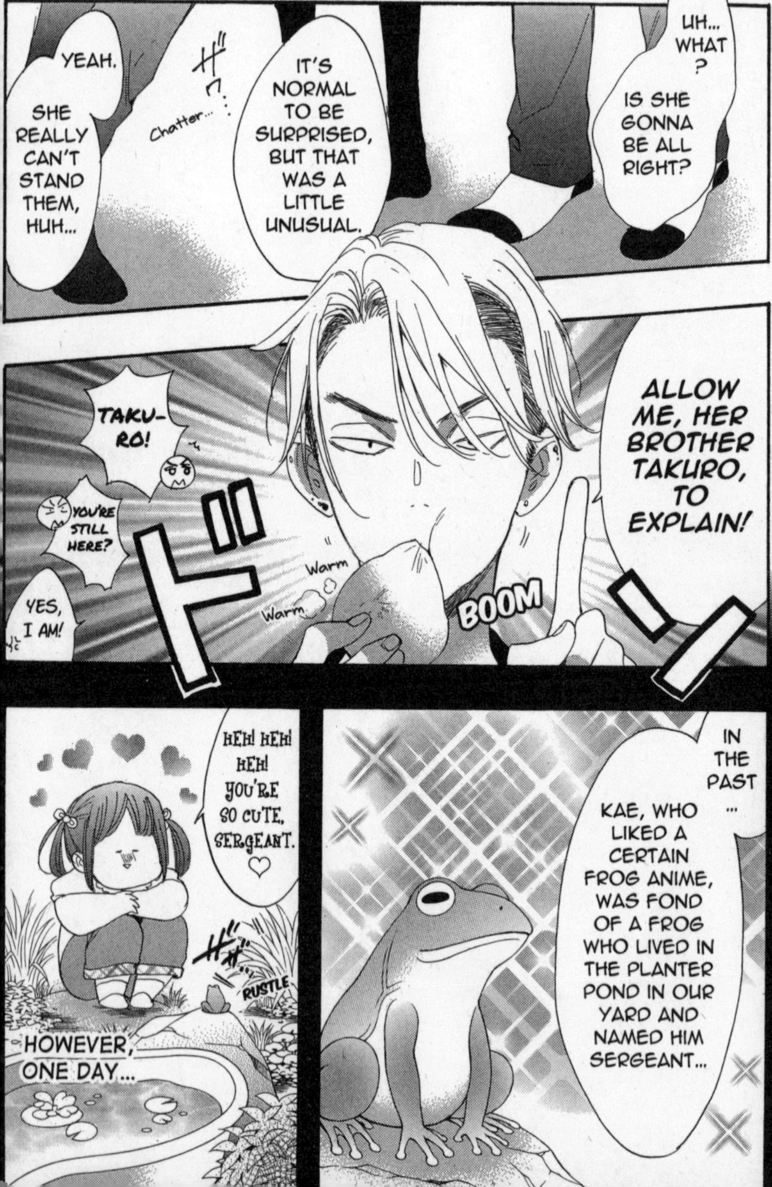
UH... WHAT?
IS SHE GONNA BE ALL RIGHT?
IT'S NORMAL TO BE SURPRISED, BUT THAT WAS A LITTLE UNUSUAL.
Chatter...
YEAH.
SHE REALLY CAN'T STAND THEM, HUH...
ALLOW ME, HER BROTHER TAKURO, TO EXPLAIN!
BOOM
Warm
Warm
TAKU-RO!
YOU'RE STILL HERE?
YES, I AM!
IN THE PAST...
KAE, WHO LIKED A CERTAIN FROG ANIME, WAS FOND OF A FROG WHO LIVED IN THE PLANTER POND IN OUR YARD AND NAMED HIM SERGEANT...
HEH! HEH! HEH! YOU'RE SO CUTE, SERGEANT. ♡
RUSTLE
HOWEVER, ONE DAY...

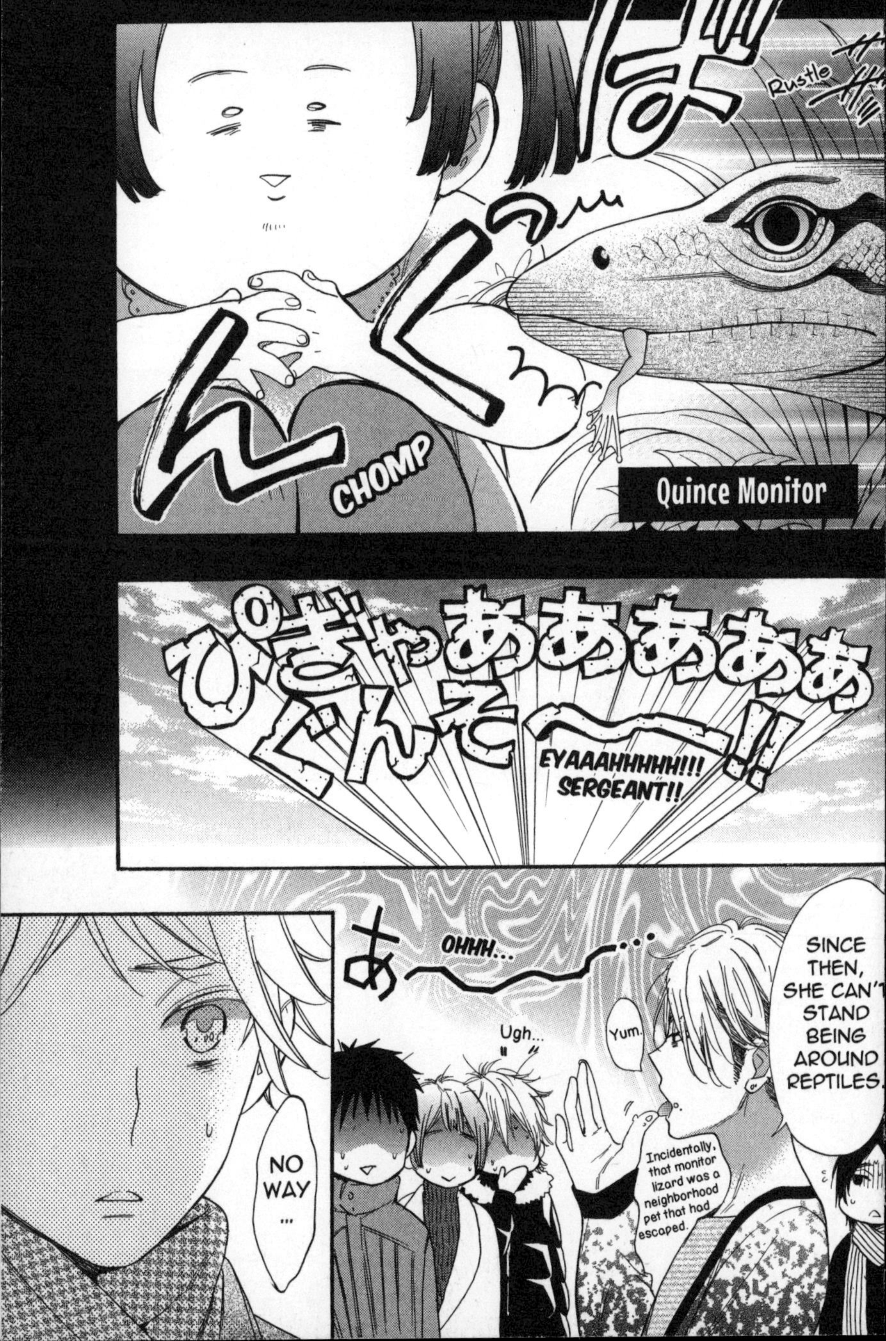
ばっ
Rustle
んぐっ
CHOMP
Quince Monitor
ぴぎゃああああああ
ぐんそ～～!!
EYAAAHHHHH!!!
SERGEANT!!
あ～～…
OHHH...
SINCE THEN, SHE CAN'T STAND BEING AROUND REPTILES.
Yum.
Ugh...
Incidentally, that monitor lizard was a neighborhood pet that had escaped.
NO WAY ...

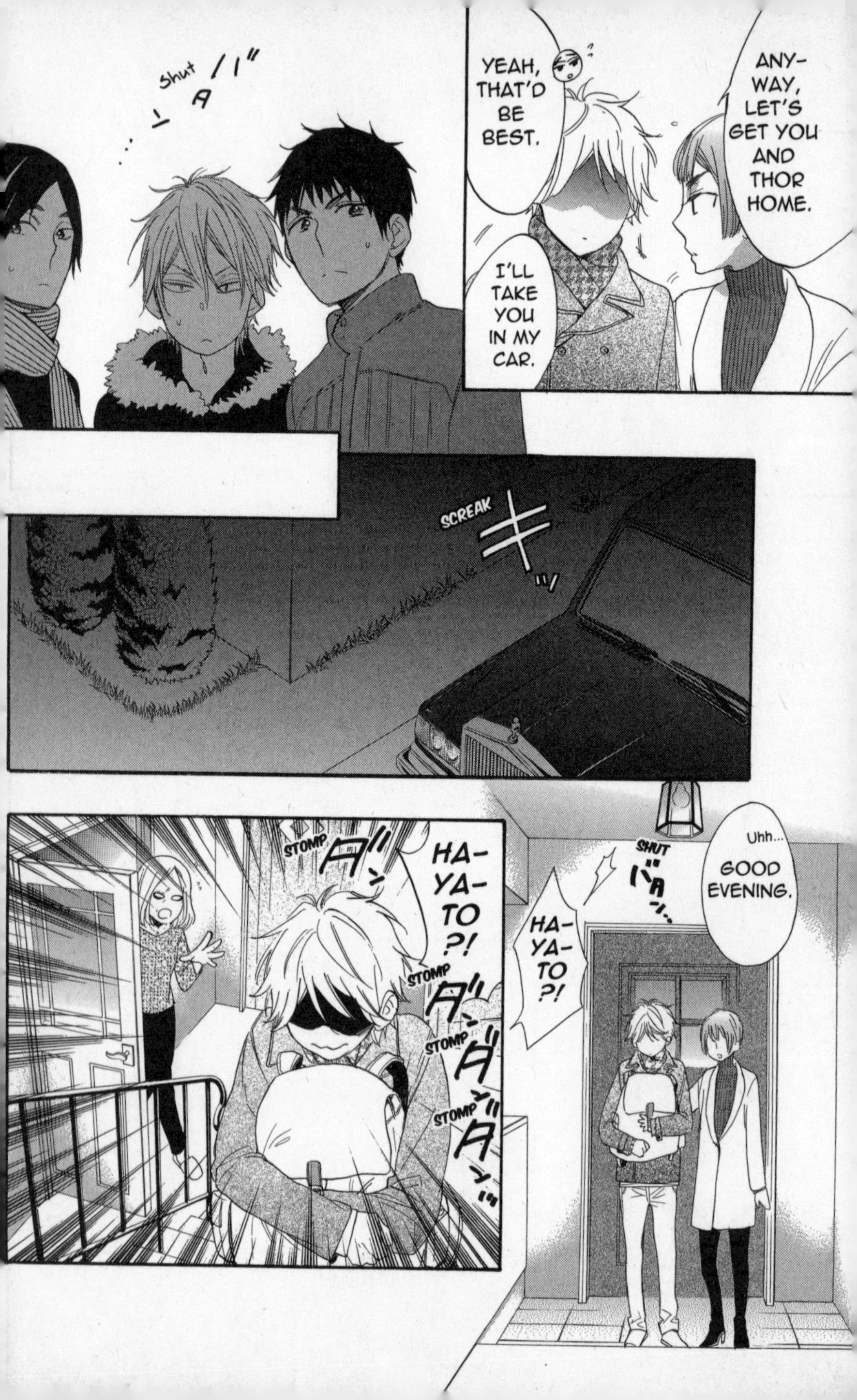
ANY-WAY, LET'S GET YOU AND THOR HOME.
YEAH, THAT'D BE BEST.
I'LL TAKE YOU IN MY CAR.
Shut
SCREAK
Uhh... GOOD EVENING.
SHUT
HA-YA-TO?!
STOMP
HA-YA-TO?!
STOMP
STOMP
STOMP

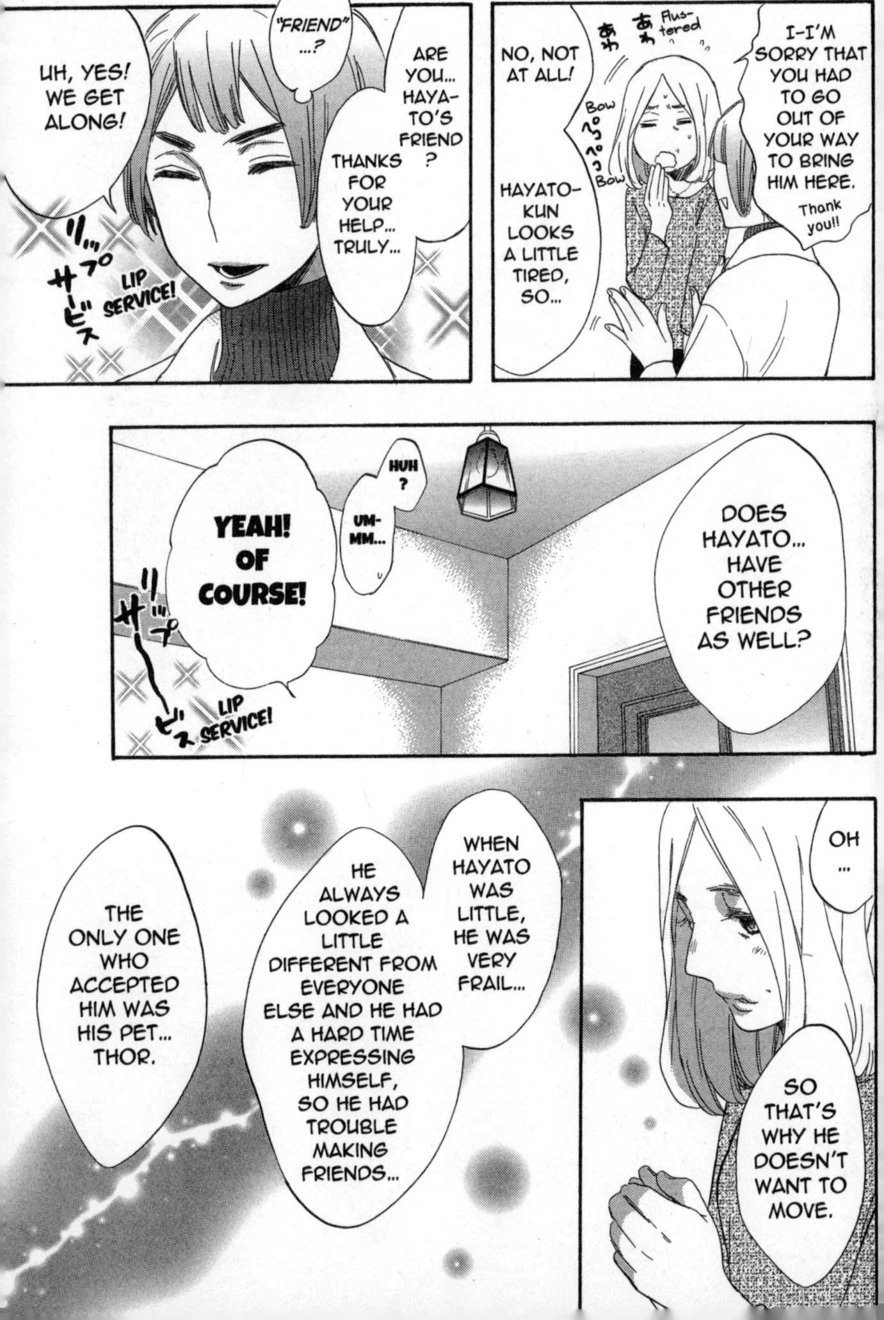
I-I'M SORRY THAT YOU HAD TO GO OUT OF YOUR WAY TO BRING HIM HERE.
Thank you!!
あわあわ Flus-tered
NO, NOT AT ALL!
ぺこぺこ Bow Bow
HAYATO-KUN LOOKS A LITTLE TIRED, SO...
ARE YOU... HAYATO'S FRIEND?
THANKS FOR YOUR HELP... TRULY...
"FRIEND" ...?
UH, YES! WE GET ALONG!
リップサービス LIP SERVICE!
DOES HAYATO... HAVE OTHER FRIENDS AS WELL?
HUH?
UM-MM...
YEAH! OF COURSE!
リップサービス LIP SERVICE!
OH ...
SO THAT'S WHY HE DOESN'T WANT TO MOVE.
WHEN HAYATO WAS LITTLE, HE WAS VERY FRAIL...
HE ALWAYS LOOKED A LITTLE DIFFERENT FROM EVERYONE ELSE AND HE HAD A HARD TIME EXPRESSING HIMSELF, SO HE HAD TROUBLE MAKING FRIENDS...
THE ONLY ONE WHO ACCEPTED HIM WAS HIS PET... THOR.

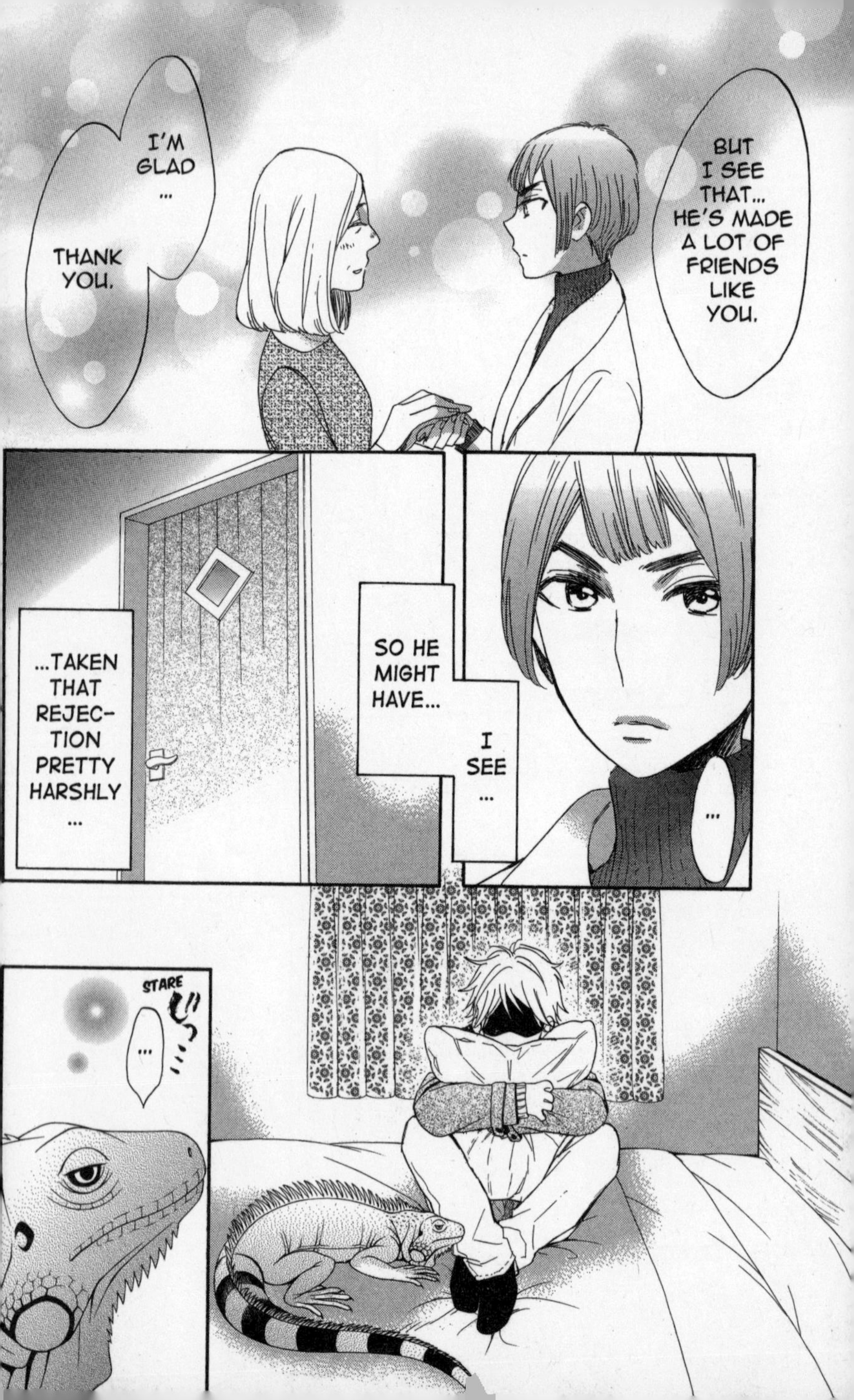
BUT I SEE THAT... HE'S MADE A LOT OF FRIENDS LIKE YOU.
I'M GLAD ...
THANK YOU.
...
I SEE ...
SO HE MIGHT HAVE...
...TAKEN THAT REJECTION PRETTY HARSHLY ...
STARE
...

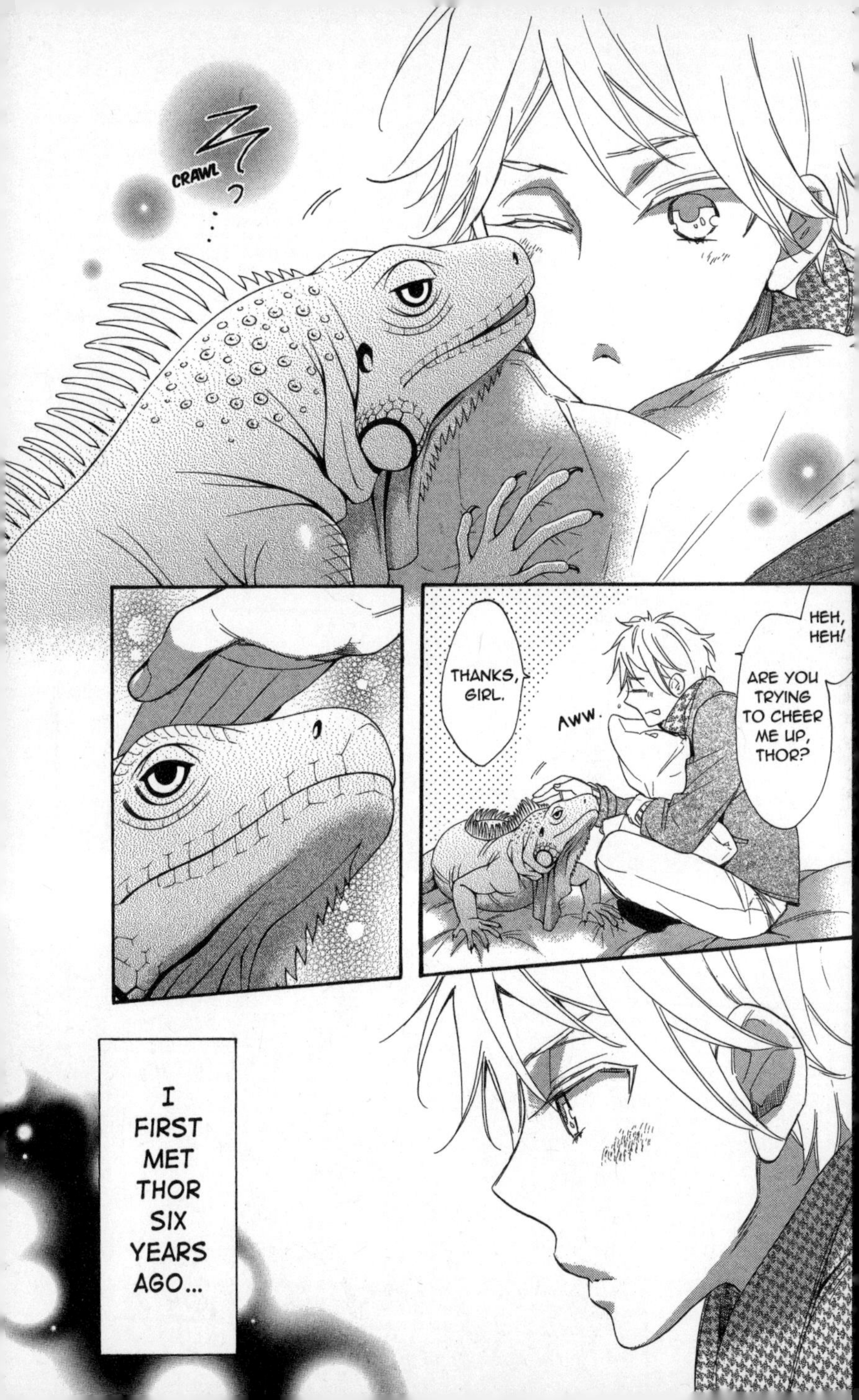
CRAWL
HEH, HEH!
ARE YOU TRYING TO CHEER ME UP, THOR?
AWW.
THANKS, GIRL.
I FIRST MET THOR SIX YEARS AGO...

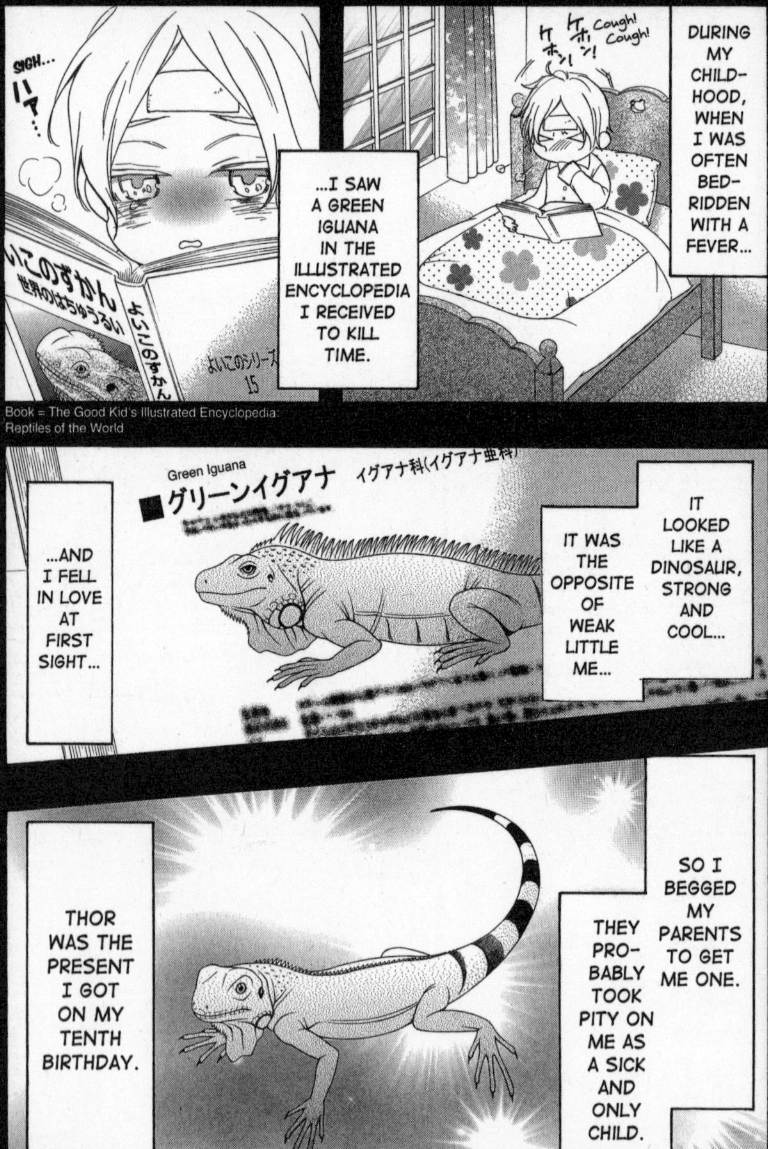
DURING MY CHILDHOOD, WHEN I WAS OFTEN BEDRIDDEN WITH A FEVER...
ケホン! ケホン!
Cough! Cough!
...I SAW A GREEN IGUANA IN THE ILLUSTRATED ENCYCLOPEDIA I RECEIVED TO KILL TIME.
SIGH...
ハァ...
よいこのずかん
世界のはちゅうるい
よいこのずかん
よいこのシリーズ
15
Book = The Good Kid's Illustrated Encyclopedia: Reptiles of the World
IT LOOKED LIKE A DINOSAUR, STRONG AND COOL...
IT WAS THE OPPOSITE OF WEAK LITTLE ME...
Green Iguana
グリーンイグアナ
イグアナ科(イグアナ亜科)
...AND I FELL IN LOVE AT FIRST SIGHT...
SO I BEGGED MY PARENTS TO GET ME ONE.
THEY PROBABLY TOOK PITY ON ME AS A SICK AND ONLY CHILD.
THOR WAS THE PRESENT I GOT ON MY TENTH BIRTHDAY.

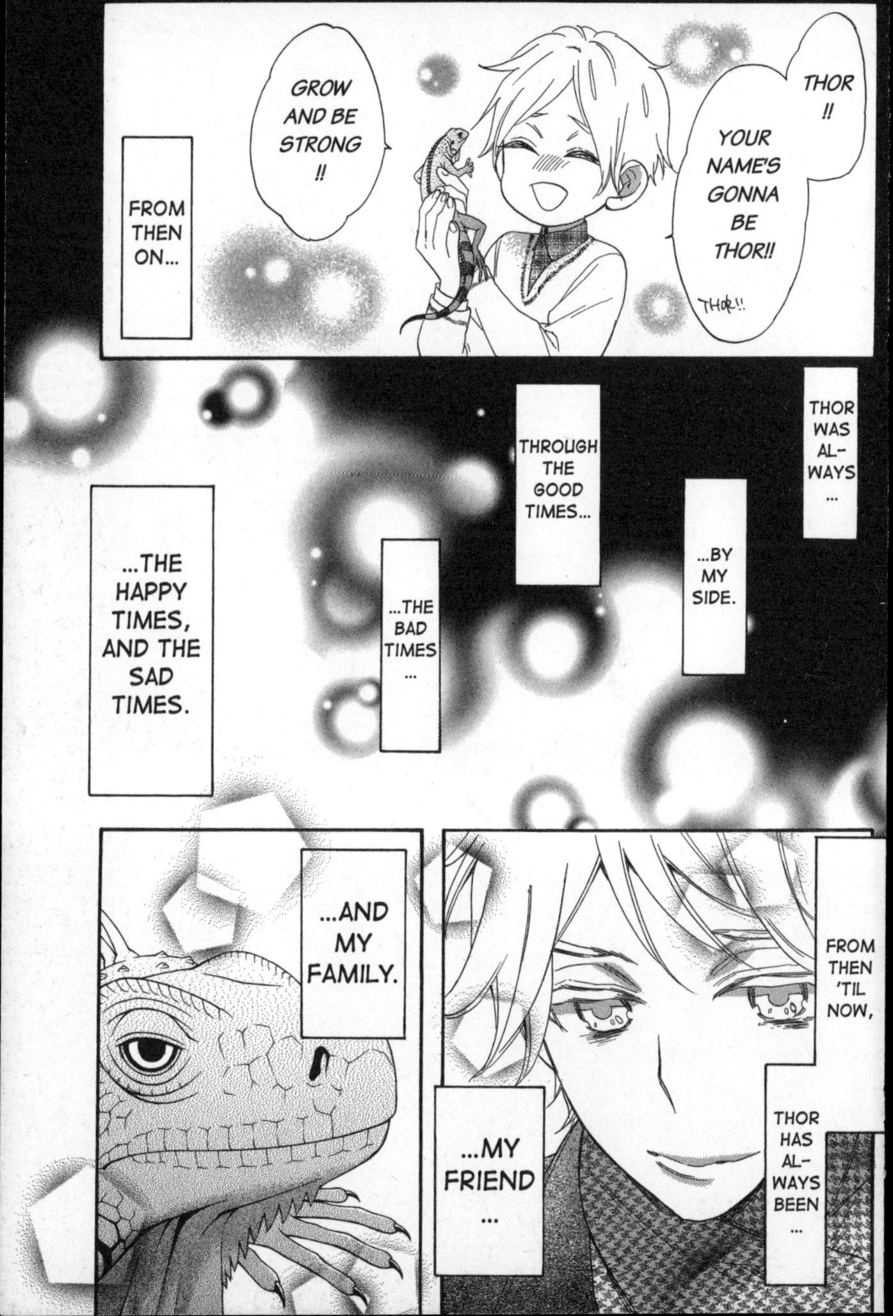
THOR !!
YOUR NAME'S GONNA BE THOR!!
THOR!!
GROW AND BE STRONG !!
FROM THEN ON...
THOR WAS AL-WAYS ...
...BY MY SIDE.
THROUGH THE GOOD TIMES...
...THE BAD TIMES ...
...THE HAPPY TIMES, AND THE SAD TIMES.
FROM THEN 'TIL NOW,
THOR HAS AL-WAYS BEEN ...
...MY FRIEND ...
...AND MY FAMILY.

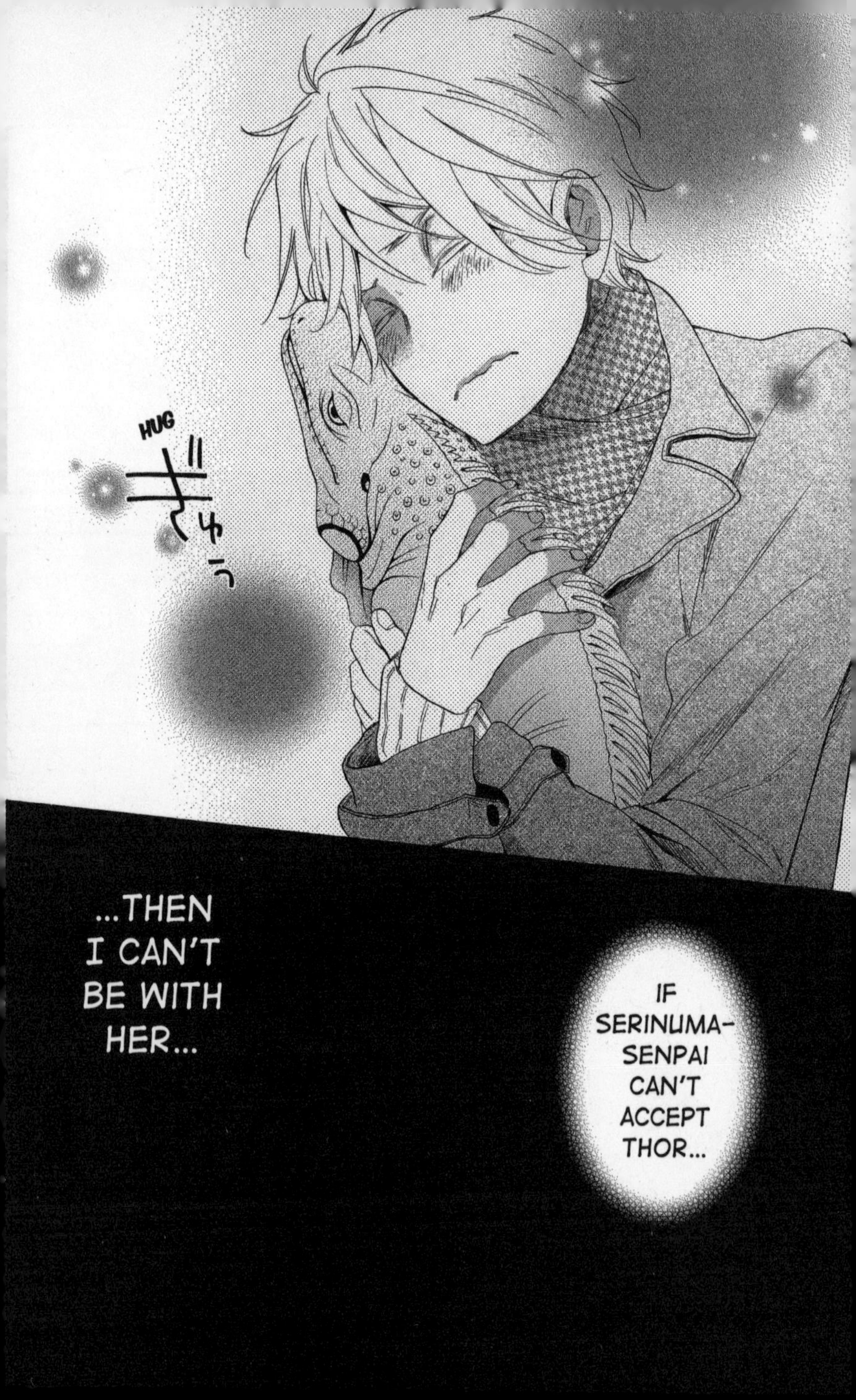
HUG
ぎゅっ
IF SERINUMA-SENPAI CAN'T ACCEPT THOR...
...THEN I CAN'T BE WITH HER...

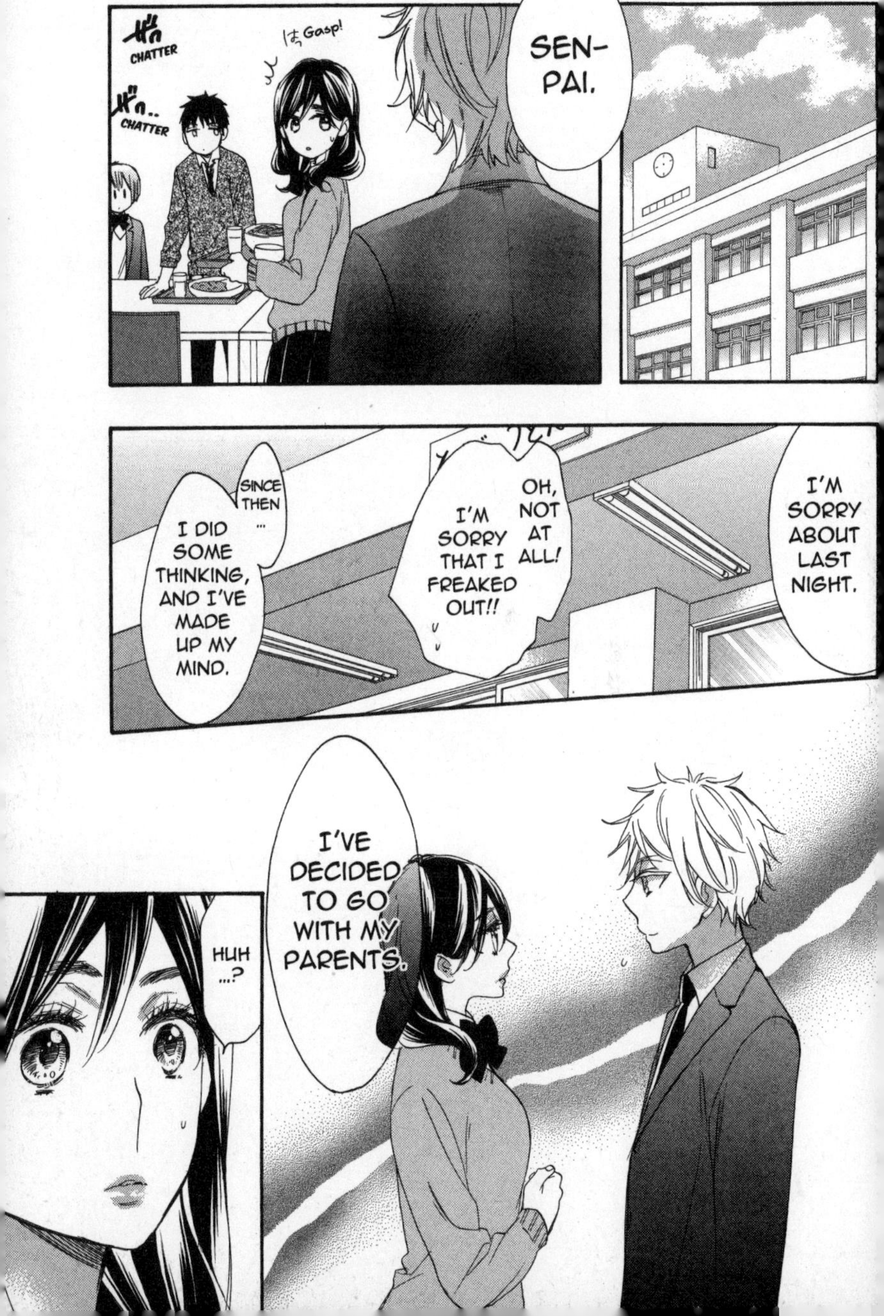
SEN-PAI.
Gasp!
CHATTER
CHATTER
I'M SORRY ABOUT LAST NIGHT.
OH, NOT AT ALL!
I'M SORRY THAT I FREAKED OUT!!
SINCE THEN...
I DID SOME THINKING, AND I'VE MADE UP MY MIND.
I'VE DECIDED TO GO WITH MY PARENTS.
HUH...?

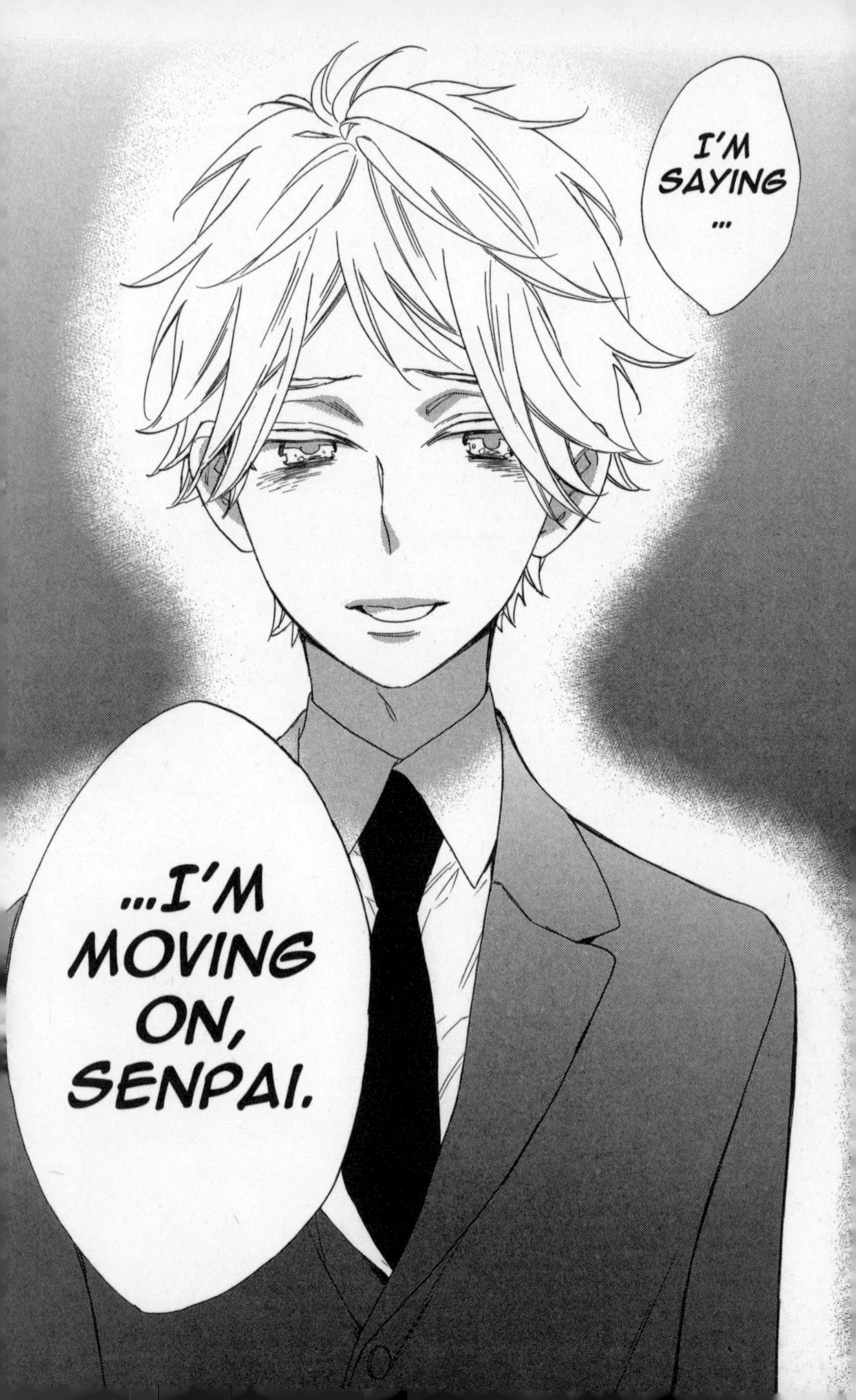
I'M SAYING ...
...I'M MOVING ON, SENPAI.

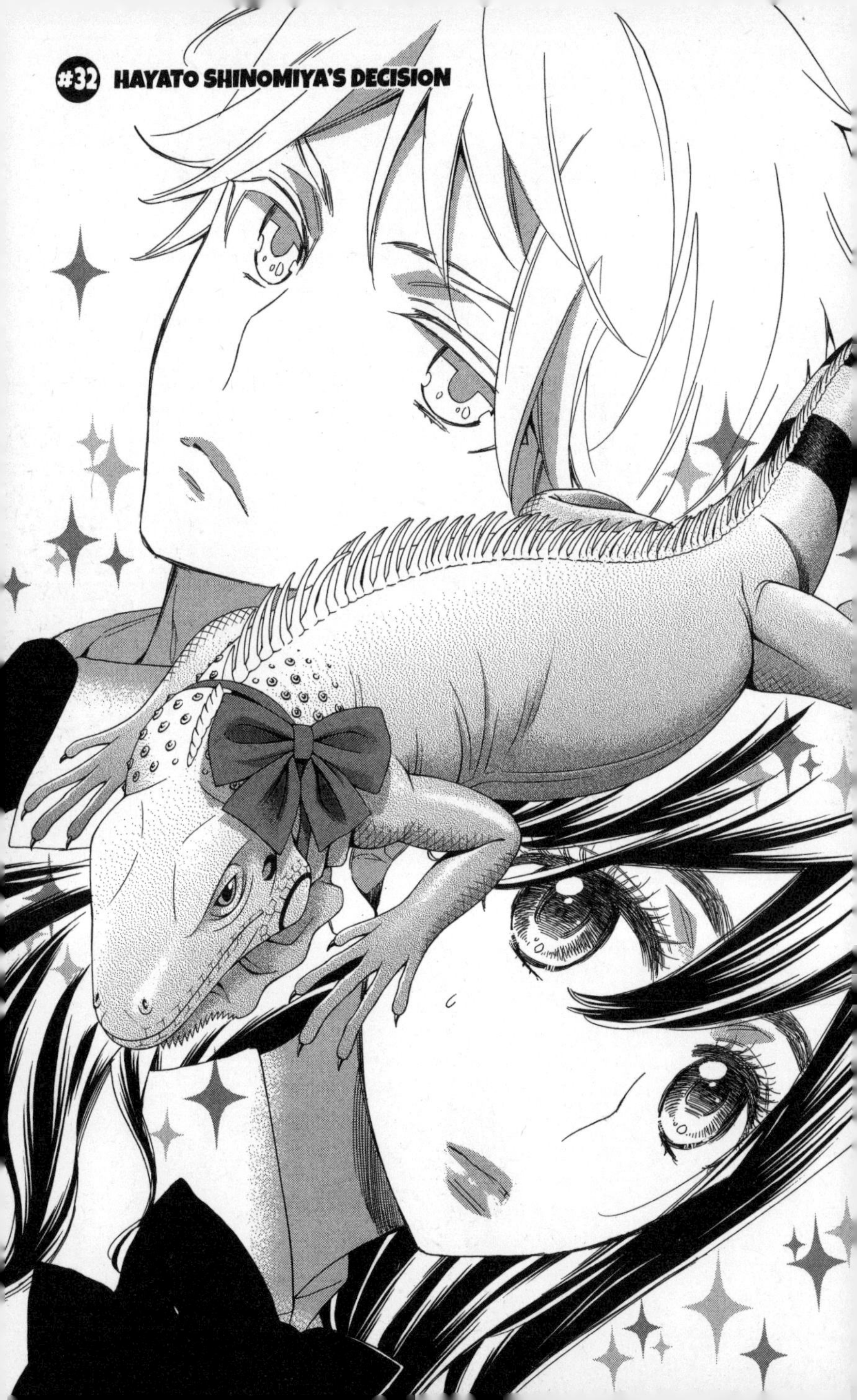
#32 HAYATO SHINOMIYA'S DECISION

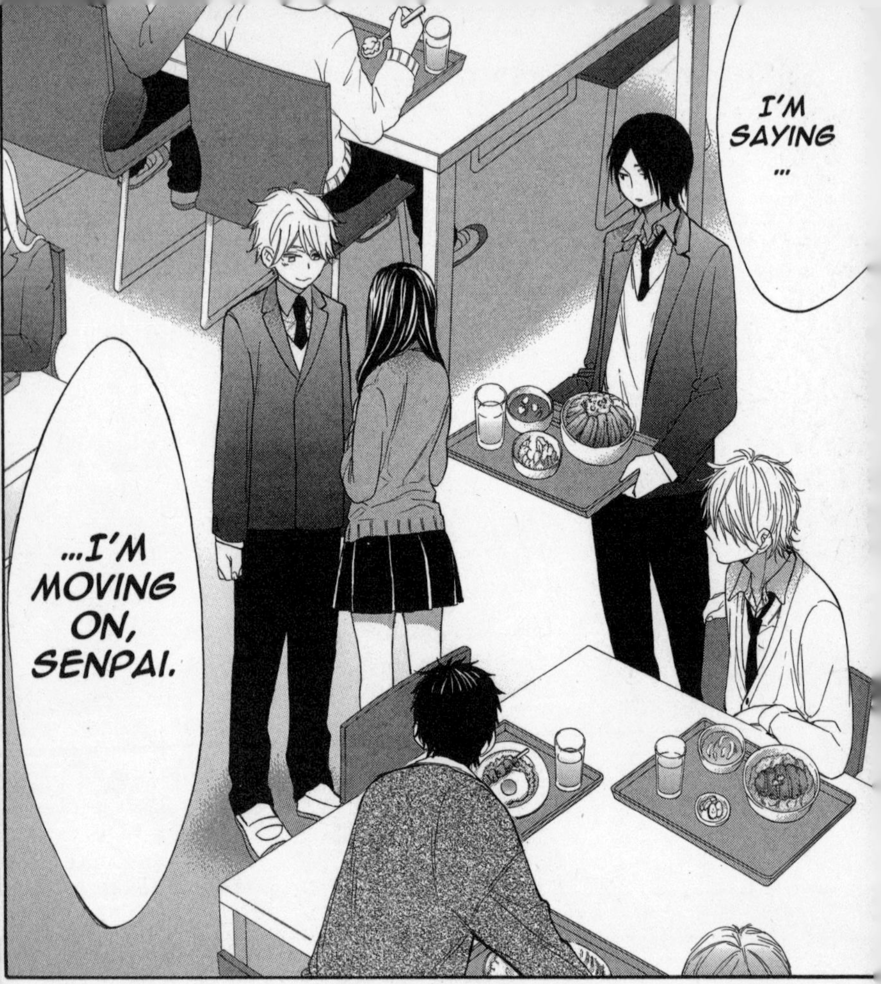
I'M SAYING ...
...I'M MOVING ON, SENPAI.

KiSS HiM, NOT ME!

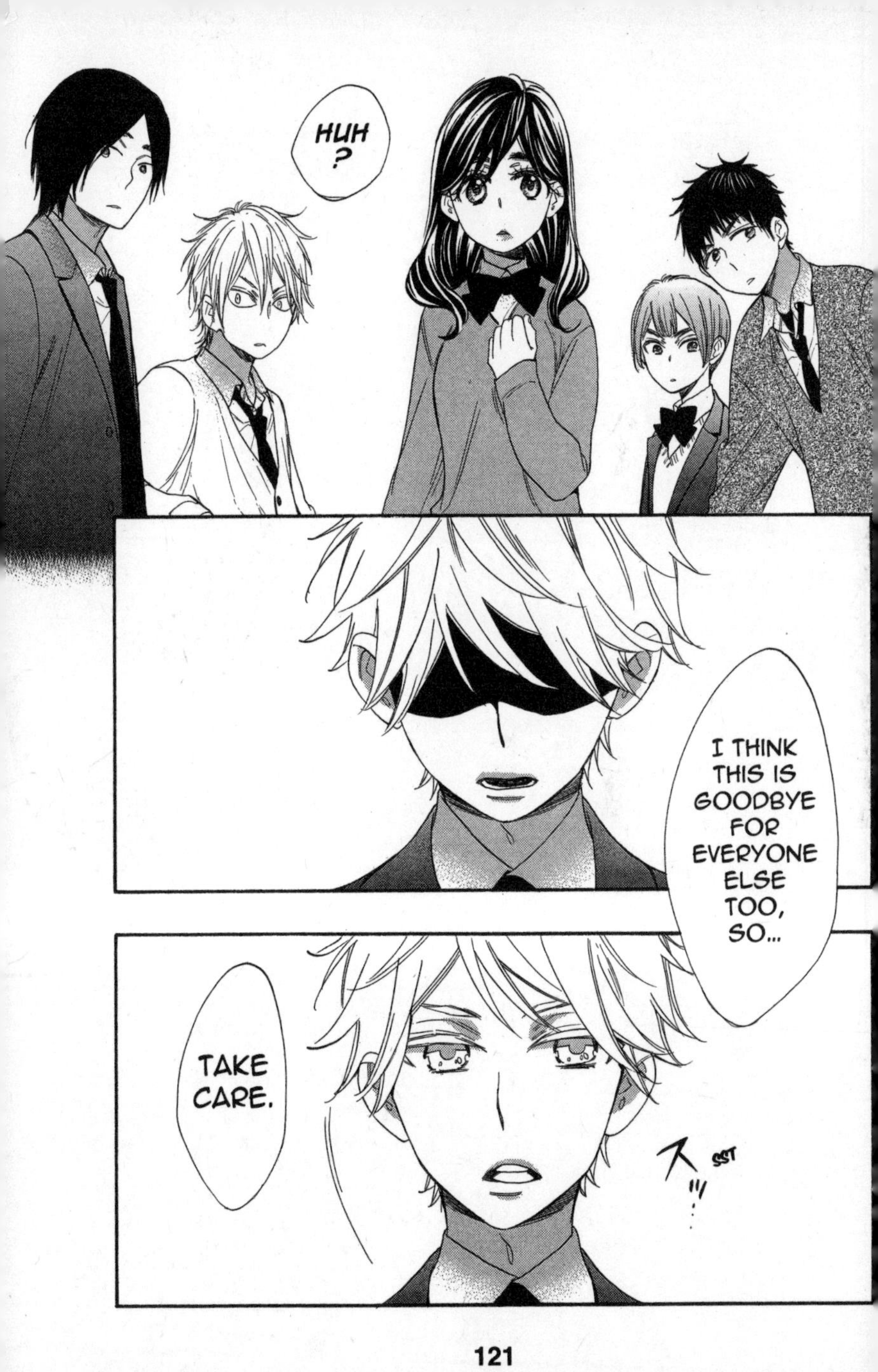
HUH ?
I THINK THIS IS GOODBYE FOR EVERYONE ELSE TOO, SO...
SST
TAKE CARE.

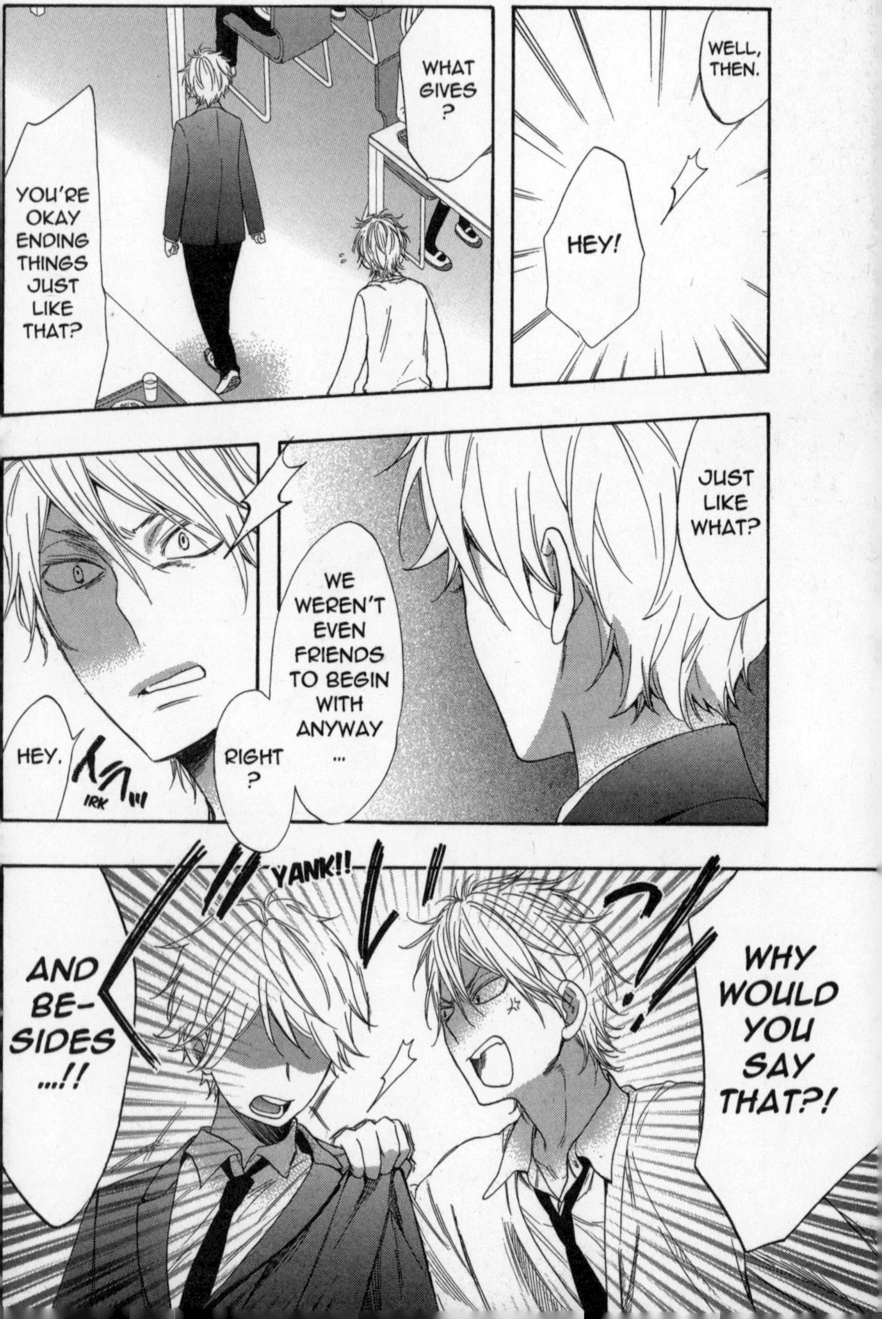
WELL, THEN.
HEY!
WHAT GIVES?
YOU'RE OKAY ENDING THINGS JUST LIKE THAT?
JUST LIKE WHAT?
WE WEREN'T EVEN FRIENDS TO BEGIN WITH ANYWAY ...
RIGHT?
HEY.
IRK
WHY WOULD YOU SAY THAT?!
YANK!!
AND BE-SIDES ...!!

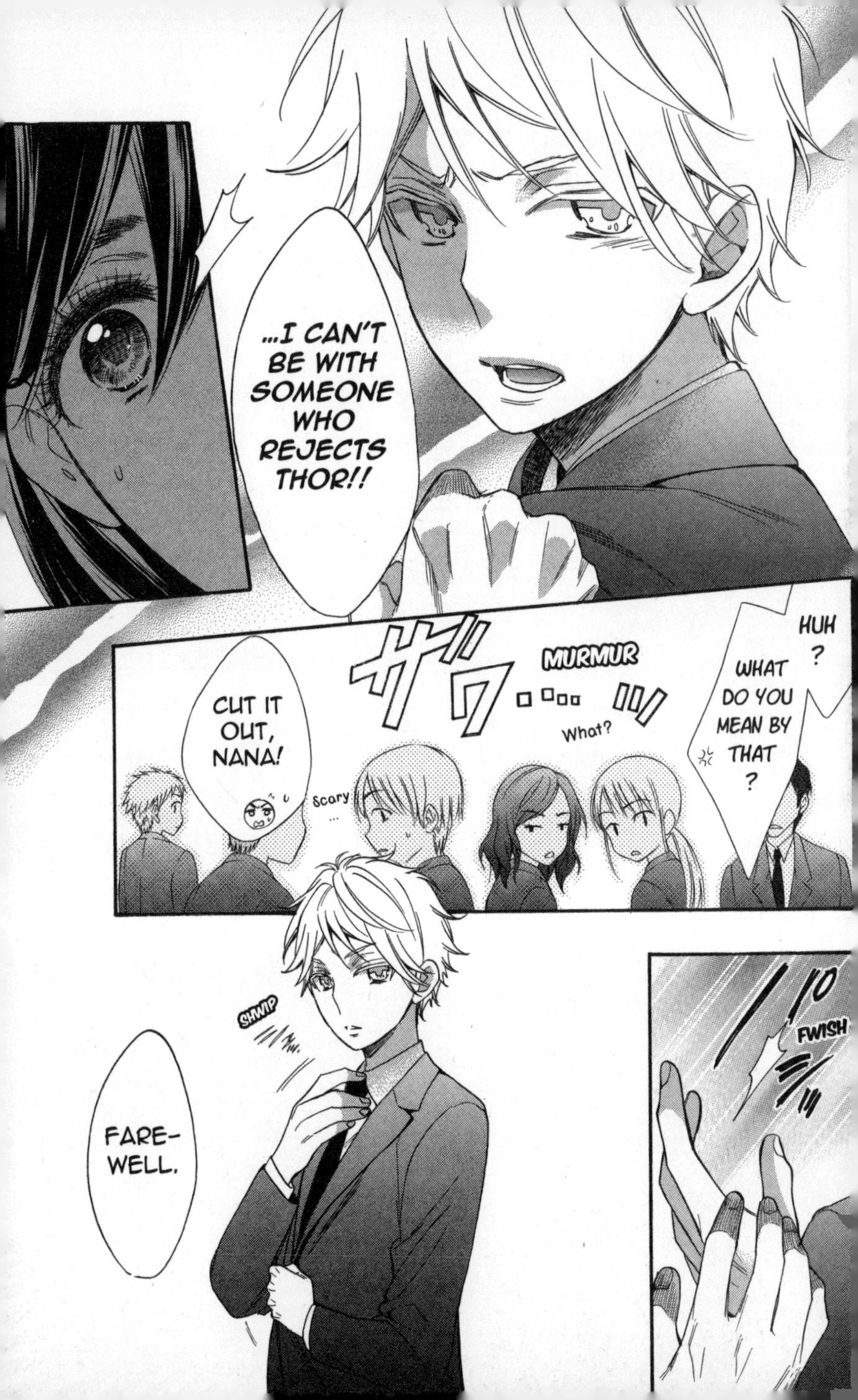
...I CAN'T BE WITH SOMEONE WHO REJECTS THOR!!
HUH?
WHAT DO YOU MEAN BY THAT?
MURMUR
What?
Scary...
CUT IT OUT, NANA!
FWISH
SHWIP
FARE-WELL.

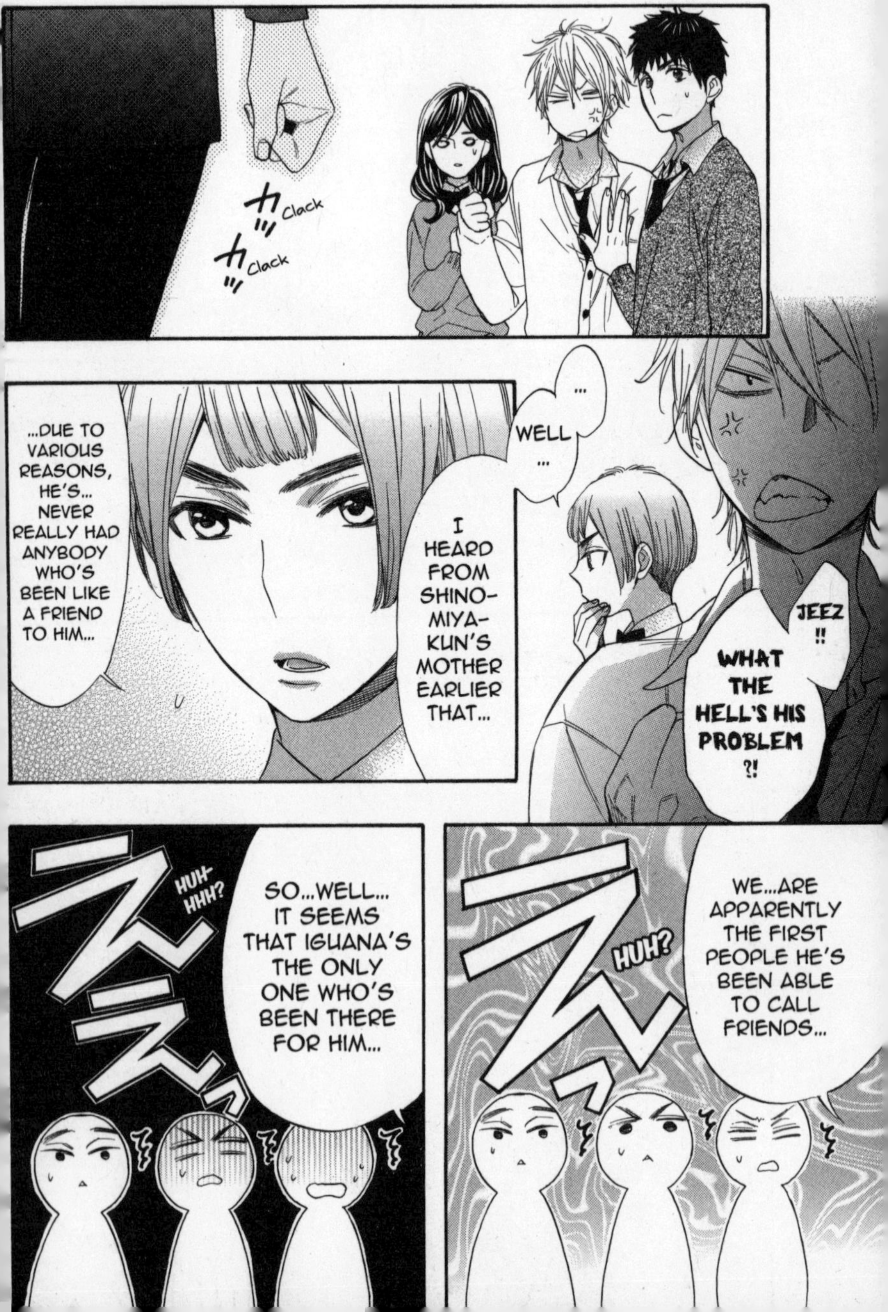

カッ Clack
カッ Clack
...
WELL ...
JEEZ !! WHAT THE HELL'S HIS PROBLEM ?!
I HEARD FROM SHINO-MIYA-KUN'S MOTHER EARLIER THAT...
...DUE TO VARIOUS REASONS, HE'S... NEVER REALLY HAD ANYBODY WHO'S BEEN LIKE A FRIEND TO HIM...
WE...ARE APPARENTLY THE FIRST PEOPLE HE'S BEEN ABLE TO CALL FRIENDS...
HUH?
SO...WELL... IT SEEMS THAT IGUANA'S THE ONLY ONE WHO'S BEEN THERE FOR HIM...
HUH-HHH?

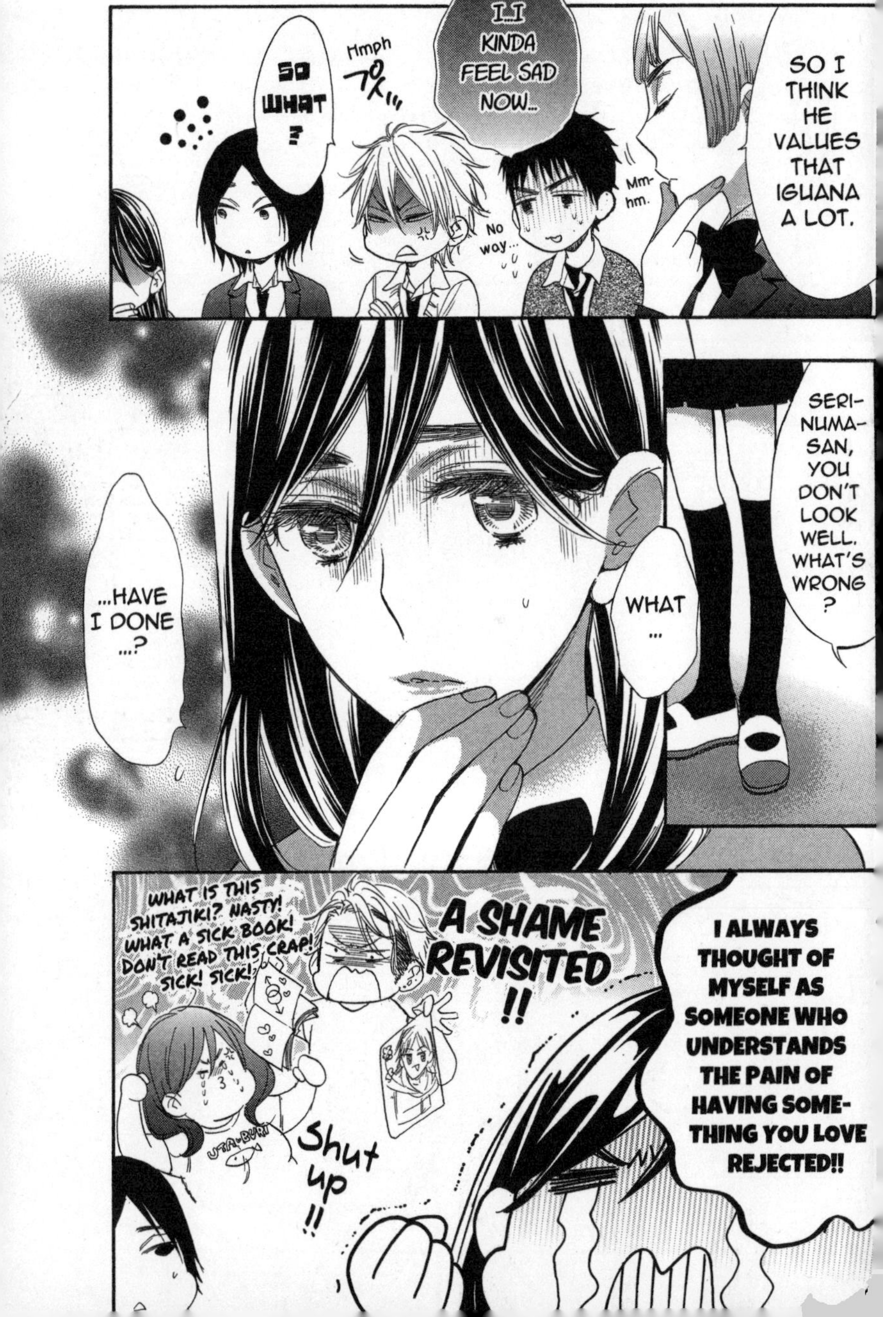
SO I THINK HE VALUES THAT IGUANA A LOT.
Mm-hm.
I...I KINDA FEEL SAD NOW...
No way...
Hmph
SO WHAT?
SERI-NUMA-SAN, YOU DON'T LOOK WELL. WHAT'S WRONG?
WHAT...
...HAVE I DONE...?
I ALWAYS THOUGHT OF MYSELF AS SOMEONE WHO UNDERSTANDS THE PAIN OF HAVING SOME-THING YOU LOVE REJECTED!!
A SHAME REVISITED!!
WHAT IS THIS SHITAJIKI? NASTY! WHAT A SICK BOOK! DON'T READ THIS CRAP! SICK! SICK!
Shut up!!
URA-BURI

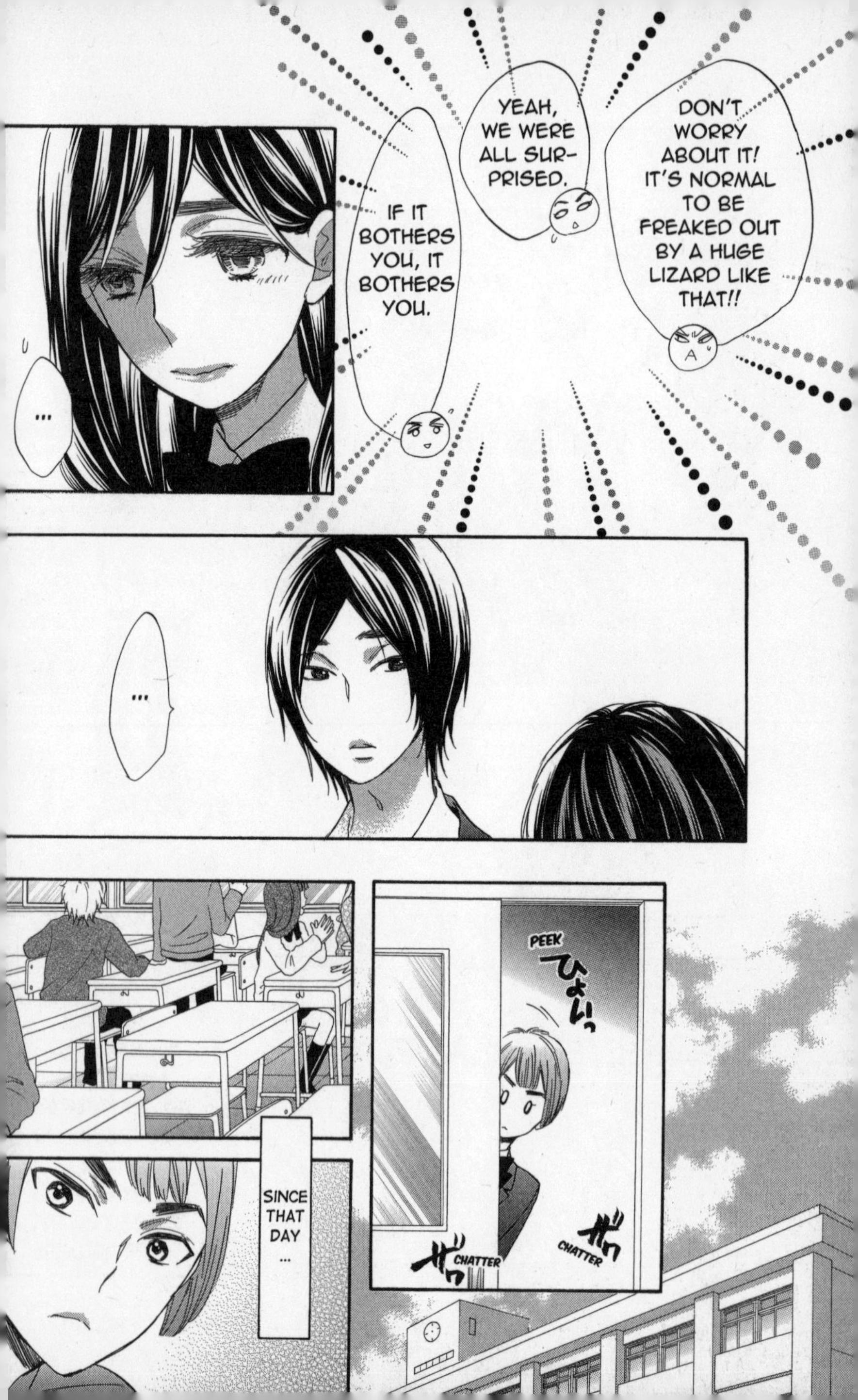
DON'T WORRY ABOUT IT! IT'S NORMAL TO BE FREAKED OUT BY A HUGE LIZARD LIKE THAT!!
YEAH, WE WERE ALL SUR-PRISED.
IF IT BOTHERS YOU, IT BOTHERS YOU.
...
...
PEEK
ひょいっ
ザワ
CHATTER
ザワ
CHATTER
SINCE THAT DAY ...

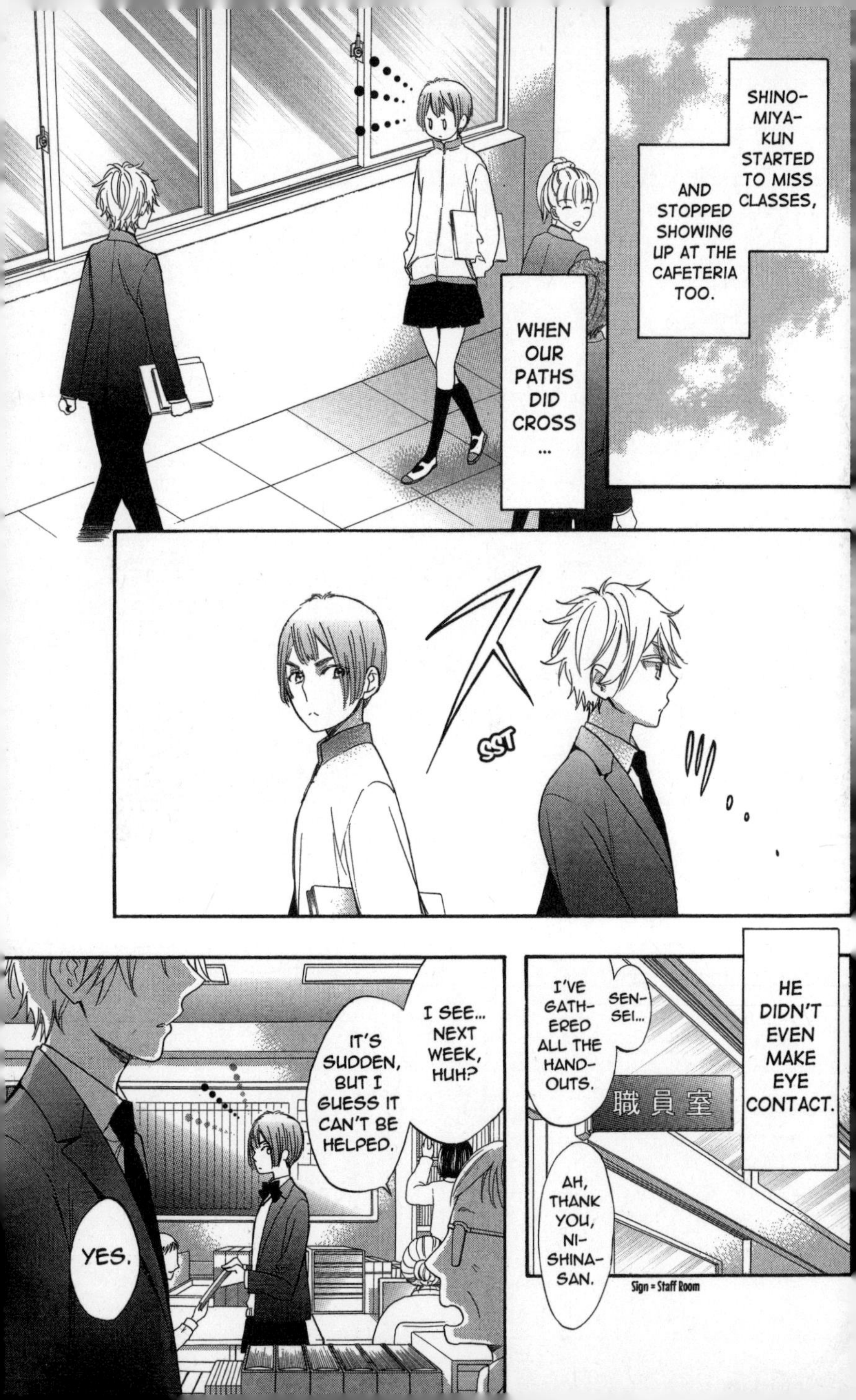
SHINOMIYA-KUN STARTED TO MISS CLASSES,
AND STOPPED SHOWING UP AT THE CAFETERIA TOO.
WHEN OUR PATHS DID CROSS...
SST
HE DIDN'T EVEN MAKE EYE CONTACT.
SENSEI...
I'VE GATHERED ALL THE HANDOUTS.
職員室
AH, THANK YOU, NISHINA-SAN.
Sign = Staff Room
I SEE... NEXT WEEK, HUH?
IT'S SUDDEN, BUT I GUESS IT CAN'T BE HELPED.
YES.

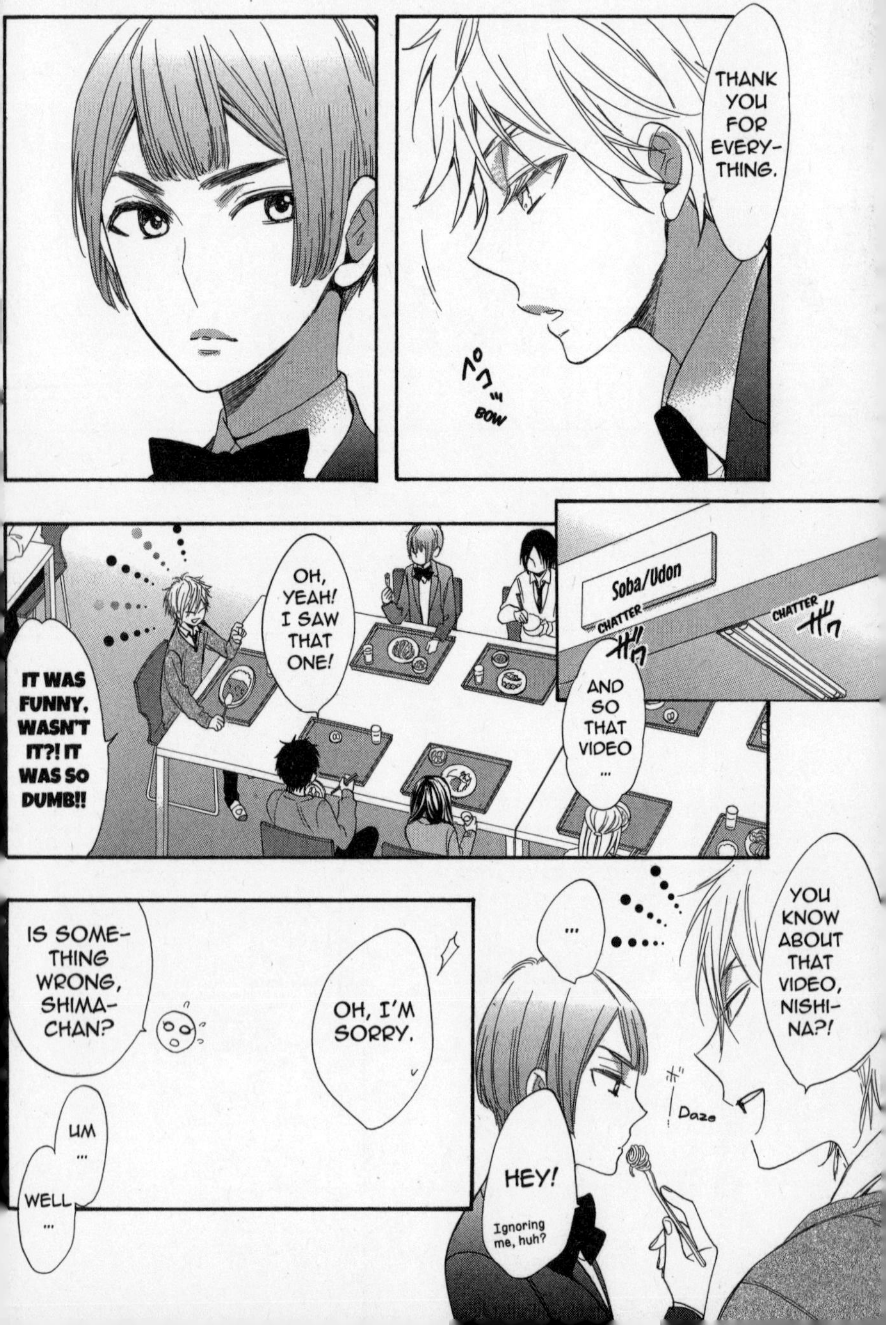

THANK YOU FOR EVERY-THING.
BOW
Soba/Udon
CHATTER
CHATTER
AND SO THAT VIDEO ...
OH, YEAH! I SAW THAT ONE!
IT WAS FUNNY, WASN'T IT?! IT WAS SO DUMB!!
YOU KNOW ABOUT THAT VIDEO, NISHINA?!
...
Daze
HEY!
Ignoring me, huh?
OH, I'M SORRY.
IS SOME-THING WRONG, SHIMA-CHAN?
UM ...
WELL ...

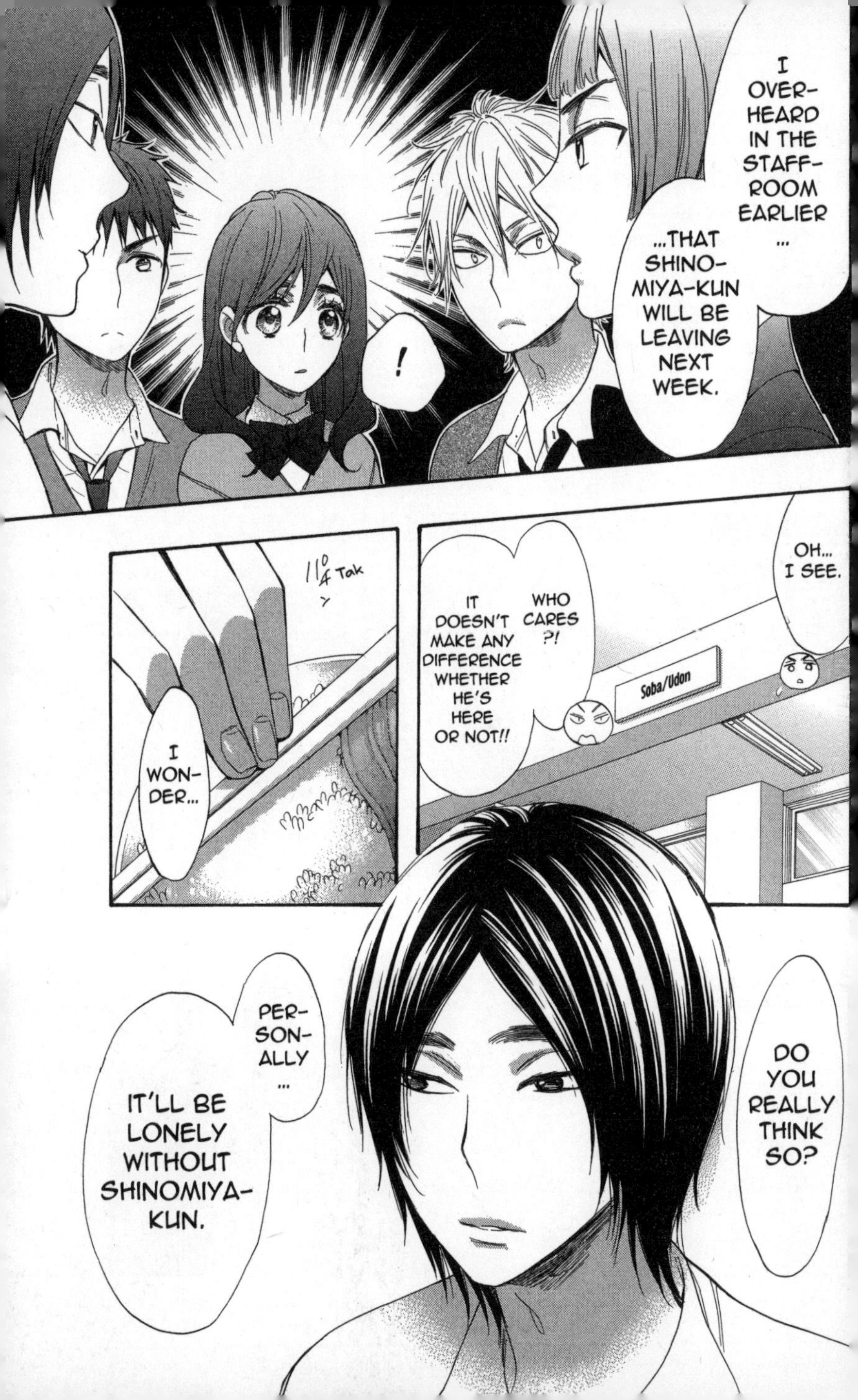
I OVERHEARD IN THE STAFFROOM EARLIER ...
...THAT SHINOMIYA-KUN WILL BE LEAVING NEXT WEEK.
!
OH... I SEE.
WHO CARES?!
IT DOESN'T MAKE ANY DIFFERENCE WHETHER HE'S HERE OR NOT!!
Soba/Udon
Tak
I WONDER...
DO YOU REALLY THINK SO?
PERSONALLY ...
IT'LL BE LONELY WITHOUT SHINOMIYA-KUN.

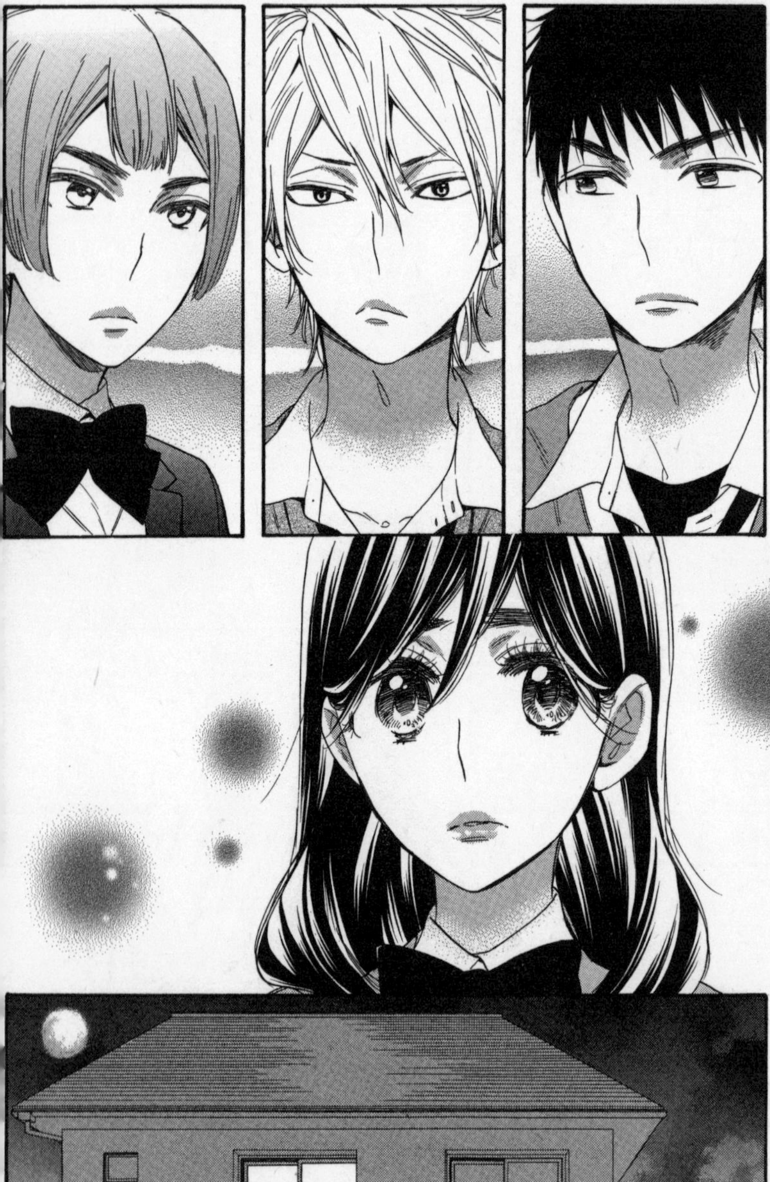

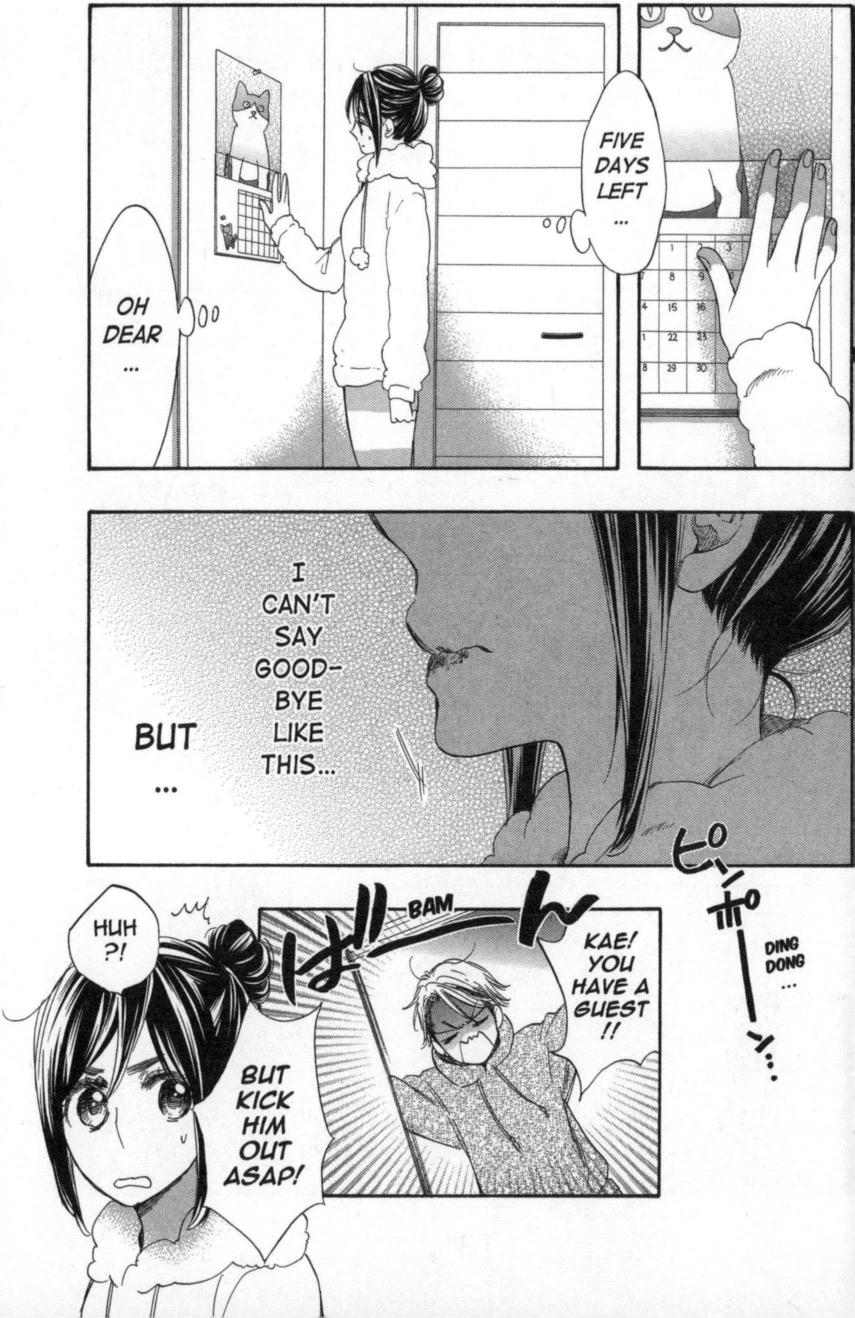
FIVE DAYS LEFT ...
OH DEAR ...
I CAN'T SAY GOOD-BYE LIKE THIS...
BUT ...
ピンポーン…
DING DONG ...
KAE! YOU HAVE A GUEST !!
ばーん
BAM
BUT KICK HIM OUT ASAP!
HUH ?!

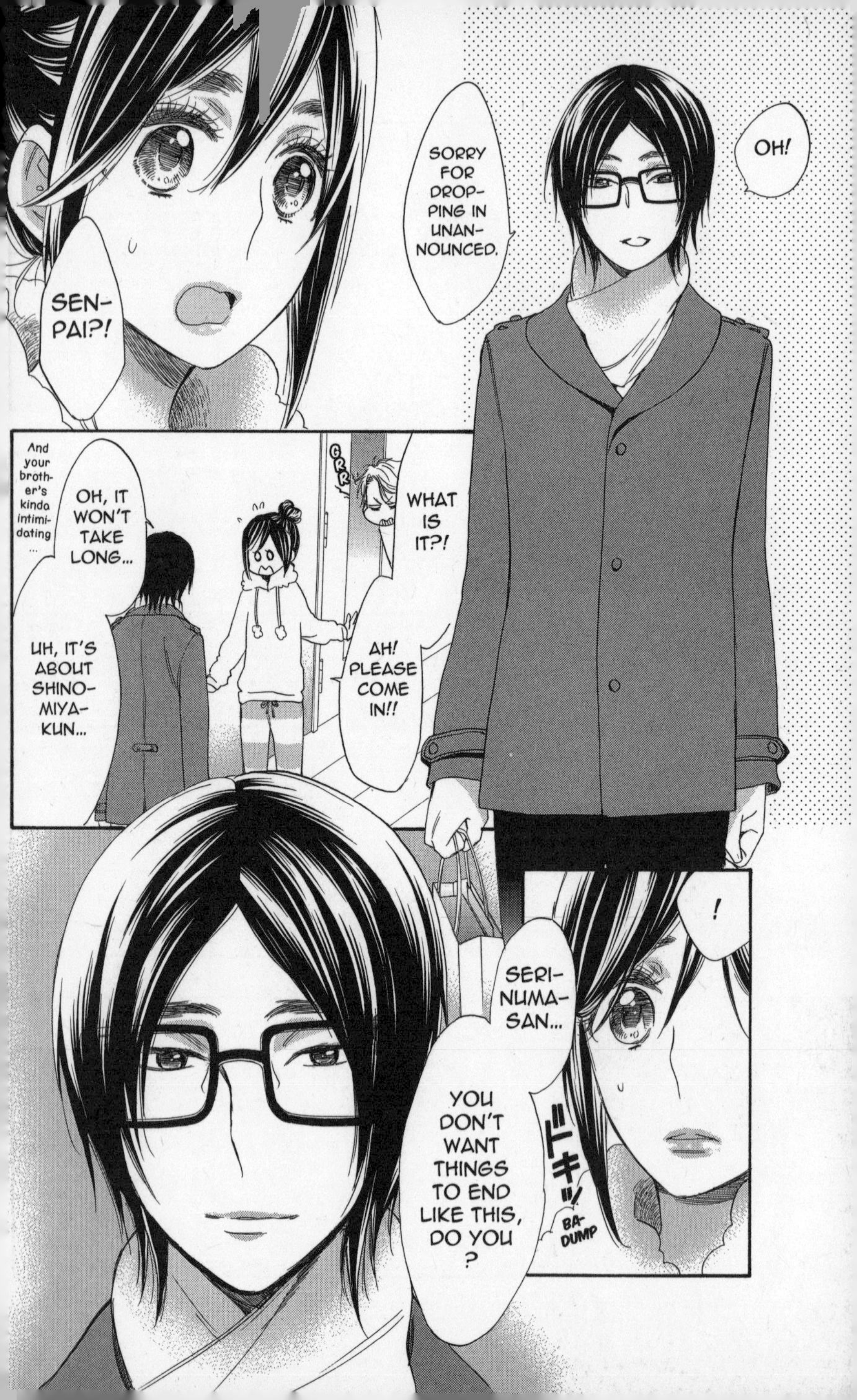
OH!
SORRY FOR DROPPING IN UNANNOUNCED.
SEN-PAI?!
WHAT IS IT?!
GRR
AH! PLEASE COME IN!!
OH, IT WON'T TAKE LONG...
UH, IT'S ABOUT SHINOMIYA-KUN...
And your brother's kinda intimidating...
!
ドキッ
BA-DUMP
SERINUMA-SAN...
YOU DON'T WANT THINGS TO END LIKE THIS, DO YOU?

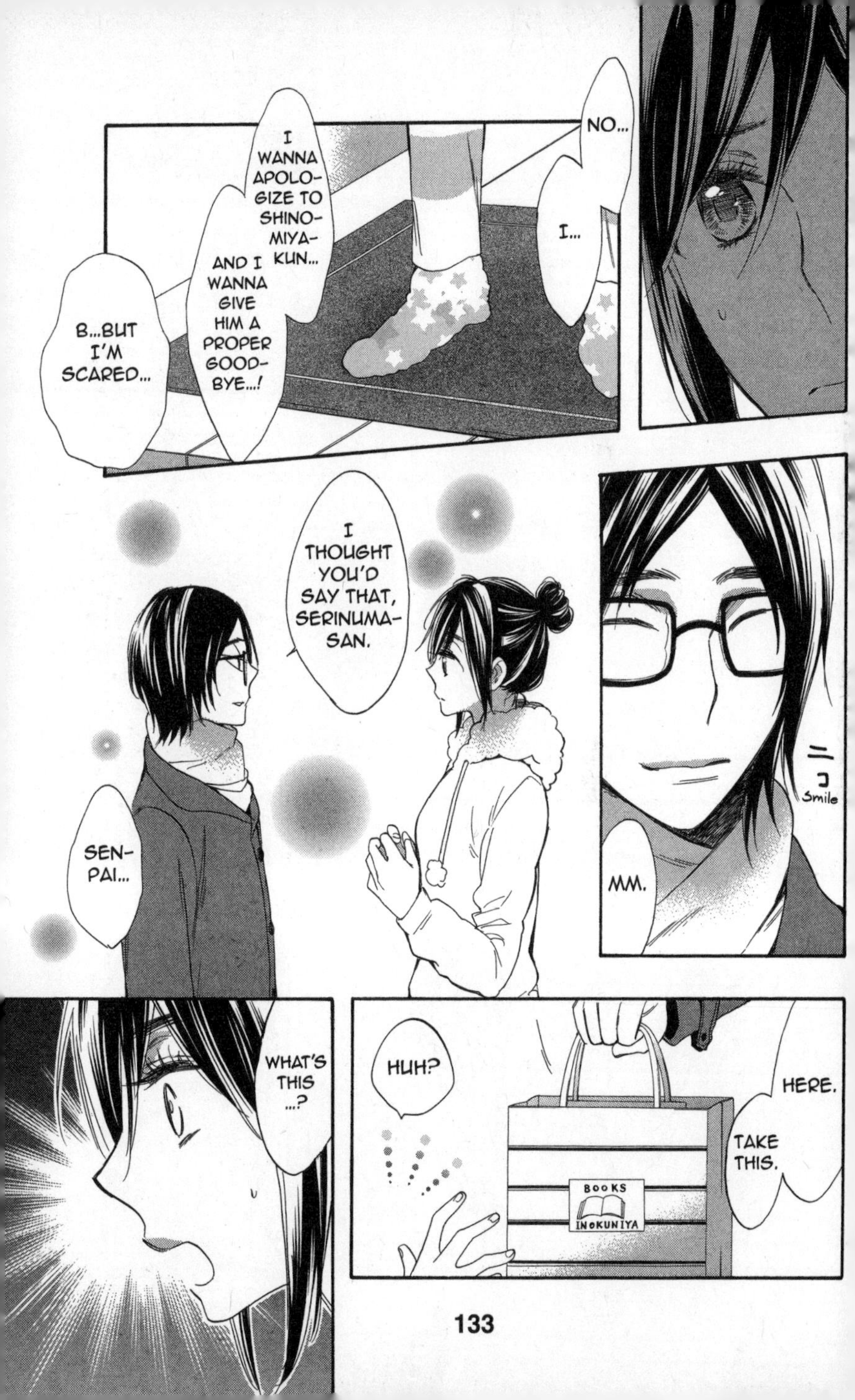
NO...
I...
I WANNA APOLOGIZE TO SHINOMIYA-KUN...
AND I WANNA GIVE HIM A PROPER GOODBYE...!
B...BUT I'M SCARED...
ニコ Smile
MM.
I THOUGHT YOU'D SAY THAT, SERINUMA-SAN.
SEN-PAI...
HERE.
TAKE THIS.
HUH?
BOOKS INOKUNIYA
WHAT'S THIS ...?

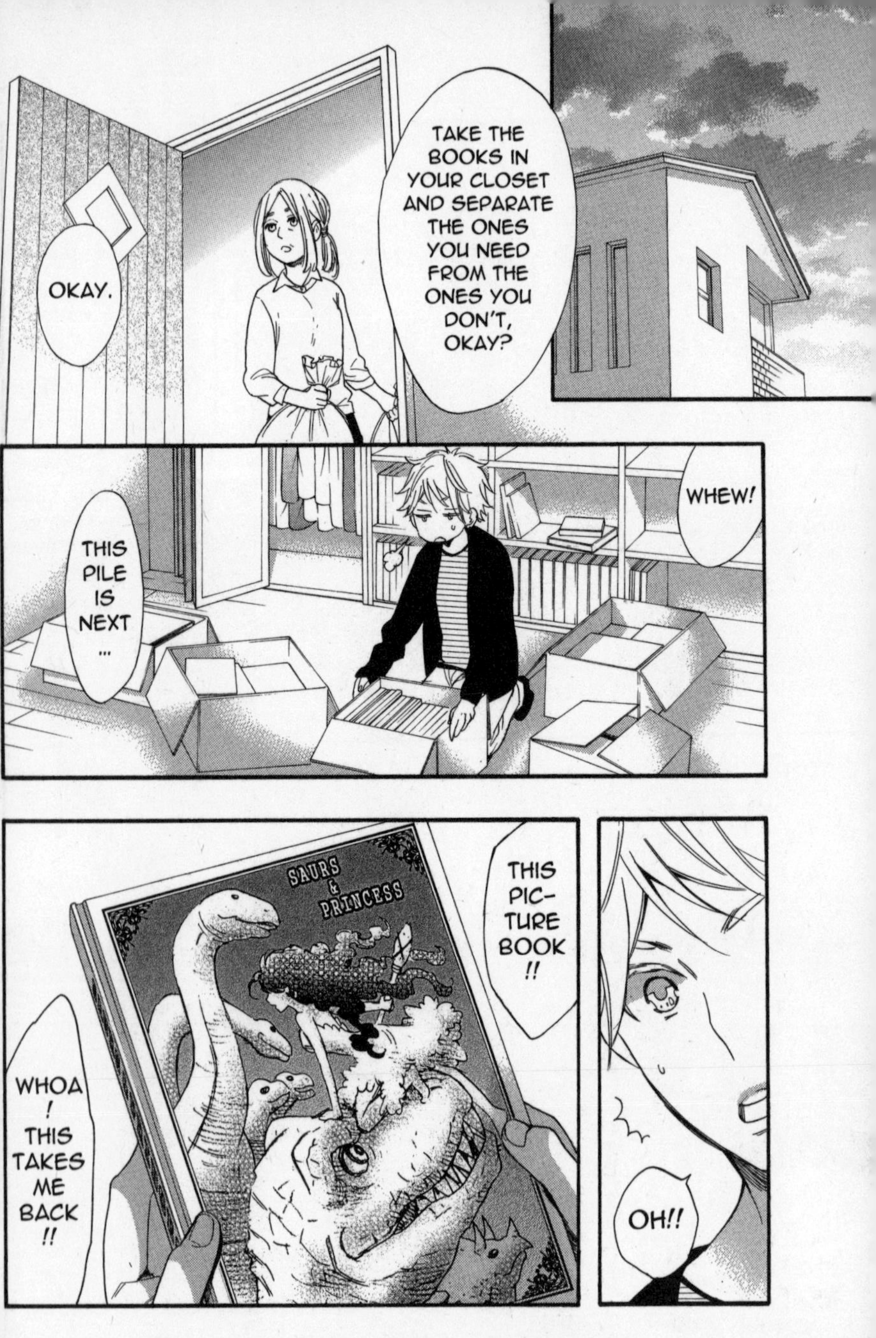
TAKE THE BOOKS IN YOUR CLOSET AND SEPARATE THE ONES YOU NEED FROM THE ONES YOU DON'T, OKAY?
OKAY.
WHEW!
THIS PILE IS NEXT ...
OH!!
THIS PIC-TURE BOOK !!
SAURS & PRINCESS
WHOA ! THIS TAKES ME BACK !!

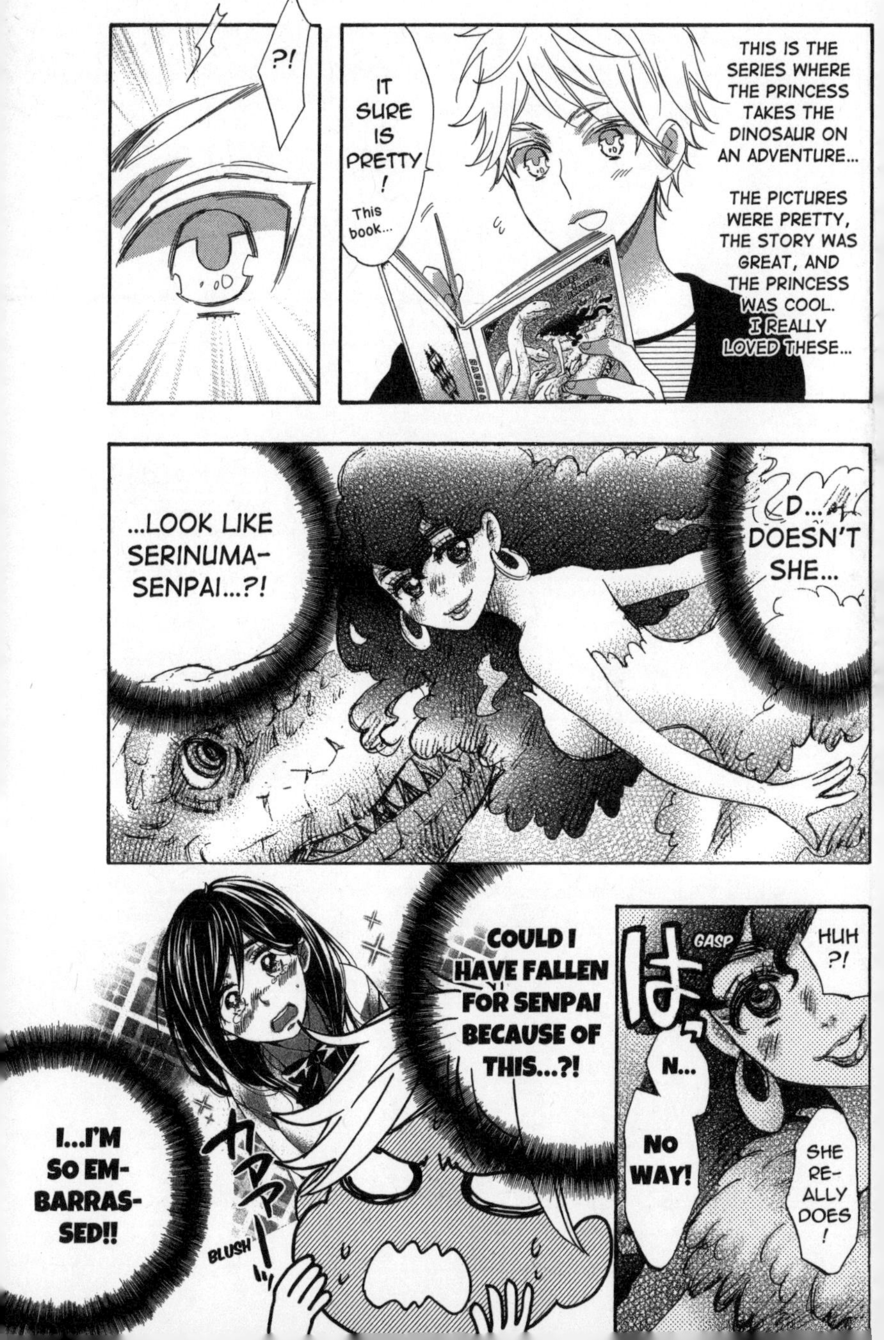
THIS IS THE SERIES WHERE THE PRINCESS TAKES THE DINOSAUR ON AN ADVENTURE...
THE PICTURES WERE PRETTY, THE STORY WAS GREAT, AND THE PRINCESS WAS COOL. I REALLY LOVED THESE...
IT SURE IS PRETTY!
This book...
?!
D... DOESN'T SHE...
...LOOK LIKE SERINUMA-SENPAI...?!
HUH?!
GASP
SHE REALLY DOES!
N... NO WAY!
COULD I HAVE FALLEN FOR SENPAI BECAUSE OF THIS...?!
BLUSH
I...I'M SO EMBARRASSED!!

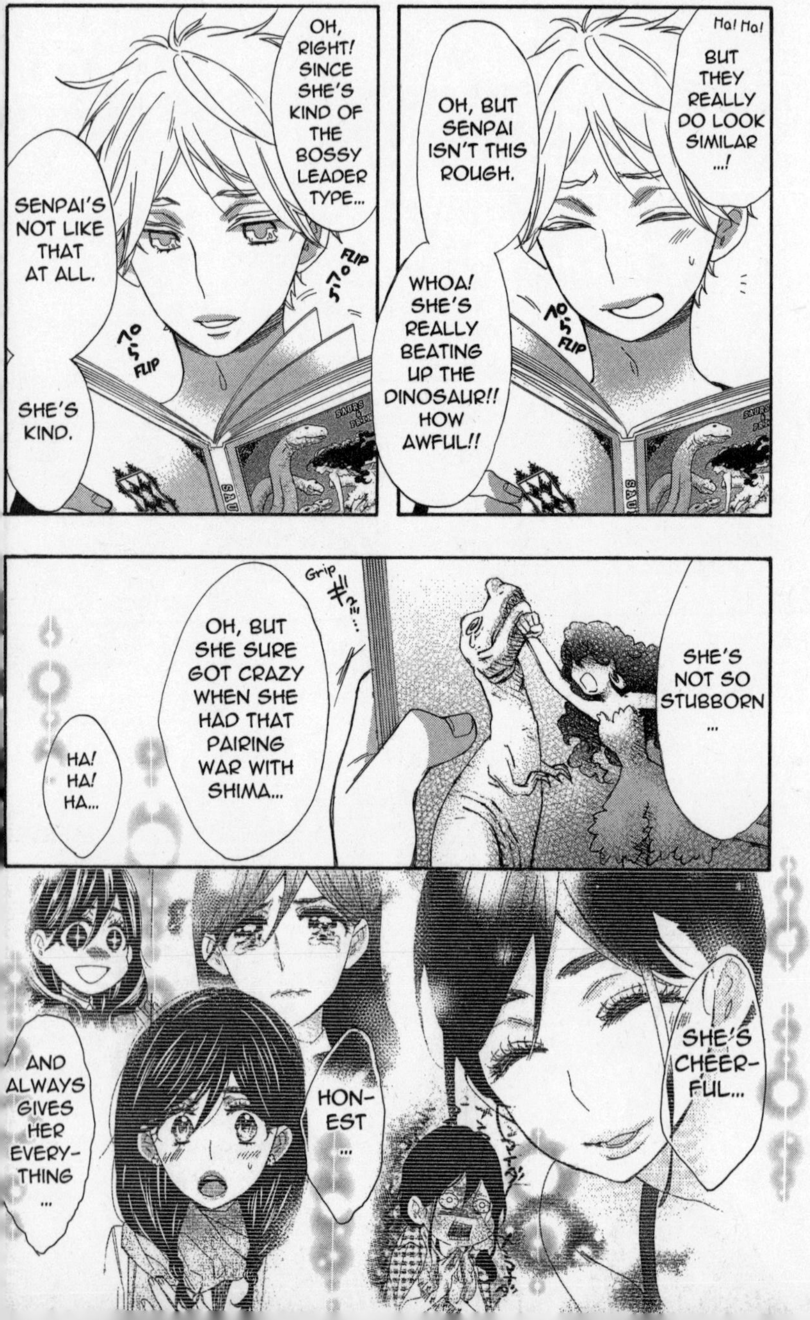
Ha! Ha!
BUT THEY REALLY DO LOOK SIMILAR ...!
OH, BUT SENPAI ISN'T THIS ROUGH.
FLIP
WHOA! SHE'S REALLY BEATING UP THE DINOSAUR!! HOW AWFUL!!
OH, RIGHT! SINCE SHE'S KIND OF THE BOSSY LEADER TYPE...
FLIP
SENPAI'S NOT LIKE THAT AT ALL.
FLIP
SHE'S KIND.
SHE'S NOT SO STUBBORN ...
Grip
OH, BUT SHE SURE GOT CRAZY WHEN SHE HAD THAT PAIRING WAR WITH SHIMA...
HA! HA! HA...
SHE'S CHEER-FUL...
HON-EST ...
AND ALWAYS GIVES HER EVERY-THING ...

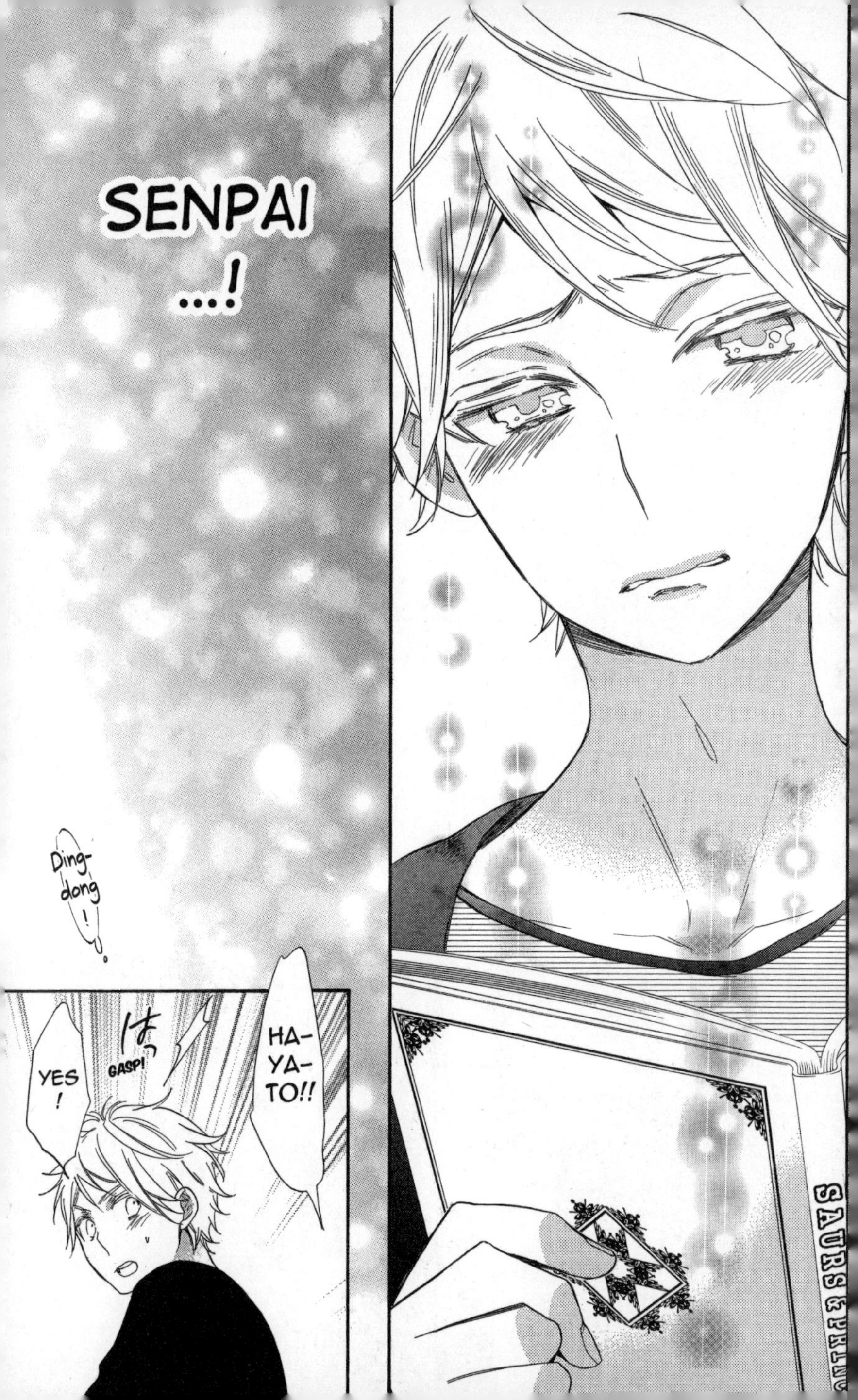

SENPAI ...!
Ding-dong!
HA-YA-TO!!
はっ
GASP!
YES!

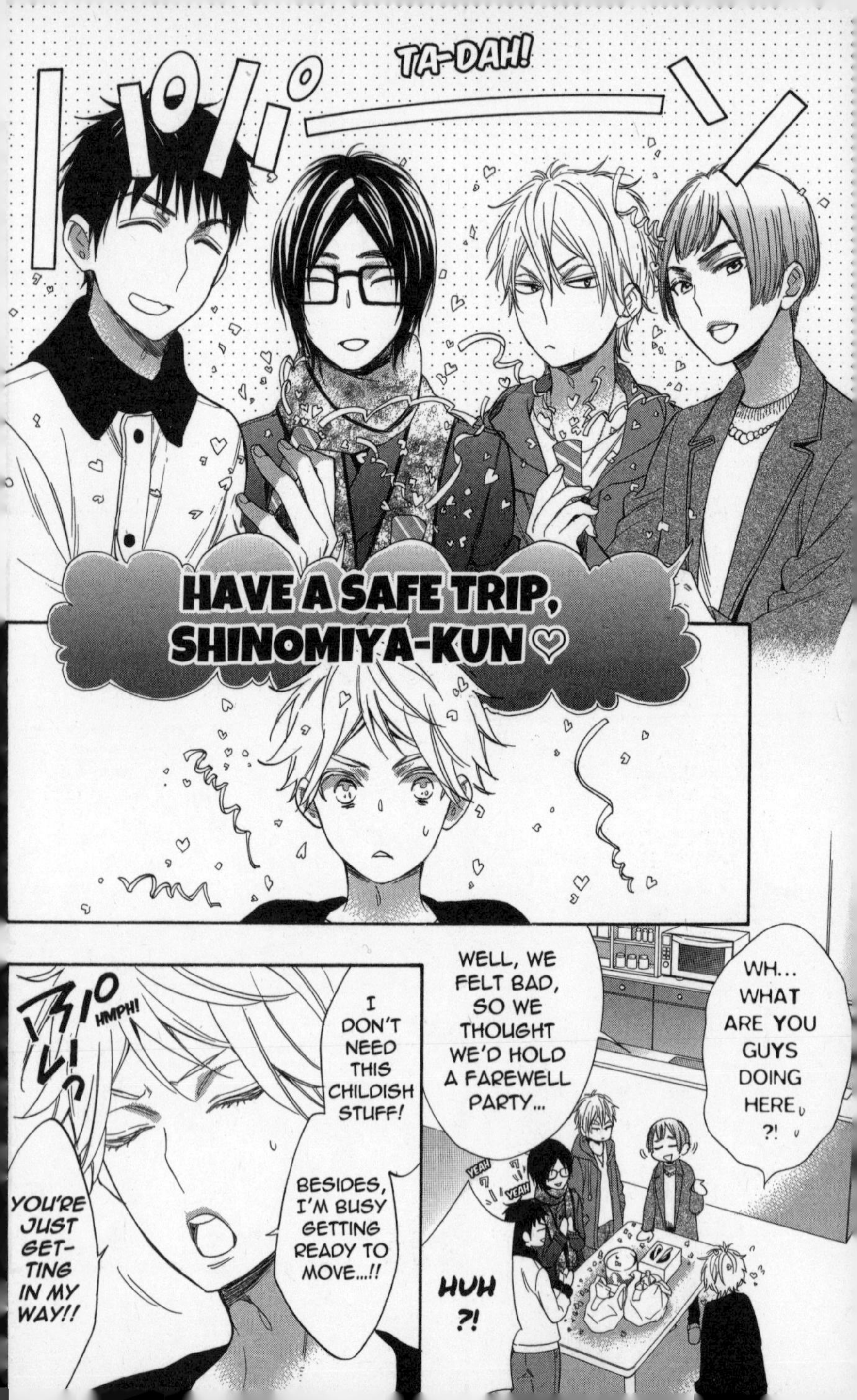
TA-DAH!
HAVE A SAFE TRIP, SHINOMIYA-KUN ♡
WH... WHAT ARE YOU GUYS DOING HERE ?!
WELL, WE FELT BAD, SO WE THOUGHT WE'D HOLD A FAREWELL PARTY...
YEAH
YEAH
HUH ?!
HMPH!
I DON'T NEED THIS CHILDISH STUFF!
BESIDES, I'M BUSY GETTING READY TO MOVE...!!
YOU'RE JUST GET-TING IN MY WAY!!

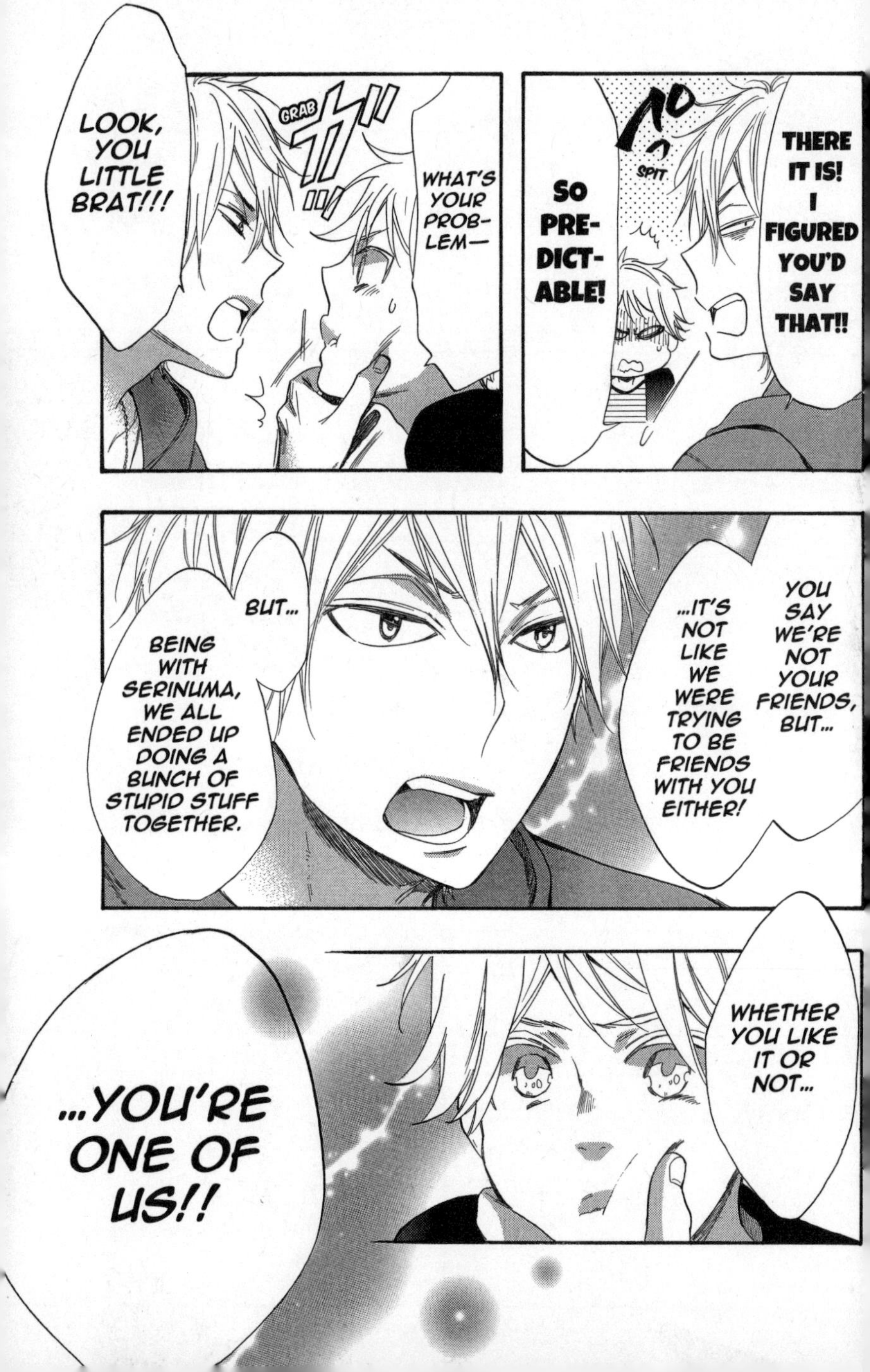
THERE IT IS! I FIGURED YOU'D SAY THAT!!
SPIT
SO PRE-DICT-ABLE!
WHAT'S YOUR PROB-LEM—
GRAB
LOOK, YOU LITTLE BRAT!!!
YOU SAY WE'RE NOT YOUR FRIENDS, BUT...
...IT'S NOT LIKE WE WERE TRYING TO BE FRIENDS WITH YOU EITHER!
BUT...
BEING WITH SERINUMA, WE ALL ENDED UP DOING A BUNCH OF STUPID STUFF TOGETHER.
WHETHER YOU LIKE IT OR NOT...
...YOU'RE ONE OF US!!

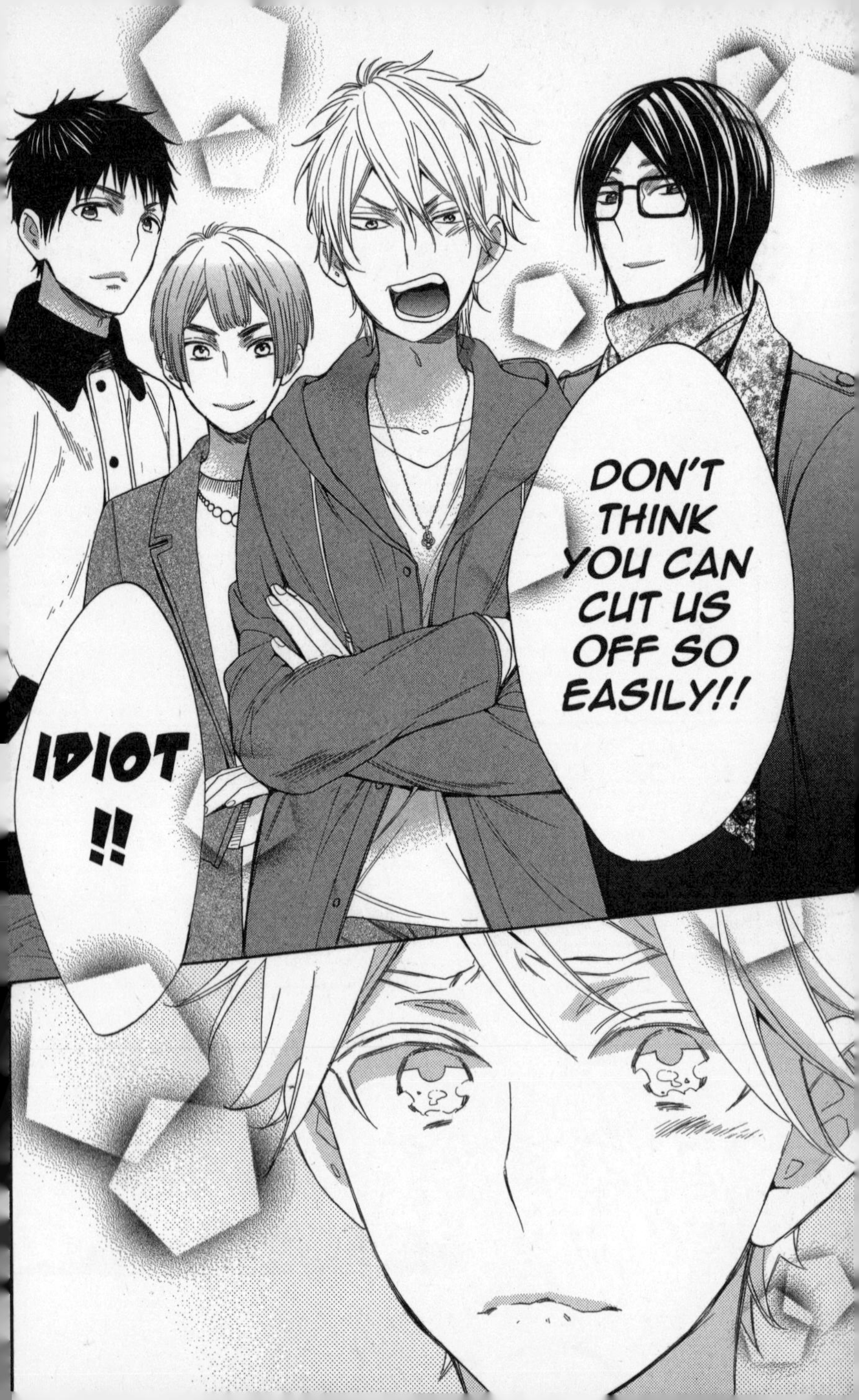
DON'T THINK YOU CAN CUT US OFF SO EASILY!!
IDIOT!!

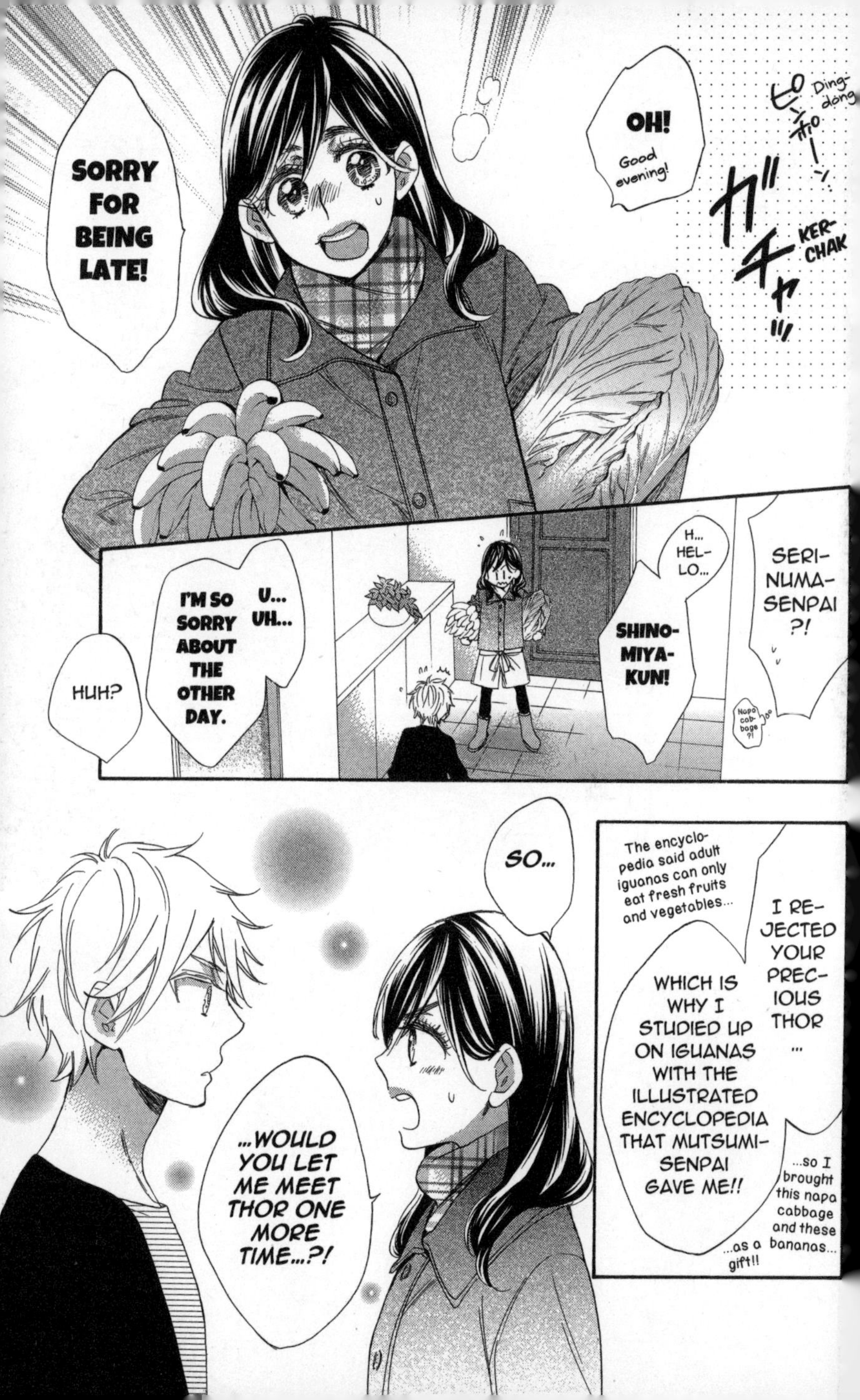
Ding-dong
KER-CHAK
OH!
Good evening!
SORRY FOR BEING LATE!
SERI-NUMA-SENPAI?!
Napa cabbage?!
H... HEL-LO...
SHINO-MIYA-KUN!
U... UH...
I'M SO SORRY ABOUT THE OTHER DAY.
HUH?
I RE-JECTED YOUR PREC-IOUS THOR...
WHICH IS WHY I STUDIED UP ON IGUANAS WITH THE ILLUSTRATED ENCYCLOPEDIA THAT MUTSUMI-SENPAI GAVE ME!!
The encyclo-pedia said adult iguanas can only eat fresh fruits and vegetables...
...so I brought this napa cabbage and these bananas...
...as a gift!!
SO...
...WOULD YOU LET ME MEET THOR ONE MORE TIME...?!

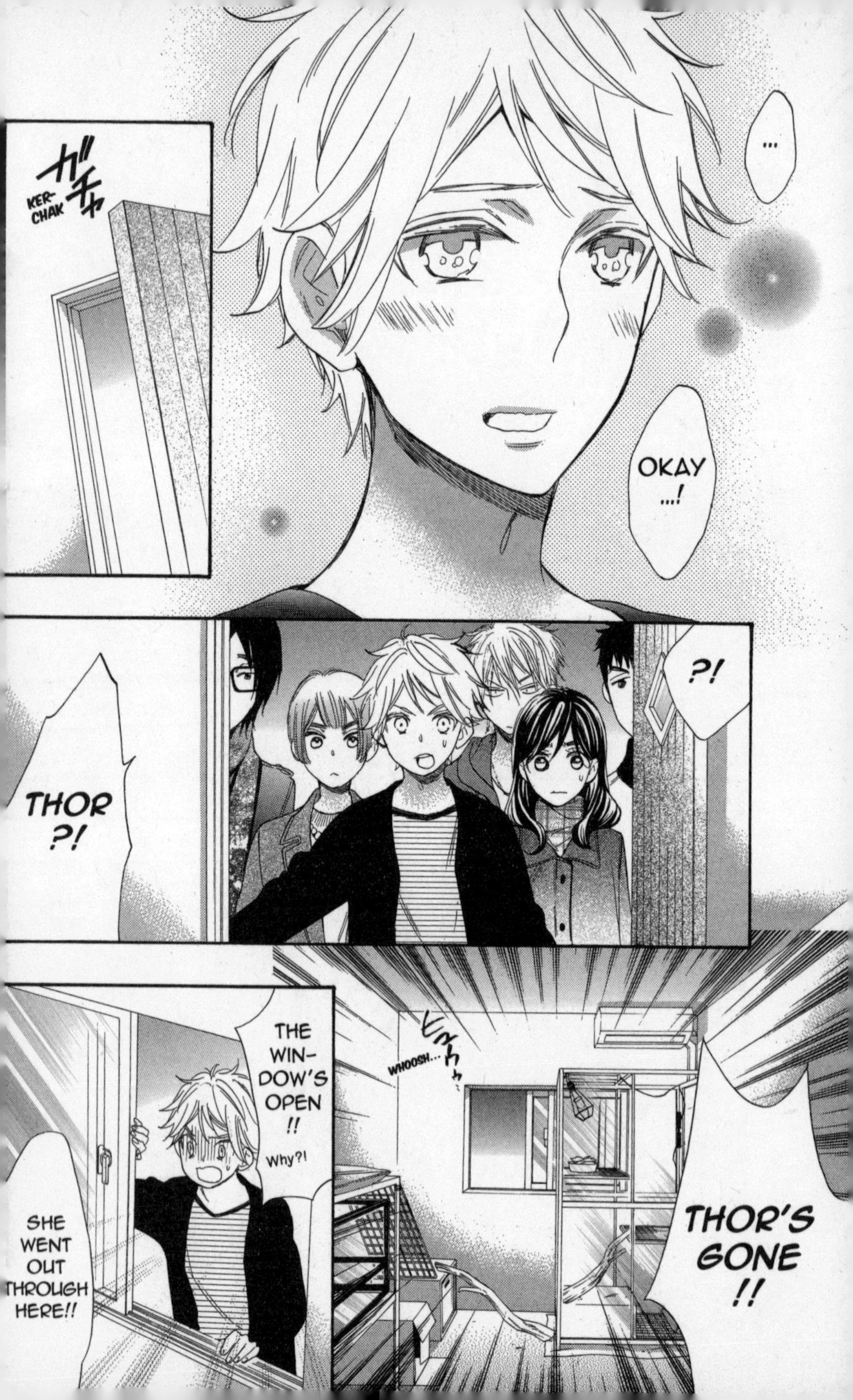
...
OKAY ...!
ガチャ
KER-CHAK
?!
THOR ?!
THOR'S GONE !!
WHOOSH...
THE WIN-DOW'S OPEN !!
Why?!
SHE WENT OUT THROUGH HERE!!

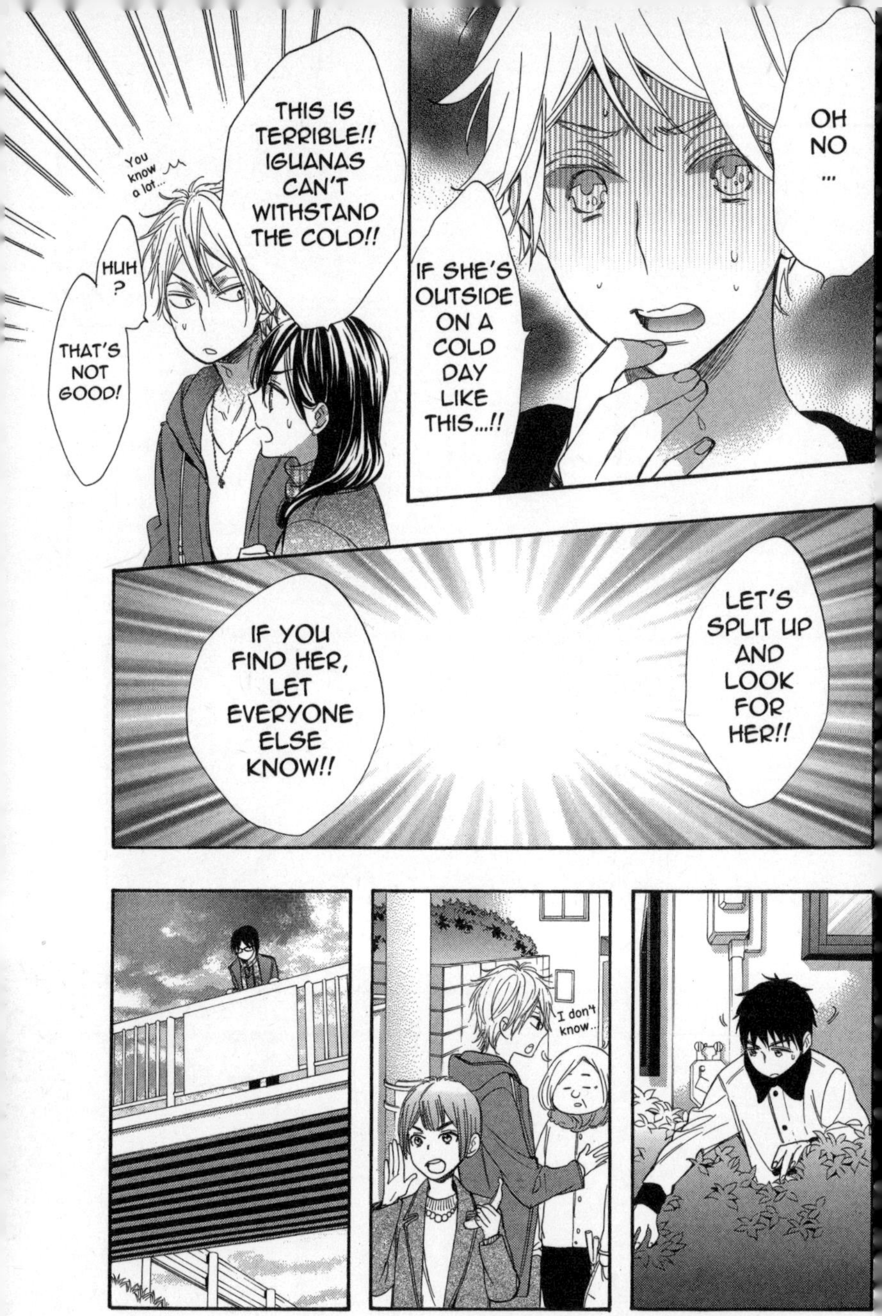
OH NO ...
IF SHE'S OUTSIDE ON A COLD DAY LIKE THIS...!!
THIS IS TERRIBLE!! IGUANAS CAN'T WITHSTAND THE COLD!!
You know a lot...
HUH ?
THAT'S NOT GOOD!
LET'S SPLIT UP AND LOOK FOR HER!!
IF YOU FIND HER, LET EVERYONE ELSE KNOW!!
I don't know...

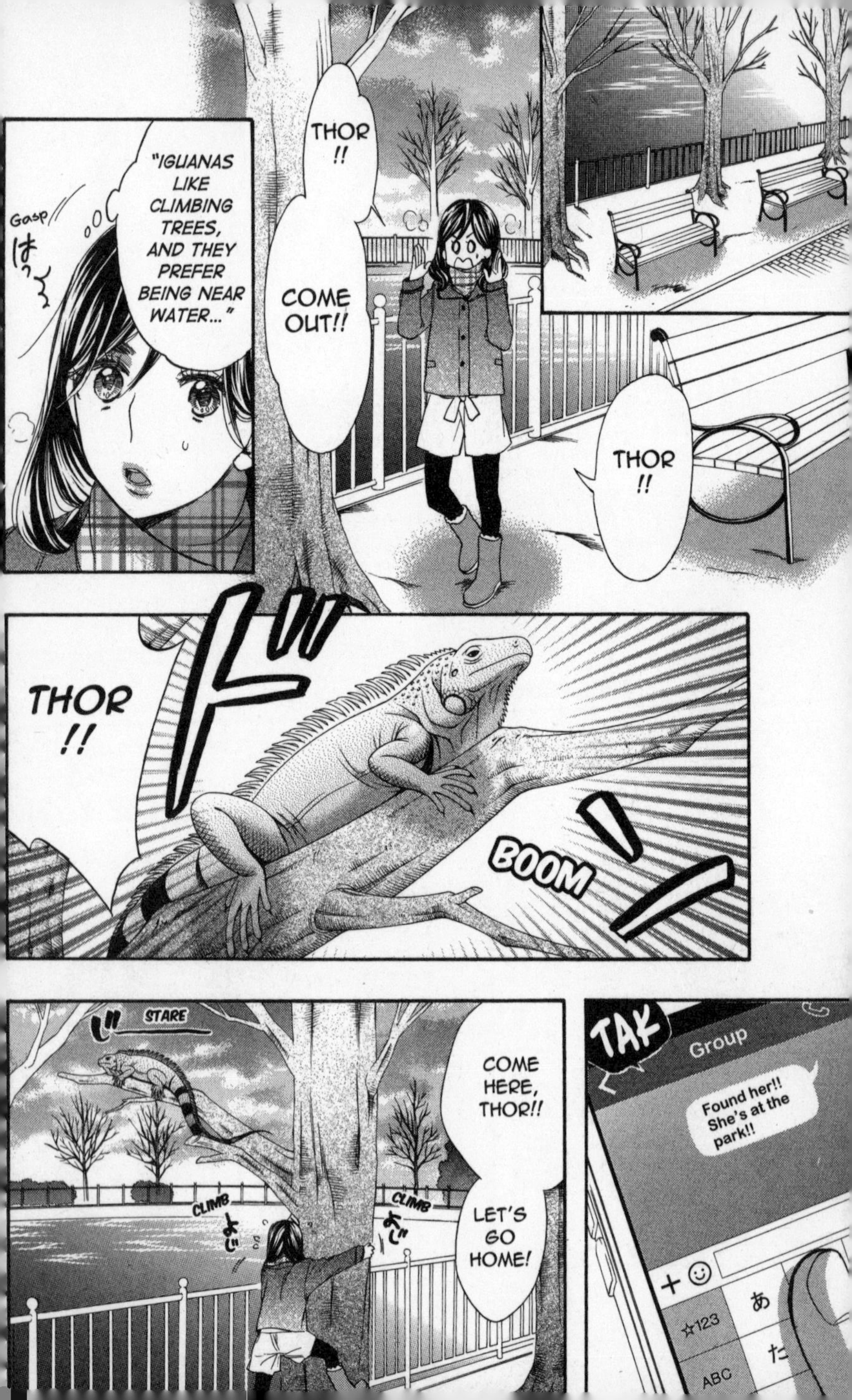
THOR !!
COME OUT!!
THOR !!
"IGUANAS LIKE CLIMBING TREES, AND THEY PREFER BEING NEAR WATER..."
Gasp
はっ
ドッ
BOOM
THOR !!
TAK
Group
Found her!! She's at the park!!
あ
☆123
た
ABC
じー
STARE
COME HERE, THOR!!
LET'S GO HOME!
CLIMB
よじ
CLIMB
よじ

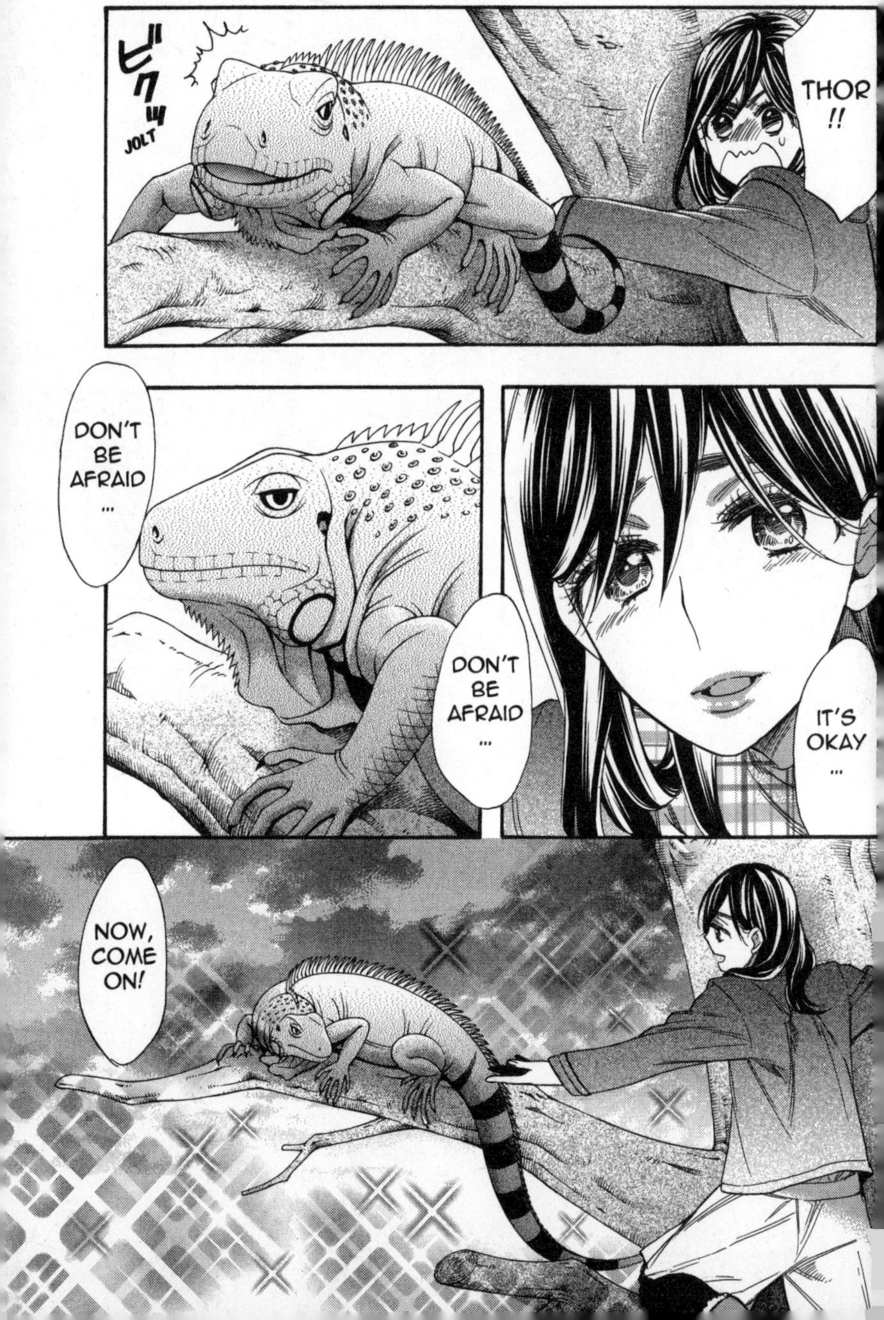
THOR!!
ビクッ
JOLT
IT'S OKAY...
DON'T BE AFRAID...
DON'T BE AFRAID...
NOW, COME ON!

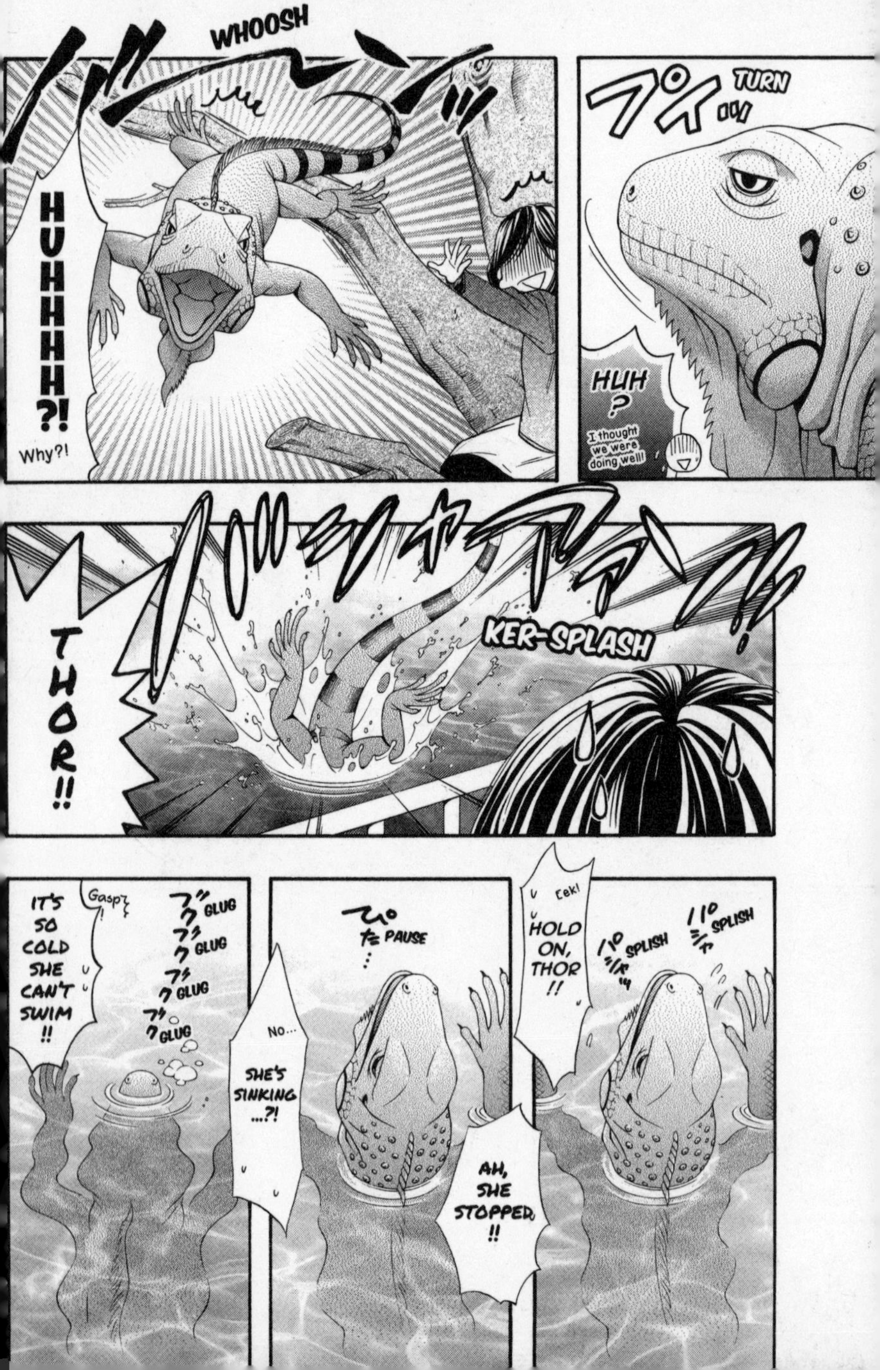
TURN
HUH ?
I thought we were doing well!
WHOOSH
HUHHHHHH ?!
Why?!
KER-SPLASH
THOR!!
Eek!
HOLD ON, THOR !!
SPLISH
SPLISH
PAUSE
...
No...
SHE'S SINKING ...?!
AH, SHE STOPPED !!
GLUG
GLUG
GLUG
GLUG
Gasp
IT'S SO COLD SHE CAN'T SWIM !!

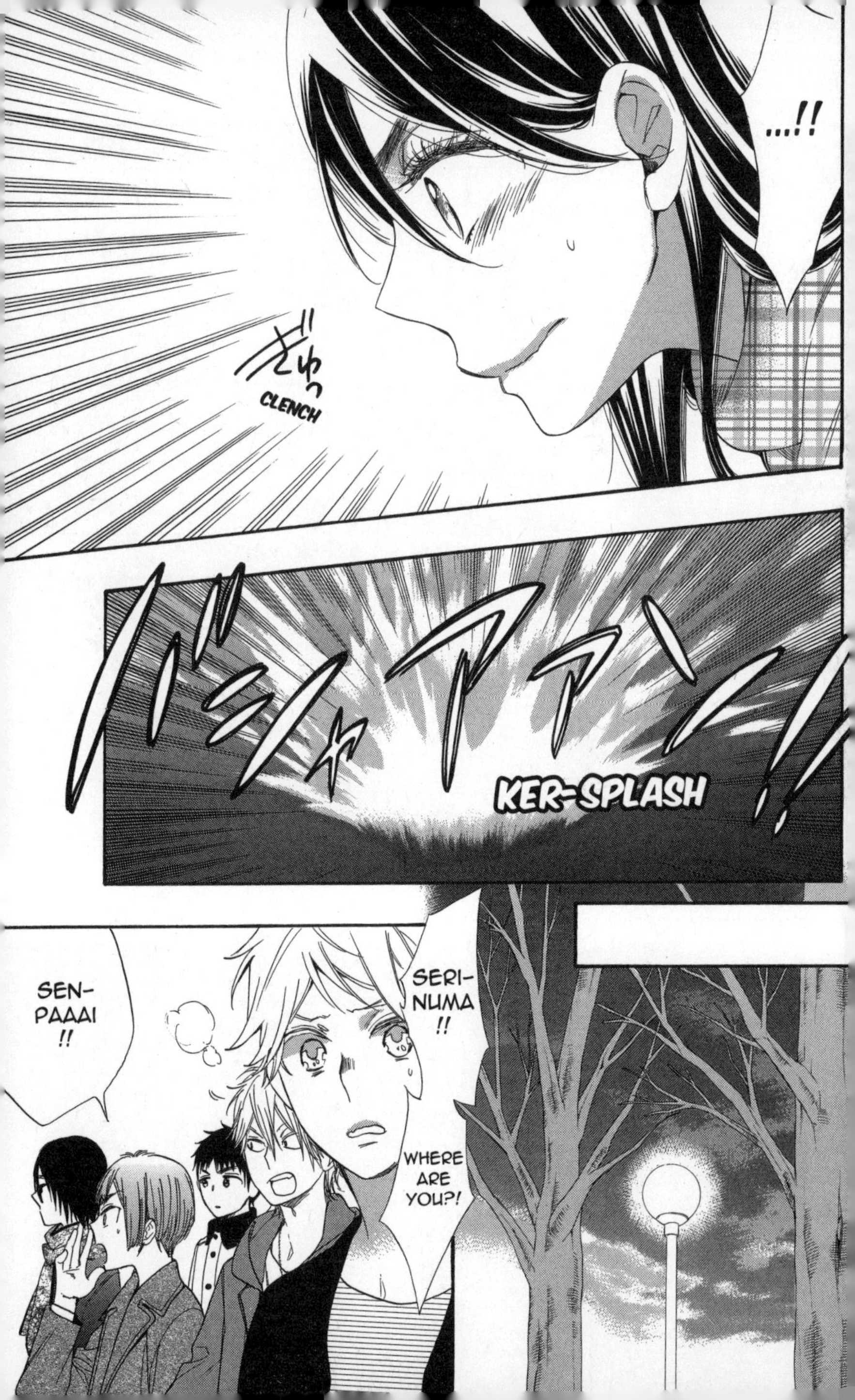
...!!
CLENCH
KER-SPLASH
SERI-NUMA !!
SEN-PAAAI !!
WHERE ARE YOU?!

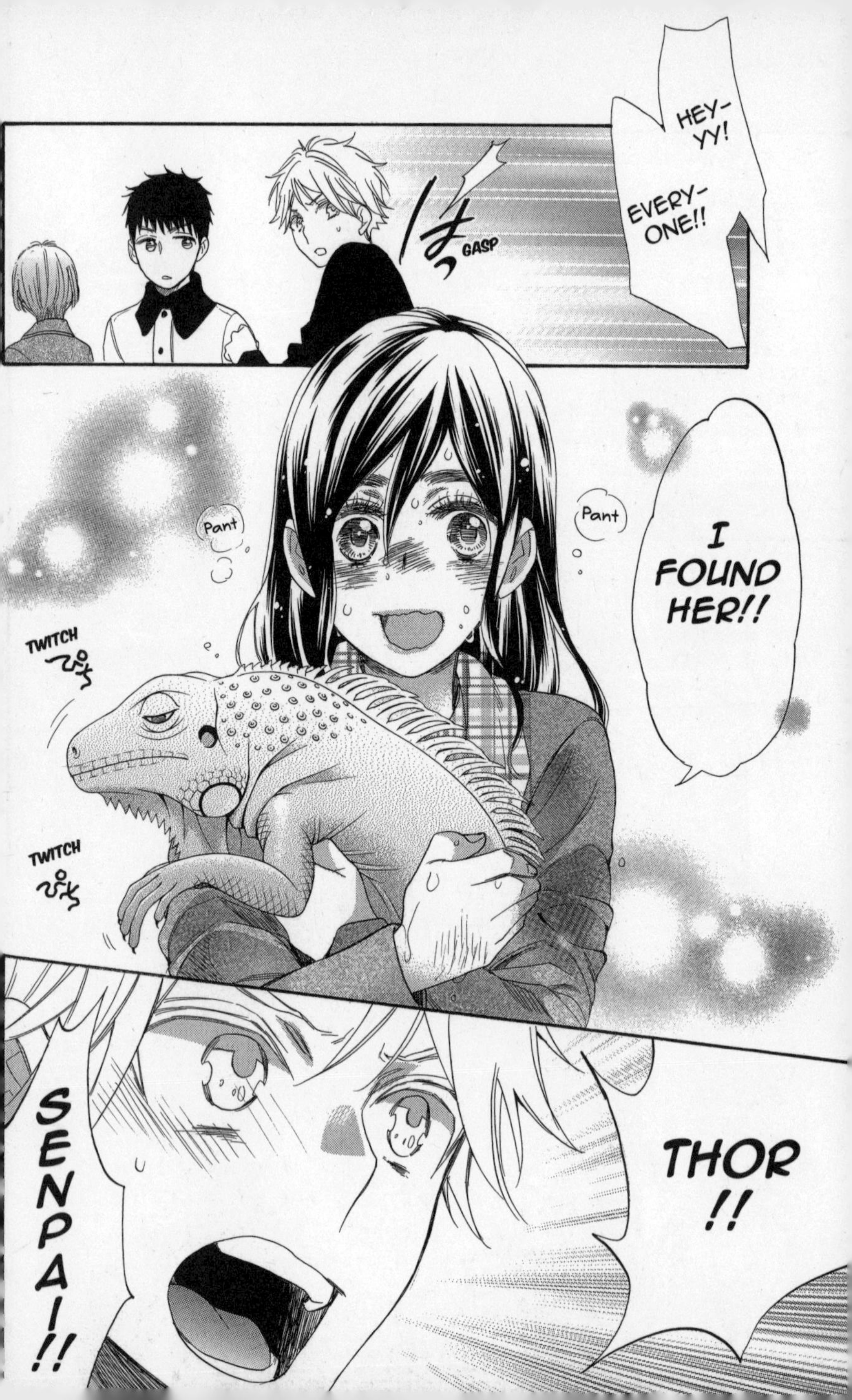
HEY-YY!
EVERY-ONE!!
はっ GASP
I FOUND HER!!
Pant
Pant
TWITCH ぴく
TWITCH ぴく
THOR!!
SENPAI!!

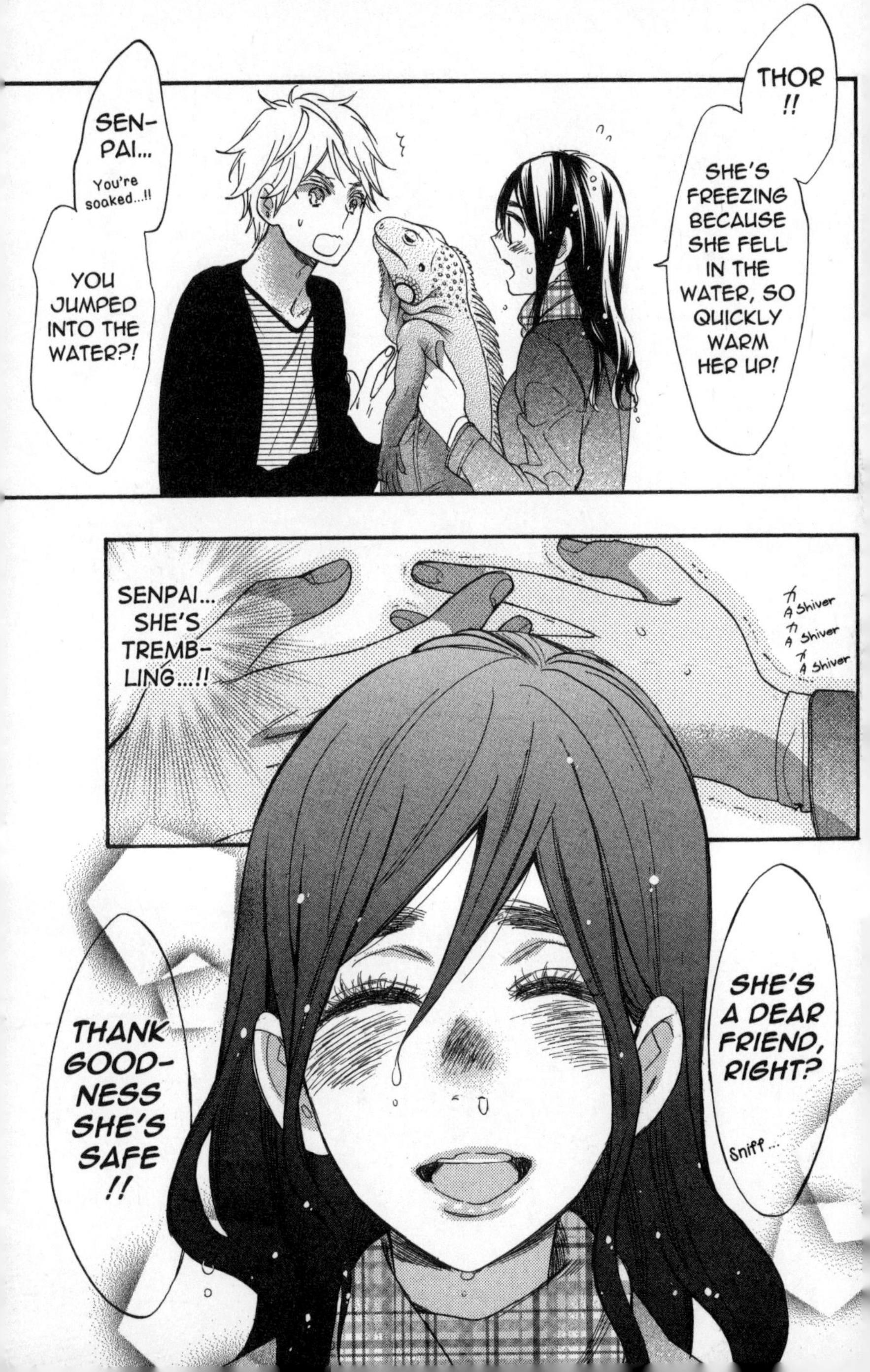
THOR !!
SHE'S FREEZING BECAUSE SHE FELL IN THE WATER, SO QUICKLY WARM HER UP!
SEN-PAI...
You're soaked...!!
YOU JUMPED INTO THE WATER?!
Shiver Shiver Shiver
SENPAI... SHE'S TREMB-LING...!!
SHE'S A DEAR FRIEND, RIGHT?
Sniff...
THANK GOOD-NESS SHE'S SAFE !!

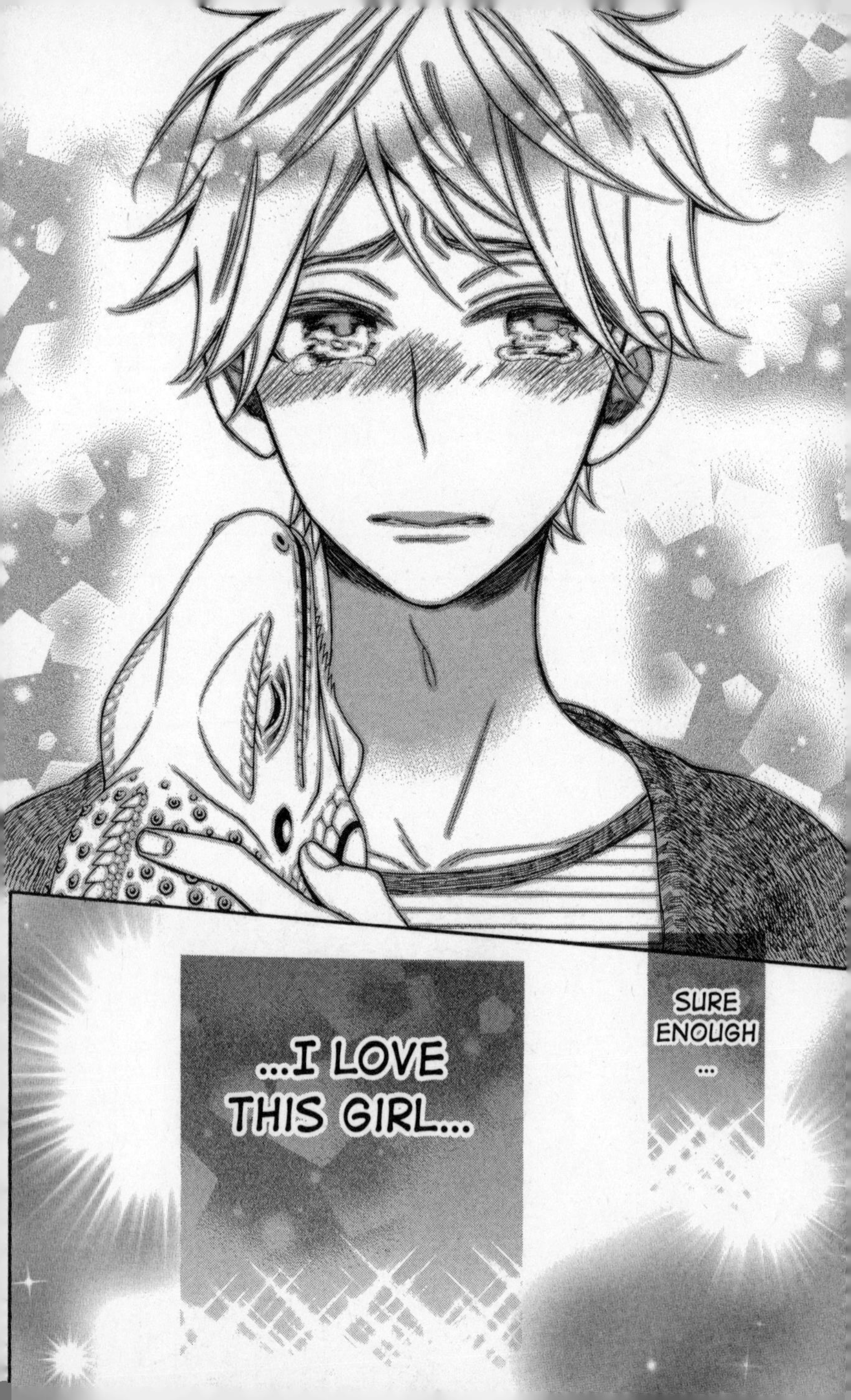
SURE ENOUGH ...
...I LOVE THIS GIRL...

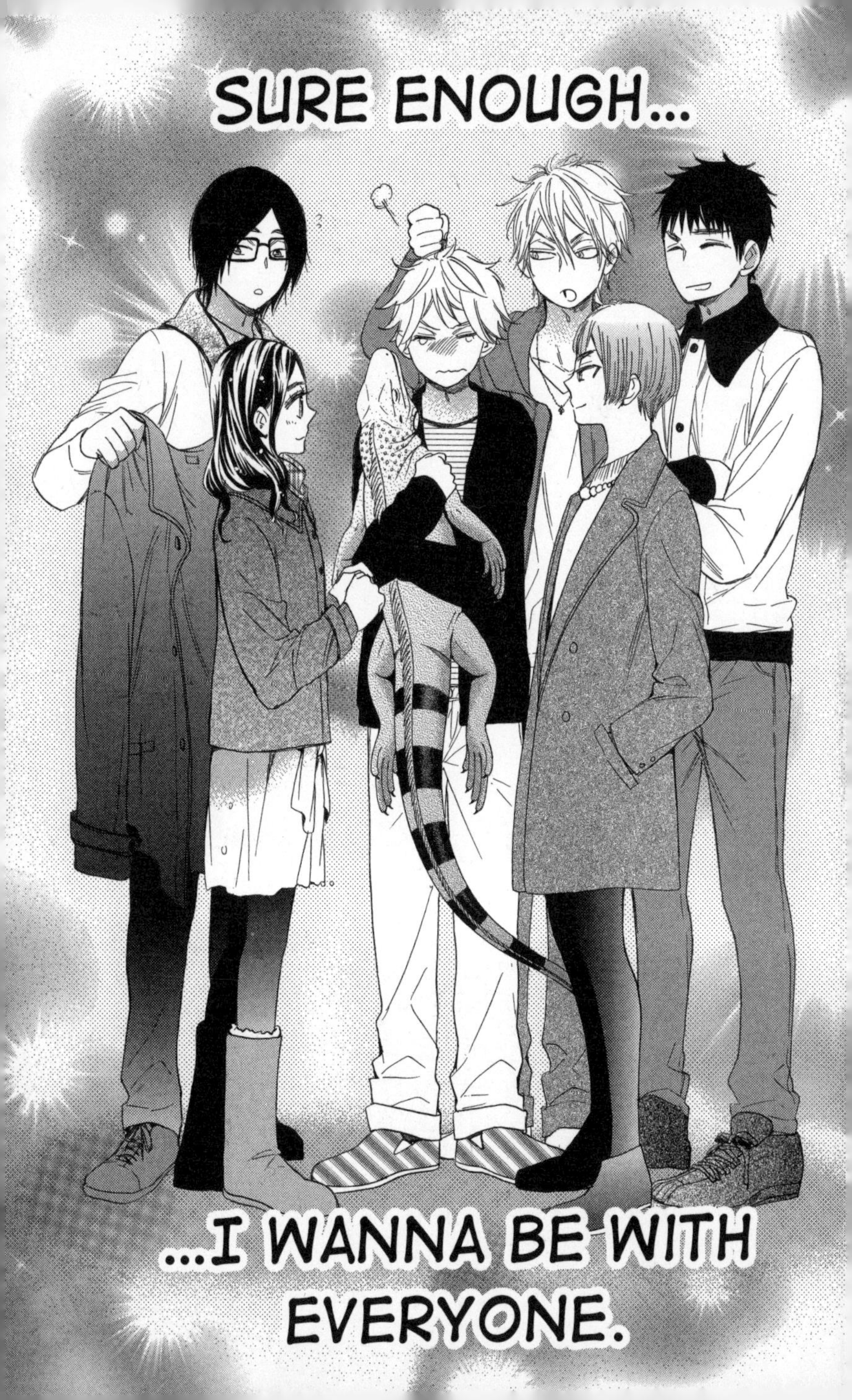
SURE ENOUGH...
...I WANNA BE WITH EVERYONE.

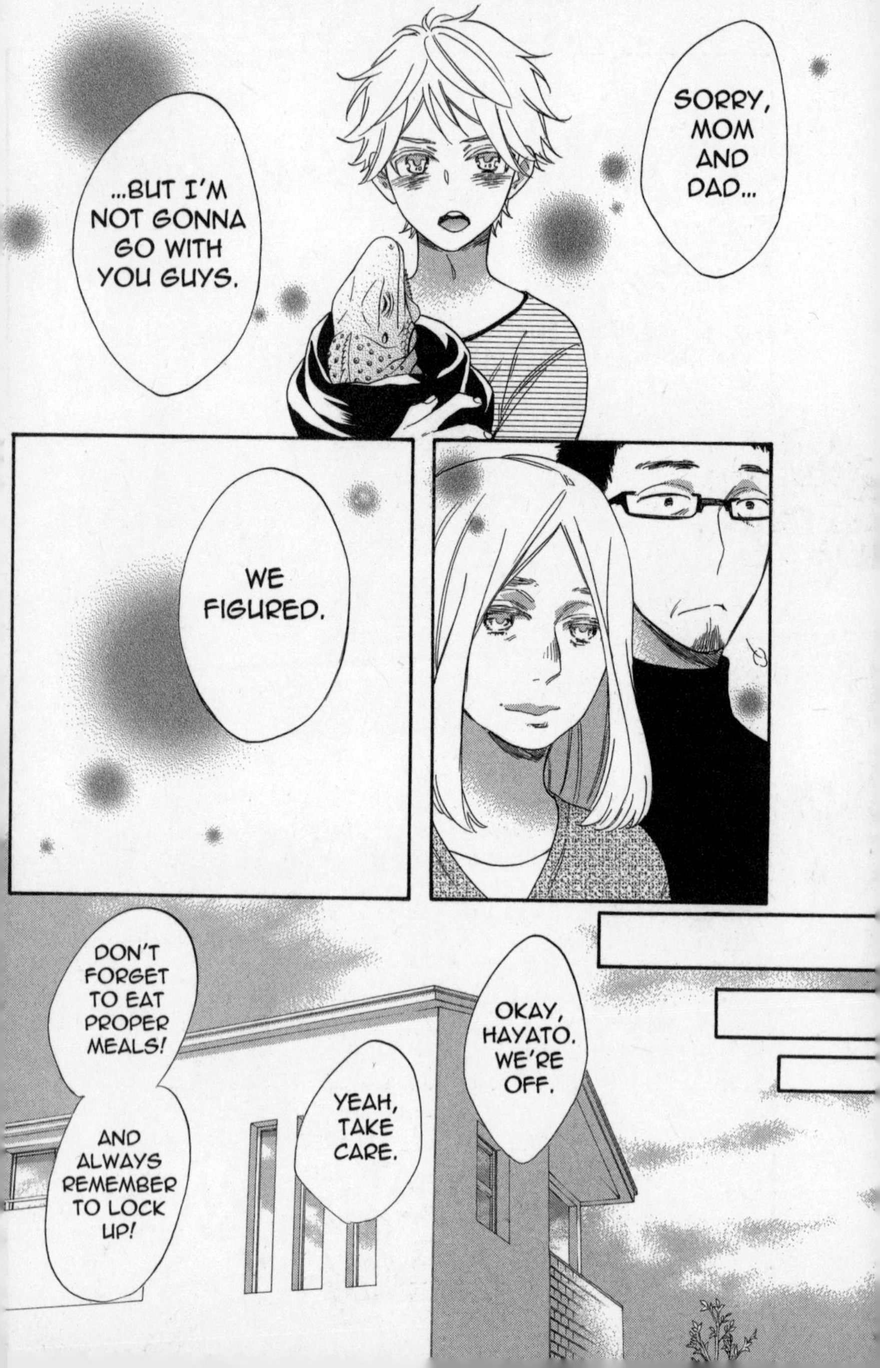
SORRY, MOM AND DAD...
...BUT I'M NOT GONNA GO WITH YOU GUYS.
WE FIGURED.
OKAY, HAYATO. WE'RE OFF.
YEAH, TAKE CARE.
DON'T FORGET TO EAT PROPER MEALS!
AND ALWAYS REMEMBER TO LOCK UP!

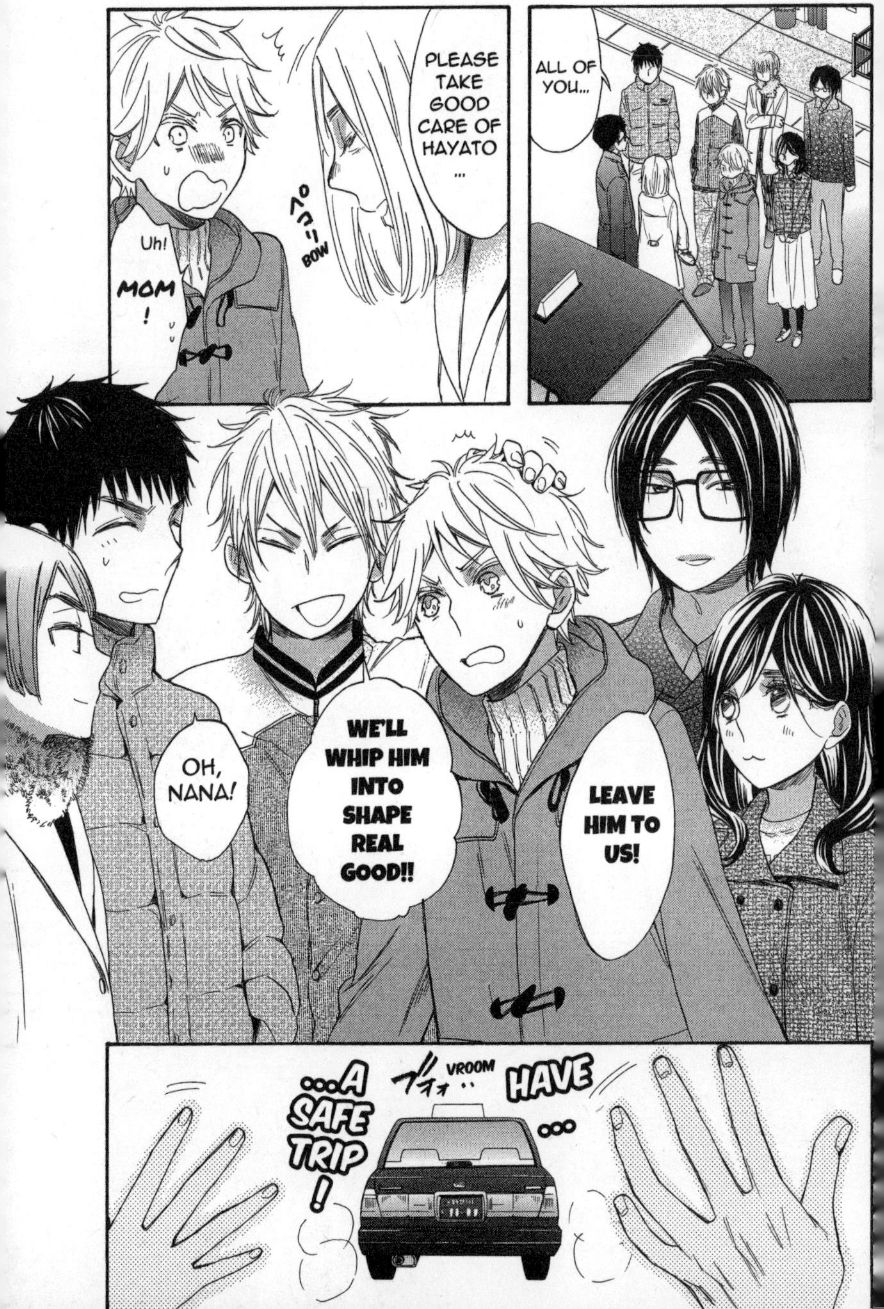
ALL OF YOU...
PLEASE TAKE GOOD CARE OF HAYATO ...
BOW
Uh!
MOM!
LEAVE HIM TO US!
WE'LL WHIP HIM INTO SHAPE REAL GOOD!!
OH, NANA!
HAVE...
VROOM
...A SAFE TRIP!

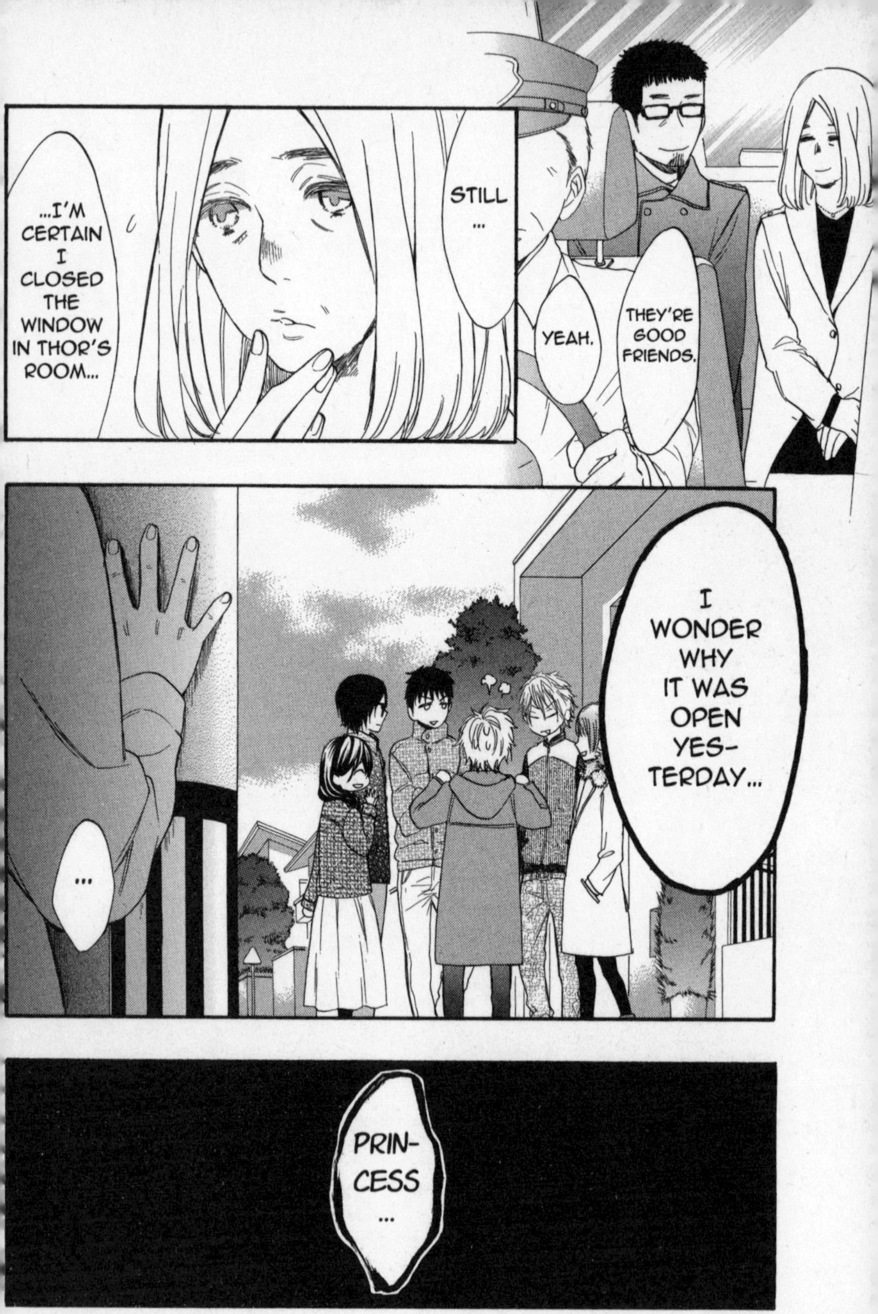
THEY'RE GOOD FRIENDS.
YEAH.
STILL ...
...I'M CERTAIN I CLOSED THE WINDOW IN THOR'S ROOM...
I WONDER WHY IT WAS OPEN YES-TERDAY...
...
PRIN-CESS ...

TO BE CONTINUED
IN VOLUME 9 OF

KiSS HiM,
NOT ME!

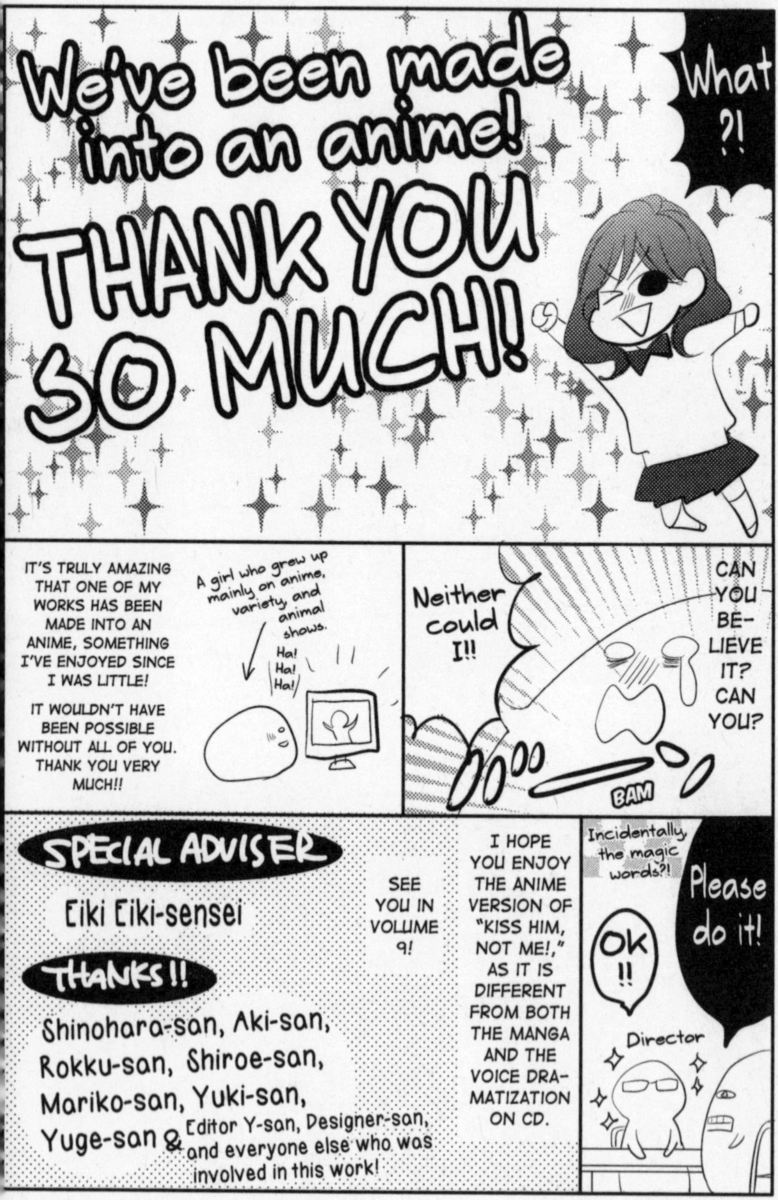
What?!
We've been made into an anime!
THANK YOU SO MUCH!
CAN YOU BE-LIEVE IT? CAN YOU?
Neither could I!!
BAM
IT'S TRULY AMAZING THAT ONE OF MY WORKS HAS BEEN MADE INTO AN ANIME, SOMETHING I'VE ENJOYED SINCE I WAS LITTLE!
IT WOULDN'T HAVE BEEN POSSIBLE WITHOUT ALL OF YOU. THANK YOU VERY MUCH!!
A girl who grew up mainly on anime, variety, and animal shows.
Ha! Ha! Ha!
Incidentally, the magic words?!
Please do it!
OK!!
Director
I HOPE YOU ENJOY THE ANIME VERSION OF "KISS HIM, NOT ME!," AS IT IS DIFFERENT FROM BOTH THE MANGA AND THE VOICE DRA-MATIZATION ON CD.
SEE YOU IN VOLUME 9!
SPECIAL ADVISER
Eiki Eiki-sensei
THANKS!!
Shinohara-san, Aki-san, Rokku-san, Shiroe-san, Mariko-san, Yuki-san, Yuge-san & Editor Y-san, Designer-san, and everyone else who was involved in this work!

AUTHOR'S NOTE

WE'E BEEN MADE
INTO AN ANIME!
THANK YOU!
I HOPE YOU ENJOY
THE SLIGHTLY DIFFERENT
KISS HIM, NOT ME! WORLDS
BETWEEN THE MANGA,
DRAMA CDS, AND ANIME!
-JUNKO

I ♥
BL

Translation Notes

Pot of salt, page 25

In this scene, Takuro carries a pot of salt and is throwing it at Nanashima. Typically, salt is thrown like this for purification, and the clearest example of this is the salt that is thrown during sumo wrestling matches. In this case, Takuro must see Nanashima as some kind of evil, and is throwing salt to exorcise him.

***Pretty Cure* shows and *bishojo kigurumi*, page 32**

The *Puri-Puri-Moon* show being peformed in the theme park appears to be a parody of the small-stage version of *Pretty Cure* (also known as *Glitter Force*). Shows like these are typically performed in theme parks and fairs, with a Power-Ranger style show (called "hero shows") for boys, and for girls, magical-girl themed shows like the one we see in this book. The *Puri-Puri-Moon* show as drawn in this volume is fairly accurate to the actual stage shows, including the presence of obnoxious, male otaku who end up being a nuisance for the parents and children that typically attend. The costumes that the peformers are wearing are a type of *kigurumi* (mascot-like costumes) called *bishojo* (beautiful girl) *kigurumi*. These are characterized by anime-girl masks instead of the typical mascot-like headpieces that are used for *kigurumi*.

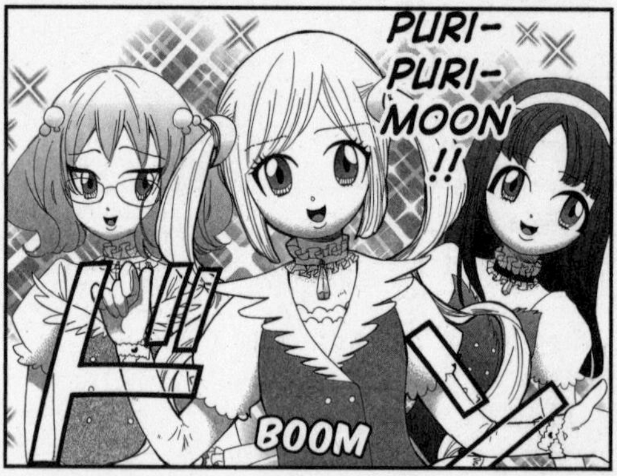
PURI-PURI-MOON!!
BOOM

***Puri-Puri-Moon* fan and idol otaku, page 35**

The superfan that disrupts Kae and Nanashima's *Puri-Puri-Moon* performance is modeled after the stereotypical image of the idol otaku. These fans, usually adult men, may passionately support their favorite pop idol at concerts by wearing a jacket (*happi*) with the idol's picture on it and headband (*hachimaki*).

***Manju* bun, page 50**

Manju is a sweet bun-like pastry that is typically filled with *anko* (boiled azuki beans and sugar). Apparently, Kae's father thinks her face resembles one of these treats.

New Year's traditions, pages 52-54

The New Year holiday is very big in Japan and is more akin to Christmas in the United States and other countries. Since many of the traditions for this holiday have been displayed in this book, we thought it would be best to give a brief descption of each:

Mochi: Pounded glutinous rice that is formed into a flattened sphere with a chewy texture. It is customary to eat mochi on New Year's Day, and you'll notice the characters eating it throughout the pages of Chapter 30.

New Year's Money (JP: *nendama*): Money that is usually gifted from relatives to young children on New Year's Day.

New Year's shrine visit (JP: *hatsumode*): A custom that involves visiting a shinto shrine for the first time of the New Year.

Fortunes: At the New Year's shrine visit, one normally buys a fortune telling—a piece of paper sold by the shrine that, when opened, reveals one of a range of possible fortunes that span from great fortune to grave misfortune.

Mitsuko in the 80s, page 54

This is actually referring to a time of oppulence for Japan called the "bubble era" or the time of the "bubble economy" that took place from 1986 until the bubble collapsed in 1992. During that time, Japanese real estate prices were greatly inflated and many people in the big cities were known for living glamorous lifestyles highlighted with disco dancing and general extravagance.

Tangerines, page 58

Tangerines are typically in season in winter and are another food that is customary to eat around the New Year's holiday.

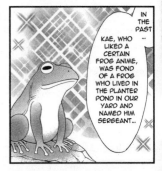

IN THE PAST ...
KAE, WHO LIKED A CERTAIN FROG ANIME, WAS FOND OF A FROG WHO LIVED IN THE PLANTER POND IN OUR YARD AND NAMED HIM SERGEANT...

A frog named Sergeant, page 108

If it's not obvious from the name, Kae's frog friend is named after *Sgt. Frog*, a currently ongoing manga series. It also had an anime that ran for 358 episodes between 2004-2011.

EYAAAHHHHH!!!, page 109

This hyperbolic reaction, written in Japanese as *pigyaa!*, is most likely a reference to *Love Live! Sunshine!!*, the most recent anime in the *Love Live!* franchise. The character Ruby Kurosawa, an easily embarrassed first-year, screams like Kae when her senpai calls her cute. Her over the top exclamation and facial expression became a meme online.

Shitajiki, page 125

Usually a piece of plastic that is placed underneath paper to prevent the indentation of other paper by a writing utensil. These are also known as pencil boards. In Japan, they are fairly common and may be decorated with art from anime and manga.

Kiss Him, Not Me volume 8 is a work of fiction. Names, characters, places, and incidents are the products of the author's imagination or are used fictitiously. Any resemblance to actual events, locales, or persons, living or dead, is entirely coincidental.

A Kodansha Comics Trade Paperback Original.

Published in the United States by Kodansha Comics, an imprint of Kodansha USA Publishing, LLC, New York.

Publication rights for this English edition arranged through Kodansha Ltd., Tokyo.

First published in Japan in 2016 by Kodansha Ltd., Tokyo, as *Watashi Ga Motete Dousunda* volume 8.

ISBN 978-1-63236-299-5

Printed in the United States of America.

www.kodanshacomics.com

9 8 7 6 5 4 3 2 1

Translation: David Rhie
Lettering: Hiroko Mizuno
Editing: Ajani Oloye
Kodansha Comics edition cover design: Phil Balsman